Wilhelm & Marion Pauck

PAUL TILLICH
His Life & Thought

The most intimate motions within the depths of our
souls are not completely our own. For they belong also to
our friends, to mankind, to the universe, and to the
Ground of all being, the aim of our life. Nothing can be
hidden ultimately. It is always reflected in the mirror in
which nothing can be concealed.

PAUL TILLICH
The Shaking of the Foundations

D1329893

WIPF & STOCK · Eugene, Oregon

Wipf and Stock Publishers
199 W 8th Ave, Suite 3
Eugene, OR 97401

Paul Tillich
His Life and Thought
By Pauck, Wilhelm and Pauck, Marion
Copyright©1976 by Pauck, Wilhelm
ISBN 13: 978-1-4982-0717-1
Publication date 2/26/2015
Previously published by Harper & Row, 1976

ACKNOWLEDGMENTS

Grateful acknowledgment is made to the following for permission to reprint selections included in this book:

CHARLES SCRIBNER'S SONS for quotations from "The Destruction of Death"; "Escape from God"; "The Yoke of Religion"; "You Are Accepted" in *The Shaking of the Foundations* by Paul Tillich, copyright © 1948 Charles Scribner's Sons: "Love is Stronger than Death"; "The Meaning of Joy"; "On Healing"; "Principalities and Powers"; "Who Are My Mother and Brothers?" in *The New Being* by Paul Tillich, copyright © 1955 Charles Scribner's Sons: "Forgetting and Being Forgotten"; "God's Pursuit of Man"; "Heal the Sick; Cast out Demons" in *The Eternal Now* by Paul Tillich, copyright © 1965 Charles Scribner's Sons. All rights reserved.

UNION THEOLOGICAL SEMINARY in New York for permission to quote the two passages from the correspondence between Henry Sloane Coffin and the Rockefeller Foundation in addition to the oral permission of John Bennett.

CHARLES W. KEGLEY and ROBERT W. BRETALL for passages from "Autobiographical Reflections" in *The Theology of Paul Tillich*, copyright © 1952 Macmillan Company.

THE EXECUTORS OF THE ESTATE OF WALTER LIPPMANN for quotation from one of his letters.

TIME LIFE PICTURE AGENCY for picture of Paul Tillich and Henry R. Luce taken by John Loengard. Copyright © 1967 Time Inc.

Additional photographs in this volume were given by the following: Claudia Bader, Wolfgang Hochheimer, Eleanor H. Kouwenhoven, Marion and Wilhelm Pauck, Maria Klein Rhine, Elisabeth Tillich Seeberger, Paul Tillich, Ilse Usener, and Gisela Walker.

We also thank Hannah Tillich and Robert Kimball, Tillich's literary executor, for granting permission to quote from Tillich's unpublished papers.

Contents

PREFACE FOR THE 2014 EDITION   iii
ORIGINAL PREFACE   v

1. DREAMING INNOCENCE (1886–1914)

    His Father's House   1
    Outside the Enchanted Garden   16
    Early Freedom   29

2. THE TURNING POINT: WORLD WAR I (1914–1918)   40

3. BETWEEN TWO WORLDS (1919–1924)

    Teacher, Theoretician   57
    Author, Journalist   65
    Religious Socialist   67
    Spiritual Breakthrough   75
    Creative Chaos   79

4. SPLENDID ISOLATION (1924–1933)

    Struggle to Survive   94
    Dance and the Demonic   98
    Early Fame   110
    Encounter with Tyranny   123

CONTENTS

5. BENEFICIAL CATASTROPHE (1933–1939)

A Second Death — 139
Shelter from the Storm — 159
An Ear to the Ground — 177

6. A BRIDGE TO THE WORLD (1939–1955)

War and Peace — 196
Return to Germany — 206
Harvest Time — 218
The Systematic Theology — 232

7. THE AMBIGUITY OF FAME (1955–1965)

The Crest of the Wave — 246
World Traveler — 258
Illness and Death — 272

A Chronology of the Life of Paul Tillich — 287

Abbreviations — 291

Notes — 292

Index — 330

Preface to the 2014 Edition

Our biography of Paul Tillich was first published in 1976 by Harper San Francisco. It was widely reviewed in USA, and published in Great Britain, Germany, and Japan. A paperback edition followed in 1989 in which minor corrections were made. I refer the reader to my preface for that edition which follows immediately after this preface.

Tragically, Wilhelm Pauck was unable to complete the second volume of our biography of Tillich. He lost a great deal of time while editing and re-working the German translation of the first volume. Grave illness and death followed. The first chapter of that proposed book, however, was completed. It is a very long one and has been included in a book of essays titled, *From Luther to Tillich*, published by Harper San Francisco in 1984. Insufficient attention has been paid to this chapter probably because it comes at the end of that collection. Outlines and notes for the second volume of our biography remain unpublished. They will eventually reside in the archives of the Luce Library in Princeton, New Jersey, taking their place in the "Wilhelm and Marion Pauck Manuscript Collection," unless some way is found to publish them.

We are pleased that Wipf and Stock is publishing again what many have referred to as "the standard" biography of Paul Tillich. Tillich's anxiety over the way his thought and writings might die with him has fortunately not been realized. Tillich's thought remains alive and intriguing to postmodern humankind. And his life in all its complexity and richness continues to fascinate us.

Marion Hausner Pauck
Mountain View, California
September 2014

Preface

Our sense of the need for a contemporary biography of Paul Tillich was first brought to his attention in the autumn of 1960 in the midst of the Greek sculpture collection of the Metropolitan Museum of Art. Two years later a concrete plan was presented to him in his office at Harvard University. Despite the fact that he had written three brief but telling autobiographies, he responded with enthusiasm, as did most of those with whom he subsequently discussed the plan. Tillich was by then at the zenith of his fame, a widely recognized public figure conscious of his image, and he was flattered that friends and colleagues were preparing to paint his portrait. Moreover, it was the spring of his last year at Harvard, and he was in the process of disposing of his books and papers. He decided to donate them to Harvard's Andover Library, where an archive was being established in his name. At the same time he yielded to the desire of his German friends to establish an archive in Göttingen, mainly for preservation of his German papers and materials. His preoccupation with the "posthumous Tillich" strengthened in him the wish to have his image preserved by those who had, for nearly a lifetime, heard his voice and seen his gestures.

The present volume draws upon sources which Tillich made directly accessible: documents in the Harvard and Göttingen archives; a multitude of interviews with members of his family, friends and colleagues; and many conversations with Tillich himself. The authors also make extensive use of Tillich's autobiographical pieces, his entire written opus, published and unpublished, as well as many contemporary works of history and literature.

Research was begun in 1963. Tillich's squirrellike tendency to preserve as much of his writing as possible made work in the archives immediately productive. Yet despite the fact that he had been a diligent collector, many documents had been lost or destroyed. A good part of what remained was in private hands. For two-thirds of Tillich's life the telephone and airplane had made letter writing almost an anachronism, and the proportionately small extant collection of correspondence turned out to be unevenly distributed over widely separated periods and yielded less valuable information than had been anticipated. Tillich almost never dated anything, and the German script and cramped handwriting of his letters, notebooks, and manuscripts, were difficult to decipher. Sometimes hours of investigation were needed to establish a single date or make out an unusual word or phrase.

In the absence of a consistently detailed and consecutive written record it was necessary to turn to living persons whose eye-witness accounts might supply the missing details. Tillich readily suggested names of persons who he felt should be visited, without restricting us to the list he supplied. Indeed, the only condition he set down was posthumous publication. He urged that the interviews be undertaken at once. Tillich was in his seventies, and several of his contemporaries (including two of his closest friends, Hermann Schafft and Alfred Fritz) had already died. Marion Pauck (née Hausner) therefore resigned her post at the Oxford University Press and proceeded, between May and August 1963, to travel through France, Germany, Switzerland, Austria, and England in order to seek out friends and acquaintances of Tillich's. The hospitality showered upon her during these months was at times overwhelming. Interviews were held in simple homes, luxurious villas, private gardens, and sidewalk cafés, on lakes and in forests, against the background of walled-in medieval towns and sprawling modern cities. The candor and devotion with which each of these men and women spoke about Tillich provided a wealth of detail covering the years from his birth until his emigration to the United

States. Although not free from error or exaggeration, the information thus obtained, as continually cross-checked, appears to have been accurate to a remarkable degree.

We list in grateful tribute the names of those who helped us: Theodor Adorno, Renate Albrecht, Eberhard Amelung, Claudia Bader, Nina Baring, Max and Hildegaard Behrmann, Emil and Susanne Blum, Walter Braune, Thea Tillich-Bülau, Paul Collmer, Willy Collmer, Gerda Erdmann, Gerhard Ebeling, Ellen von Frankenberg, Emmy Frey, Hanno Gelau, Nelly Gelb, Margot Hahl, Eduard Heimann, Alexander and Ellen Höchberg, Wolfgang Hochheimer, Max Horkheimer, Kurt Leese, Waltraut Seeberger Lefèbre, Gunther and Claire Loewenfeld, Heinrich Meinhof, Marianne von Machui-Pallat, Adolf Müller, Erika Opelt, Erich Pfeiffer, Harald and Dorothea Poelchau, Lilly Pincus, August Rathmann, Carl Heinz Ratschow, Margot von Reuthern, Ernst Rhein, Maria Klein Rhine, Eberhard Röhricht, Ruth Schmidt, Heide Seeberger Schütz, Erhard and Elisabeth Seeberger, Hans-Jürgen and Barbara Seeberger, Gertie Siemsen, Fedor Stepun, Gertraut Stöber, Ilse Usener, Friedrich Vorwerk, Cora Wächter, Gisela Walker, and Marie-Luise Werner.

Interviews were undertaken in America: on the eastern seaboard at Columbia, Harvard, and Yale universities, and at Union Theological Seminary in New York; in the Midwest, at the University of Chicago; and in the Far West, at Stanford University. The men and women consulted were as cooperative and hospitable as their European counterparts. They represented many fields of endeavor: they were artists, economists, historians, philosophers, psychiatrists, scientists, and theologians. They stressed Tillich's gradual and astounding success as an emigré and tended to relegate his personal life to the background. Although profound affection for Tillich was apparent at almost every turn, the interviews were often sober and critical in content and tone. The authors hereby gratefully acknowledge the assistance given by James Luther Adams, Ruth Nanda Anshen, John C. Bennett, Robert McAfee Brown, Gotthard Booth, Winston Davis, John Dillenberger, Tom Faw Driver, Horace Friess, Kurt Goldstein, Robert T.

Handy, Mary Heilner, Albert Hofstadter, Hanya Holm, Hans Huth, Joseph M. Kitagawa, Richard Kroner, Paul Lee, Paul L. Lehmann, Adolf Löwe, Rollo May, John T. McNeill, Samuel Miller, Albert T. Mollegen, Reinhold and Ursula Niebuhr, Albert C. Outler, Kenneth Pease, Nathan M. Pusey, John Hermann Randall, Jr., Elinor Roberts, Werner Rode, Roger Shinn, Joseph Sittler, John E. Smith, Clifford Stanley, Robert Ulich, Henry P. and Elizabeth Van Dusen, Hugh Van Dusen, Carl Hermann Voss, Daniel Day Williams, Clark Williamson, and Elisabeth Moore Wood.

Our interviews with Tillich himself were the most fruitful of all. He recalled vivid details about his childhood; he spoke freely of his relationships with family and friends; he described with calculated objectivity his intellectual and professional career, and—surprisingly—rarely repeated what he had written or said elsewhere. He set straight unreliable myths maintained by oral tradition and proved often to have a more accurate memory of the past and its meaning than many who had shared it with him. His greatest fault was his inability to recall dates exactly; his greatest virtue, his lack of self-deception. Aware that his personal life was unconventional and fearful that his work might be undermined on that account, he took special care to recall and illuminate the details of his personal development.

After Tillich's death, the need to order and catalogue the materials in the archives prevented rapid progress of our work. Major illness and two moves between the east and west coasts interfered even further. Then in 1973 the appearance of Hannah Tillich's autobiography and Rollo May's personal memoir reinforced our conviction that a complete biography of Paul Tillich was greatly needed. In the spring of 1975 we were finally able to complete our labors.

Our original plan to publish a biography of Tillich emphasizing the main trends of his life and showing the origin and growth of his thought has resulted in two separate volumes which, although each is in itself an organic whole, are interdependent. Volume I depicts

Tillich's life against the background of his thought. Volume II analyses his thought against the background of his life.. The first volume is primarily the work of Marion Pauck, the second of Wilhelm Pauck, but since the whole work has been the product of constant collaboration, we both assume full responsibility for both volumes. A bibliography will be included at the end of Volume II.

Our work on the whole enterprise was made possible by the generous aid of many persons to whom we are especially indebted: Eleanor H. Kouwenhoven, whose private gift financed the first trip to Europe; John M. Musser, president of the General Service Foundation, for a large grant which has helped to underwrite many expenses since 1965; Vanderbilt University, whose research grant made possible two visits to the Harvard Archive; Robert Kimball, literary executor of the Paul Tillich estate, for his readiness to give us access to the Harvard Archive after Tillich's death and for permitting us to quote from Tillich's unpublished papers; Kenneth Pease, for his competent and kindly help in finding our way through the contents of the archive; James Tanis, head of the Andover Library during Tillich's last years at Harvard, and Maria Grossmann, Tanis's successor, who made available their services in friendly, professional fashion; Renate Albrecht, the indefatigable editor of Tillich's *Gesammelte Werke*, and Gertraut Stöber, the archivist in Göttingen, whose industry put valuable materials at our disposal; Jaroslav Pelikan, for stimulating discussions at the start of our work; Carl Hermann Voss, for his consistent and willing assistance throughout the years; Henry P. Van Dusen, for his energetic encouragement. Above all we thank James Luther Adams—who, Tillich said, knew his writings even better than he himself did—for his countless favors and steadfast friendship. We express gratitude to Clayton E. Carlson, Marie Cantlon, and Richard Lucas of Harper & Row, for their unfailing patience, enthusiasm, and support, and to Annabel Learned, our copy editor, for her unflagging diligence.

Finally, we are grateful to Paul Tillich for his confidence in us.

When we bade him farewell after talking about the biography for the last time, in the summer of 1965, he said: "I am in safe hands."

WILHELM AND MARION PAUCK

Palo Alto, California
1 September 1975

Preface to the Paperback Edition

The paperback edition of our biography of Paul Tillich is a faithful rendition of the original work first published in 1976. The few corrections which have been made concern mostly dates and names of persons and places.

Several minor changes have also been made: where documentary evidence turned out to be unreliable; where there is conflicting evidence among documents in the two Tillich archives or in private hands; and, finally, where new documents have become available. In each of the above instances, appropriate changes and/or additions have been made in the text and/or in the reference notes.

It is important to note that neither the corrections nor the changes have significantly altered the portrait of Paul Tillich which my late husband, Wilhelm Pauck, and I painted in these pages. Indeed, the passage of time and the continuing publication of articles and books about Tillich and his thought have deepened our conviction that our portrait is a true and balanced one.

It is tragic that my husband's long illness and death in 1981 prevented him from completing the second volume of our biography which was to have been a history and analysis of Tillich's thought. The first third of Pauck's unfinished manuscript was published posthumously in a collection of enduring essays entitled, *From Luther to Tillich*, edited by Marion Pauck (Harper & Row, 1984). In the last chapter of this collection, "Paul Tillich: Heir of the Nineteenth Century," Pauck traces the spiritual and intellectual development of the young Tillich; yet most of what is written there applies also to the mature Tillich.

Another publication by Wilhelm Pauck regarded by many scholars to be the most incisive essay on Tillich in print, and entitled "To Be or Not to Be: Tillich on the Meaning of Life," was published in *The Thought of Paul Tillich*, edited by James Luther Adams, Wilhelm Pauck, and Roger Shinn (Harper & Row, 1985). These two chapters and the volumes in which they appear make excellent companions to our biography.

The fact that this biography has been published not only in the United States of America but also in Great Britain, The Federal Republic of Germany, and Japan, is a source of genuine satisfaction to us. It is clear that more than 100 years after Tillich's birth and nearly 24 years after his death, his life and thought, and the era of prolific historical and theological scholarship of which he was an outstanding representative, continue to demand serious attention.

14 March 1989   MARION PAUCK
                                                 Palo Alto, California

1

Dreaming Innocence (1886-1914)

His Father's House

Paul Tillich was born on 20 August 1886 in a parish house in Starzeddel,[1] a village in the district of Guben near Berlin, Germany. This little place, where ruins from the Bronze Age have been uncovered, now belongs to Poland and is called Starosiedle, meaning "Old Homestead." Tillich's parents, Johannes Oskar and Wilhelmina Mathilde, née Dürselen, were married in October, 1885. He was then twenty-eight, she was twenty-five. Paul was their first child.[2] Born at half-past midnight, the infant nearly perished on the same day. Announcing the event to his parents, Johannes Tillich wrote:

> Little Paul is still alive but his life is a continuous struggle with death; perhaps, but only perhaps, will this young life be victorious. Yet his breathing may stop at any moment. We have already given him up three times this night . . . he lay in a death struggle for nearly seven hours, then his body became warm again—to our terror, I must say. The excitement, the wavering between fear and hope are nearly killing us too, despite all self-control.[3]

In this first experience of his existence, Paul Tillich's lifelong dread of death—this melancholy preoccupation—may have had its beginning. As a child he was struck by the question, "Why is there something rather than nothing?" As a boy he repressed the knowledge of the untimely death of his mother. As a young man, in World War I, he experienced the death of a civilization and was transformed by it.

For the mature Tillich, death represented the "absolutely unknown," "the darkness in which there is no light at all," "the real and ultimate object of fear from which all other fears derive their power,"[4] "the anxiety of being eternally forgotten"[5]—death meant parting, separation, isolation, and opposition.[6] Tillich felt uneasy in the presence of the dying, partly because he was fearful of his own death; partly because he could not conceive that he would himself one day no longer be.[7] For Tillich, death was never a friend or an achievement, but a stranger to be unmasked;[8] yet he never thought of it as the ultimate victor. "For love," he said, "is stronger than death."[9] The infant who won his early struggle over death became the man whose statement, "Being overcomes nonbeing," is the very entrance to his thought.

The infant survived and was baptized by his father, a Lutheran pastor, on 12 September 1886. In the fashion of the time, Tillich was given two middle names, Johannes for his father, Oskar for his paternal grandfather. He never used all his names; for most of his life he was known as Paul J. Tillich, and after fame overtook him late in life, simply Paul Tillich. As a child he was called Paulchen, as a young man Paul; in his maturity he was known as Paulus.

The Tillich family name first appears in official records of the thirteenth century in middle and east Germany.[10] Until the Hussite wars, when Slavic elements were absorbed, the Tillichs were all German. The earliest of whom details are known were two brothers, Johannes and Theodricus, both of whom studied at the Augustinian monastery, St. Moritz vor den Toren von Naumburg. By 1392 Johannes was a monk, later he became a prior. He studied in Prague in 1384, during the lifetime of John Huss. Theodricus was at the St. Moritz monastery at the University of Leipzig from 1410 onward. He was a provost, a lecturer at the university, and the author of two histories. He was especially respected by his monastic brethren for having planted vineyards in the Saaleberg hills near Naumburg, an achievement for which he and his brother were given a lifelong benefice.

In the 1630s all relatives of one George Tielich, except for two older uncles, were wiped out within a week by the plague. This ancestor was born in 1624, around the time of Jacob Boehme, and lived to be seventy-four. His youngest brother, called Paulus, did not survive infancy. George studied theology at the University of Leipzig in 1648, and became a minister. He was criticized for discussing politics too freely in the pulpit and was dismissed from one of his pastorates for reasons unknown.

The Tillich family produced musicians and manufacturers as well as monks and ministers; many of them were blessed with double talents. Indeed, the name Tillich, originally "Dietrich," means "rich or powerful folk." This power or talent expressed itself to an unusual degree in the immediate forebears of Paul Tillich. His great-grandfather Wilhelm, known by his second name Samuel, was a skilled musician who played the flute, clarinet, guitar, and violin. Married twice, he raised a family of six and supported himself by selling cloth. Oskar, his youngest son, born in 1828, owned a copper and silver workshop; he made a great deal of money—all of which he lost before World War I—and lived to the ripe age of eighty-six. It is probably to Oskar's wife that Tillich refers when he mentions a grandmother who built barricades in the revolution of 1848, from whom he surmises he may have inherited a drop of socialist blood.[11]

Johannes Tillich, Oskar's son and Paul's father, was the first Lutheran pastor in the Tillich family.[12] Good-looking, with small features, he wore a black beard which he kept expertly trimmed. He moved gracefully and was clever with his hands, but tended to be melancholy and meditative, was a hypochondriac, and incessantly smoked cigars, unlike his son who never smoked. A pastor and church administrator, Johannes included in his functions that of school inspector and superintendent of thirty ministers. He examined candidates for the ministry, was a traditionalist Lutheran of decided views, and ultimately became a *Konsistorialrat*, i.e., member of the Consistory of the Province of Brandenburg of the Evangelical Church of Prussia, with headquarters in Berlin.

He was a dignified man and, partly because of his elevated position, exuded an air of authority. Some, including his son Paul, thought of him as more strict than in fact he was. He was a master of exact formulation and greatly relished debate. He never openly criticized, but discussed quietly. Philosophy, particularly the tensions between Greek and Christian thought, fascinated him. In this intellectual adventure he included his son in early exchanges.

Johannes was also endowed with a lively musical talent. He performed on the piano, composed, and wrote poems which he set to music. He thought up lullabies for his grandchildren, and they adored him. It was through music that Johannes Tillich learned to know himself, as his son came to know himself through painting. The family often played chamber music in the evenings, and although Paul did not inherit his father's musical talent, he was taught at an early age by his mother to play simple pieces on the piano. At the annual family gathering, Johannes alternated in providing music and joining in the dance.[13]

Johannes Tillich was a typical Prussian or German father. He regarded it as improper to express satisfaction directly to his son, but it was important for him to praise his son to other people. Moreover, he played the customary role of the parent: the father had to be the figure of authority. In this, as in everything else, he was a pillar of Prussian society. While Paul greatly respected and sometimes feared him, he also loved him; indeed, their relationship was softened by a benevolent, even sentimental understanding, a protective and secret pride. The same may be said of Johannes's attitudes toward his two daughters, who in turn respected and loved him. He urged them to carve out professions of their own, with a liberality of mind unusual for his time.

4

The image of Mathilde Dürselen Tillich, Paul's mother, is ghostly; very little is remembered about her. Her face was narrow and long, with small serious eyes and a generous but sad mouth. Her background was liberal and bourgeois. Her father, Gustav, was a Rhenish *bon vivant* who lived to the age of ninety and was inordinately fond of women. Tillich loved his grandfather Dürselen, who called him Paulichen or Paulchen ("little Paul"), and felt he had inherited from him his great affection for women. A popular man, Dürselen enjoyed drinking beer at the *Wirtshaus* at dusk.

The survival of all Tillich's grandparents until 1900, except for Mathilde's mother, Amalia, provided a link with the nineteenth century as far back as Goethe and Napoleon—a link to which Tillich remained sentimentally attached all his life.

Tillich's father was strict but his mother was inflexible. She was a "Calvinist," especially about eating, and had an absolute idea that the children must get out into the open air every day. One Christmas day, Tillich's father successfully interceded for them, saying it would be nice for them to stay at home and play with their new toys. Nevertheless, young Paul adored his mother. "My whole life was embedded in her," he once said. "I couldn't imagine any other woman." Shortly before her death he said to her, "I would like to marry you." She died of cancer when she was forty-three.

As a small child, Tillich played in a beautiful garden outside the parish house in Starzeddel where he was born; Tillich's father enlarged the garden by having a barn removed. Nearby was a great park belonging to the lord of the manor, Prince Schöneich Carolath. From a certain window in the parish house, young Paul could see a stork's nest on a neighboring roof and note the arrival and departure of the birds. A stone wall separated the garden from a girls' school; there were chickens in the courtyard there. Tillich played with other small children in the village. In the long winter, they battled with snowballs; in the milder seasons they played hide-and-seek, robber and princess, and a wild game somewhat similar to hockey. In 1888, Tillich's sister Johanna Marie was born,[14] and in 1891 the entire family moved to Schönfliess, where Johannes Tillich became a superindent.

Schönfliess was a tiny medieval town with a population of about three thousand. There was a large, very old and beautiful church, an old city hall, and many ancient houses, none more than two stories high. The streets were paved with cobblestones; grass grew between them. There were no automobiles, of course, and the only transportation was by horse and carriage. Indeed, Schönfliess was famous for its horse market. The town children were always infinitely happy to be free from school for a day when horses were sold.

When Tillich was not playing with his young sisters (Elisabeth Johanna Mathilda was born in 1893[15]) his favorite sport was to walk along the top of the town wall, as Goethe in his own childhood had done in Frankfort, and survey the realm. Late in life, he still dreamed of that wall, remembering the turrets and towers that marked the entrance to the town.

Outside the town, nearby, was a lake where the boy and his father sailed; his father held the tiller while young Tillich handled the foresail. Once there was a terrible storm and they were forced to leave the boat on shore at some distance and walk home, returning only the next day to sail it back. Tillich remembered the waves and wind on the water. One night he dreamed that tremendous waves from the lake were rushing up over the wall to engulf the town. On another occasion when Tillich, out alone, came home very late from the lake, his father, who had been fearing he had drowned, spanked him. It was the only time his father punished him in this way.

The years in Schönfliess were orderly, quiet, simple. In the fall, Paul and his sisters roamed over farms and fields. They pulled up weeds, built a hut, made a fire of potato leaves. They played "soldier." Tillich had a gun which he had made himself, and used an old iron·pipe for a cannon as they ran about the land. He was a protector to his young sisters, helping them overcome their timidity. In winter, he packed them on a sled and pushed them around town. One day he bribed Elisabeth with a bonbon to cross a field of snow; it magically removed her anxiety. When she was older he taught her to play chess. She later married a Lutheran pastor, Erhard Seeberger, and bore him a son and two daughters, but remained Tillich's proud and adoring young sister throughout her life.

With his other sister, Johanna, he shared a deeper, almost mystical relationship. They fought a good deal in the early years. Indeed Tillich, a serious, somewhat spoiled child, occasionally had terrible fits of temper, but his anger never lasted long and he did not bear grudges. As time went on, these siblings became of "one heart, one mind." Johanna was an unusually beautiful girl, with philosophical inclinations and a passion for wild flowers. As she was about to be confirmed, Tillich caused her anguish by asking her critical questions; it is said he roused doubt in her mind about her faith.[16]

Tillich's schooling began when he was six. He attended the grammar school that stood opposite the Gothic church where his father was pastor. Instruction in religion was an obligatory part of the curriculum; for four hours a week Paul was taught the catechism, hymns, and Bible stories. Time was measured by the Christian festivals—the year was the church year, and the greatest time of the year, for him at least, was Advent and Christmas. He loved to build, and, in the typical month-long preparations for the German Christmas, would construct a church with a candle in it. This was his offering, placed under the Christmas tree. At other times, he made *crèches*. The building was done very carefully, systematically, with great finesse, using small red, white, and blue squares or blocks from a *Steinbaukasten*.* He spent hours making the thing perfect. Balance was his goal. By the time he was fourteen or fifteen this and similar constructions were his favorite hobby.

The indelible impression made by the Christian symbols on Tillich's receptive mind was for him a first experience of the holy as

* Child's box of "stone" (composition) blocks, often ample in number and quite varied. Even adults found them creative and picturesque.

an indestructible good. He later said that this was the foundation of all his religious and theological work.[17] When he was eight, in his initial glimpse of the Baltic Sea, he wrestled for the first time with the idea of the infinite.[18] He was already fascinated by Christian dogmatics and devoured popular books on philosophy during his preconfirmation instruction. The thought of the infinite disturbed him; it was not just an idea, it was an experience. He was not so much being taught about religion as being grasped by it. In the center of the town stood the church; in the center of the year was the festival of Christmas; all else revolved around this place and this event. His feelings for the ecclesiastical and sacramental were for him part of the fabric of life from the very beginning.

Tillich's friends at school were boys who came from a less privileged class.[19] The Tillichs were far from wealthy, indeed actually poor, but because his father's church district included members of the old landed nobility with whom he and his wife had social contact, young Paul visited the manor houses too and played with their children. He was proud of this; also conscious of the tension between the two sets of friends, at an early age he developed a sense of guilt about the underprivileged. When he was ten, for example, he used his enormous young energy to help some Polish workers load sand onto a truck near the railway station.

His first close friend, however, was the son of a noble family whose forefathers had served the kings of Prussia, Eckart von Sydow. This boy presided at the growing sophistication of Tillich's childhood, opening up new worlds beyond the sheltered life of the stuffy parish house, luring him to joys hitherto unknown. He taught Paul to play chess and checkers, sitting in the branches of a tree. He introduced him to Darwin, suddenly saying one day, "You know, we're all descendants of monkeys." This was a terrible shock to young Tillich. Von Sydow grew into a man of rare intellectual ability, whose books on classical and modern art got a wide response.[20] In 1912 this old friend opened Tillich's eyes to the work of Sigmund Freud, and after World War I introduced him to Expressionist painting. In the 1920s the two men had a terrible row, which made Tillich disconsolate until they were reconciled.

Then, in a boyish gesture, he sent von Sydow a sheaf of red roses.

Tillich's sense of identification with the Prussian nobility was entirely natural. The times were Wilhelminian: once his father accepted a call to Berlin, young Tillich saw there the reigning Kaiser, Wilhelm II. The capital was a booming industrial city at the heart of the growing German empire. It was the turn of the century: cannon were fired at midnight to mark the moment. The boy's father took him out into the Berlin streets that night to behold the bright celebrations. The bustling, dynamic metropolis which the youth had seen only on annual visits to his grandparents now became his home. Walking to school each morning he passed through the produce market (*Markthalle*) where food and flowers were sold; the variety of sights and smells nourished his later love for French cooking, wine, and the bohemian aspect of life. The activity of the city, the crowds, the many sights and sounds, the largeness of its environment with its lakes and woods, allured and excited his imagination. Most of all he was transported by the view of the Kaiser and his parades, as indeed was every boy in Berlin.

Before World War I, the annual Kaiser maneuvers of guard regiments took place in the city every May. The plumes on the helmets of the cuirassiers, the pennants of the lancers, the units of splendidly uniformed men marching to the sound of fife and drum in sparkling sunshine (obligatory Kaiser weather), even the whirling dust under the horses' hooves, were for all small Berlin boys an ineradicably grand experience. Tillich never forgot it, and his heart, no less than his father's, was filled with royalist patriotism. Johannes Tillich was chosen to accompany the Kaiser to Palestine in 1898 for the consecration of the Church of the Redeemer in Jerusalem. The event must have meant a great deal to him, for a piece of olive wood he brought back from the Holy Land remained always on his desk.

The Tillichs moved to Berlin because Johannes had been appointed minister and superintendent of the *Bethlehemgemeinde*; at the same time he was made a member of the consistory of the province of Brandenburg. In this capacity, he examined ministerial candidates in the field of philosophy. A somewhat remote figure now, he was far more occupied than he had been in Schönfliess, yet found time for his son. Every day at three in the afternoon, after his nap, he tutored him in Latin. It was the only thing in this otherwise lovely period of the boy's life that marred his day. His father was usually in a bad mood on waking, either morning or afternoon.

Tillich's *Gymnasium* or higher schooling had already begun before the family moved from Schönfliess. In 1898 he was sent to Königsberg to attend the "Humanistic" *Gymnasium* there, living meanwhile in a boardinghouse run by an old lady. His loneliness in his room was assuaged only by reading the Bible given him on his first birthday, his most precious possession. At the *Gymnasium* he learned the humanities, especially Latin and Greek, to prepare for the university. In Berlin he attended the Friedrich Wilhelm *Gymnasium*, beginning his training there on 4 January 1901. Although he has written several imaginative and precise autobiographical pieces and recorded so much concerning his later youth and development,[21] Tillich has said amazingly little about his *Gymnasium* years. This is difficult to explain, since most people so vividly remember their teachers, friends, and particularly the mischievous capers in which, between the ages of twelve and seventeen, they tend to engage. Perhaps in Tillich's case the move to Berlin was responsible. It meant a switch from school to school, from country to city. His grades were not outstanding, but *genügend* or adequate. A certain preoccupation with higher academic demands probably seized him in the effort to do well. His memories of the time are therefore not of people and events but of his thorough training in Latin and Greek. Later he was inordinately proud of his command of these languages and frequently built his lectures and sermons around the Latin or Greek etymology of a word or phrase.

Tillich's memory of these years was blurred not only by the demands of a new life in city and school but by certain emotional problems of his adolescence. His memories were of emotional upheaval and intellectual adjustment. The difficulties he experienced in coming to terms with reality led him "into a life of fantasy at an early age. Between fourteen and seventeen" (he wrote later), "I withdrew as often as possible into imaginary worlds which seemed to be truer than the world outside. In time, that romantic imagination was transformed into philosophic imagination."[22] In his realm of idle dreaming and fantasy Tillich was not unlike other adolescents, except that his need to escape reality was more extreme. His identification with figures like Hamlet, for example, nearly endangered his health.

> Even after my infatuation with Hamlet, which lasted for some time, I preserved the capacity for complete identification with other creatures of poetic fancy. The specific mood, the color as it were, of certain weeks or months of my life, would be determined by one literary work or the other. Later this was especially true of novels, which I read infrequently but with great intensity.[23]

Tillich's "romantic imagination" or capacity for dreamy fantasy was formulated only much later in philosophical language, however. During his adolescence it was nourished by sailing, by wandering through the pleasant Brandenburg countryside, which remained his favorite landscape, and by playing in the garden behind his home in the Neuenburgerstrasse. Cultivated by his mother, who disliked the city, this little paradise was a rarity few people in Berlin possessed. Like the enchanted garden of Oscar Wilde's fairy tale,[24] it was framed by a high wall on three sides and the house on the other: no one could look into it, but the children could look out. Climbing the wall was a grapevine already there when the Tillichs moved into the house. It grew year after year, faithfully producing grapes which the children picked and ate. There was a ladder leaning against the wall upon the broad top of which they often sat overlooking their domain. The most beautiful tree in the garden was a walnut, near which they planted lilies, violets, and other flowers. Paul at this age had a remarkable ability to play happily here for many hours with his sisters and the young friends who came to the house, most of them girls and all younger than himself. He played croquet and boccia with them, and invented guessing games for their amusement.

The turmoil of the boy's spirit during these adolescent years seems to have been intensified by questions which arose in his mind regarding the Christian faith. These often ran counter to the authority of his father's orthodox views. He therefore sought out the friendship and counsel of a young man, Erich Harder, who had come into his life already in 1899. Harder, then around twenty, was Johannes Tillich's vicar or assistant, a Wingolf member,* theologically a liberal. He was intelligent, benevolent, and kind—a contrast in some respects to Johannes Tillich, whose certainty was sometimes threatening, particularly to a doubter. It is said that Johannes fought like a bull during theological congresses, for example, and was so sure of his own position that he once said, "Uns kann nichts geschehen, wir sind allem gewachsen." [Nothing can happen to us, we are prepared for everything.]²⁵ While there may have been more faith than arrogance in the elder Tillich's attitude, it produced feelings of awe in the young inquiring mind of his son. And so Paul poured out his heart to Harder, who became his mentor and father confessor. Harder permitted him the luxury of doubt, and thus helped him at a crucial time in his development. The vicar, who was genuinely Lutheran, made the fundamentals of theology, particularly justification by faith, clear to Tillich. He was a joyous, open, quiet, and balanced man, especially good at listening and then patiently explaining his opinion. He once took the boy on a walking trip from Berlin to Eberswalde; the two wandered for days, and it was an experience Tillich never forgot. To the end of his life he remembered Harder gratefully as a highly cultivated man and a free spirit.

Tillich's unconscious sophistication in questions of the Christian faith was demonstrated by the time of his confirmation, which took place on 23 March 1902. He was confirmed by his father in the Bethlehemskirche in Berlin. In later years, he wrote about this event:

When I was of the age to receive confirmation and full membership in the Church, I was told to choose a passage from the Bible as the

* A student corporation, further explained on pp. 20ff.

expression of my personal approach to the Biblical message and to the Christian Church. Every confirmee was obliged to do so, and to recite the passage before the congregation. When I chose the words, "Come unto me all ye that labor and are heavy laden," I was asked with a kind of astonishment and even irony why I had chosen that particular passage. For I was living under happy conditions, and being only fifteen years old was without any apparent labor and burden. I could not answer at that time; I felt a little embarrassed, but basically right. And I was right, indeed; every child is right in responding immediately to these words; every adult is right in responding to them in all periods of his life. . . . Returning for the first time in my life to the passage of my early choice, I feel just as grasped by it as at that time, but infinitely more embarrassed by its majesty, profundity, and inexhaustible meaning.[26]

On the same occasion, Tillich's father presented him with a motto for his future life, and he felt, he says, that these words were just what he was looking for. They were, "The truth will make you free." (John 8:32)[27] Tillich felt at the time that the other confirmands were equally receptive to this motto; it warned them not to lose their passion for truth in adulthood. It was a passion which in Tillich himself never abated. Nor did he shrink from heavy burdens of labor; his drive to excel was as great as his energy.

In 1903, a year after he was confirmed, Tillich's mother died of cancer. He always left the impression that her death occurred when he was an extremely young child. The facts contradict this, for he was already seventeen. After her death, his father exercised such unchallenged influence upon him that he often felt overwhelmed. He became involved therefore in a deep inner struggle to free himself from his father's authority, which for a time he identified with the authority of revelation. For this reason, each new level of personal and intellectual autonomy he reached was colored by a sense of guilt.[28]

The burden of guilt thus experienced in Tillich's earliest attempts to find independence was never entirely overcome. Neither the ongoing quiet discussions between him and his father nor the great pride the father took in his son's achievements seem to have provided the necessary cure. Yet the letters between them, written during his university years and after, reveal a deeply moving mutual tenderness, understanding, and concern, suggesting that Tillich's fears of disapproval were somehow exaggerated and out of proportion. Even when he had reached maturity this was so: he demonstrated a respect tinged with awe toward all men in positions of authority, and often dreamed that he was teaching a classroom filled with divinity students each of whom wore a clerical collar and had the face of his father.[29]

Tillich's loss of his mother took on an even more exotic turn: he repressed the fact of her death and did not speak of her to anyone. This was and would remain his way of dealing with the death of those he greatly loved. He sought her forever after in every Demeter or Persephone he pursued. He continued to worship her by transferring his obsessive love to the sea and to the sun. After their mother's death, Tillich and his sister Johanna drew exceedingly close to each other, sharing their innermost thoughts and feelings. He called her "Woman" or "Wumming," she called him, "My boy." More than anyone else she became his "ideal."[30]

Johannes Tillich was deeply saddened by his wife's death and for a time became a rather remote figure in the family. A housekeeper, "Tante Toni" [Aunt Toni] joined the ménage, but the children—Tillich as well as his sisters—seem to have suffered from neglect. They were not well-groomed and were often pale, stayed up too late, frequently looked very tired. Left to their own devices, they were only occasionally interrupted in their work or play by the appearance of their preoccupied father.

During his last years at the *Gymnasium*, Tillich and his friends often sailed with passionate pleasure on the Wannsee. One day a strong wind came up. Tillich rose up in the boat and said, "Let's invent a sail." To the delight of his companions, he took the cape he was wearing and stood holding it against the wind. On Sundays the young people took long walks in the pine forests of the Mark Brandenburg,* singing together and stopping for picnics. Often Til-

---

* i.e. the territory around Berlin, ruled for centuries by the Hohenzollern dynasty.

lich, unusually serious and introspective, engaged the others in philosophical discussions. Sometimes, showing his puckish lighter side, he went off alone with three or four girls, who had to cook for him while he pretended to be a pasha! He called the girls his "harem," but the term was innocent.

Occasionally, dances and house concerts enlivened the Tillich home. Family and friends took part, The younger Tillich always cut an awkward figure on the dance floor: he wore white gloves and a dark suit and never knew what to do with his hands. He was taught to dance the quadrille, waltz, polka, Polonaise, contra, and the Rhineländer. A younger cousin, distantly related, attended these dances and looked forward to them all year; she always danced the first dance, a Polonaise, with the father and the last, a waltz, with the son. On one such occasion, the father said to her, speaking of Paul, "Some day he will be a very important man."

During the last year of his *Gymnasium* training. Tillich came upon Schwegler's *Geschichte der Philosophie* [History of Philosophy] in the dusty corner of a country preacher's bookstore, and found Fichte's *Theory of Sciences* among a wagonload of books on a Berlin street. He also purchased Kant's *Critique of Pure Reason* from a bookshop for fifty German pennies. He read these books over and over again and later claimed that they had introduced him to the most difficult parts of German philosophy. The discussions he had with his father and his perusal of these three volumes enabled him from the very beginning of his university career to converse intelligently with older students and young instructors about idealism and realism, freedom and determinism, God and the world.

In his eighteenth year, following in his father's footsteps, Tillich was headed for a career in the ministry. At the same time his own desire to become a philosopher, a desire he had nourished since his mother's death, began to sprout. When he graduated from the *Gymnasium* in the late summer of 1904, it was said of him: *Interessiert sich für Philosophie* [Is interested in philosophy].[31]

Outside the Enchanted Garden

Tillich began his theological study at the University of Berlin in the winter semester of 1904.[32]* He studied Assyrian under Professor Friedrich Delitzsch and took a course in the history of philosophy given by the famous Hegelian Adolf Lasson. But the most important events in his life that winter occurred outside the classroom. He met for the first time Hermann Schafft, who later became his closest friend. And one day, by chance and destiny, he discovered the *Collected Works* of Friedrich Wilhelm Joseph Schelling in a bookstore in the Friedrichstrasse. At the time he impulsively purchased the set, Tillich knew only a little of the history of philosophy and was eager to learn more. Yet this "seduction," as he later described it, led to his doctoral dissertation. His romance with Schelling lasted well beyond the original encounter and the dissertation; it determined his entire philosophical point of view.

In Germany at this time, theological study lasted at least three years, usually four. The matriculation or entrance examinations were followed by preparation for the first theological examination. This normally took a year or more, of which half was spent in the major work of writing a dissertation.

Theological study was divided into three sections: that of exegetical and historical matters during the first year, systematics during the second, and practical theology (preaching, counseling, and religious education) in the third. Students were given sufficient academic freedom to specialize in their own field of interest. More important perhaps was the fact that the order of study was not held to rigidly. There was a certain mobility, permitting a student to put in some time in several universities. Thus Tillich spent one semester each at Berlin and Tübingen, and two whole years in Halle.

Academic life was individualistic; the sexes were kept separated,

---

* The spring and fall terms familiar in the U.S. in the old two-term academic year were known in Germany as winter and summer semesters.

and relationships were rather impersonal. There was little social communication between students and professors except for the rather stiff obligatory Sunday afternoon calls. This was in part the result of the distance customarily maintained between the generations. Young people were expected to show formal respect to their elders, whether parents or teachers. These rigid mores inevitably produced certain inhibitions, and students found genuine community only in the student corporations. Tillich joined the Wingolf society, and we shall see shortly what it meant to him.[33]

The era was still one of social stability, unprecedented peace, and prosperity. The automobile and electricity, technology in general, had not yet come into their own. It was in this overall setting that Tillich's university training took place. During the summer semester of 1905, when he went to Tübingen, he took courses on the Gospel of John, in church history, psychology, and basic problems of philosophy. But he seems to have concentrated more on enjoying the countryside than on study. Tübingen was then a very small town surrounded by hills and woods. In May 1905 he wrote to his father of his rambles there.

> The only misery I feel is that I do so little work. In the morning I attend classes, and afternoons I take long walks. For I cannot bring myself to stay at home when the sky is sunny and cloudless, and when Nature provides me with a new and unknown wonder with every step I take. For hours I roam, usually alone, through unknown woods, fields, and hills, and revel in what I have been painfully without for half a year. The blossoms on the fruit trees are already at their peak, the gooseberries are beginning to ripen, the oaks are all green. For the first time the riddle of why poets rave so much about the month of May is solved for me.[34]

This soulful little paean signaled the beginning of Tillich's lifelong self-conscious reflection on the wonders of the natural world. While the sea absorbed his romantic attention more than any other aspect of nature, as the finite bordering on the infinite, his emotional life was interwoven with landscapes, earth, weather, fields of grain, forms of clouds, the sound of wind, the smell of flowers in spring and potato plants in the fall, the silence of the woods. He read Schelling's philosophy of nature surrounded by nature; what Schelling said, Tillich made his own. Yet it was not Schelling's influence alone that inspired his mystical participation in the beauty around him. The poets made their impact. The incomparable Goethe, to be sure, Tillich did not particularly like; he found him too scientific, insufficiently existential, not "on the boundary." In his maturity he revised this judgment. But Hölderlin, Novalis, Rilke, not to mention Stefan George, spoke to his heart. His own attitude was not scientific; he did not identify the flowers and the trees, nor did he dissect plants under a microscope. His immersion in nature was worshipful and meditative. He was proud of knowing the names of mountains he had climbed, but this is as far as his explorations went. On the lighter side, he once confessed that he was a pagan as far as trees were concerned. On the dark side, he beheld nature as tragic. Within its beauty lay the ugliness of death and the incomprehensible suffering of animals.

A melancholy air hung over this first springtime away from Berlin; there was an absence of joy and merriment. His mother had died two years before, and Tillich's sense at this time of mourning and yearning for a lost good was later incorporated by poetic analogy into many of his sermons. He lived apart in Tübingen, he was a "loner" and reserved. Student gossip spread the rumor that he had read Kant's *Critique of Pure Reason* while in the *Gymnasium*. He gave the impression of being an unworldly bookworm, was rather pale, thin, and delicate. A month after his poetic letter to his father, he telegraphed for permission to undergo an operation; he was suffering from an excruciatingly painful middle-ear infection. The surgery itself went well, but the whole experience was an ordeal. Tillich lay in the hospital for a long time convalescing, and a fellow student, Alfred Fritz, who came to pay a friendly call found him far too much alone and decided to keep him company.[35] "Frede," as he was known, read aloud to him from Wilhelm Raabe's *Schwarze Galeere*. After his recovery, Tillich remained weak and had to go home. The two met again in Halle, where Tillich sought Fritz out later that year. They became

18

close friends and ultimately brothers-in-law. What struck Frede about this rather serious theological student even at their first meeting was a quality many others were to discover in Tillich: underneath the seemingly bloodless mask of learning lived a child-like and endearing openness to the world.

In the winter semester of 1905, Tillich began his course of study at the University of Halle. The theological faculty there was second only to that of Berlin (far better than Leipzig, which was limited denominationally), and only Marburg could compete with it. At Halle two traditions—the pietism of August Hermann Francke and the rationalism of Christian Wolff and the Enlight-enment—existed side by side.

Tillich once said that while all the teachers at Halle were great, the greatest was Martin Kähler, then the grand old man of the faculty.[36] Kähler had been a passionate devotee of Goethe before awakening to the Pauline-Lutheran doctrine of justification by faith, which led to his rejection of Goethe as a heathen. It was from Kähler that Tillich gained the insight that man is justified by grace through faith, not only as a sinner but even as a doubter. The discovery of this idea brought him immense relief.

Kähler was a man of overpowering intellectual, moral, and religious authority. Tillich's enthusiasm for him is described by his friend Meinhof, a medical student several years his junior, whom he persuaded to accompany him to class: "You absolutely *must* come with me to hear the old boy."[37] Meinhof went along and was not disappointed. Kähler's classes were always filled to capacity, seventy or more students jammed into the large auditorium in Halle to hear him. He had sharply cut features, with thin lips tightly pressed together and long white hair hanging to his collar. He was very difficult to understand, but until his death in 1912 was the most popular lecturer on the faculty.

Tillich's second most influential teacher was Fritz Medicus, a lecturer in philosophy who later transferred to Zurich. This scholar's work on Fichte had contributed to a renaissance of German idealism—that is, of the thought of Kant, Hegel, Schelling, and

Fichte. His knowledge of German classical philosophy was mediated to Tillich in these years. The categories of Fichte in which Medicus trained all his students enabled Tillich to attack Lütgert's theology. Tillich regarded Lütgert as the other outstanding theologian on the faculty but felt that his ideas were insufficiently independent. Medicus was a *Privatdozent* in Tillich's time and therefore not much older than those he taught; the two maintained friendly relations all their lives, the teacher proud of his student, while the student never forgot the debt he owed his teacher.

Tillich's recollection of his teachers was marked by gratitude, but his memories of his experience as a Wingolfite bordered on the romantic.[38] Student societies have existed since the Middle Ages and the founding of universities in Germany. Accidental friendships, social needs, scientific and practical drives, political, patriotic, and religious ideas have at various times impelled young people to join together. In the beginning, those with common ideas were bound, more or less closely, as the case might be, into larger groups called "nations" or smaller groups called "provinces." By the sixteenth century, these groups were called *Bursen*. Each student lived in a *Burse* and was called a *Bursarius*; the term eventually became the German word *Bursche*, meaning young man or comrade. *Bursen* flourished during Reformation times, but the Thirty Year's War brought them to an end. At some time before 1815, the forerunner of the Wingolf group had been founded as a German *Burschenschaft*. It stressed the unity of Germany, love of the fatherland, and respect for Christianity.

The Wingolf Fellowship, still alive in present-day Germany, was established around 1830, not as a resurrected *Burschenschaft* but as a loosely religious society, a new form of student life. The name has its origins in the Nordic *vin*, meaning friend, and *Golf* meaning house, thus Wingolf means "Friendship House." From the beginning it was a nondueling Christian group which adopted as its motto the Greek phrase, *Di henos panta*, meaning "All through one." The individual groups at Halle, Erlangen, Bonn, Berlin, and other universities ultimately united, and the struggle between them for definition of purpose brought about the eventual development of the Wingolfite philosophy. At national conventions at the Wartburg the principles were hammered out.*

The purpose of the corporation was to provide a lasting community for university students, which found its central focus in the formal *Kneipabende,* or social evenings. At these gatherings personal discussion between students flourished. There was beer drinking and much singing. The songs from the Wingolf songbook were largely student and marching songs, and the new young members of the society memorized them all and sang them when they went on long hikes.

Older members of the Wingolf group were called *Burschen* or comrades, while those recently accepted were *Füchse* or foxes—a reference to the time when younger members had to serve the older and thus be as sly as foxes dealing with their superiors. Each incoming member was given the opportunity to attach himself to an older member, who might or might not accept the honor. A special relation, sometimes merely formal, often more personal, thus developed between the older student, called *Leibbursch* or guardian, and the younger, called *Leibfux* or ward. The maturer student was responsible for his protégé—showed him the ropes, prepared him for the inevitable problems of university life, and concerned himself with the spiritual state of his charge. The younger student was expected to run errands for his "guardian" or do him special favors, though in Tillich's day such obligations were not rigidly enforced. Indeed when Tillich was elected first officer of the society, his own *Leibfux,* Heinrich Meinhof, made a special plea to him to ban the practice of forcing the *Leibfüxe* to polish the shoes of their elders. This Tillich granted.

Officers of the corporation were elected at annual gatherings. There were three of them, each called X–1, X–2, and X–3, or the first, second, and third "chargé." The first chargé was president, in charge of all conventions and final arbiter of all disputes, including questions of membership. The second chargé introduced new members to the statutes or rules, and communicated the spirit

* Wartburg: a castle in Thuringia where Martin Luther was confined in 1521–23 and translated the New Testament into German.

of the group to them. The third planned the *Kneipabende*. Tillich often declared that his election as first chargé was the greatest experience of his life up to that time.

He joined the society when he arrived in Halle, a medieval town which lies south of Berlin. In speaking of it later, he made much of the fact that this was the first time in his life that he had freely chosen membership in any community. At the same time, he was aware that he had picked the Wingolf society at least in part because his father was a member. In many letters to his father (in atrocious handwriting) he reported on Wingolf meetings in some detail, mentioning the principles under discussion and describing his own role in the organization.

Tillich also reported quite regularly on his studies, his relations with his teachers and fellow students, and the condition of his health. The latter part of most letters was filled with requests for food packages, particularly a hard sausage for which he had a lifelong passion, as well as chocolate and cocoa. Occasionally— not very often—he asked for money. The most characteristic aspect of these letters is that they show how close Tillich was to his father and what remarkable confidence he had in him. In July 1907, for example, on the occasion of Johannes Tillich's fiftieth birthday, his son wrote as follows:

> I very much regret that on your fiftieth birthday I must confine myself to a letter in order to express to you my heartiest best wishes, but the thoughts and feelings that naturally stir in me on such a day are no different than if I were with you. It is chiefly gratitude toward God that moves me today, gratitude toward God who has preserved you so mercifully for us despite illness and much labor. I pray that you will be ours for a long time to come. For you are mother and father to us at one and the same time and this means the most precious good we have on this earth. May you be given during the next year, and indeed the next decade, full strength and health on which we so much depend. Most particularly I want to thank you for all that you have meant to me during my student years. For the beautiful and best part of our conversations is that you allowed me to work with you freely and without compulsion and thus led me more and

more toward what is most precious to you. You cannot know what a joy it was for me that it was possible for both of us standing shoulder to shoulder to fight for the same goal. And my greatest wish for the future is that this may remain so, giving me independence and yet unity with you.[39]

Tillich's reference to "standing shoulder to shoulder" concerned a national convention of the German Wingolf at the Wartburg which his father also attended. There were approximately twenty-five units in the German Wingolf at this time. The one in Halle was considered orthodox, those in Marburg and Göttingen liberal. The students exchanged views with one another and wrote from group to group defining and clarifying the tenets on which the fraternity was to be based. In Halle, moreover, there were two main groups of which the intellectually more alert was led by Tillich. Its motto was "Zwar . . . aber," or "Yes indeed . . . but. . . ." Tillich, known not only for his superior knowledge of philosophy but also for his ability to sharpen points of logic as the principles were hammered out, was relied on to come up with the final formulations. When he got stuck, he said to his astonished fellow students, "I'll have to sit down in front of my stove and think this problem through." The phrase impressed all who heard it with its originality!

Besides sharpness of mind, Tillich was known for a sort of ambivalent moralism. He was both tolerant and rigid in his attitudes. On the subject of alcohol, for example, he showed some liberality. Once he was first chargé, he advocated freedom in the matter of drinking—that is, supported the principle that to drink or not was a question of individual conscience. But indulging to the point of intoxication was strictly forbidden.

With respect to sex, however, he came close to being priggish. On one occasion a fellow member confessed to having had sexual relations with a girl. Since it was absolutely against the Wingolf code to have such relationships, the confession became a *cause célèbre,* and in the uproar that followed, Tillich found himself at the head of the stricter group. They won, and the erring student was expelled. In protest over Tillich's attitude another member resigned. Incidentally, while girls were invited to attend Wingolf festivals, they did so as guest-observers, so to speak, rather than as participants. The female sex, as Tillich later euphemistically put it, was out of bounds for him and his fellow students. In the absence of closer contact with women no doubt some degree of erotic transfer occurred within the society. While there was no overt homosexuality, a certain erotic element was present in the Wingolf friendships.

Tillich's closest personal friends, both of whom he met in the fellowship, were Hermann Schafft and Alfred Fritz. Schafft was three years older than Tillich, who had been immediately drawn to him when they first met in Berlin. Among the many interesting faces he noticed during that winter semester of 1904–5, Schafft's struck him with great power.[40] The fact that he was older gave him an aura of dignity and authority. A point in the rules prevented Tillich from asking him to be his *Leibbursch*; instead, Schafft became his *pater en pneumati* or spiritual father in everything except philosophical or theological matters, in which Tillich was and remained independent. Long after they grew old, Schafft remained the "father" and Tillich the "son." Their friendship lasted for fifty-five years, and in many ways, although Tillich's special genius for friendship won him numerous other intimates, Schafft remained the closest of all.

After their first meeting in Berlin, Schafft and Tillich met again in Halle. There both belonged to the "Zwar . . . aber" group, with Tillich as head and Schafft as the power behind the throne. The personal influence he exercised, not only on Tillich but on the student body in general, was considerable. He was the *paparum papa*: the father of the fathers, or pope.

Schafft's position of authority was tempered by a marvelous sense of humor, which he expressed in cartoons and doggerel verse. No one took umbrage, for his wit was not malicious but merely poked very good fun. He liked to tease, and the students liked to laugh. Tillich himself was never able to invent jokes; his sense of humor was awkward at best, but he relished laughter and enjoyed drollery of someone else's creating.

Schafft was high-strung, energetic yet often sickly. A minister's son, he himself became a pastor and worked throughout his life with young people; he was greatly interested in them and eager to help. While Tillich patiently observed, listened, and then spoke his mind on intellectual matters, Schafft was resolute, practical, and simple—an able administrative type. He was unbourgeois, yet not bohemian; he gave Tillich a sense of direction which at the time he badly needed. Schafft was not a flatterer, and indeed, throughout Tillich's life most of his intimate friends were precisely those who did not flatter him, serving as antidotes to the many acquaintances who did.

Tillich was keenly aware of his great dependence on Schafft. In the early 1930s he wrote him from America, "How deeply you live in me can perhaps become clear to you when I tell you that I dream about you more often than anyone else in Germany."[41] In his late years, Schafft lived in shabby elegance, generously giving his clothes away to those who needed them. A musical man and a superb dancer, he married late—at sixty—and to Tillich's delight and surprise produced three children. When he died of a heart attack in 1959, Tillich felt an immeasurable loss. His gratitude for their friendship of over half a century despite external separations, exile, and war was enormous. "Our friendship was never endangered," he wrote, "and is among the most precious things of my life."[42]

In Halle, Alfred Fritz became Tillich's second intimate friend. An inseparable trio was thus formed, with "Frede" in the middle. A quiet, simple, reserved man with great pastoral gifts, he married Johanna Tillich, to the surprise of nearly everyone, and bravely bore the pain of her early death, which shattered and permanently saddened him. Of their union only one child, Gisela Walker, survives. After Johanna's death, Fritz married Trude Horn, who had for a time been Johannes Tillich's housekeeper; she was a practical, uncomplicated woman who lived until the 1950s. Fritz himself died in 1963; he was at the time head of a deaconesses' house in Teltow, East Berlin.[43]

Other, less intimate but similarly loyal friendships were formed in the Wingolf association. Ernst Rhein was one of Tillich's walking companions: a small, jolly young man whom the students called "Vater Rhein," in a pun on the river. Rhein sought Tillich out to discuss philosophy and theology and was greatly impressed by the way he went about learning Hebrew, systematically memorizing the roots of Hebrew vocabulary from the lexicon. His most vivid memory of all was of Tillich carrying around with him an edition of Kant's *Critique of Pure Reason*, in three pocket-sized volumes.

Tillich's *Leibfux*, Heinrich Meinhof, first laid eyes upon him after Tillich had been elected first chargé. It was in the spring of 1907 that Meinhof entered a beer tavern where members of the Wingolf fraternity had gathered for the first meeting of the new semester. He found himself deeply moved by the spectacle unfolding before him. First chargé Tillich made his appearance: he was tall, slender, ascetic-looking, despite a uniform of leather boots rising above his knees, white trousers, a black velvet jacket, and long white cuffs which reached his elbows. Attached to the top of his right shoulder, swinging diagonally across his chest and fastened at the waist, was a sash of black, white, and gold, the Wingolf colors. On his tamlike hat waved a plume. One hand was on his sheathed sword. Tillich, who greatly enjoyed wearing his uniform, walked to the president's chair, and said, "*Omnes ad loca. Feierliche Semester—Antrittskneipe incipit.*" [The inaugural festivities now begin.]

Tillich then delivered the opening address. His manner and words so moved Meinhof that he decided on the spot to ask him to be his *Leibbursch*. Tillich accepted, much to the amazement of other fraternity brothers, who had criticized Meinhof for aiming too high. The relationship between the two reflected Tillich's generous concern for the serious young student. In Meinhof's fraternity songbook he wrote this little dedication:

> Be joyous! And give others joy!
> And when it is difficult for you to
> do so, then do not think of the fact

that you are a student but remember
that you are a Christian. 7 June 1907.
From the speech at your reception,
Your Leibbursch,
Paul Tillich X.[44]

This friendship, too, endured for a lifetime. Indeed, it must be said
that Tillich's special talent for friendship was marked by an extraordinary ability to make it last. Once he decided to be a friend,
he remained one. He rarely deserted any friend, man or woman,
and the quality that drew or attracted him at first encounter remained alive for him through all subsequent meetings. While the
best friendships deepened and were sometimes radically transformed, their original inspiration was never relegated to the past.

During these years, Tillich was aware of his own psychological
danger from rather strongly overtheoretical, meditative, and con-
templative tendencies, and in an effort to avoid the ill effects of
such an escape from reality he threw himself into whatever practical tasks confronted him. His participation in the Wingolf became
a day-to-day involvement. It had already provided him with a
community of friendships; now it gave him the opportunity to
participate in "practical politics."

In 1907 the entire body of the association, comprising all local
units throughout Germany, was greatly aroused by a controversy
concerning the conditions for membership. There was disagreement on the interpretation of the Christian principle to which
every local group, and indeed every individual member, was
expected to adhere. The issue focused on the Apostles' Creed, and
the question was whether each group and member of the fellowship should be required to accept its articles as a binding statement
of faith. After much debate, which finally culminated in a vote
taken at one of the national conventions at the castle Wartburg,
it was decided that literal adherence to Christian creeds and principles should not be required, but that local groups should formulate statutes which would affirm loyalty to the Christian faith,
expecting individual members to accept this as a condition of

membership, but allowing for personal hesitation to the point of doubt.

Tillich, supported by the Wingolf members at Halle, assumed a rather orthodox stance and insisted that no action be taken that would lower Christian standards. He even went so far as to demand that the national convention adopt basic principles which would then have to be accepted by each local group, but in this he failed. He and his friends had to agree to allow different interpretations of fundamental principles by the several local groups, with a recommendation of mutual fraternal recognition by all.

Tillich proved himself a capable and industrious leader. He won the admiration of friends and comrades, who were proud of his clarity of thought. He himself gladly and gratefully remembered the months of his leadership until the end of his life. He often mentioned his belief that he had learned more about ideas, as well as personal relationships, from the responsibilities connected with his Wingolf membership than from the best programs of formal education.

On completing his fourth semester at Halle, Tillich returned to Berlin to finish the required course of study and prepare for the examinations that would give him entrance into the profession of the ministry. On 22 October 1907, he again matriculated at the University of Berlin. He was now twenty-one years old. During the next fourteen months he took courses leading to a doctoral degree and crammed earnestly for his initial theological examination—the first obligatory step toward ordination. Once a student (*theologiae studiosus*) had passed the first, largely academic, theological examination, he was considered a theological candidate (*theologiae candidatus*). A second, more practical theological examination was then required, and if the candidate passed this final test he could be ordained. The examinations leading to the Christian ministry were given by the *Konsistorium* (of which Johannes Tillich was a member) and were quite different from university examinations. Indeed, tension frequently developed between the church and the university in this regard. Many professors were considered too liberal to be trusted with the responsibility of examining ministerial candidates, and most churchmen were considered too conservative by the university professors. In addition to the rigorous preparation needed for the examinations, a ministerial candidate had to spend a year studying liturgics, preaching, and the catechism at some seminary for preachers before ordination could take place.

Early Freedom

Tillich's plan to complete the practical requirements of theological training was temporarily postponed when he accepted an invitation to become an assistant to Pastor Ernst Klein, a superintendent of schools and a friend of his father's. Klein had taken on additional administrative duties and needed an assistant to help him in his congregation in Lichtenrade, a rural village near Berlin.

Tillich arrived there on 1 January 1909,[45] and remained until the autumn. These months were for him an idyll which he ever after sought to recapture. On the day of his arrival, at lunch, he met for the first time Carl Richard Wegener, called Dox by his friends. The relationship that developed between the two young men first involved them in intellectual interchange, later in ecclesiastical and political enterprise, and still later in a tragic love triangle. Three years older than Tillich, Wegener, a perceptive, sharp observer had already earned his doctorate. His influence on Tillich was considered destructive by some, but for Tillich himself it represented one of the great liberating forces of his life. In Lichtenrade they lived in adjoining rooms on the north side of the manse, and at night the door between them usually remained open and they "symphilosophied" into the small hours. This term (meaning simply to philosophize with one another) they lifted from Schleiermacher, who had engaged in philosophical discussions with the poet Friedrich Schlegel when *they* had lived together.

Toward morning, Tillich frequently groaned so loudly with nightmares that Wegener sometimes threw a boot through the door to wake him. Once Tillich dreamt that he was in the garden in Schönfliess and was climbing the apple tree, when he saw his father coming. His father climbed the tree in order to bring him down, while Tillich went higher and higher and eventually found himself on the topmost fragile branch. His father reached for his heel, and in that split second Tillich screamed and flew through the air, waking before he reached the ground.

Wegener had met Johannes Tillich and thought of him as the "Grand Inquisitor."[46] He once remarked that Karl Barth's perception had been accurate when he described Tillich's theology as an expression of opposition to and fear of the Grand Inquisitor; Wegener's appraisal was similar, except that he substituted for that figure the Freudian phrase "fear-of-father complex." It amounted to the same thing.

Two other intellectual friends who occasionally visited Tillich in Lichtenrade were Emanuel Hirsch and Kurt Leese. Like Wegener, they played a continuing and important role in Tillich's development. Hirsch, the son of Pastor Albert Hirsch and two years younger than Paul, had spent his youth in Berlin, where he was educated. In 1906 he began his theological studies at the Friedrich Wilhelm University. Despite his father's effort to keep him from exposure to anything but orthodox Christianity, he found himself attracted to the liberal theologians there who were influenced by historical criticism. Hirsch was greatly under the sway of Fichte and Luther, and was for a long time Karl Holl's only doctoral student.

Hirsch and Tillich met in 1908 at a Wingolf meeting in Berlin. They were drawn together by their classical education as well as by their common talent for definition and analysis. Friends who accompanied them on long walks in Berlin said it was almost impossible to tell their thinking apart, it was so nearly identical. This provides a clue to the bitterness of their later split. As long as the friendship lasted, it yielded untold richness and intellectual stimulation for both. Hirsch suffered terrible tragedy in his life: as a young man he went blind in one eye, and later a barber's razor accidentally lacerated the other. In old age, he became totally blind. Yet despite these progressive handicaps, he wrote and translated voluminously until his death in 1973. Hirsch's knowledge was encyclopedic; an authentic genius, he combined mastery in historical theology with the skills of a systematic theologian.

Born on 6 July 1887, Kurt Leese was the son of a privy councilor who opened his home to Tillich and Wegener in 1913 when they inaugurated their *Vernunft-Abende* or evenings of discussion, later in Berlin. He, too, became a minister. He was close to Tillich but rather critical of him. They exchanged ideas, sent each other the books they wrote, and reacted to each other's development in a correspondence which lasted until Leese's death in 1965. After World War II, Leese abandoned the Christian ministry and taught philosophy at the University of Hamburg. He was sharply critical of Tillich's connections with the church, maintaining that his thought, as it had developed, implied an inevitable break with that institution.

Tillich spent the months in Lichtenrade preoccupied with Schelling. He sat on a veranda looking out upon green fields and surrounded by blooming linden trees which gave off a honeyed fragrance, endlessly writing out excerpts from Schelling for his dissertation: "Mysticism and Guilt Consciousness in Schelling's Philosophical Development." Nature intoxicated him as never before; later, in America, he tried to duplicate the Lichtenrade experience in his East Hampton home on Long Island, where he grew trees, dined outdoors, and worked for hours in his garden.

Tillich taught the younger boys and occasionally preached. The boys were hard to control and he did not find his task with them easy. But his talent for play finally won them over. He built sand boxes and trains for them, and a garden bench which he painted green. He bought firecrackers which his little friends were permitted to set off on special festival days. He played chess with Pastor Klein, whose young daughter Maria later became his good friend and ardent admirer. He took long walks with his friends, bicycled through the Neumark to see his beloved Schönfliess, and on rare occasions, when he needed greater diversion, went to Berlin.

In that center of German culture were innumerable small circles of literary persons, artists, actors, actresses, philosophers, film-makers, and so on, who met in salons, at private homes, in conventions, or at cafés.[47] Whether at the Romanisches Café, which writers preferred, or the Café Josty, which Tillich frequented, varied clusters of persons formed and talked and talked. The most exciting part of cultural life, however, was the theater, dominated at this time by Max Reinhardt, whose productions of Shakespeare's *Hamlet* or Gorki's *Nachtasyl*, with Alexander Moissi in the main role, were sold out for many nights. Globe-trotters, diplomats, Americans such as Mark Twain, came to see and be spellbound. Tillich partook of this life as eagerly as anyone, seating himself at the Café Josty for hours, writing in the open, watching the passing faces, talking with friends, strangers, even prostitutes, who had a piquant fascination for him: they were part of his "parish" and yet bizarre. In the evenings he went to the theater. Back in Lichtenrade again, he tried to incorporate the vivid action of Berlin life in sermons written in the quiet of the garden. But the irony, the sharp, dry humor of Berliners, the rejection of all affectation, the crisp cynicism, all this he somehow failed to make his own. For when in the autumn of 1909 he was in Berlin once again, he wrote to Mrs. Klein, wife of the pastor, to thank her for this idyll, now of the past, and said,

> I would like to express again to you and Pastor Klein my most cordial thanks for all you have given me to remember, all the enrichment I have received from you, and all the resources of power on which I shall draw for a long time to come, I hope. The whole time in Lichtenrade was a golden age full of an undisturbed enjoyment of nature and spiritual lightheartedness.[48]

In the spring of that same year, 1909, Tillich had passed his first theological or church board examination. There is no record of his grade, but since theological students were expected to attain high marks, it may be safely assumed that he had done very well. He was now a theological candidate, and in the fall, when the idyll in Lichtenrade had come to an end, he returned to Berlin and proceeded to satisfy the final requirements for his university degree and for the Christian ministry.

It is interesting to note, in passing, that unlike his father, Johannes, Paul Tillich did not receive any *formal* ministerial education. In his day, Johannes had been trained in the Berliner *Domstift*,[49] a college for preachers founded in 1854 by Friedrich Wilhelm IV, whose piety and interest in the church had moved him to provide an adequate number of preachers for the city of Berlin. The king had a dormitory built near the cathedral, where properly prepared ministerial candidates lived and worked together. At his time they were trained primarily to lead the largely unchurched masses back to the church. Later the Domstift became essentially a school for preachers. Until 1919 it was called the *königliche Domkandidatenstift* or "royal training school for preachers." Life in the seminary was highly structured: the day began and ended with a service of prayer; courses were given in biblical and homiletical exegesis; and a weekly preaching seminar was led by the dean.

Paul Tillich learned to preach superbly well under much more informal circumstances. The sermons he wrote and delivered during World War I, as well as the chapel talks and Sunday sermons given in America, were the fruit of his natural talent, the influence and example of his father, and his own personal and professional experience. As a young vicar, for example, his contacts with members of the several congregations he served, rich or poor, ignorant or worldly wise, brought him into immediate contact with human problems. Unlike his father whose faith was sure and unquestioning, Tillich's disposition was and remained precarious: doubts often assailed him. Thus he responded with particular relish to the confusions and questions of parishioners and friends. Moreover, as he struggled during this year in Berlin, to finish his dissertation, he began to realize that many Christians did not understand the language in which he had been taught to communicate the gospel. Perhaps for the first time in his life he confronted the harsh fact which later inspired him to use nontraditional language to communicate the meaning of biblical revelation. He was also made acutely conscious of the enormous gap between rich and poor, and the uneasiness which he felt about the condition of poverty became one of the factors that later led him into the movement of religious socialism. This tension between the heady atmosphere of Schellingian philosophy on the one hand and the hard problems of the pastor's parish on the other produced in him in due course the need to address them both.

In the course of the year, Tillich had completed a dissertation on Schelling written in partial fulfillment of the requirements for the degree of Licentiate of Theology, the highest academic theological degree that could be earned in Germany at the time. Then a new opportunity presented itself. The city of Berlin announced that it would award a stipend to any candidate for the degree of doctor of philosophy who had published a work in philosophy before 1 August 1910.

Tillich decided to stand for the doctorate also and compete for the stipend, and so wrote a second dissertation based on his Schelling studies. In that day it was customary for a doctoral candidate to work independently and then submit the completed dissertation to a professor, who would sponsor it, approve it, and recommend the candidate to the faculty. It was of course Medicus at Halle who had inspired in Tillich his great affection for and interest in German idealist philosophy, but Medicus was a *Privatdozent* and thus unable to sponsor him. For this and other reasons which remain obscure—perhaps through a connection his father made for him—Tillich submitted this second piece of writing on Schelling to the University of Breslau. It was entitled, "The Conception of the History of Religions in Schelling's Positive Philosophy: Its Prepositions and Principles." On the recommendation of Professor Eugen Kühnemann, a specialist in German idealist literature, that university accepted his work and awarded him the degree of Doctor of Philosophy.[50] On Monday, 22 August 1910, 15 twelve-thirty in the afternoon, two days after his twenty-fourth birthday, Tillich gave his inaugural lecture in the music salon of the University of Breslau. It was entitled, "Freedom as a Philosophical Principle in Fichte." The degree qualified him to lecture in the field of *philosophy* and earned him the Berlin stipend.

A little over a year later, on 16 December 1911, Tillich took the final examination for the degree of Licentiate of Theology. He had submitted his original dissertation on Schelling to the University of Halle, entitled, as noted earlier, "Mysticism and Guilt Conscious-ness in Schelling's Philosophical Development." Early in 1912 that university awarded him the Licentiate of Theology degree, which qualified him to teach *theology* on the university level. His aca-demic training was now behind him.

Tillich's ministerial training had continued along parallel lines with his academic education: a procedure entirely customary in Germany at the time. After his graduation from the university he served as vicar attached to Dr. Lang, a superintendent of the church district of Nauen, a suburb near Berlin. On 27 July 1912 he passed the final church board examination. He was ordained in St. Matthew's Evangelical Church, Berlin, on 18 August 1912, two days before his twenty-sixth birthday. For the next two years he worked as assistant preacher in the Moabit or workers' section of Berlin.[51] It was an assignment he urgently required in order to support himself.

The marriage of Tillich's sister to Alfred Fritz enlivened the autumn of 1912. Tillich was overjoyed. He had of course known of their plans for some time. For four years the couple had been secretly engaged, at the insistence of Johannes Tillich, who had regarded his twenty-year-old daughter as too young for immediate marriage. He also shared the customary feeling that the groom should be professionally established before undertaking domestic responsibilities. During the intervening period the couple cor-responded and saw each other often, yet no one outside the family suspected their attachment. When the engagement was announced, many who did not know the quiet, unassuming pastor well ex-pressed surprise. For Emanuel Hirsch the surprise was a painful one. He too had fallen in love with Johanna, and had determined to ask for her hand, but waited too long and suffered despair at the knowledge. Johanna, for her part, had never considered him as more than a friend.[52]

This elder of Tillich's two sisters had large blue eyes, dark blond hair, and an upturned nose. Womanly for her age, she was exceedingly attractive to men. She had a strong predilection for Grieg's piano music and played for her brother by the hour while he studied or wrote. In later life he sought to duplicate this experience: failing the presence of a woman willing and able to play for him, he sometimes worked against the sound of musical recordings. Johanna's passion for art expressed itself in frequent visits to galleries and museums, and her intellectual interests involved her in lengthy discussions with a variety of young men. Admirably suited for the life of a salon, she did not readily adapt to the role of the German *Hausfrau*, and after her marriage, which was inordinately happy, it was noted that her household was casually run; she preferred intellectual discussions with her own and her husband's friends to doing the daily chores. Since Tillich and his sister had experienced together, in articulate exchange, the pains and pleasures of growing into adulthood, he felt that she understood him better than anyone else. He was therefore much pleased when she married his friend Frede, whom he also greatly loved.[53]

By 1912 Tillich had decided to become a professor, and it was to this goal that he bent his energies while working as an assistant minister in the Moabit. On the surface it looked as though he had not yet chosen between the pastorate and a professorship, but in fact his mind was already made up. He might ask a friend, "What do you think I should do?"—but only for the sake of once again weighing the pros and cons. It was a habit he carried into old age.

In 1913 he began negotiations with the University of Halle to apply for a post on that faculty. He sought permission, in other words, to teach or lecture at the university level. In order to obtain it, he had to write a *Habilitationsschrift*, or qualifying thesis. This represented the final prerequisite to becoming a member of a German university faculty. Once it was written, the candidate had to submit to a colloquium with the faculty. Tillich chose to write on "the concept of the supernatural in German theology during the period of the Enlightenment," and for the next two years he labored on the thesis in his spare time.

This cannot have been easy, since his work in the Moabit kept him rather fully occupied. Once again he was faced with the task of communicating with the poor, but he experienced similar problems with the intelligentsia with whom he now came in professional contact for the first time. While teaching a confirmation class, he discovered for example that the word "faith" no longer had meaning. And he realized, perhaps for the first time, not only that a question implies an answer, but that an answer always presupposes a question, and that the human question and the Christian answer are inevitably related and must always move in concert. This discovery determined his way of being a theologian: early in his process of development he cast his lot with the apologetic theologians, namely those who attempt to interpret the Christian faith by means of reasonable explanation. Tillich understood this to mean that one must learn "to defend oneself before an opponent with a *common criterion in view*."[54]

He and his friend Richard Wegener, conscious of the need for apologetics and working with the permission of the church administration, inaugurated a series of evening meetings which they jestingly dubbed *Vernunft–Abende* or "evenings of reason."[55] They found sponsors who were willing to open their homes to the members of these discussion groups: artists, businessmen, society women, students, philosophers, lawyers—Roman Catholics, Protestants, and Jews. Tillich and Wegener spoke to such groups on a variety of topics which they planned together, sometimes at the Englisches Café in Berlin. While Wegener helped to define the subject matter of the lectures and discussions, it was Tillich who presented most of them. He spoke on "The Courage to Find Truth," "The Protest of Doubt," "The Mysticism of Art and Religious Mysticism," "Mysticism and Consciousness of Guilt," "Culture and Religion," and so on. For a while they both thought that a reconciliation between traditional Christianity and modern secularism could be achieved by the formation of a new ministerial office for which "apologists" should be trained. Indeed, they thought of founding a new religious order for that purpose. But the "evenings of reason" lasted only a little over a year. Wegener in particular began to doubt their real value, since they were being infiltrated by lecturers from the audience and the discussions were becoming too general in tone.

In the meantime, Tillich had been informed by his father that the position of inspector or head of a theological students' seminary was available in Bonn. Professor Ecke had been in touch with Johannes Tillich and it was fairly certain that the younger Tillich would get the job if he applied for it.[56] The position would have given him a place to live, an income of 1,500 German marks, and most important of all, time to complete a paper for presentation to the theological faculty at Halle enabling him to qualify for a position of *Privatdozent*. Wegener, among others, pressed him to go to Bonn, urging him to write one book and project six more.[57] But the job did not materialize when it was discovered that Tillich was a bachelor; it was essential that the inspector be a married man. He was not too disappointed, for by then he had decided that he did not want to live in a small city.

At twenty-seven he had already clearly demonstrated intellectual gifts of a high order, but in his emotional life he was a late bloomer. He had held faithfully to the vow of his Wingolf days, remaining only casually related to members of the opposite sex. Wegener the skeptic, who enjoyed breaking rules, tried to influence him in the direction of liberation from his vow and from his father's authority. A sort of inner freedom was beginning to develop at this time, but his outer freedom was limited. He had gone often to the Friedrichstrasse and the Kürfurstendamm, sat at cafés and observed the world around him, yet was not a participant in it.

It was in this state of incipient self-consciousness that he encountered Margarethe Karla Mathilda Katharina Maria Wever, called Grethi. She was daughter of the administrator of an agricultural estate named Butterfelde, south of Stettin, now in Polish territory. Tillich had begun to divide his time between his father's house in Berlin and his sister's in Butterfelde, where Frede Fritz was pastor, and on one of these visits he accidentally met Grethi. They got to know each other on the water. He was still a passionate sailor and when staying with the Fritzes used to go out on the Moriner Lake, where Grethi had a rowboat. She was small, with dark hair and features which bore a striking resemblance to Johanna. Two years younger than Tillich, she had unconventional views of life; some say she pursued him with seductive wiles. One of his younger friends, herself enamoured of him, tried to stop the romance: "I hope that one day you will have a wife who does not think very highly of herself but feels she is very weak and small and yet understands all your interests. Your entire life is a search for God, and I believe Grethi is not exactly a type with a seeking nature."[58] But Tillich found Grethi irresistibly attractive and felt he was in love for the first time in his life. Their engagement was announced in January 1914.[59] While there is no record of Johannes Tillich's reaction to his son's choice, Grethi Wever's father seems to have been skeptical about the match: "The most extreme opposites have once again been mutually attracted to one another and will lead, we hope, to a happy marriage."[60]

Happiness was not a part of any man's destiny in 1914. Spring and summer passed, the thunderclouds of World War I gathering overhead broke open in August. Tillich and Grethi Wever were married on 28 September in Butterfelde,[61] probably in her parents' home. In his heart he swore her absolute fidelity. On 1 October he volunteered for military service. The years of his "dreaming innocence" were over forever.

2

The Turning Point:
World War I
(1914-1918)

The peace and stability of the Wilhelminian era was irreparably shattered by the shot fired at Sarajevo. Forty years of tranquility had transformed Germany into a powerful and enormously prosperous empire, in which the bourgeoisie had burst into unprecedented flower. However, militarism and aggressive nationalism had won the day not only in Germany but everywhere in Europe despite repeated peace conferences. The great world of pomp and circumstance, of affluence and power, of unbroken cultural traditions, was destined to die. The destruction that took place during the next four years brought a fruitful period of history to an end, changing the entire world scene. Yet not a single German, nor for that matter Frenchman or Englishman, who volunteered would realize this for a long time.

When war broke out, young men signed up to fight in a spirit of nearly ecstatic joy, exalted by nationalistic fervor.[1] Tillich was no exception. He said much later that when he and other German soldiers went into World War I, "most of them shared the popular belief in a nice God who would make everything turn out for the best."[2] And when they saw that everything in fact turned out for the worst, the ecstasy turned to despair and their God to ash.

At the beginning of the war Tillich was a shy, grown boy, truly a "dreaming innocent." He was a German patriot, a proud Prussian,[3] as eager to fight for his country as anyone else, but politically naïve. When he returned to Berlin four years later he was utterly transformed. The traditional monarchist had become a religious socialist, the Christian believer a cultural pessimist, and the repressed puritanical boy a "wild man."[4] These years represent *the* turning point in Paul Tillich's life—the first, last, and only one.

On volunteering, Tillich was appointed chaplain and assigned to the Fourth Artillery Regiment of the Seventh Reserve Division. He served until January 1919.[5] In October of the first year of the war he moved with an army transport to the western front. During the next three weeks he led nineteen worship services, under trees, in caves, and in trenches, all under fire. (In a report to his commanding general he suggested holding services indoors in future.) On 3 December his father received a telegram: "Today I was given the Iron Cross. Paul."

Events at home and on the battlefield were intermingled in Tillich's memory of the war. On 16 November a telegram announced the birth of Johanna and Frede Fritz's first child, named Eckart Paul Johannes. At the beginning there was frequent communication with his family. He received in fact an endless number of packages, telegrams, letters, and notes. On his part, as with most Germans, there was still the expectation of a brief and victorious campaign. From the beginning, too, Tillich had friendly relations with the soldiers to whom he ministered; they made him feel more needed than he had ever felt in peacetime. He spent many nights sleeping in the trenches with his superior officers, who were eager for company and many of whom eventually became his friends. There was the fascination, moreover, of new comradeship with people from other levels of society. Ordinarily, during these years, Tillich would have moved in academic or university circles, but the war threw him into contact with all kinds of people; he learned to know their idiosyncrasies, their dialects, their personalities, how they lived and how they died. There were artists, pharmacists, manufacturers; there were steel workers and postal clerks, butchers and newspaper publishers; in a word, the world.[6] And there was the unheroic, mechanical, everyday drudgery of military life, with its extreme boredom and total absence of thrill. The shock and horror of death and the endlessness of fighting waited in the dim future. For the present, war meant exchange of gunfire and small troop maneuvers behind the lines.

When Tillich arrived to join his division, it had been withdrawn from the front for a rest period; from its more retired position one could see the towers of Soissons. His officers were immediately impressed by the young theologian from Berlin sent to serve and comfort their troops. He was small, slender, reserved, and markedly shy when not on duty. He behaved like a member of an aristocratic family; a spiritual veil seemed to cover his young personality, and the self-conscious dignity of the clergyman was missing. He seemed unaware of the world outside—was just a boy, out on his first mission.

The young Roman Catholic chaplain Father Kapell, Tillich's colleague, was a thickset man with clever eyes and nimble movements who immediately felt at home everywhere. He was well versed in theological matters but ignorant when it came to philosophy and "eternal searching," a child of this world who did not wish to be anything else.

When the division was moved again, these two sharply contrasting persons volunteered to go to the front, and for the next two years shared the pain and joy of the troops in the very front lines. They, too, inevitably became soldiers. For all of them, officers, soldiers, and chaplains alike, were headed in the same direction: toward the hell of the greatest battles of the war.

As a soldier Tillich discovered the true meaning of Schiller's phrase *kein bleibend Quartier* [no permanent quarters]. The constant grouping and regrouping of units and the need to find new quarters made everyday things exceedingly important. Supplies taken for granted in peacetime were carefully transported from one stopping-place to another, and the acquisition of scarce foods or drink became cause for celebration. One day some Bavarian beer arrived, and some of the officers decided to set up a bar in the accommodations into which they had just settled. On this occasion Tillich displayed a hidden talent: he applied himself with great industry to the task of decorating the barroom, which was then festively inaugurated. The brigadier general was guest of honor, his adjutant functioned as bartender, Father Kapell as waiter, and Tillich chose for himself the title "guest from Königsberg." The meaning of this? His recognition of how much on this wide earth was still unfamiliar territory, and that he was just beginning to learn a little about it. He was still a "guest" in the universe opening up before him.

This idyll, as a fellow soldier called it, lasted into the spring and summer of 1915. It was a time of waiting, of boredom, of playing chess and writing letters.[7] On 22 February Tillich wrote to Maria Klein, his friend from Lichtenrade, in melancholy vein, "True experience has its roots in suffering, and happiness is a blossom which opens itself up only now and then."[8] In early March he complained in somewhat bragging fashion to his father that enemy fire was too passive, and this was hard to bear; he would rather be shot at than forced to wait! Everything seemed to him "grey on grey." Between that time and early April he was kept busy, nevertheless, for he led thirty-one worship services.[9]

In August the celebration of his twenty-ninth birthday broke the mood of sadness and produced in Tillich mingled sensations of pleasure and pride. For the first time in his existence he consciously attributed importance to the day, and for the rest of his life made much of it; indeed, it became a second Christmas for him. "In earlier years," he wrote his father on 21 August, "I mostly forgot about my birthday and was amazed when someone reminded me that I would soon be a year older. This time I thought about my birthday throughout August and was curious about it, wondering how the day would turn out."[10]

In fact, a two-day feast had been prepared in his honor. On the eve of his natal day he enjoyed a celebration with the officers of his division. They ate partridge, scared up in the fields, and drank French wine and champagne and feasted in the billiard room. (They were billeted at the moment in a large, comfortable manor house. There was even a chandelier!) His friend, Adjutant Erich Pfeiffer, set up a bar in an unprepossessing room which he and other officers had cleverly transformed by dint of papering the walls. There were four tables, with two to five seats at each, and even music to which Pfeiffer and Schwarzkopf, a flyer, danced.

On the twentieth itself the soldiers congratulated him and they all went horseback riding. At the party afterward, the general— "His Excellency"—standing in the entrance of the room, a yellow rose in his hand, delivered a little birthday speech wishing Tillich the attainment of his academic goals. He then led him to the birthday table, where there was a cake decorated with a wreath and twenty-nine candles and flanked by black and white knights, symbols of the chess games played by the officers. The general then wished Tillich much happiness, good luck, and a blessing for the coming year. After the celebration, Tillich gave a lecture on Russia, pointing out on wall maps he had brought in the various places in Europe where battles were raging. That night he heard the thunderous roar of cannon in the distance as he read the Ninetieth Psalm—"which I let sound forth in my soul every birthday and every New Year's day."[11]

> Lord, thou hast been our refuge
>   from generation to generation,
> Before the mountains were brought forth
>   or earth and world were born in travail,
>   from age to age everlasting thou art God.
>   Psalm 90:1,2

In October the waiting, the greyness, and the feasting came to an end. On the seventh Tillich wrote his father, "Tomorrow, the Champagne."* For the next six months his division was quartered in deep trenches. Villages in a wide circle had been destroyed and there were no civilians to be seen. Their food came only from field

---

* Northeastern region of France.

kitchens; the coffee was not real coffee, the tea not real tea. In the winter now and then alcohol was available. All this could somehow be borne; the worst business was with the roads. Fall and winter rains had transformed the chalky earth into a viscous mass. Boots sank into the ground in spite of the wooden planks put down to provide support. At night rats could be heard scuttling over the same planks.

It was during these months that Tillich became a genuine frontline soldier. His duties were as difficult and dangerous as anyone else's, but he showed neither nervousness nor fear, nor did he ever shirk his task. This fact did not elude the awareness of his fellow soldiers. Many reports and communiqués acknowledged his courageous participation.

On 30 and 31 October, the German armies attacked near Tahure. Many officers and countless men were killed. Mass burials followed. Tillich became a grave-digger as well as pastor. He preached a sermon in Tahure which he considered the best of his war sermons. It was based on 2 Corinthians 4:17–18: "Our troubles are slight and short-lived; and their outcome an eternal glory which outweighs them far. Meanwhile our eyes are fixed, not on things that are seen, but on the things that are unseen: for what is seen passes away; what is unseen is eternal." He continually comforted the men by praising them for their courage in the face of blood and death in the cold rain and on the slimy earth. And he pointed to St. Paul's suffering, even as their own, emphasizing that in spite of it Paul rejoiced in the eternal. He asked the soldiers,

Why this murder day after day, why this nameless suffering, why the bleeding and bleeding again. . . . yet we must remain responsible to ourselves and to all others: for the sake of love for and devotion to our homeland, for the sake of pride, pride in being Germans, and for the sake of the bond of community which ties our spirit to the spirit of our nation, for the sake of the glory of the German fatherland . . . all these things are unseen and yet they are true and real and worth a thousand times more than food and drink, than clothing and reward, than rest and comfortable living; for what is seen passes away but what is unseen is eternal.

He sought to inspire them:

Your heroism, your pain, my dear comrades, bear eternity in them. They have a brilliance and a glory which will light up when all earthly brilliance is sunk in dust and rot.

Finally, he urged them on to new selfless action—

And so we all, old and new troops, bound together in one spirit, desire to hold out in new flaming enthusiasm and remain strong and cheerful, and take away victory from the enemy without and the enemy within our own hearts, and we want to hold to the invisible despite the visible.[12]

The first days of November 1915 continued to be engulfed in blood and death. Some of the best officers in Tillich's division died, men who had befriended him and to whom he felt intimately bound. An inner grimness filled his spirit as he threw the sticky claylike soil upon coffins closed over men in their best years, men he regarded as worthy and good. He no longer thought of his own death; he felt he was already in death, gripped by its force. He did not know that this was only the beginning of the violence and horror by which he was to be shaken, only the beginning of suffering, of inconceivable human misery.[13]

By December a note of resignation had crept into the letters to his father. "Do not expect peace for a year or two," he wrote. "Whether or not I shall then be able to be intellectually productive is very doubtful, and it is still more doubtful whether there will be enough money in Germany to nourish a *Privatdozent*. But all that is far, far in the future."[14] The idea was beginning to grow in him as in others that the war would not be over quickly—indeed, that its end was not even remotely in view.

Christmas came, and the Seventh Division was in Aure, a little village where Tillich celebrated Christmas Eve in a half-destroyed church. The front was quiet. Those not on duty in the trenches hurried to participate: the church was soon jammed with soldiers. Tillich had managed (how remained his secret) to decorate the church despite the barren surroundings. But what the soldiers

46

found unique and unforgettable about this evening was his words. They were simple, clear, and moving. He related the Christmas message to the situation in which they all found themselves and to the hope for an honorable and early peace. This undogmatic simplicity won many hearts. Tillich's way of proclaiming the word of God was different from what his hearers were used to. His interpretation was freer, yet not less penetrating or even inspiring. He himself experienced "close identity" with his listeners. Yet for him Christmas had something tortured about it. He noted that what comforted the men was not religious hope; it was the hope of peace that gave them strength to live.

On 13 January he wrote his father urging him to come to Halle, where he would be giving his trial lecture on 2 or 3 February (he had obtained leave for this purpose, and had been preparing his lecture even in the trenches). He said it was inwardly impossible as yet for him to come to Berlin.[15]

The early months of 1916 were reasonably quiet. The battles on the front were reduced to skirmishes for position. More "comfortable" quarters could be constructed for the troops and a barracks was built for the general's staff. Tillich volunteered to decorate it. Somehow—again this remained his secret—he managed to find material for curtains and even tablecloths. He cut out good pictures from art magazines, which were readily available together with other reading materials, and decorated the walls. The study of art, especially history of painting, had become for him a primary means of escape from the horrors of war. He bought some art books in a military bookstore; though the reproductions were poor, he became so immersed in them that he could forget the ugliness around him. For the moment his absorption was merely an escape, but by the end of the war it had become vastly more important to him.

Perhaps most significant of all were the quiet hours during which he debated and philosophized to his heart's content. A change had come over him. His earlier reserve had been stripped away; he was now an experienced comrade-in-arms, who understood everything that concerned the ordinary soldier. For he had begun to think about the exploitation of the common man at the hands of powers he had always taken for granted: the landed aristocracy, the army, and the church.

These were in many ways the best weeks of Tillich's war years, and they reached their high point in May 1916. The Seventh Division was pulled away from the front to a remote and lovely region almost completely untouched by the conflict. Someone remembered a well-known castle nearby: Blanchefosse. Three men of the general's staff and the two chaplains undertook to investigate what treasures still remained there. In the castle courtyard the men, who had seen neither a civilian nor a woman for over seven months, were greeted by an unusual sight: a hundred or so young women and girls, nicely dressed, at work in the courtyard and park grounds. Some were preparing the castle rooms. At the arrival of the five men they quickly dropped their work and surrounded them, showing particular interest in the two chaplains, to whom all talked at once, excitedly gesticulating—they had endless complaints and demands to put forward.

Despite the hubbub and the language difficulty, the French women soon managed to make themselves clear: German civilians had been imprisoned by the French in a concentration camp nearby, and the Germans were retaliating by confining the youth of Lille to the castle. It was believed that a commission of the Red Cross had arrived to see justice done.

The women spoke with the voice of French nationalism, "You started the war! You dragged us to this place!" The Germans replied in kind, "For years you encircled us!* You wanted revenge for the annexation of Alsace Lorraine in 1871." A miniature peace conference ensued. In his role as mediator, Tillich was in his element. He calmed the discussants until they understood and respected one another's position. Citizens of warring nations talked quietly with one another.

But the victory of reason was short-lived, and the "peace conference" soon came to an end. Within a few weeks the Seventh

---

* Reference is here made to the coalition between France and Russia.

Division was in Verdun. This was a garrison town of northeastern France between Paris and Metz. The Germans had taken a position there in February 1916, hoping to break through to Paris. Indeed, in the months that followed this became the primary objective of the German campaign. The failure to attain it had a far-reaching influence on the course of the war, and the battle itself became the most concentrated of the entire conflict, not to say of human history. The exorbitant use of men and material, the intense bombardment lasting month upon month, the relentless struggle for every foot of soil, can be compared only to the siege of Stalingrad in World War II. Hundreds of thousands of men on both sides were killed and nearly a whole generation wasted.

The Seventh Division became involved in the battle for Verdun in late May. In the weeks that followed the division achieved a stunning victory: they stormed the Cailette Forest. In June Tillich wrote to his father, "We are on the west bank of the Meuse. East of the River our troops are storming the Cailette Forest and Fort Douaumont, near Verdun."[16] A day later, he wrote, "Hell rages around us. It's unimaginable." For three and a half weeks the division repulsed all counterattacks by the enemy. Bit by bit they pushed the line forward, suffering enormous casualties.

For Tillich, it remained to visit the wounded, comfort the dying, and bury the fallen. His emotional and mental anguish was beyond words—yet the verses of Romans 8:38–39, "For I am sure that neither death, nor life, nor angels, nor principalities, nor things present, nor things to come, nor powers, nor height, nor depth, nor anything else in all creation, will be able to separate us from the love of God in Christ Jesus our Lord," were much stronger, he later wrote, "than the sound of exploding shells, of weeping at open graves, of the sighs of the sick, of the moaning of the dying."[17] He was inexpressibly relieved when toward the end of June, the division was removed from battle. This time, however, Tillich's nerves had failed him. He recovered swiftly nevertheless, for by 3 July he was in Halle presenting a learned paper to the theological faculty for discussion, and on 20 July, again in Halle, he presented the trial lecture he had originally hoped to deliver in

February. After this, he was appointed *Privatdozent* of theology.

When Tillich returned to the front in August, the division was once again sent to the Champagne, occupying a quiet section of the front line. During the following months, he recovered some of his *joie de vivre*. He often philosophized and debated with other staff officers during the late summer and autumn evenings, and on one such occasion he and the brigadier sharply clashed. His Excellency was known for his striking personality. Before the war he had held a high position in Berlin; he was very dogmatic and favored ecclesiastical authority, and the young free-thinking Tillich did not greatly please him. Tillich did not conform to the general's notion of an ideal army chaplain. They had had differences of opinion all along, but Adjutant Pfeiffer had always been able to bridge the gap. On this occasion he had been called away, and the inevitable break occurred.

At issue was the power of prayer. The general was of the opinion that prayer could indeed protect a soldier from enemy fire. Tillich argued openly against this, freely defending his views to his military superior. It proved too much for the general to take. How could a chaplain, he asked, belittle the very power he himself described as having a miraculous result? Tillich was, in effect, forced to emigrate for the first time. In October he was transferred from the staff of the Fourth Artillery Regiment to the Medical Corps of the Seventh Division. He remained attached to that unit for the remainder of the war, stationed in northern France until the end, living through the offenses at Amiens and Aisne- Marne and the final defeat in the Champagne.

The transfer took place on 5 October 1916. Tillich found himself housed in a magnificent French baronial castle situated in a park. For a few weeks his life was pleasantly relaxed, filled with chess games, parties, and even the company of young women. On 15 October, together with a group of officers, he visited the town of Cambrai and went sightseeing there. The interlude revived his spirits only temporarily. The war, which from the beginning had alternated periods of rest with those of attack and counterattack, again claimed him, this time in the trenches. He found himself once more in the fray, dragging wounded men from the front, running back and forth like a madman between the wounded and the dying, not caring for his own safety. When his friend Bartenstein was killed, Tillich was unable to speak at his burial and only read the liturgy. While the battle continued, he slept in the trenches for hours at a time. Then he collapsed, and was relieved and sent to a hospital. Reporting to his father all that had happened, he wrote, ". . . but the Butte de Tahure is safely in our hands." In late November, overtaken by darkness of spirit, he wrote to Maria Klein,

> I have constantly the most immediate and very strong feeling that I am no longer alive. Therefore I don't take life seriously. To find someone, to become joyful, to recognize God, all these things are things of life. But life itself is not dependable ground. It isn't only that *I* might die any day, but rather that everyone dies, *really* dies, you too,—and then the suffering of mankind—I am an utter eschatologist—not that I have childish fantasies of the death of the world, but rather that I am experiencing the actual death of this our time. I preach almost exclusively "the end." . . . Now and then I overcome all the suffering by pasting pictures into books and working scientifically on a system of the sciences.[18]

In one sense, Tillich never fully recovered from his intense suffering in the face of death. When a friend sent him a picture of herself in a white dress, sitting on a lawn, he wrote to her saying he found it inconceivable that something like that still existed. His mood was like that of the later popular ballad, "Where Have All the Flowers Gone?" To his family he wrote, "We are experiencing the most terrible catastrophes, the end of the world order . . . it is coming to an end, and this end is accompanied by deepest pain."[19]

The awareness of endless individual deaths and of the death of an entire order of civilization were parallel. Tillich later described this as his "personal *kairos*,"[20] meaning that something new and unexpected had broken into his life at a time when he was ripe to be changed by it and to act on account of it. He claimed later that this transformation took place in one night in 1915, but it was actually a cumulative metamorphosis. Nor did he alone experience it. Painters like Franz Marc, whom Tillich came to admire, and dramatists like Carl Zuckmayer, and many others on both sides recorded the same transformation in their war letters or memoirs.[21] Awakening and enlightenment followed upon suffering and thus clarified thought. Romantic young patriots became sharp, sober men, for the first time without illusion and without hope.

For Tillich the traditional concept of God had become invalid, and he now found final liberation from this concept in Nietzsche. At the age of thirty, in a French forest, he began to read *Thus Spake Zarathustra*, and the ecstatic affirmation of existence he found in that poem, and which became so prevalent after the war as a reaction to the years of hunger and death, put him into a state of exultation. Like many other soldiers who also read Nietzsche, Tillich found himself lured back to passion and to life. Nietzsche's rejection of bourgeois hypocrisy in particular attracted him. He became wildly addicted to life's vivid joys while on leave, and like any other soldier confessed his desire to suck the last sweetness out of existence. On the battlefield he had had to repress everything that made life rich and vital; on leave he sought to compensate for this deprivation. He was torn between the casual girls a soldier could easily find and the one "true love" waiting at home.[22] His preoccupation with the future and his work intermingled with memories of an innocent past now forever out of reach. His mood slowly shifted from standing in hell and death to wondering about what lay ahead, and what role he would play in the new order.

Came 1917 in Germany: the "turnip winter." People were starving, their hunger stilled only by the lowly turnip, served up on German tables in every conceivable way—as soup, as a vegetable, as jam, even as coffee. In January Tillich wrote his father not of war or famine, but of his new destiny, comparing it with his father's own and neatly summarizing their different and identical talents.

The hardest thing for you as for me is to be a pastor and a preacher, whereas we are both ideally suited to intellectual work. You are a born *Konsistorialrat* and I am a born Professor. But destiny has ordained that you must always be a preacher, and I, if not always, for a great part of my life.[23]

His growing self-awareness moved him in the same letter to mention that pictures had come to mean to him what music had always meant to his father, and that he suddenly realized that he was able to learn from such things, too.

In April America entered the war, making the outlook for peace more bleak than ever. In May Tillich's father celebrated his sixtieth birthday, and Tillich wrote him recalling the garden in the Neuenburgerstrasse—"that was a world—a whole world of bliss and innocence untouched by reality."[24] He began to wonder whether he could link his destiny to the church. Did he have a right to do so?[25] The church had supported the regime responsible for the endless war in which he was still helplessly caught.

Then in August, when another chaplain had been secured to assist him, Tillich resumed intellectual work; he again became a scholar. He started to fill the greatest gap in his knowledge by reading modern philosophy from beginning to end. When he wrote his friend Hirsch later in 1917, he said he had come so far that he could now survey the literature of modern philosophy, sense its direction with considerable clarity, and understand its chief problems. He declared that the work of Husserl, Scheler, and Ebbinghaus interested him most. He had accomplished so much in a short time, he told Hirsch, because he had managed to cut himself off inwardly from the war and had achieved therefore a certain peace of mind.[26]

Yet his state of mind was not as serene as he then described it. Frequently alternating between hope and despair, he wondered aloud whether philosophy was his true calling. To become a philosopher seemed a "terrible curse" on the one hand, and on the other, inevitable. More and more he grappled with the awareness that the concept of God that had crumbled on the battlefield—

namely, of a God who would make everything turn out for the best—needed to be replaced. In early December he wrote, "I have long since come to the paradox of *faith without God,* by thinking through the idea of justification by faith to its logical conclusion. . . ."[27]

He was in search of a new definition, but only part of him had rejected the old one. His sentimental longing for it is reflected in his Christmas letter to his father, in which he writes, ". . . the most beautiful gift we have received from you is that we have such memories of Christmas, and that we can hand them on to others."[28] It was like his longing for the tranquility and unbroken culture of the nineteenth century—despite his criticisms of it, his yearning for it was never entirely stilled.

One last bloodbath awaited him: his first and last victory and the final defeat. In April 1918 Tillich's nerves failed once more.[29] It was not as terrible for him as after Verdun, he wrote from the hospital, but the difference was that this time he could not stand it any more. He was overcome by the need to make an end to his war service and return home, for he feared he would collapse again. He realized at the same time that it would be difficult, both inwardly and practically, to secure a release, but if it could be done, he said, the burden of responsibility he no longer felt able to carry would fall from his spirit. He asked his father to see if the consistory could call him back to Berlin and give him a job which would not demand too much of him; he was certain that he would be ill for months to come. "Body and soul are broken and can never be entirely repaired, but that is a small sacrifice in comparison with millions who have given their lives."[30]

He had seen too much ugliness and horror, as had all other soldiers, ever to be the same again. He felt close to insanity. Every death was like the first—he wanted to make an end of it all. There he was, sitting in the mud, while his friend Friedrich Büchsel, only three years older, was already a full professor in Rostock.

On 1 May 1918 Tillich asked to be relieved from army service. His application was rejected. At the end of the month, in a complete change of mood, he expressed a strong sense of victory.

Today or tomorrow our troops will reach the Marne, and we follow behind. The wounded are in good spirits; everything is different, everything entirely different and much, much better than before. Our regiments are magnificent and I am grateful to the chief of chaplains for forcing me to experience this. This is the first time in war that we have experienced something of victory and advance. The result is that we are fresh and joyful again despite all losses! And in spite of many scenes of horror.[31]

For a moment the romantic patriot reemerged in warm affirmation. But mood and victory were short-lived. On 10 June Tillich won the Iron Cross First Class. He was very proud that General Balkmeister, commander of the division, personally pinned the medal on his uniform. That was "very nice," he wrote his father.[32] In July he came home for a few days' leave. On 1 August he was assigned to Spandau, a military base in west Berlin, as army chaplain until the end of the war.

Events moved swiftly. The German High Command sued for an armistice. On 9 November the war came to an end, and on the eleventh an armistice was declared. The fighting had lasted for more than four years. All great nations had been involved in it, with sixty-five million men under arms. More than eight and one-half million soldiers were dead, more than twenty-one million wounded, and nearly eight million were taken prisoner or were missing. Germany alone counted one and three-quarter million dead, over four million casualties, and over one million were taken prisoner or were missing. The German national debt was reckoned at forty-four billion dollars.[33]

German troops returning to their defeated homeland marched into a revolution and civil war. Inflation was in the making. An epoch of stability, social order, and security was giving way to a new uncharted world. Tillich did not personally witness the final collapse of the German army, but he saw the revolution taking place in Berlin: there was shooting in the streets during an uprising of workers. He found himself more sympathetic with their cause than he had ever imagined he could be.

A new feeling began to grow within him during these months.

At first he felt that the end of European culture had come, and was depressed and pessimistic. But now he started to think clearly about all that had happened, and came to the conclusion that this end was the inevitable consequence of social developments, nothing less than the breakdown of capitalism. His mood of depression and defeat was followed by one of anger at the society that had permitted such a world conflict to occur. He had seen the gap between officers and the common soldier at the front; he had beheld the contrast between the gains of war profiteers and the losses of the mass of the people. During the last months of the war, in Berlin, he saw the distress and burden put on the people's shoulders by those in power who themselves had not borne it in equal measure. It was then and not earlier (as he sometimes later boasted) that Tillich fully comprehended the consequences of nationalism—they were to be seen all around him. He sometimes felt them within his own being. "I was a barbarian when I returned from the war until a friend introduced me to a few psychoanalytic tricks of living," he later said.[34]

And as the nightmares of war slowly turned into shadows obscured by the looming outline of the immediate future, he knew that he wanted to be a partner in rebuilding Western civilization. The guilt feelings he may have had about surviving the worst battles of the war were hidden under the restless energies of an impatient, ambitious man. He was pessimistic about the future, to be sure, but physically whole and filled with vigor and courage. In this state of mind, and with a certain clarity of purpose, Tillich took up his work where he had left it, more determined than ever to become a professor. Everything else was of secondary importance.

3

Between Two Worlds
(1919-1924)

Teacher, Theoretician

Tillich spent the next six years in Berlin, the city he once described as "homeland and mythos."[1] As capital of a defeated nation it was permeated by the aftermath of war. The people were nervous and hungry, the streets filled with beggars and cripples. Drugpushers and swindlers wore horn-rimmed glasses and combed their hair back flat in what was called the Bolshevik manner, their necks cleanly shaven and powdered. A cynical, half-insolent tone was adopted generally, masking a terrible insecurity. Women wore their hair very short; their shapeless dresses did not reach to the knee; old-fashioned or beautiful clothes had been sacrificed to the war. At the beginning of the twenties, Berlin smelled of cheap perfume and gasoline. There was a sense of hysteria everywhere as new inflationary levels were reached, soon every day, then hour by hour.[2]

The city was drab. Houses were being rebuilt; for a time scaffolding seemed a permanent part of the scene. The brilliance of the imperial epoch had been tarnished, but Berlin slowly became the center of the most vibrant cultural life in Europe. From the

57

ashes of defeat a phoenix was beginning to rise. The city became a magnet.[3] Composers, journalists, actors, painters were drawn to it. With its superb orchestras, forty theaters, and over a hundred newspapers and journals, it attracted the talented and the ambitious. Names such as Kandinsky and Klee, Brecht and Wedekind, Rilke and George, Furtwängler and Walter, Ullstein and Fischer, suggest the impressive list of those active in the city at the time. All shared in a cultural flowering which was marked essentially by experimentation, not only in the arts but in all spheres of life: government, science, sexual mores. The old was challenged, the new yet to be born. It was a time of unrest and poverty, yet of burgeoning activity, when bourgeois concepts of thought and behavior were being shattered.

Against this background Tillich began to carve out his career. All the elements that shaped his later success sprang into being at this time; a pattern was cut which was never substantially altered. He combined teaching at the university, his first love, with lecturing outside it; he combined writing serious articles, essays, and book reviews with the publication of fugitive journalistic pieces; he sought the company of esoteric intellectual groups which shared his own interests: politics, religious socialism, painting, economics, the theater, and later depth psychology.

Variety of interest was one of Tillich's basic traits, experiment another. He was involved only theoretically in postwar reconstruction and the search for a viable form of government, but was personally entangled in the rich confusion around him, experiencing to the full the fears and expectations, the excitement and despair of the social ferment. His hesitant participation in bohemian ways was both an inspiration and a problem to him. For unconventional modes of life and expression became a part of the fabric of his existence; his relations with women in particular inspired him with a sense of freedom, then nearly cut him off from the established society of which he was critical but in which he needed to work—and for which, indeed, he always maintained a childlike respect.

The trauma of which he had written his father in the last year of the war, as something permanent and beyond repair, became apparent in thought as well as emotion. Caught between the conservative Christian traditions of the nineteenth century and the bold radical creativity marking the new style of the twentieth, he could not side with either the one or the other. He sought to combine the two. Freud's psychoanalysis, Cézanne's Expressionistic Impressionism,* Marx's socialism, all became material for his Christian apologetic theology. He said neither yes nor no: he said both. The split did indeed remain, despite his great efforts to heal or hide it—much later he called it "the boundary." His great gift for synthesis, analogous to Proustian recollection, gradually produced a written work marked by bright clarity on the one hand and dark obfuscation on the other. His work and his life alternated between wisdom and foolishness, between order and turbulence.

While still an army chaplain in Spandau, in November 1918 Tillich had resumed negotiations with Professor Lütgert at the University of Halle,[4] who informed him that it had been decided no longer to maintain the seminary for theological candidates that Tillich had expected to head. He advised him therefore to transfer his record of qualification from Halle to the University of Berlin, where he might be able to find a job.

On 1 January 1919, Tillich was released from army service. A friend of his father's, Bishop Gustav Haendler of Berlin, became Tillich's sponsor, appointing him as one of his vicars. The position, which Tillich later described as a sinecure, enable him to earn some money while establishing himself; when the appointment ran out, Hugo Simon, a banker and friend, supported him for a year. In those days, the post of *Privatdozent* was somewhat analogous to that of an instructor in an American university. He was not paid a full salary but was entitled to receive the fees paid by his students. In other words, he was given the opportunity to establish himself as a scholar and lecturer. He was expected to launch his reputation through publishing books and articles, and to demonstrate his competence to become a professor. It was a cruel system at best, especially since it assumed that a *Privatdozent* had a private income. In times of inflation and economic chaos it

* Cézanne, too, was on the boundary between Expressionism and Impressionism.

was a desperate situation in which to find oneself. Tillich was fortunate that Haendler stepped in to enable him to continue his career without further interruption. To his meager sources of support, he decided to add the income from renting rooms in his Taunusstrasse apartment. He was able to manage, but he was poor. In fact, his struggle for an adequate income played no small part in the years that followed.[5]

Early in January 1919 Tillich gave his inaugural address at the University of Berlin, entitled "The Existence of God and the Psychology of Religion."[6] Somewhat later he met his first class, which to his delight consisted of twenty-five, later thirty, men and women. The course he called "Christianity and the Social Problems of the Present." The topic reflected his determination to come to terms with the new world around him. He concentrated on a discussion of the religious and philosophical grounds of various political parties, exploring the democratic, conservative, anarchistic, liberal, and socialist groups. For his historical material he relied for the most part on Troeltsch's *The Social Teaching of the Christian Churches*, a work he regarded as the greatest theological contribution since Harnack's *History of Dogma*, and which he highly recommended to all, urging his friends Fritz and Schafft to buy it despite the high price.[7]

It soon became clear to his classroom audience that Tillich had endured the demons and horrors of war even as they had, but that he seemed unconquered by them. He stood with both feet in the present, wrestling with immediate problems and communicating his certainty that something new was in the making.[8] This expression of faith together with his favorable attitude toward socialism was part of his early appeal. Many alert and intelligent young people of the time tended to be prosocialist; there seemed to them no viable alternative.

But it was more than the content of his early teaching that impressed his first students: it was the form and his personal presence. The same traits that ultimately prompted an American colleague to characterize Tillich as a "genius-teacher" were already there at the start of his career. His physical presence is a case in point—it was unprepossessing. During the first year he came to class dressed in his army greys with the Iron Cross on his chest. He wore a mustache and blonde horn-rimmed glasses so thick that they gave him the appearance of being extremely nearsighted. The combination of uniform and mustache made him look older than he was, and his narrow face unduly enlarged his nose. After a year, when he could afford it, he bought a dark blue suit, wore a tie, and appeared clean-shaven. He was swiftly transformed both inwardly and outwardly into a modern young man of the big city.

He was just under six feet tall, and thin, and when he wanted to emphasize certain passages he thrust his hands straight up in the air; there was an almost ecstatic quality in the motion, a student later reported. He was always punctual, appearing with black notebook in hand and surveying his audience before he began to speak. He moved quickly and energetically in those days; even when reading from his notebook he spoke with a sparkling rapidity. Each lecture, neither too long nor too short, was written out to fit the hour, leaving time for questions. With his intensity, while not really handsome he exuded great charm. After the lecture, even when foolish questions were asked, he managed to find in them some sort of highly perceptive comment.[9] As the bell sounded he walked out the door, usually surrounded by a bevy of girls.

Lecturing was a passion to which Tillich remained enslaved all his life. This activity, he wrote after forty years of teaching, had from the start given him "the greatest anxiety and the greatest happiness." Each time he walked up to the podium or pulpit he did so "with fear and trembling," his lips tightly compressed, his breathing heavy. Contact with the audience gave him immediate relief, "a sense of joy," the satisfaction of "creative communion." But beyond this, the exchange of questions and answers remained for him the "most inspiring" aspect of all.[10] When he wrote these much-quoted lines he did not exaggerate; indeed, the knowledge that an audience awaited him sometimes cured him of illness in the twinkling of an eye.

Association with his students, which he carefully nurtured from the beginning, did not stop at the classroom door. It was carried over into social evenings in his apartment in the Friedenau section of Berlin. There at semimonthly meetings he entertained fifteen or twenty young men and women, seating them at separate tables, forbidding them tobacco or alcohol, and serving lemonade. The discussions that took place from eight o'clock on began with Tillich's newest ideas, which he introduced and thus tested. In a Socratic manner he asked questions, trying to elicit what the students knew of contemporary books and ideas. He naturally knew more than they, but because they were articulate and responsive their varied reaction not only helped to provide him with a sense of what was going on outside his own realm, but also gave him a sounding board and ultimately a following.

Yet he relied less on secondhand information than was later alleged. He read voluminously. The myth that subsequently developed to the effect that he "no longer read" originated with himself and was in fact true, but did not apply in the twenties. He read everything new: Karl Barth's *Romans*, Ernst Troeltsch's *Historism and Its Problems*, Max Weber's *Economy and Society*, Heinrich Scholz's *Philosophy of Religion*, all were on his list. He was working on a book on *The System of the Sciences* and at the same time planning a system of theology. His purpose, therefore, in asking students about what was going on in seminar and lecture hall was not idle. He wanted to get a picture of all possible disciplines, to know what was happening outside his own field.

What he read, Tillich never forgot, and thus he built up a vast storehouse of knowledge from which to fashion his own thought. It was not his desire or interest to become a precise, exact scholar; he preferred to be an architect, using ideas as a builder uses bricks to make a new edifice. It was a bold ambition, but it came naturally to him to think in a systematic way.[11]

There was in him too the tendency to learn by osmosis, to "pick" other people's brains. It was a conscious habit, a deliberate approach which increased as the years passed. If he wanted to be *au courant* he asked an expert: the historian, the biologist, the sociologist, the psychologist. Sometimes he took up the words of others into his work, often without benefit of footnote. He absorbed what another had written and made it his own, creating something new in the process. It was, some said, like the making of a bell: the hot lavalike fluid pouring into the hard form, emerging new and shining with a clarity of tone that went out to all who would listen. When his great work, the *Systematic Theology*, was finished late in life, some compared it to "pure poetry" but found it unacceptable as theology. Others suspected that the peculiar mixture of old and new masked some sort of deception, did not rest on sound intellectual ground. Still others found him the most seminal theologian of the twentieth century.[12]

In any case, from the first Tillich earnestly desired to be understood, and after each lecture would ask, "How did I do?" or "What do you think?" or "How was it?" It was a question he asked in various forms of student and colleague, friend and sometimes even foe, for the rest of his life, even when he had become internationally known. It was not a pose; he wanted the other person's opinion, and his early students—perhaps all his students —loved him for what they felt as the compliment he paid them.

His first students remembered him too for his witty, jovial, relevant remarks, his readiness to laugh, his quick movements and goodness of heart. Kindness and gentleness were reflected in his tone of voice as well as his gestures. His sometimes demonic vitality and energy lay hidden below a benevolent manner which increased as the years went by; the troubled, hard, broken look of the twenties was slowly replaced by a quieter, softer, fuller disposition. As he grew older, his physical movements grew less excited, his speech slower; he became heavy and bearlike, with hands folded behind him, his eyes fastened on a manuscript, his voice sometimes weary.

He remained, however, extraordinarily sensitive to audience reaction, noting faces in his classroom, responding to the slightest nuance of expression. In Berlin, Marburg, Frankfort, and New York it was always the same. After a lecture he might ask a student, "What was bothering you?" or say, "I know what you were thinking," or "Let's discuss this! What you say interests me greatly." Discussion and friendship often grew out of such seemingly casual encounters. There were those, too, who never made any impression on him whatever—whom he might meet a dozen times and still not remember or recognize. To these he seemed neither gentle nor kind, but strangely uncomfortable and preoccupied.

Tillich's early students pleased him and he relished the contact with them, remaining lifelong friends with some, even being influenced by their ideas (particularly with respect to socialism). But almost at once he sought a larger audience, partly in order to earn more money. He lectured for example at the *Hochschule für Politik,* or Institute of Politics. Yet it must be said that he would have tried to broaden his audience even had he been a man of wealth; the fact that he was poor simply increased the inner pressure. He liked nothing so much as having before him a gathering of people to speak to. He was in some respects driven by the desire for applause. If there is a single note to be sounded about the paradoxical personality of Paul Tillich, true from beginning to end, it is this: he had an enormous need to succeed. His work was unabashedly his own "ultimate concern," and the devotion he poured into it was accompanied by temporary neglect of wife, family, friends, and muses. It was a price he was willing to pay, and which many were willing to accept, impressed as they were by his industry and genius, and won by his great personal charm or charisma.

His first outstanding public lecture, indeed the first public presentation of his own creative thought, took place on 16 April 1919 when he appeared before the Kant Society in Berlin. He spoke "On the Idea of a Theology of Culture." This was a notion which remained in the center of his interest throughout his life. In this particular lecture he asked how the specific functions of faith, cult, community, and church were related to the functions of culture: namely, to science, art, ethics, society, and state. How, he wondered, is the religious sphere related to the secular? The startling note he sounded was that religion was not a special sphere and function in man's life but the dimension of depth in all of life's functions. He laid down the thesis he was to explicate in detail in nearly all his later works: "Religion is the substance of culture, and culture is the form of religion."[13] He applied some of these ideas in a new and extraordinary way to painting, as we shall see.

This first lecture, with its unusual contention that religious experience must not be separated from the secular, was well received, and in virtue of this success Tillich was invited to speak at conferences, in schools, at the Kant Society, and to participate in small discussion groups. There he found the stimulus and criticism of his peers a necessary antidote to working alone. Among the many subjects to which he addressed himself during the twenties were: socialism, the *kairos* (a concept he developed in the religious socialist circle), youth and religion, anthroposophy, the masses and the spirit, church and culture, doubt and justification, and many others.

Author, Journalist

Since Tillich never lectured without a manuscript or notes, he found it relatively easy to publish a great deal. Writing came naturally to him: he thought with pencil in hand. He often said of the essays and articles he wrote between 1919 and 1933—the years that include all his German publications—that they were "screws in the rock."[14] The rock, of course, was his systematic theology, and the analogy is from mountain climbing. Tillich was convinced that these small attempts, these "screws in the rock," were the ideal, perhaps even the only way for him and for others to reach the top. In his case at least the theory proved true. He wrote voluminously, publishing larger volumes only after he had tested ideas in smaller essays. He explored and developed and expanded, writing steadily over a lifetime, and published his theological system only at the end.

While the act of writing came easily to him, it was not entirely effortless. He sometimes experienced great inner turmoil or torment, familiar to all who wield the pen. In the early twenties, while staying in Kampen on the island of Sylt, one of his favorite vacation spots, he spent fourteen days working on a little piece entitled, "Über Formkraft in der Abendländischen Geistesgeschichte" [The Formative Power in Western Intellectual History]. He wrote to a friend about the agonies of creation:

> I worked for fourteen days on this piece. In the end I could not sleep any more because the spirits of the dream world drove me further. I thought of the idea about fourteen days ago and I have not yet recovered from the experience. There were quite a number of new concepts which entered my mind and with which somehow I had to come to terms, ideas like "demonic" and "theocratic."[15]

This experience of the torture of creation was not unique. In Tillich's case it was coupled with an immense ability to concentrate no matter where he was: on the beach, seated atop a sand castle in a wicker chair, or on a rock overlooking the ocean; later, in his sometimes noisy New York office or in his favorite spot, the quiet and lovely grape arbor of his East Hampton home. Nothing penetrated his consciousness or disturbed him when he was caught up in formulating his ideas. *The Religious Situation,* his first successful book, was partly written on the beach at Sylt, and friends who observed him later reported that he seemed absolutely transported with joy as he labored to bring forth his ideas in the midst of myriad sights and sounds. He had visions of jewels and flowers while he looked at the sea; he delighted in the movement of people on the beach, though separate from them, surveying all from his wicker chair.[16]

Tillich's written work varies from being extremely abstract, which makes it difficult to read, to being imaginative, which gives it an elusive quality. It is marked by great learning and a keen perception of the human condition. He made endless distinctions, relied on his excellent grasp of the history of philosophy and Christian doctrine, and finally caught all his ideas in the net of philosophical presuppositions worked out during his lifetime. He had a considerable flair for a catchy title and a feel for the contemporary mind. He tended to compress what he had to say and to avoid elaboration, in sharp contrast to his contemporary Karl Barth,

66

who was tempted to great expansion of his thought. Like many popular authors, Tillich wrote and published too much, frequently repeating the same stimulating, provocative ideas. This occurred especially at the end of his life as a consequence of belated fame. In Berlin in the twenties the story was different. He was interested in establishing his name, in having his ideas discussed and disseminated; each publication, whether book review or essay, represented an important achievement in which he rejoiced. Writing for publication remained for him a permanent necessity, but he never thought of himself primarily as a writer, who worked and produced in isolation. His books, monographs, and articles were generally products of lengthy and exhaustive discussions with others—friends, colleagues, and students. Tillich loved debates; even as a student he was proud when he emerged the victor from a heated discussion. Later on, particularly in the years immediately after World War I, he derived great satisfaction from the fact that terms he had created and phrases he had been the first to formulate, mainly in political discussions, were adopted by his friends and associates.

Religious Socialist

Politics was unavoidably a subject of foremost importance in Germany at the time. Tillich became deeply interested. He did not get involved in active party politics, but developed a passion for political and sociological analysis. Thus his writing and teaching acquired both vitality and urgency. He spent much time and effort trying to understand what was happening to Germany and how postwar reconstruction of its social-political order could best proceed. Thus he became an activist of sorts.

Political experiment under the auspices of the Weimar Republic dominated German life from 1919 until 1933. Monarchical rule had disappeared overnight when the Kaiser fled into voluntary exile. The new German government was headed by six Socialists; Friedrich Ebert was chancellor. There were at once great gains for workers, including the right of collective bargaining and the eight-hour day. There was a brief revolutionary interruption, but by the middle of January 1919 Ebert was president, a position he occupied until 1925. A new constitution was drafted and adopted by a large majority of the National Assembly against the opposition of the Independent Socialists, the German People's Party, and the German National Party.

From the outset the fate of the government seemed uncertain. Ebert was possessed of a calm dignity and good common sense. The Weimar officials were clearheaded men of personal integrity and good will, but they were inexperienced in the art of political propaganda and the rituals of international diplomacy. Yet in the early years the feeling of hope that a new and better world was possible prevailed over Spenglerian despair, at least in the hearts of men like Tillich.

In the spring of 1919, some friends whom he had met at various political gatherings that winter invited him to deliver a lecture at a meeting of the Independent Socialist Party to which they belonged. The party was to the left of the Social Democratic Party (then in power), but to the right of the Communists. Tillich's appearance before this group on 14 May angered the Protestant Consistory of Brandenburg, which identified itself with the feudal-capitalist order despite the lost war. Defeat and revolution made no change in its attitude. The church remained what it had been in prewar days: antidemocratic, antipacifist, and antisocialist.

It is not surprising therefore that Superintendent Bartels, as spokesman of the consistory, at once reprimanded Tillich. What disturbed him was not so much what Tillich had said in the lecture as the fact that an ordained Protestant clergyman had appeared at a radical socialist party gathering.

By way of self-defense Tillich sent Bartels the substance of his lecture, given under the title "Christianity and Socialism." On the one hand, he rejected every attempt to identify Christianity with a particular social order, a view he felt deprived religion of its inward personal character. On the other, he asserted that Christianity carried with it the duty and the will to shape the life of humanity in terms of justice and liberty, rejecting oppression. He then set forth many ideas he was to develop and elaborate in succeeding years.

On 12 July Superintendent Bartels replied in a manner Tillich described as being "soft as a plum."[17] His tone was in fact sharp, but he took no action against Tillich. He wrote that he found himself unable to agree with many of the points the latter had made and did not in any case have time for a detailed response. He further regarded Tillich's thought as essentially unclear, and emphasized the danger of mixing religion and politics. Obviously many church members, he wrote, were disturbed or offended by the fact that a clergyman had attended a radical-socialist meeting. He warned Tillich not to attend such gatherings again. Tillich's lecture was published later in the year in a brochure entitled *Socialism as a Question of the Church*,[18] but there is no record of his having repeated the offense.

Indeed, he went to great pains to explain to his friends, in a circular letter dated September 1919, that he had not joined—and had no intention of joining—the Independent Socialist party, though he now chose to vote in its favor, finding neither the Social Democrats nor the Communists to his liking. He qualified his political commitment even further by maintaining that his approval of the Independent Socialists did not mean he accepted their procedures; in fact he leveled incisive criticisms at their methods of agitation. Nevertheless, he was convinced that the greatest socialist energy and the best potential for constructive change were in that quarter. What Tillich wanted was a new order of society born of Christianity and socialism, in which the destructive powers of capitalism and nationalism would be undone. It was this hope that prompted him to join the religious socialist movement.

Already before the war religious socialist groups had sprung into being all over Germany. The term "religious socialism" was first employed by Christoph Blumhardt, Hermann Kutter, and Leonhard Ragaz, founders of the movement. The members of the several groups which went by that name felt that the socialist parties in the various countries of Europe, but particularly in Switzerland and Germany, should be supported in the name of religion. They differed greatly among themselves as to the implementation of this idea. Moreover, some were Christians, others not; some wished to work through the church alone, others outside it; some were theologians, others pastors, philosophers, or economists.

In September 1919 a three-day conference of all Continental religious socialists took place in Tambach, Germany. One of the three main speakers was Karl Barth, the young Swiss theologian destined to dominate twentieth-century Protestant theology until forced to share the spotlight with Tillich and the great American theologian, Reinhold Niebuhr. A last-minute replacement, Barth was not yet well known. He had just published the first and disturbing edition of his *Commentary on Romans*. He urged his listeners to identify themselves with the Christian church, to work through it without linking it to any political party or social program. Some applauded this idea, others fled from the scene in despair. It soon became evident that the variety and multiplicity of notions set forth by those in attendance would make it impossible to form a united and therefore politically effective movement. Religious socialism, therefore, came to express itself in Germany and elsewhere in small individual groups that met sporadically and mapped out various programs for reform.

Tillich joined a group which had sprung up in Berlin in 1920 under the leadership of Günther Dehn and Karl Mennicke.[19] Known variously as the Berlin group or *"kairos* circle," it never exceeded ten or twelve in number. The regular members of this small circle were, in the words of Eduard Heimann, "naive, optimistic, esoteric, eccentric academicians" who gathered to discuss the problems of the world, which they regarded as now open to new creative possibilities. The defeat of Germany was seen by them all as a sign and opportunity to create new conditions for international survival and self-governance.

Dehn was a pastor, perhaps the only active minister of the group, and was later called to teach practical theology at the University of Halle. Nazi students rioted in opposition to this appointment because they resented a pacifist speech he had made in 1928.

He remained with the Berlin group for only a short time, sensing that the debates among the members were too theoretical to be politically effective. Karl Mennicke worked as a minister and social worker in the Moabit or workers' section of Berlin. He was, as a matter of fact, an exceedingly practical man, who relished talking until three in the morning with workers about their special personal and social problems. During the Nazi period he fled to Holland, where he organized a folk school and was active in adult education. In World War II he survived in the underground, returning afterward to Germany to teach social pedagogy at the University of Frankfort.

In addition to Dehn and Mennicke, Adolf Löwe, Eduard Heimann, Alexander Rüstow, and Arnold Wolfers were regular members of the *kairos* group. Rüstow, an historian and economist whose dogmatic manner irritated Tillich and whose debating habits occasionally threatened to split the group, came from a military family. For a time he was a Communist; ultimately he converted to socialism. Arnold Wolfers was a Swiss lawyer who became director of the Berlin Institute of Politics. He emigrated to America in 1933, and taught political science at Yale University.

Rüstow and Wolfers were Protestants, but Adolf Löwe the economic technician and later a professor of economics, was a believing, non-Orthodox Jew. He remained attached to Tillich from their first meeting, combining lifelong devotion with an insistent critique. On the evening when Tillich introduced his idea of the *kairos* to the religious-socialist group, Löwe returned with him to his Friedenau apartment, challenging and debating, then staying until dawn to discuss the Book of Job. Tillich was stimulated by such "attack" as he called it, to refine, expound, and elaborate his ideas.

Whenever Tillich wrote or talked about the rich and rewarding friendships he maintained with Jews, he was referring primarily to Löwe. The ceaseless dialogue between the two was enlivened by a recurring argument about Judaism and Christianity which finally persuaded Tillich that it was useless, even destructive, to attempt to convert any Jewish believer to the Christian faith. Löwe maintained that the world had not been transformed by Jesus Christ, who therefore could not have been the Messiah. He remained a Jew, waiting for the Messiah's coming. Dismissed from his post on political rather than racial grounds, a fact of which he was proud, Löwe escaped to Switzerland in 1933 after the Nazi takeover. He taught for a while at the University of Manchester in England, to which he sought unsuccessfully to lure Tillich, and rounded out his career at the New School for Social Research in New York.

Eduard Heimann, another Jewish intellectual, was markedly different from Löwe. An economist with great interest in history and philosophy, he was a profoundly religious, kindly man who identified himself with the Christian vocation more deeply than many baptized Christians. He became a professor of economics at the University of Hamburg, but in 1933 emigrated to the United States and joined the graduate faculty at the New School for Social Research. After his retirement he gave one course each year at Union Theological Seminary, returning in the 1960s to Germany, where he taught at the University of Hamburg until his death.

In the early twenties this Berlin group met fortnightly. Mennicke was the organizer and soul of the group; in time Tillich became its head. Their discussions dealt with problems of the postwar situation, attempting to read the signs of the times. They were highly conscious of the irretrievable breakdown of the old order and would give no support to those who, despite the catastrophic end of the war, endeavored to bring about a restoration of the former system: feudalism and the monarchy, capitalism and the firm divisions of the social classes. They turned away in particular from the churches, which appeared to be chiefly concerned with preserving their institutional power, and thus found themselves in opposition especially to Lutheranism because it retreated from responsible social and political action behind the walls of political conservatism as well as social and cultural tradition.

Tillich and his friends identified themselves ever increasingly with socialism, although they decided at the time not to join any socialist party or participate in political campaigns. They felt their own function as spokesmen of the prophetic strain in the religious tradition of the West, reviving the social message of the Hebrew prophets and the spirit of radical reformers down to the religious socialists of their own day. Yet they did not believe anything good would come of a mere alliance between Christians (or Jews) and socialists, or from a Christian infiltration of the socialist parties. They were also doubtful whether the conglomeration of socialists actually possessed the power or ability to bring about a transformation of society through real change in the economic processes of supply and demand, the production and distribution of wealth, and particularly relations between the property-owning upper and middle classes and the proletariat. The German socialist parties had become too hardened, they thought, in their attitudes and modes of behavior, chiefly by reason of the unavoidable necessity of parliamentary maneuvering, but partly also because of the influence of their own party propaganda on their program. Tillich and his group concluded that all social classes, but especially the churches and the workers, needed to be restructured through the affirmation and observance of first principles: namely, the direction of all religious practice toward the holy and the determination of all social action by justice.

They feared nothing so much as oversimplified utopianism; they shrank therefore from the Marxist and Bolshevist expectation of the inevitable dictatorship of the proletariat, and with equal force rejected proposals by religious groups and individuals for the establishment of the Kingdom of God on earth.

But they became more and more united in the conviction that the disaster of World War I had provided the setting for decisive acts of renewal. Tillich expressed this by a reinterpretation of the New Testament idea of the *kairos*, the moment of timely action when the eternal (what ought to be) breaks into time (the prevailing situation), resulting in the emergence of something new out of old and dying conditions.[20] The idea of the *kairos* thus became the focus of all deliberations among the Berlin religious socialists and the central point of their philosophy of history and their proposals for responsible historical action.

More and more frequently referred to as "the *kairos* circle,"

Tillich and his colleagues sought to propagate their ideas on the lecture platform of the Institute of Politics in Berlin as well as by the publication of a small journal entitled *Blätter für den Religiösen Sozialismus* [Leaves (or Pages) for Religious Socialism], edited by Karl Mennicke and published until 1926. Of high quality, the little magazine consisted of editorials, articles, and book reviews. It had a limited circulation, depended on a financial subsidy, and enjoyed slight influence outside the academic world.

In 1930 a journal called *Neue Blätter Für den Sozialismus* [New Leaves, etc.] was founded and put into the hands of August Rathmann. A former worker intent on studying law in order to help change the German political structure, Rathmann—a student of Heimann's—had first met Löwe, Tillich, and others at their *Akademische Woche* or "Academic Week" in October 1925.[21] At this conference papers read by the various members of the circle included Tillich's "The Religious Situation," which later became part of his first well-known book. Tillich, for his part, hoped that the young socialist might give a practical direction to the theoretical work in which he and the *kairos* group had thus far been engaged. He persuaded Rathmann to edit the new magazine in place of Mennicke, who had already left Berlin, and Rathmann devoted himself to the task with industry and skill.

For Tillich, the friendships which had sprung up in the twenties and his interest in politics lived on beyond the demise of the group. The idea of the *kairos* became a cornerstone of his theology. In his autobiographical writings and in his later years on the lecture platform he tended to exaggerate out of all proportion the size and influence of the religious socialist group to which he had belonged. To the unenlightened, he seemed to have been the spearhead of a political party which represented a genuine threat to Hitler and the National Socialists. This was clearly not the case. But while the national importance and actual influence of the *kairos* circle were minimal, the ideas it generated were not, and the hours Tillich spent expressing them to his friends, or on the lecture platform, or in published articles, were of inestimable value to him personally.

His tendency to generalize his own experience, making it larger than it was in fact, is in part responsible for this lopsided historical recollection.

Spiritual Breakthrough

Tillich's passion for the visual arts, like his political self-consciousness, was born during the war. His decision to support socialism and become involved in the religious socialist movement may be understood as a form of rebellion against his father's devotion to the royalist cause. His love of architecture (he toyed at one time with the idea of becoming an architect), of sculpture, and especially of painting was merely a different way of arriving at self-knowledge. For it was not through music, in which his father excelled and for which he had no talent, but during his adolescence through literature, and as an adult through painting that Tillich understood himself.[22]

Painting captured his fantasy from the moment in which he discovered that he could escape the destruction, horror, and ugliness of war through the vision of beauty. Once formed, the attachment developed, deepened, and endured. While the visual arts played a continuing and important role in his creative imagination and influenced his writing directly during the 1920s, they rarely became the sole object of formal analysis. Tillich knew he was an amateur, not a professional art critic or even an artist. Yet he enjoyed, particularly in his old age, lecturing about art in the classroom and talking about it informally with his friends. He generally translated his visual experience into theological ideas, introducing them obliquely into his work.

In 1919 Tillich was still learning about this new world into which he had accidentally stumbled. His old friend and childhood guide, Eckart von Sydow, now an art historian, who had once introduced him to Darwin and Freud, opened the door for him to the world of Expressionist painting. Tillich's interest had developed from a primitive state of escapism to the study of art history.

During the war, moreover, on his last furlough he had had an experience of revelation standing before Botticelli's "Madonna with Singing Angels."[23] The Berlin collection was then housed in the Kaiser Friedrich Museum, itself a beautiful building on the river Spree. The painting hung alone on a wall opposite the entrance, and the setting lent itself to wonder and awe. As Tillich stood before the work he felt suddenly grasped not only by its great beauty and power but by the reality of the absolute. He felt he was looking not merely at angels but at the holy itself. It was not the painting's religious subject—Madonna, Infant, and angels —but the combination of color, texture, expression, and balance that communicated the absolute to him. In this magical moment, to which he often referred, he apprehended somthing else: it was possible to experience the absolute—in his words, to be grasped by it—through something other than mere ecclesiastical symbols and signs.

Tillich's introduction to Expressionist painting was equally fateful. The painters of that movement were motivated by a personal, intuitive approach. They did not attempt to present nature as the external, objective phenomenon perceived by the eye, but rather to reveal the inner impression it makes upon the observer. They were interested not in the given exterior but in the laws that hold sway behind it. Transcendental, not external reality fascinated them; they sought to disclose it.

Van Gogh "revealed the creative dynamics in color and light," while Munch "showed the cosmic dread present in nature and mankind," but it was Cézanne whose work displayed expressionism *and* impressionism, that Tillich especially admired, as one who "battled with the form that depicted self-sufficient finitude and restored to things their real metaphysical meaning."[24]

Tillich concluded that the struggle of the Expressionist painters was precisely like his own. It seemed to him that the religious art of capitalist society was empty primarily because it had reduced traditional religious symbols to the level of middle-class morality, while Expressionism had a mystical, religious character independent of its subject matter. An apple painted by Cézanne seemed to him more sacred than a painting of Jesus by Uhde, for example.

Style or form, Tillich maintained, not subject matter revealed transcendent reality.[25]

In the spring of 1921 he expressed some of these ideas in his classroom lectures.[26] The painting that concerned him most was Marc's "Turm der Blauen Pferde" [Tower of the Blue Horses]. Marc, six years older than Tillich, had been killed early in the war near Verdun. He had wished originally to be a theologian, but after enrolling in a language school in Munich suddenly decided to become a painter. He rejected the human body as too ugly to depict, and studied the anatomy of animals instead. He wanted to paint simple things, which alone, he felt, contained the symbolism, pathos, and mystery of nature. His colors became so bold, his style so abstract, that paintings of a deer, a horse, or a leopard seemed to represent all deer, all horses, all leopards. Tillich emphasized this element: namely, that the horses were not horses but rather the "essence of horse." For him, the paintings represented a "breakthrough of content in form and color."[27]

This was the word Tillich used to describe what the Expressionists were doing. Their bitter struggle with middle-class taste was analogous to his own rebellion against middle-class morality and conventional theology, and they therefore appealed to him in a special way. They made him see how a work of art may produce profound delight through disregard and even destruction of form. This conception of the "breakthrough" came to dominate Tillich's theory of revelation, as he himself has vividly described.[28]

Once this style of Expressionism in painting had been replaced by the Neue Sachlichkeit or New Realism, Tillich coined the phrase gläubiger Realismus [believing realism], a concept central to his book, The Religious Situation. What he had in mind was a "realism based on faith," which he saw developing out of Expressionist art and believed would determine the spirit and mood of cultural life. The impact made by Expressionism on Tillich's imagination was never exceeded in intensity or duration by any other style of painting, although he was open to a great variety of art forms throughout his life. Coming as it did immediately after the war, the special attraction of this movement (especially its German phase) for Tillich lay in its courageous revelation of a disrupted society, of guilt, of ugliness, of death, also of beauty and depth. Perhaps this explains why he held fast to his conviction that painting more than any other of the arts not only mirrors the present but likewise provides clues to the future.

To be sure, Tillich conceived of all art as the highest form of play: it was the genuinely creative realm of the imagination.[29] But he considered painting the fullest of all forms. It reflected for him the inmost character of man's spiritual condition. It was a prophetic art and the expression of the most beatific mode of human freedom. He concluded that the only genuine kind of painting, the only painting worthy of the term "great," is that which allows the power of being to shine through the forms and colors on the canvas; anything else was for him a sort of dishonest or "beautified" realism. Thus Tillich was led from his study of painting to the insight that became the major theme of his philosophy of religion: namely, as we have already noted, that religion "is the substance of culture," while culture is the form through which religion expresses itself.

Thus the world of art was a prophetic instrument for Tillich as well as an inspiration. Though he remained an amateur, and sometimes uttered the subjective and exaggerated views of the self-educated layman to the embarrassment of the expert, his reactions to specific pictures or pieces of architecture are interesting because they reveal so much about himself. He regarded Grünewald's "Crucifixion" with its depiction of Christ's horrible wounds as "the most religious of all paintings."[30] He called Picasso's "Guernica" a great Protestant painting, perhaps the greatest of modern times, later qualifying this absolute statement by admitting that the radicalism of the Protestant question rather than the Protestant answer was to be found in this masterpiece.[31] The "gold ground" of Byzantine art revealed "the holy" to Tillich more than anything else except perhaps the stained-glass windows of Gothic cathedrals, which "permitted the light of God's spirit to penetrate man's darkness."[32] The cathedral at Chartres was his favorite example of the consummate perfection of the medieval art form. In his old age Tillich noted that Matisse's chapel at Vence was sublime in its simplicity, but had been designed by someone with no inner relationship to the Christian church, and therefore an important element was missing.[33] He was convinced that the old church architects knew that "aesthetic expressiveness is more than a beautifying addition to the life of worship."[34]

Tillich was a delightful companion in an art gallery or museum; he talked little but was visibly absorbed and markedly relaxed. Throughout his life he made pilgrimages to great art collections all over the world, returning to them again and again, often in the company of friends. Once in Paris in the 1930s, standing before the Cathedral of Notre Dame and looking up at the stone figures and gargoyles, he said, "The saints are sitting on their demons."[35]

Creative Chaos

In Berlin immediately after the war, Tillich was struggling with his own demons. The builder of pyramids in the sand, the architect of philosophical systems, gripped by passion for order and consistency, lived in a private world of "creative chaos."[36] It was a term he himself later used to cover the state of general disorder he shared with many young intellectuals of the time. In his case it meant a broken marriage and the tangled relations that followed from it. For in the years 1919 to 1924 a tale of considerable conflict, confusion, and anguish acted itself out against the backdrop of his Taunusstrasse apartment—known as the *Katastrophen-Diele* or Disaster Bar. His friend Eckart von Sydow hit upon this appellation. A *Diele*—literally a floor—was a type of little bar to be found at the time on almost any corner in Berlin. The disasters that occurred while Tillich lived there included an abortion (the sight of blood so frightened him that he was forever after opposed to abortion in principle), the birth of a baby, a dreadful robbery, and most important of all, the departure of his wife Grethi.[37]

When Tillich married Grethi Wever in 1914, he came to marriage still faithful to his Wingolfite vow of chastity. He was in his twenty-seventh year, and the vow had not been easy to keep. He had always found women alluring. As a boy he had loved nothing so much as to be in the kitchen and read or write while his mother cleaned vegetables or fruit. Her presence soothed him and made it easier for him to work.[38] As a young man, he had wandered in the Mark country with his "harem" of young girl friends, philosophizing with them, enjoying their attention. After his mother's death, moreover, he became exceedingly attached to his sister Johanna, with whom he shared his private thoughts, whom he trusted, and on whom he depended. There are hints that he was in love with her.[39]

Nor had women ever been oblivious to him. The attentions he craved and won through his boyish helplessness, his humanity and charm, were showered upon him by mother, sisters, and friends. By the time of his marriage he was a sought-after bachelor, outwardly proper and respectable but inwardly chafing under the burden of an enormous sensuality and sensitivity. The vow of chastity was not a yoke that made his burden lighter but a prison from which he incessantly yearned to escape.

In choosing to marry Grethi, Tillich found only temporary release from his prison. She was unconventional in thought and action and thus doubly attractive to him; she scoffed at the idea of monogamy, ridiculed his wish to be faithful only to her. During the war she became attracted to his friend Richard Wegener, with whom she had an affair, and to whom she bore two children. The first died in infancy; the second lived and bore Tillichs' name. Grethi left Tillich in the spring of 1919, but against all expectation Wegener did not marry her once she was free.

Deserted by his wife, whom he still found attractive but no longer loved, and betrayed by his friend, for whom he felt no bitterness either then or later, Tillich arranged for a divorce which would neither ruin Wegener's career nor saddle Tillich himself with the burden of the child that was not his. Wegener was not named the father in the divorce decree, which was granted on grounds of Grethi's desertion. A separate agreement was drawn up

requiring Wegener to support the child for a time. Grethi meanwhile came into a small sum of money through the sale of her
father's land, but she raised the child alone and never remarried.
After the divorce became official on 22 February 1921, Tillich and
Grethi went their separate ways.[40] Wegener himself forsook the
ministry and entered the teaching profession, ultimately holding
high positions in the field of education. While he remained on
good terms with Tillich, who continued to love him despite his
role in the breakdown of his marriage, Wegener was increasingly
critical of Tillich's theology and way of life.

The broken marriage was symptomatic of Tillich's inability to
give himself entirely, but the divorce, which he disliked to mention
in his later years, set him free to plunge into a life he euphemistically called "the Bohème." His apartment was transformed into a
"pension" for struggling artists and students. His father's former
housekeeper, Aunt Toni, cooked, cleaned, and sewed for him. He
was grateful to have someone who tended to the chores which he
himself was unable and unwilling to manage. Meals were shared in
common with the roomers, some of whom were not always reliable
when time for payment came around. In one instance Tillich lent
an artist some of his own funds so that he could manage. His most
prominent boarder was Christian Hermann, a psychoanalyst, who
paid for his lodging through a brief and incomplete analysis.[41]

Now Tillich began to enrich his emotional and imaginative side
through stimuli hitherto only superficially encouraged: the mystical, the demonic (a power he defined as creative and destructive at
the same time), and the erotic.[42] He was drawn to the revolutionary theater of Piscator as well as to the distinguished and fashionable classical productions of Max Reinhardt. He read the poetry of
Rilke and Stefan George and continued his habit, begun before the
war, of writing in cafés where he often met his men and women
friends. He seemed to avoid the world of music, and fled the
joyless existence to which his conformity with the law and convention of the church had confined him. Much later he wrote of the
meaning of joy for him,

Many Christians . . . try to hide their feeling of joy, or they try to avoid joys which are too intense. . . . Such an experience of the suppression of joy, and guilt about joy in the Christian groups, almost drove me to a break with Christianity. What passes for joy in these groups is an emaciated intentionally childish, unexciting, unecstatic thing, without color and danger, without heights and depths.[43]

Tillich's genius for friendship with women as well as with men coincided in these years with his great appetite for play, distraction, and amusement; it developed along new, intense lines in the postwar atmosphere of freedom. He was a bachelor once more, though with serious problems, who enjoyed the company of several interesting, intelligent women. Since it was no longer fashionable to be introduced to eligible women in the homes of their parents or the drawing rooms of friends and relatives, where before the war many marriages had been arranged, romances flourished in local bars and cafés, or people met at large balls where great numbers freely commingled. Tillich found the new ways enticing. He was in no particular hurry to remarry, but his monastic ties no longer bound him. He was thus drawn into a multiplicity of erotic adventures with a number of young women who were easily attracted to him and who also enjoyed the new freedom and yielded to the appeal of the metropolis. They met him at cafés, or as students in his classroom, or as strangers at a ball. The women he liked and who liked him were usually intellectual and interested in one of the various worlds that fascinated him: politics, psychoanalysis, painting, the arts and literature. Despising conventional beauty, Tillich preferred an interesting face or an unusual expression.

But while he took satisfaction and pleasure in those who were drawn to him, he was no Don Juan. Some of his friendships remained platonic, some pastoral, some merely professional. Yet his flight from the law—as represented by Wingolfite moralism and his father's authoritative, bourgeois manner—drew him into more than one unconventional relationship. As a consequence of his belated sensual awakening he encountered "manifold fears, expectations, ecstasies and despairs."[44] Rejection of the demands of chastity did not free him as he had hoped but thrust him into captivity of a different sort: namely, of chaos. His response on many levels to more than one woman meant for him a confusion rather than a solution. Moreover, each time he felt he was falling in love he discovered that the woman had already been promised to another and was not able to give herself entirely to him. The unavailable attracted him.

Yet he clung to his new way of life, for he had convinced himself that his work suffered when he was deprived of the experience of the erotic, whether actual or sublimated. In 1924 he wrote,

> There is no doubt that I am sometimes in danger of wanting to force certain deductions which lack the freshness of spontaneous views of reality. I am aware of this danger and I try to avoid it by getting involved in many different forms of vitality; I am in an uninterrupted connection with nature, and I refresh it every year with the greatest energy. Since my student days I have enjoyed close friendships. I have come to know the Bohème; I went through the war; I got involved in politics; I became fascinated by the art of painting, and, in the course of this winter, with greatest passion by music.[45]

Without such stimulation Tillich could not produce. The combination of an overlong monastic existence and the new casual satisfaction, however, wrought in him new feelings of guilt. "The gift of freedom," he later wrote, "implies the danger of servitude; the abundance of life implies the danger of sickness."[46] The abundance of relationships in these years produced in him a sort of sickness.

His guilt was double: he felt guilty in relation to each woman, and thus never deserted a single one whom he learned to know well; he felt guilty also in relation to the moral code, of which he never entirely rid himself and which continued to exert its power over him. For a time he convinced himself that the dangers of paganism were less than the pangs of earlier confinement. Thus he chose the fascination of variety and freedom of expression over against the monotony of the single, monogamous, bourgeois condition. At the same time, the choice created in him a fear that if his chaotic existence continued too long, he would find neither rest nor resolution of his conflict.[47]

Nor did Tillich seek to hide his way of life from the world. Gossip spread among his students to other universities in Germany. Emanuel Hirsch, himself now happily married, in whom Tillich confided his notion that while marriage was perhaps the ideal form of love between a man and a woman it was not the only possible form, implored him to change his ways and seek a balance in his relations with women—to treat them as sisters, as Hirsch himself did, and not as a means to productive intellectuality. He reminded Tillich of his own suffering, his unrequited love for Johanna, and remonstrated with him. Hirsch wondered whether Tillich still had the right to belong to the Wingolf fraternity; he doubted that there could be any prospects for him in the theological world, and suggested that he turn to philosophy instead.[48]

Tillich's friend Büchsel feared that the rumors of Tillich's divorce and the women in his life would result in his excommunication from the church. Hermann Schafft, no stranger to Tillich's predicament and always ready to enliven the scene with humor, gave him a picture of the temptations of St. Anthony showing the saint seated at a table with an open Bible, surrounded by devils and tempted by a woman. It hung, together with a reproduction of Grünewald's "Altar" and a Schmidt-Rottluff print, in Tillich's cave-like study.[49]

Tillich rationalized his not unsullied reputation. He was keenly grateful to Hirsch for his honesty and love, and admired his personal strength, which he went so far as to call a heroic religious ethic. Yet he rejected his advice. He did not want to pay the high price of the loss of nature, the demonic, the world of art, intuitive truth, and mysticism. So far as his own reputation was concerned, he felt that to have one at all was a blessing. He sensed that the split between his life and his work must be overcome, but knew at the same time that he could never return to the old ways from which he had freed himself in such tortuous fashion.

Then on 5 January 1920 Tillich experienced a terrible loss. His sister Johanna died in childbirth, through the carelessness of a midwife who in a moment of difficulty failed to seek the aid of a doctor. It was Johanna's third child; she had wanted four. As was the custom then, the elaborate funeral, including a sermon, was followed by a burial at which an ordained minister or family friend spoke a few words. At the graveside, Pastor Büttner of Bremen said that "she was a seeker, a genuinely homesick person."[50]

Friends who saw Tillich immediately after Johanna's death noted that he looked wretched and refused even to speak. Despite his habitual effort to forget those he loved as quickly as possible after they died, for weeks he was wrapped in terrible depression and gloom. His younger sister Elisabeth, herself married to Erhard Seeberger, a minister, and with a growing young family, was deeply concerned over her brother's despondent state of mind. In February she urged him to attend a Mardi Gras ball, and he did so.[51]

Thus Tillich, dressed in a cutaway and turban, went alone to the Academy of Arts in the Prinz Albrecht Strasse,[52] where he encountered a handsome young woman with magnificent large eyes and a deep melodious voice. Her name was Hannah Werner; she was wearing green stockings and she immediately fascinated him. She taught art at a school in Neukölln, a suburb of Berlin where she had studied and where her father had once been a superintendent of schools. Born on 17 May 1896 in the town of Rothenburg (she died on 27 October 1988 in East Hampton, N.Y.), she was ten years younger than Tillich, one of a family of five. As a child she had been temperamental, introspective, and preferred to play with boys. She had developed a taste for literature and wrote poetry; while her involvement with the world of painting played an important role in their relationship, it was not the first thing that attracted Tillich to her.

He told her about his sister's death, struck by the fact that she bore the same name.[53] When the costume party was over he invited her to his apartment. Resisting at first, she yielded to his wish, and in the months that followed there developed between them a tempestuous romance which, in all its anguish, passion, and contradiction, Tillich forever regarded as the supreme love of his life. She attended his lectures; they walked in the Grunewald, a park not far from Tillich's Friedenau apartment, discussing art, poetry, and philosophy; they fell increasingly in love.

But when spring came, Hannah confessed that she was already engaged to another man—Albert Gottschow, also an art teacher—and felt duty-bound to marry him. Despite Frede Fritz's intervention on Tillich's behalf (he and Tillich hoped she would wait until Tillich's divorce became final and then marry him), she decided to go ahead with her marriage to Gottschow. It is not absolutely clear why she made this decision—she said she did not trust Tillich, but at the same time promised to come back to him a year later.[54]

On 13 July 1920 in the university town of Marburg, where her parents then lived, she married Gottschow, who was completely ignorant of her relationship to Tillich.[55] She and Tillich kept in touch in the months that followed through a clandestine correspondence in which he urged her to return to him. In the spring of 1921 she accordingly left Greiz, where she and Albert were living, and—pretending to visit her sister Marie-Luise, who lived in Berlin—returned to Tillich for a night. Their ecstatic reunion convinced her that she was as much in love with Tillich as he with her.[56] Nevertheless, she returned to her husband. It was not until several months later, when she discovered that she was bearing Albert's child, that she finally yielded to Tillich's more and more urgent pleading. For in her abandonment of him he was in constant fear of slipping back into the bewildering, chaotic existence from which he was convinced she could save him.

Hannah left Albert, this time permanently. She lived for a time in Frede Fritz's home, then moved to Marburg, where on 5 June 1922 she gave birth to a boy. She then moved back to Berlin to live in the immediate neighborhood of Tillich's apartment. Gottschow, who had been devastated by her departure, for which he was totally unprepared, at first refused to grant the divorce she requested, but after the death of their child, who had been put into a nursing home in the city and had been neglected there, he acceded to her wish. The divorce was granted in December 1923; she married Tillich on 22 March 1924 in the home of Erhard Seeberger, the officiating minister and now her brother-in-law.[57]

The marriage was unhappy from the beginning.[58] The gap between expectation and fulfillment was and remained deep for both husband and wife. Tillich was convinced that Hannah was the answer to his conflict regarding women and their place in his life. He felt that she alone could save him from the nightmare of a multiplicity of relationships, to which his openness, sensitiveness, and warmth of nature made him prone. In the winter of 1920 he had fallen utterly and completely in love with her; he was intoxicated by her, and pursued her relentlessly until she finally yielded. He felt, moreover, that in her he had found a woman who could accept him as he was, who would forgive his faults as well as applaud his virtues. He was attracted by her unconventional ways, her disdain of the bourgeois, perhaps most of all by her almost boundless and unpredictable wildness. And he found her intellectually stimulating; her intuitive grasp of things supplemented his logical, rational way of thinking.

But there was a fatal expectation on his part: that in no circumstances would he ever again be bound by the restraints of stultifying bourgeois existence. He did not seek to return to the confusion of life between his two marriages, to be sure, but wanted to be free in his marriage—free to relate to the infinite possibilities of life that provide vital fulfillment—and refused to regard his wife as the absolute law which would imprison him once more. The threat of jealousy in particular angered him. It was with the understanding on his part that she was prepared to forgive him for his weakness and accept him as he accepted her that he married this inexperienced young woman, who did not entirely comprehend what Tillich expected of her, or envision the implications of it for their life together.

For the truth is that despite Hannah's inclination toward the unconventional, despite her ability to express herself with great abandon, she was from the outset of their marriage often jealous of Tillich and his friends, male or female.[59] She expected him to be absolutely faithful to her, and in this was immediately disappointed. He felt strongly that love must never be exclusive or possessive. For him, then and later, fidelity meant *not to be possessive.* Marriage, therefore, did not imply being exclusively bound to a single person but rather being closely related to others as well.

He doubted, moreover, that an absolute vow was possible. "I deny the possibility of a vow because of the finitude of the finite. A vow, if it is an absolute commitment, would make the moment in which we make it infinite or absolute. Other moments come which reveal the relativity of the moment in which this decision was once made."[60] On love he wrote, "Fulfilled love is, at the same time, extreme happiness and the end of happiness. The separation is overcome. But without the separation there is no love and no life."[61]

Tillich's conviction that no vow can be made absolute, and his idea that those who are separated are driven toward one another by love, combined with his thought that the end of happiness is the overcoming of the very separation without which love and life are impossible, form a crystal-clear image of his own life.[62] He alternated between relationships with various friends, trying to keep them secret from his wife, whose jealousy he feared but to whom he could make no absolute vow and to whom he always returned as "the only woman I could have married."[63] Love was more interesting, marriage more bearable for him on these terms; it also became more complicated. For Hannah, marriage became a battleground on which she felt constantly driven to fight for her husband's exclusive attention. A pattern developed of stormy scenes, passionate reunions, life together when they traveled, life partly apart at home. Moreover, her inability to hide her jealousy of even the most innocent meetings between Tillich and his friends, men or women—her fear that he might be taken away from her—matched his inability to keep his fatal attraction for and by other women a secret. His obsession was as transparent as her distrust; they suffered together.

In an effort to avenge and compensate for her suffering and become independent, Hannah threw herself into a series of extramarital relationships over the years.[64] But they did not cure her jealousy. When this solution proved illusory she sought peace, finding solace in yoga, in painting, in her private friendships, and finally refuge in their East Hampton home near the sea, to which Tillich too was inevitably drawn. She bore his children, she accompanied him into exile, together with him she learned to live in a new country, where their lives became more separate as his life touched wider circles. Toward the end of their life together, with its harmonies and tensions, its fertile and barren stretches, its certainties and doubts, its ecstasies and despairs, they entered calm if not entirely untroubled waters. Her jealousy never disappeared; his need for play, distraction, and attention always persisted. As his dependence on her grew, and her compassion for him deepened, there was often mirrored in their deeply-lined faces a new and tender understanding.[65]

Tillich never gave himself entirely to his friends any more than he gave himself entirely to his wife. But to each one he gave something individual; in each he discovered something new and different. His manner was gentle, his generosity great, his concern for the other was intertwined with the inevitable admiration he received and of which he had insatiable need. His friendships with women, especially since he was a theologian, presented a particular agony as well as a keen pleasure.[66] On the one hand, he openly admired women—all women. It made no difference whether it was a waitress in a French restaurant or a student in the classroom, the wife of a colleague or a sophisticated worldling who conducted a salon. He enjoyed talking with each one, admiring each one, having each respond to him, but did not become friends with them all.

Indeed, some women were offended by his advances and quickly rejected him; others wanted much more than he was ready or willing to give. The lasting friendships were with women who were intellectually stimulating, interesting, unusual, open to him, and with whom he felt comfortable himself. Their work, their state of mind, and their development were of genuine interest to him. He comforted them and sympathized in their days of sorrow, he celebrated their joys and successes, he advised them, encouraged them to fulfill themselves in their personal as well as their professional lives. He preached to them incessantly to avoid the pitfalls of compulsive self-giving, which he felt was the great danger implicit in the monogamous relationship. He urged them to remain open, even as he was, to the infinite experiences of life.

In the presence of real friends, male or female, he put the image of the "great theologian" aside, although his work and its effect inevitably became part of the fabric of every relation. His presence in a life sometimes created disorder; in his belated youth, in his period of sensual awakening, the seeds he sowed were often wild. But as he grew older he allowed the erotic, which he felt to be part and parcel of every relationship, to express itself only rarely. He did not wish to involve the woman any more than himself in too great an interdependence. If she objected, he did not force himself upon her. But because his magnetic power was so great, he attracted the lonely and the confused as well as the strong and highly motivated, the single as well as the married. If the woman was unmarried and a serious suitor appeared on the scene, he maintained his friendship from a distance, not wanting to prevent a possible union. Yet there were those, even so, who were hurt by his power, indeed overwhelmed by it.

Tillich entered each friendship with a special anxiety of which he was never altogether free. Those who knew of his fatal weakness, those close to him, accepted him as he was; he did not fear their judgment. They would not give him away. His overriding fear was that his story might one day be made public and bring ruin upon his work, if it were misrepresented and misunderstood. He thus seldom wrote directly about his conception of marriage or sex, but he dropped hints, and the observing reader will find them scattered throughout his work. In 1926, in his book *The Religious Situation*, he criticized the church's support of the "hypocrisy of bourgeois conventionality," urging that it come to grips with the task of "offering a solution which will point to the transcendent sphere but which will not be purely legal and conventional."[67] He knew that breaking the conventional moral law was a danger for the woman as well as for himself; on the other hand, he felt it was too simple to avoid a relationship merely because the possibility of marriage did not exist. Did he prevent marriages? Did he destroy them? He sought to assuage his feelings of guilt by a rule which he developed over the years: it did not matter so much what happened between two people so long as *agape* was not absent from the relationship.

> Sexual desire is not evil as desire, and the breaking of the conventional law is not evil as the breaking of conventional laws, but sexual desire and sexual autonomy are evil if they bypass the centre of the other person—in other words, if they are not united with the two other qualities of love, and if they are not under the ultimate criterion of the agape quality of love. Agape seeks the other one in his centre. Agape sees him as God sees him. Agape elevates libido into the divine unity of love, power, and justice.[68]

But Tillich's uneasy conscience continued to plague him even as he sometimes succeeded, sometimes failed to live up to his rule of *agape* in his many friendships, or in relation to his wife and family.

The Tillich marriage never worked well, but it never failed entirely; like Picasso's "Guernica," by which Tillich was so fascinated, it remained in the same place but was in constant danger of falling apart. Indeed "Guernica," which for Tillich exhibited a world of "guilt, anxiety, and despair," with its incongruous mixture of empathy and sadism within a normal rectangular frame, may be understood as a symbol of Tillich's own physical frame which was a nice square containing such odd assortments of incompatible values and tendencies. This explains in part why he is seen in such differing ways by different people. For he alternated between the one and the many, the Christian and the pagan, law and grace: in his personal life, too, he remained "on the boundary." And because these values were so incompatible they produced in him a burden of tragic guilt, about which he wrote,

> We must risk tragic guilt in becoming free from father and mother and brothers and sisters. And we know today better than many generations before us what that means, how infinitely difficult it is and that nobody does it without carrying scars in his soul his whole life. For it is not only the real father or mother or brother or sister from whom we must become free in order to come into our own. It is something much more refined, the image of them, which from our earliest childhood has impregnated our souls.[69]

Tillich expressed his guilt and anxiety in other ways: by the constant manipulation of paper clips or by play with sand castles. The incompatible fragments, the conflicts of his life, the bits and pieces of his ideas were most constructively used or manipulated in his system of theology—it is pertinent to recall here that its basic theme is reunion with Being itself. It was not by accident or without genuine meaning that Tillich dedicated the last volume of his *Systematic Theology* to "Hannah the companion of my life." For he always insisted that he could never have married any other woman, despite her negative attitude toward theology and the church. He said she was a magnificent person whom no one understood, whom only he could fathom. He depended on her: she took care of him, fed him, typed for him when he had no secretary, made room for his work.[70] She sympathized with his desire to be applauded and to be at the center; she was inordinately proud of his achievements. She provided irrational, mystical, passionate, unpredictable elements in his life which greatly enriched him. It was as his traveling companion that she believed he most accepted her.[71] Tragically, she felt fully appreciated only at the end of their life together. Tillich remained fearful of her rages, fascinated by her outbursts, angered and frustrated by repeated misunderstandings, but sure in his knowledge that she was his great love: he spoke in her defense, on her behalf. In their last years their shared experience bound them together in an interdependence that overcame all disharmony.

Tillich worked out what he called his "erotic solution" in the 1920s, and the unusual, unconventional, nonconformist pattern he created for himself, which at first provided him with escape from the demands of the law, gradually became a new law for him. Both his marriage and his personality remain paradoxical and mysterious, eluding final or complete definition. Precisely those weaknesses in himself to which he had ultimately to become reconciled in exceedingly painful fashion made him so believable, fascinating, and elusive as a productive thinker and as a human being.

In his old age Tillich concluded that love was tragic and marriage sad. His self-doubt was great. He wrote, "I speak of the ecstasy of living that includes participation in the highest and the lowest of life in one and the same experience. This demands courage and passion but it also can be a flight from God."⁷² Was his way, he wondered, a flight from God? Was his way of saying yes to life "in spite of insecurities of daily existence and the breakdown of meaning" the right way?⁷³ The self-doubt and conflict about which he was remarkably clear and conscious lasted until his dying day, and against the background of that consciousness the words of what many regard as his greatest sermon take on poignant meaning. It is entitled, "You Are Accepted," and on the original manuscript in his own handwriting are the words, "For Myself! 20 August 1946." It was his sixtieth birthday, and he wrote,

Grace strikes us when we are in great pain and restlessness. It strikes us when we walk through the dark valley of a meaningless and empty life. It strikes us when we feel that our separation is deeper than usual, because we feel we have violated another life, a life which we have loved, or from which we were estranged. It strikes us when our disgust for our own being, our indifference, our weakness, our hostility, and our lack of direction and composure have become intolerable to us. It strikes us when, year after year, the longed-for perfection of life does not appear, when the old compulsions reign within us as they have for decades, when despair destroys all joy and courage. Sometimes at that moment a wave of light breaks into our darkness, and it is as though a voice were saying: "You are accepted, accepted by that which is greater than you, and the name of which you do not know. Do not ask for the name now; perhaps you will find it later. Do not try to do anything now; perhaps later you will do much. Do not seek for anything; do not perform anything; do not intend anything. *Simply accept the fact that you are accepted!*"⁷⁴

4

Splendid Isolation
(1924-1933)

Struggle to Survive

In the spring of 1924, shortly after their marriage, Paul and Hannah Tillich moved to Marburg on the river Lahn, an enchanting university town steeped in the atmosphere of the Middle Ages, nestled in the Hessian hills sixty miles north of Frankfort on the Main. A castle crowns the highest of the surrounding hills, from which all of Marburg can be seen: there in 1529 Luther and Zwingli conferred on the subject of the Real Presence. In the valley below, dominating the horizon, is the famous Gothic church erected in memory of Elisabeth of Thuringia and named after her, the *Elisabethkirche*.

The Philip's University of Marburg, to which Tillich had been called in order to replace the ailing theologian Rudolf Otto, has been famous since the time of the Reformation as the first Protestant university.* Despite this fact and in spite of its illustrious faculty, Tillich hesitated to accept the offer. He thought of Marburg as a provincial town; he shrank from its smallness, being reluctant to leave the freedom and fascination of the large city of

---

* Founded by Philip of Hesse in 1527.

94

Berlin. Carl Becker, Prussian Minister of Education, who greatly respected Tillich and bore him warm affection, in negotiations which took place in late 1923 urged him to accept the Marburg associate professorship.[1] The post was higher than that of *Privatdozent,* and while its benefits were not nearly as great as those of a full professorship—it did not include tenure, for example—the salary was better. Moreover, Becker was convinced that Tillich would soon be promoted to a higher rank once he had established himself. At the University of Berlin chances for promotion were slim: it was a faculty reserved for professors at the height of their career. Bowing to these realities, Tillich finally accepted the appointment, which he later freely admitted had been valuable to him.

He taught at Marburg for three semesters, and his experience during this brief period, though painful, helped him to establish himself. The majority of the Marburg students were Barthians. Unlike his students at the University of Berlin, who from the beginning had been responsive to Tillich's political and cultural interests, they expected him to address himself to the theological upheaval caused by Karl Barth, in which Rudolf Bultmann, the professor of New Testament who later became world-famous as advocate of the exegetical program of demythologization, and the philosopher Martin Heidegger, later one of the chief spokesmen of Existentialism, were involved. Both had only recently come to Marburg, and like Tillich they stood at the beginning of their careers. They greatly impressed their students, who tended to identify themselves with their teaching to such a degree that they rejected or at least radically neglected all other views, particularly those connected with theological or cultural liberalism.

Tillich was aware that he would have to struggle to maintain himself. Yet he ignored the wishes of his Barthian students and insisted on developing his own ideas. He began to formulate his systematic theology and gave a course on it during his last term. In the first two he concentrated on philosophy of religion and the Protestant mystics.

Tillich's thought was by now mature, and he began to use his own terminology in the classroom—it was his way of challenging the Barthians, he later said. His vocabulary at first baffled, then fascinated the students.[2] By the end of his Marburg stay the number of those who attached themselves to him had grown to thirty. They were enchanted by his unusual and to them novel way of talking about faith and about God. Tillich did not speak of God, with Otto, as the "wholly other," or with Barth as the "unknown stranger," but as *das Unbedingte*," or "the Unconditioned," a phrase he substituted for the Absolute. To this he always added that he who is grasped by faith in God is filled with confidence, marching forward as it were like soldiers, *mit klingendem Spiel*, i.e., to the sound of fife and drum. Tillich had borrowed the phrase from Nietzsche. Those who first heard this expression from him were forever after bound in their imaginations to its emotionally charged association.

Tillich's students were also delighted and surprised by his personal attentions. Measured by German standards his manner was casual. He included them in his private parties, introduced them to art and the dance, and welcomed them generally as friendly equals. He listened to their problems and helped them in making personal decisions. Already he was proving himself gifted in counseling a student of uncertain mind as to how he might best apply his talents. He encouraged many to spend a year in Berlin or some other big city for the sake of practical experience, urging them to return to their studies only after such exposure to the world in which they would labor. One of his students was Harald Poelchau, who later became Tillich's assistant at the University of Frankfort and still later acquired fame as chaplain in the Plötzensee Prison, where during the Nazi period, like an angel of the Lord with his pale blue eyes and blonde hair, he accompanied hundreds of Nazi victims to their deaths, showing great compassion, understanding, and Christian love. He recalled in his old age that it was Tillich who knew even before he himself did what he should do with his life.

The beauty of the countryside lured Tillich to take long walks through the fields and over the hills with his students, debating with them about theology and the history of dogma. He seemed young to them at thirty-eight, with his narrow, long face and his "sad, philosophical eyes."[3] Indeed, there was more than a hint of sadness in Tillich during these months. A terrible nightmare revealed to him the degree of guilt he carried about with him as the result of the events leading up to his second marriage; at the same time, and more acutely in outward life, he felt depressed because he was faced with such a tremendous intellectual challenge and feared he might not be able to meet it.[4] Moreover, Marburg's provincialism, its lack of many social opportunities or possibilities, and its sharp contrast to Berlin proved a heavy burden to him, and even more so to his wife. After a trip to Italy in August and September of 1924 as a belated honeymoon, partially financed by royalties from a recently published book and by the friendly help of a colleague, Professor von Soden, the Tillichs found Marburg even narrower than before.

On this trip Tillich was exposed for the first time to Italy and to the world of his favorite pre-Socratic philosophers Parmenides and Heraclitus. The Tillichs traveled on a freighter embarking at Sicily, stopping at various places along the way. At Syracuse, they admired the Greek theatre; at Girgenti, the temples; in Ravenna and Rome, the ancient mosaics of the "gold ground."[5] Tillich found the last so exciting that he dreamed about them for months afterward. His first direct encounter with the ancient world of art, like his first view of Botticelli's "Madonna with Singing Angels" in Berlin, called up from within him an immediate, deep, and permanent echo which he later recorded in his work. He acquired postcards of what he had seen and saved them for a lifetime, using them when he lectured on the "image of man," a course he gave with the utmost relish as late in his days as Harvard University.

On his return to Marburg, Tillich made the most of the few but good friendships that developed there. His colleagues were in fact not much older than he, but merely gave that appearance. Rudolf Otto, author of *The Idea of the Holy*, was perhaps closest to Tillich, and in later years whenever he used the phrase "the idea of the holy" he thought of the wonderful times he had spent with Otto in Marburg as they walked through the hills and woods to-

97

gether for hours on end. They discussed problems of Christianity and Asiatic religions, they talked of the demonic (Otto either supported or inspired Tillich's ideas on the subject), and also the ecstatic. It was an association in which Hannah, too, shared and thus doubly rewarding.[6]

Tillich's other close friend was Friedrich Spiegelberg, a wealthy German historian of religions in whose garden the Tillichs sought frequent and welcome refuge. Aside from Spiegelberg, Otto, and the ongoing association with his students, however, Tillich seems to have had only the most casual relations in Marburg.[7] He became acquainted with Bultmann, but only from a distance. Heidegger was open only to the most formal relations. Indeed, the only "conversation" Tillich seems to have had with him was by way of points made in the course of lectures, transported back and forth from classroom to classroom by student gossip. But Heidegger's thought made a profound impression on Tillich, at first unconsciously. There are some who feel that had it not been for Heidegger's *Being and Time,* Tillich would never have developed his ontology as he did. In any case, neither in Marburg nor later did the two men become personal friends.

Carl Becker's prediction that Tillich's move to Marburg would benefit his career soon proved accurate. In 1926 he was greatly helped by the publication of his little book entitled *The Religious Situation,* in the *Wege des Wissens,* or "Ways to Knowledge" series designed by the Ullstein firm of publishers for popular sale. It was, as Tillich often remarked, his first genuine success: he called it "the original impact" that made his name known all over Germany.[8]

Dance and the Demonic

It was ironically not a theologian but a philosopher who helped advance Tillich to a full professorship, albeit not at the university level. This was Richard Kroner, a well-to-do member of the faculty of the Institute of Technology in Dresden. Kroner's special interest was the field of German idealism, in which he had demonstrated his sovereign expertise by a work entitled *From Kant to Hegel.* Kroner had however also read widely in the field of theology. He had interested himself in Barth, Otto, Brunstäd, and Tillich, whose work on Schelling as well as *The System of the Sciences* had greatly impressed him. He decided that Tillich, whom he had not met personally, was a "kind of genius"[9] and urged Robert Ulich, in the ministry of education for Saxony, to appoint him to a vacant post at the institute, where a newly established Department of Humanities was being developed. It was hoped that the department would flourish and eventually be recognized by the German universities as being on an equal level of academic excellence. Kroner, one of the first members of the new department, was thus in a good position to recommend names to the ministry. When he met Tillich personally, he was even more impressed by him. Tillich was persuasive, productive, convinced of what he said.

Ulich, who had the responsibility of appointing new faculty members upon appropriate recommendation, had already met Tillich personally in 1918 and 1919 at a conference for religion and adult education which took place in Simbach in those years.[10] At the time, he had been impressed by the originality of Tillich's contribution to the discussion. He did not therefore need to be persuaded of Tillich's talents, and invited him to his office to discuss the terms of the contract, at the same time warning him to be discreet in the presence of one of his associates who was a political reactionary, with whom Ulich's relations were nevertheless good and whom he did not wish to offend. Ulich was aware of Tillich's socialist leanings, which he enthusiastically shared. Tillich shrewdly kept his political views to himself, and by 1 May 1925 a contract was drawn up. Tillich was appointed to a full professorship of religious studies in the Department of the Humanities of the Dresden Institute of Technology. Although the appointment was not to a university, and the department's future was uncertain, Tillich was moved to accept the offer not only because it included an advance in position and salary, but also, because it enabled him to return to a large city, a desire in which his wife ardently concurred. Indeed, shortly before this decision, he had turned down an offer to teach theology at the University of Giessen which seemed to him as provincial as Marburg.

In the summer of 1925, before their move to Dresden, the Tillichs spent five weeks in Kampen, on the island of Sylt in the North Sea. He was unusually happy that summer. His book was a success, he had become a full professor, and he felt equal to the challenges he would find in Dresden. He dug for hours in the sand, building huge castles in an effort to keep his waistline trim. In the afternoon he wrote endlessly, and in the evening he and Hannah joined the artists, dancers, and intellectuals who frequented Kampen in drinking large amounts of red wine and champagne. These weeks of visual delight in the pounding surf, the high dunes, the grey-green grass, the fields of bright purple heather, and the tall clay cliffs, were his preparation for the move to Dresden.[11]

It was an exquisitely beautiful city. Its baroque and rococo architecture as well as its great art treasures made it known as "the Florence of the Elbe" or "the German Paris." The Semper Gallery housed famous paintings, among them works by Raphael, Correggio, Titian, Rubens, and Rembrandt. Dresden's musical tradition matched its physical beauty. Weber and Wagner each in his time had conducted at the opera house; Felix Mendelssohn for years directed the work of the conservatory, and died in Dresden. Two public theaters were easily reached by modern transportation, including buses and trains which made it entirely unnecessary to own a car. As if these allurements were not enough, the countryside round about, particularly the nearby hills (called the "Saxon Switzerland"), made it nearly perfect. Tillich felt the city was ideal for him not only because of its artistic attractions and spacious openness, but also because of the lively social life into which he was immediately drawn.[12]

The Dresden Institute, where Tillich taught between 1925 and 1929,[13] was breaking new ground in providing higher education for potential public-school teachers. The addition of the new Department of Humanities, an attempt to widen the scope of its students, was a bold experiment in modern education. Tillich was intrigued by it, as were his colleagues, all men of high achievement. Richard Kroner was one; Fedor Stepun, a Russian nobleman who had come to Germany on the second wave of those fleeing the Bolshevik revolution, another. Together with Kroner, Tillich urged the appointment of Stepun to the faculty because he was a statesman, a poet, a philosopher, a novelist, and an incandescent orator. He was invited to teach sociology. Viktor Klemperer, who taught Romance languages, and Christian Janentzki, who taught Germanic languages, were two other well-known members of the humanities division.

From the beginning, Tillich and his colleagues drew sizable classroom audiences. In addition to the potential teachers who made up the nucleus of the student body, nonmatriculated adults were attracted to the institute. The open atmosphere made itself felt particularly in Tillich's classes. Even his seminars, normally attended by qualified students only, included people who had long since outgrown the student generation. They had met Tillich at social gatherings or cultural conferences, found him attractive as a human being, and wished to become acquainted with his ideas.

Once again Tillich was thrust into the comfortable, natural role of apologetic theologian. On the one hand, he gave courses on "The Chief Problems of Christianity" and "The Religious Meaning of Being;" on the other, he taught "Religion and Art," or "The Religious Meaning of History." Nor did he abandon his interest in current affairs. He lectured widely on a variety of topics: "The Meaning of Social Conditions for Intellectual Life," or "The State as Expectation and Demand," or "Lessing and the Idea of the Education of the Human Race."

Three of Tillich's most able students first studied with him in Dresden. They were immediately attracted by his stance in apologetics. One was Renate Albrecht, who in the 1950s became chief editor of Tillich's massive *Collected Works*. A second was Gertraut Stöber, later caretaker of the Tillich Archive in Göttingen, Germany. Nina Baring, the third student, was a lonely, troubled woman whose near-blindness toward the end of her life did not prevent her from brilliantly translating many of Tillich's American writings into German. Tillich wrote a sermon for her entitled "Come and See." These and many other students came from strict pietistic backgrounds, and Tillich's thought appealed to them because it was so open, liberal, and undogmatic. His way of discussing matters of faith and religion freed them from their own legalistic upbringing. They did not therefore share the criticism of one of the nonmatriculated auditors, a baroness, who once said to Tillich, "I am always enchanted by what you say, but someday you will come to God."[14]

Tillich's reputation as a scholar and effective teacher transcended any suspicion that he was not orthodox. At the end of his first semester in Dresden, the University of Halle bestowed upon him an honorary degree of Doctor of Theology, through the good offices of his former teacher Wilhelm Lütgert, dean of the theological faculty there. The citation read:

> The theological faculty of Halle has unanimously voted to grant the Professor of the Philosophy of Religion at the Dresden Institute of Technology, Paul Tillich, Lic. Theol., Ph.D., the rights and privileges of the degree Doctor of Theology, *honoris causa*. With conceptual acuteness and dialectical skill he has developed a program in the philosophy of religion and placed it in the framework of general scholarship. Through his teaching he has instilled in his students his own enthusiastic interest in his goal, namely to combine philosophy and sociology with living religion.
>
> 24 December 1925[15]

Two months later, on 17 February 1926, Tillich became a father. For weeks in advance he had felt so much anxiety about the coming event that he asked a friend to keep an eye on his wife and report to him the instant the first labor pain occurred. His brother-in-law Frede Fritz came to Dresden and took him out for a long walk to keep his mind off his wife's agony. Liesel, Hannah Tillich's younger sister, had come to help nurse the baby and was present when she was born.[16] In October, after considerable dispute between the parents regarding her name, the baby was christened by her father Erdmuthe Christiane.

She was born in the Tillich apartment at Elisenstrasse 11. A friend employed by the Academy of Arts and Crafts in Dresden had, at the Tillichs' request, renovated the dark old rooms. The dining room was sand-colored and furnished with early Victorian chairs. The living room was pink, hung with blue curtains. The bathroom walls were of all possible shades of pink and red. In order to produce a modern effect, the legs were cut off an octagonal table and two old couches in the living room; those who sat on them felt as though they were sitting on the floor. Tillich's study was crowded with the same heavy oak furniture he had had in Berlin, but the walls were yellow and the curtains bright red, his favorite color. Friends lent the Tillichs modern paintings and they frequently changed them around, or got new ones, to provide constantly new scenes, moods, and effects.

People coming for the first time to the Tillich's apartment were asked to look at each room and say which they liked best and why. Psychoanalytic interpretation followed. After-dinner discussions about social economics, painting, and psychoanalysis gave Tillich an opportunity to analyze, mediate, and define. He tended in those days to interpret other people's dreams in the most sinister fashion.[17]

Heinrich Goesch, a frequent guest, was well-acquainted with Freudian psychoanalysis and influenced Tillich's preoccupation with the interpretation of dreams. A professor of architecture at the Dresden Arts and Crafts School, Goesch was a handsome man with large eyes and a Roman head. He had studied law for a time and practiced it; later he was drawn to philosophy and architecture. He also wrote poetry and was a passionate advocate of the poet Stefan George. He was so talented, so versatile, that some regarded him as a dilettante or even a charlatan. Tillich himself felt that Goesch was a disorganized genius, unable to produce, by which he meant that Goesch wrote very little. But Goesch in fact was not interested in making an impression on others, since his almost magical, sometimes demonic influence made itself felt through personal conversation, in which he excelled. His clear understanding and spiritual richness made him a good listener:

Tillich expanded in his presence. He was always grateful to Goesch for having introduced him to a few "psychoanalytic rules of living" but he did not follow his advice to submit to a rigorous psychoanalysis himself. Goesch, who was born in Mecklenburg, died of pneumonia in 1930 at the age of fifty.[18]

While Goesch and others enjoyed the effect of the modern and unusual decor, some felt extremely uncomfortable in the Tillichs' *avant garde* quarters. One such was Tillich's friend and close associate, Richard Kroner—a man with classical tastes. He and his wife Alice rented a villa built in Biedermayer style, with two stories in front, three in back. It had a huge terrace where their guests danced in the moonlight, overlooking a beautiful garden with wide lawns and groups of trees running down to the Elbe River. In this romantic setting the Kroners gave many lavish, cultivated parties.[19] At one of these, to which sixty persons came and which lasted all night, Tillich was especially happy. He danced and sang, and his friend Kroner thought he had never seen him so happy. Kroner, who in his dignified and elegant way was a very different sort of man, nevertheless admired him greatly, and yet at the same time was puzzled by him. He was much surprised when Tillich once confessed to him that he feared he was a great sinner. When Kroner asked him why, Tillich replied, "Because I love women, drinking, and dancing."[20]

It was at a masked ball given by the Kroners that Tillich met two young members of the Steinweg Dance School, an offshoot of the Mary Wigman School of the Dance. Mary Wigman was recognized as the founder of modern dance in Europe. She was a gaunt-looking woman with strong features, not at all the type of a conventional ballerina. To her, the function of dance was not to entertain but to communicate. Often criticized for her use of ugly and distorted movements, she put expressiveness above prettiness, and her work was predominantly introspective and somber. Many regarded her as part of the Expressionist movement.

In Dresden in 1920 she had founded the Mary Wigman Central Institute, where she trained dancers and experimented in choreography. Three years later, she won wide recognition and acclaim by performing "Scenes from a Dance Drama" with a large group.

Cora Wächter and Ellen Frankenberg, the two young dancers whom Tillich met at Kroner's masked ball, promptly invited him to watch them work at their school. The group had no money, no costumes, no coal, but they had a pianist and were working on improvised, expressionistic dances. Tillich and Goesch went together to the rehearsals, watched the dancers improvise, and marveled at them. The dancers marveled too, for they felt they were being "discovered." They were natural, unintellectual, unselfconscious beings and thought it quite mysterious and delightful that a professor of theology and a "magician psychologist," as they called Goesch, should find them so interesting.

Tillich on his part was fascinated by the way the young people were so completely absorbed in their creative dancing. They found it so easy to be themselves. They did not discuss or argue, but acted. They did not observe, they participated. He said to them that what they were doing was more religious than many stated religious functions.

From time to time the Tillichs invited the dance group members to their home, where the dancers improvised on Bach motifs. The Tillichs and their guests sometimes joined in and improvised with them, but although Tillich himself danced with great gusto, he drew the line when it came to gymnastics. He refused to bend down, fearing that this motion might injure his head. But at the Kroners' villa when the dancers were invited to entertain there, Tillich was in his element, dancing out of sheer joy in movement and often choosing a Steinweg group dancer for his partner.[21]

Relying on these and similar experiences, Tillich wrote an essay about the modern dance entitled "Dance and Religion." For him the essence of the new form was the combination of individual and group movements, which he described as an "almost mystical unity." Moreover, it seemed to him in full agreement with the great works of Expressionist painting. It confirmed his understanding of religion as "the spiritual substance of culture" and culture as "the expression of religion. The dance awoke in me the unanswered question of how the lost unity of cult and dance could grow again on the stony, dry earth of Protestantism."[22]

The dancers who had first introduced Tillich to their world and who occasionally came to hear him lecture in Dresden did not understand what he was saying, but they admired him greatly. This was true also of one of the prominent students of the Wigman Dance School: Hanya Holm. Tillich had first met her at Kampen, in 1921. There, while building a sand castle, Tillich had playfully carried her little son around on his shovel. In Dresden they met again at the house of an influential banker who enjoyed playing host to a heterogeneous group of painters, musicians, and lawyers. Tillich often spoke of religious matters to fifty or seventy-five people gathered there. He felt particularly happy, he used to say, with these open-minded cultural enthusiasts who were so responsive to his ideas. In 1936, when Tillich and Hanya Holm were both in New York, she made an appointment with him to ask his advice. His uncanny logic was something on which she felt able to depend. Her problem at the time concerned her inability to complete a dance called "Trend." She described it to Tillich, who saw the problem at once, pointing out that she had three major themes in her dance and therefore the whole was unclear. He suggested that she work on one of the themes and abandon the other two. As soon as he pointed this out, she realized why the dance had been either too short or too long, and solved her problem.[23]

Tillich's new passion for the dance never became a substitute for his interest in painting. One of the nonmatriculated students in his class at the Dresden Institute of Technology was instrumental in introducing him to the artists themselves. Her name was Ida Bienert. She and her husband Erwin invited him to their house to lecture, ultimately including his entire seminar. They were wealthy patrons of modern painting and owned a large modern collection, including works by Kandinsky and Klee. They gave big parties which Tillich and Hannah frequently attended, and enjoyed opening their home to struggling young intellectuals as a place to live. (At one of the Bienert soirées, Tillich met Paul Klee, of whom he later recalled only that he had huge eyes.) The Bienerts were the first in a long succession of wealthy friends who "lionized" Tillich. He enjoyed the attention, and always carefully cultivated wealthy persons despite his socialist leanings. His intellectual friends, whom he often kept separate from his wealthy acquaintances, tended to regard such attachments as signs of Tillich's vanity and weakness.

Stepun especially was openly critical of his participation in high life, and even more of his temptation to success, which he feared might ruin him. A deeply religious man, whose belief in an absolute God was mirrored in his adoration of and fidelity to his wife Natasha, Stepun believed that a man who had absolute faith must love only one woman. He felt that Tillich's unorthodox thought, his use of the phrase "ultimate concern" rather than "faith," and his attempt to interpret Christianity through Schelling were like "making a swan out of a crab." He doubted that Tillich could be called a Christian. Tillich was intensely aware of this criticism, but he returned Stepun's love and the two got on famously.[24]

Kroner shared Stepun's conviction that Tillich was not a Christian, and that his thought was heretical because it was overly influenced by Hegel and most particularly Schelling. But he admired his honesty: Tillich told the world what he really thought; other theologians did not.

Partly because the suspicion of heresy hung over Tillich in theological circles, and partly too because his Dresden post had drawn him out of the mainstream of theological development, after a time he began to fear he was drifting away from his true calling: theology. He therefore accepted an adjunct professorship of systematic theology at the University of Leipzig, where he taught from 1927 to 1929. In June 1927 he presented his inaugural address in Leipzig, entitled "The Idea of Revelation."[25] Fortnightly, after this, he shuttled between Dresden and Leipzig, giving seminars there along more traditional theological lines: "The Religious Meaning of Being," "The Religious Experience," "The Religious Meaning of History."

Stepun and Tillich shared a friendly joke about the Greek Orthodox teaching on salvation: the "bag of grace" which they said was readily available to all sinners. Tillich envied Stepun's admissibility to this privilege and jokingly added that all he had in his cellar was a "bag of demons." It was conversation of this sort as well as his own observation of him that prompted Kroner to call Tillich a "demonic saint and saintly demon,"[26] neatly capturing the ways of a man whose benign appearance and generous humanity sometimes gave way to the darker forces of his inner self. Tillich himself wrote articulately about the demonic as "a power in personal and social life that is creative and destructive at the same time. In the New Testament, men possessed by demons are said to know more about Jesus than those who are normal, but they know it as a condemnation of themselves because they are divided against themselves."[27]

While vacationing in Paris in 1926 in the company of Eckart von Sydow, Christian Hermann, and Marie-Luise Werner, his psychoanalyst sister-in-law, Tillich completed the long essay, published later in the year, entitled *Das Dämonische* [The Demonic], which he later cherished as among the few truly original contributions he felt he had made. It was in Schelling's thought that he first stumbled upon the idea of the demonic as the irrational potential in God, and to the Schellingian interpretation he remained faithful. His teacher Fritz Medicus,[28] among others, was greatly taken by the essay, and the concept itself became the subject of an interesting exchange between Tillich and Max Scheler two years later.

Early in 1928 Tillich attended a "European Conference" in Crissier, near Geneva, Switzerland. The hosts were a wealthy banker and a baron who opened their mansion to the many distinguished international guests. There were receptions, lectures, and excursions throughout the week, but the high point of the conference was a lecture by Max Scheler, philosopher and sociologist, famous for his *Wissenssoziologie* or "sociology of knowledge."[29] Like Tillich, Scheler combined a dislike for industrial, bourgeois society with a yearning for the past. He romanticized medieval feudalism; although World War I had made him a socialist, he had great admiration for the nobility. In 1928, in order to recover from

a heart attack and prepare for his move to the University of Frankfort, where he had accepted the chair in philosophy left vacant by
the retirement of Hans Cornelius, Scheler went to Switzerland, and
it was during his visit there that he attended the meetings at Crissier.

On the afternoon of Scheler's lecture Tillich, who had had lively
exchanges with him all week, engaged him in a passionate discussion about the demonic, a concept which Scheler in his pessimistic
mood interpreted very differently from Tillich, who felt he could
affirm the demonic in the form of the "unity of the ground and the
abyss in the tension between both elements." While details of the
discussion were not preserved, there remains the memory of two
men stimulating one another to intellectual showmanship on opposite sides. The contrast between them was startling. They differed in aspect as well as outlook, like creatures from two different planets. Scheler was thickset, almost fascinatingly ugly, with a
broad face in which the small muscles and prematurely deep lines
reminded onlookers of the picture of Dorian Gray: a soul tor-
mented by raging passions. As he spoke, he was seized by spontaneous, brilliant formulations, apparently altogether unrelated to
what he had carefully thought out beforehand. He could be ob-
sessed by an idea, and gave the impression that afternoon that he
had long since experienced all the fires of hell.

Tillich, the younger man, was slender, and with his thick, dark-
blond hair and benevolent face, looked more like a student than a
professor. He was much more thoughtful and serious than Scheler,
and he too spoke spontaneously. He was interested in the split in
personality implied by the demonic and in the boundary situation,
a phrase which had already crept into his vocabulary. For his part
Scheler, nearing the end of his life of tension between modern
secular morality and traditional Christian ethics, was preoccupied
with the partial truth of every world view and the limitations of
every individual perspective.[30]

It was the first and last time that the two men met. In mid-April
Scheler went to Frankfort to look for a place to live. On 19 May
1928 he died of a stroke at the age of fifty-four. The chair of

philosophy at the University of Frankfort to which he had been appointed, but which he had never occupied, was again vacant. Within a year it was filled by Tillich.

Early Fame

The University of Frankfort was established in 1914 in the city of Frankfort on the Main, Goethe's birthplace. The house in which he was born, destroyed during World War II and faithfully restored with its original fittings, is still along with the Goethe museum the greatest attraction of the modern city. Always a thriving commercial center, where the Rothschild family began its banking business, Frankfort became an industrial town in modern times. Firms such as I. G. Farben made it their headquarters.

Several scientific institutes provided the nucleus around which, after World War I, new faculties were formed in order to create a university. Unlike traditional Prussian state universities, it was in part privately financed, and its curator* was responsible to Frankfort's Lord Mayor, who served as ex officio head of the *curatorium*. Under the leadership of Kurt Riezler, who became curator in 1928 and helped organize a forward-looking, largely Jewish faculty, the new university rapidly became progressive. Its tone and program were in fact so liberal that by the 1930s it was known, especially in fascist circles, as the "red university."[31]

Carl Becker, still minister of education in Prussia,[32] had chosen Riezler for this sensitive and influential post because of his experience in the diplomatic service as well as for his reputation as a fine classical scholar. Riezler therefore began work on 4 June 1928 both as curator and as honorary professor and member of the philosophical faculty.

Riezler, who had been secretary to the imperial chancellor von Bethmann-Hollweg, narrowly escaped assassination in 1918 while serving in the German legation in Moscow. From 1919 to 1920 he

---

* i.e. highest administrative officer. His office was distinguished from that of the rector, the highest academic official who "represented" the university.

was director of the office of Reichspresident Ebert. Disenchanted with politics, he returned to private life before accepting the post at Frankfort, where he proved a shrewd and practical administrator. His wife was the daughter of the famous German Impressionist painter Max Liebermann.

One of Riezler's first problems was to find a successor to the Kantian logician, Hans Cornelius. He was looking for someone who could "provide an entering door to philosophy"[33] by relating it to contemporary affairs and when Carl Becker now put forward Paul Tillich's name he found this entirely agreeable. By March 1929 negotiations were underway. Tillich was invited to the office of Werner Richter, the autocratic and powerful director of the Prussian Ministry of Education, to discuss the terms of the contract, which Tillich soon discovered were highly favorable.[34]

His salary was to be larger than he had received in Dresden, partly because the university was willing to guarantee 7,500 German marks in addition to the normal salary, regardless of the number of students who presented themselves. Each professor received a percentage of the registration fees, and the 7,500 marks were Tillich's estimated percentage. A high salary was a thing of no small moment to him, for he often said to his friends that he and his wife were at times so hard put to it for money that it would seem almost easier to survive by opening a small bar than to continue in the academic world. It was a complaint he made throughout his career, whether poor or well off; it was in the same class with his repeatedly expressed fear that he simply could not keep up with his mail, or bear the burden of increasing demands on his time—it was all too much for him.

But the wry complaint regarding income in the 1920s was not exaggerated. Germany had been through an inflation of catastrophic proportions, when people rushed out to buy bread or shoes the moment they could lay hands on money, for if they waited as long as an hour or more it would shrink to half its value. Despite the monetary reform introduced by the government in 1923, the political and economic situation continued to worsen, even after the so-called Dawes Plan had been adopted in order to reduce the reparations imposed on Germany by the Allies after World War I.

Tillich's personal relation to money in his case magnified the strains felt by every German citizen. At all times in his life his attitude toward money was puzzling and unrealistic. He was always depressed when he did not have enough, but equally eager and ready to work in order to earn it, finding ingenious ways of raising it when most needed. Once he had acquired an adequate sum for the moment, however, he was strangely uninterested in putting any aside in the form of savings; he spent it freely on himself and his family, either on a trip to Italy or other foreign parts, or on a new set of books for which he had yearned, or even—in his later years—on costly red wine.

The new salary arrangements at the University of Frankfort[35] were therefore of particular value to Tillich, who never learned how to balance his budget. Moreover, he was in debt to the Ministry of Education for the costs of his moves from Berlin to Marburg and Dresden, to the tune of over 2,000 German marks. (Most of this indebtedness was resolved when the decision was made in 1930 that anyone who had taught at a post for less than five years need not return the loan.) The university also provided an allowance for housing, so that the Tillichs could look forward to finding a pleasant apartment, either in the city itself or in one of the neighboring suburbs, renowned for their beauty, surrounded as they were by the Taunus hills.

In addition to the generous financial arrangements, Tillich, already forty-three, was overjoyed by the prospect of becoming for the first time a full professor at an accredited German university. He was given the opportunity to teach precisely what he wanted and to exercise a certain measure of influence over important decisions concerning faculty appointments and curriculum. He did not hesitate. In March 1929, he resigned from the faculty of the Dresden Institute of Technology, which had failed to become an accredited university, so that other faculty members including Kroner and Stepun were also leaving.[36] Richard Kroner went to Kiel and Fedor Stepun to Munich, while Tillich accepted the post in Frankfort under the title of Professor of Philosophy and Sociology. In June 1929 he gave his inaugural lecture on "Philosophy and Destiny."

Tillich always wrote and spoke of being the successor of Scheler in Frankfort rather than of Cornelius, which he technically was. What he meant was that he was Scheler's spiritual successor in a way he could not have been to Cornelius. He and Scheler, Tillich insisted, shared an interest in ethics, personality, history, and philosophy, while with Kantian logic as represented by Cornelius he felt no such kinship.[37]

Tillich's former teacher and friend Fritz Medicus, who had observed Tillich's popularity at a seminar in Davos during the summer of 1928, wrote a tremendously enthusiastic piece for the *Neue Zürcher Zeitung*, the leading Swiss newspaper, proclaiming that the appointment of Tillich to Scheler's chair was the beginning of a new philosophical era.[38] His experience in Davos convinced him that his former pupil, whom he described as a genius, had rescued the Schellingian philosophy from the dusty theory in which it was held captive and transformed it into meaning for a responsible way of life. Moreover, he felt that Tillich himself had experienced the yes and no of dialectical existence to such an extent that he could communicate the experience, directly eliciting a necessarily positive response from colleagues and students. Medicus declared that philosophy had become the center of all intellectual inquiry, and that Tillich was now the "coming man" in this field.

Tillich's formal task at the University of Frankfort was in fact to teach social education, and in his lectures and seminars between the years 1929 and 1933 he thus emphasized the aspects of social ethics, historical action, and political direction rather than the speculative or metaphysical interests of the thinkers with whom he dealt in the classroom. More than ever he felt obliged to make philosophical questions existential for the numerous students for whom philosophical courses were mandatory. He was also forced during these years to create new courses, and accordingly worked with greater industry than he had ever done before. He gave courses on Kant, Hegel, and Schelling, on Locke and Thomas Aquinas. He lectured on "Being and Action," "The Masses and the Spirit," "Philosophy of Religion," and "The History of Philosophy." He offered a course on questions of systematic theology only during his last semester in Frankfort and then only in an informal, colloquial way.[39]

The period at Frankfort turned out to be the richest and most successful of Tillich's German career. From the beginning, as Medicus had predicted, he attracted a large and enthusiastic group of students, which steadily increased. In these years, which he and his illustrious colleagues (to whom he referred as "glorious") described later in ever more glowing and romantic reminiscences as the "golden age" of German university life, Tillich deepened and refined his teaching skills.[40] He sought the truth, as of old, in his nonauthoritarian way. That was unusual for a theologian. His colleagues soon learned that he had somehow freed himself from the stuffy moralism of his Protestant background. Moreover, he did not merely teach his students; he lived with them and mobilized their intellectual forces. The largeness of his nature, the broadmindedness that gave others confidence to speak their own minds, became more and more evident.[41]

As the leader of a seminar or wherever he gathered and interpreted answers to questions, he inevitably went beyond the question asked and by his enthusiastic introductory response, "Oh, that's a most interesting point!" made the most foolish student sound far more intelligent than he often was. As a teacher, he did precisely what he did in his friendships with men or women: he made potential spiritual riches actual. This interaction was achieved not merely through the renunciation of authoritarianism. An even more potent factor was his ability to listen to the other person and take him seriously. His lack of bigotry rested on a much greater quality, the gift of openness. It lured his hearers to say things, utter ideas, they had not sensed were in them—ideas which until that moment had lain silent and dormant.[42] Yet for those who listened to him carefully over a long period of time, there came the sometimes startling realization that he did not answer the question that had been asked at all, but used it rather as a platform from which to give a brief homily or lecture in miniature, ineluctably absorbing the inquiry into his own systematic thought. It was a subtle thing, not always recognized by those who were mesmerized by his genius for marshaling a great variety of ideas into immediate, spontaneous organization.

Whereas Tillich enjoyed great popularity in the classroom, he was feared as an examiner, not because he turned against the student but because he asked awkward questions, making especially those inexpert in philosophy feel uncomfortable, helpless, and ignorant. Moreover, he showed great impatience and annoyance when a student used his own—i.e., Tillich's—terminology to answer a question. He felt somehow that this meant the student had not understood either the question or the answer and was hiding behind words.[43]

Tillich responded warmly to all his students but fastened special attention upon a select few who were able to sustain a relationship with him beyond the classroom. One of these was Harald Poelchau, whom he had imported from Berlin to facilitate the writing of Poelchau's dissertation and to provide himself with an assistant. It was in the seminars and lecture halls of Frankfort that Poelchau first noticed the new openness in his former teacher, who at Marburg had been much more reserved. A second assistant was the brilliant and versatile Theodor Wiesengrund, known by his *nom de plume* Adorno, or as Teddy. Adorno was already a doctoral candidate when Tillich arrived on the scene in the summer of 1929. Curious to hear the new faculty member, he squeezed into the last row of a crowded lecture hall where Tillich was holding forth on early Greek philosophy. The subject that day was Plato. Adorno listened intently, unaware that he was being observed. On the following day, he and Tillich were introduced at the home of Gabrielle Oppenheim, a wealthy and cultured lady who presided, at lunches and dinners, over a salon to which all intellectuals were welcome.

Tillich immediately seized Adorno, saying that he had seen him in class the day before, and describing in the greatest detail precisely how Adorno had reacted to every statement he had made. Adorno, amazed at Tillich's power of observation, was immediately captivated. He came to know intimately what he then only sensed, namely, that he was in the presence of someone who had enormous intuition and an extraordinary capacity to register other people's reactions to him. He concluded that Tillich was provided with a special set of permanently live antennae. He also noticed something else about him: how he concentrated exclusively and absolutely on the person to whom he was talking, and what a powerful magnetic effect such concentration had on the object of this intense attention.[44]

Adorno decided to write his dissertation under Tillich's sponsorship, choosing Sören Kierkegaard's aesthetics as his subject. Oral tradition has spread the charming tale that when Tillich read the work, which was written in a difficult and murky style, he said to its author, "I can't understand a word, but it's wonderful." Tillich did not agree with Adorno's conclusions, but he defended him in the oral examination and gave him an A. He made a similar remark on another occasion, when Adorno burst upon him during a nap with urgent news. "Yes—what's the matter?" said Tillich, rousing himself and fixing his eye upon the younger man. "I've just discovered the meaning of humor," Adorno blurted out in excitement. "Humor is hope seen once more." Tillich responded—not surprisingly—"I don't understand a word you're saying."[45]

Their friendship, which included many hours of meaningful exchange in which Tillich understood precisely what Adorno was talking about but did not always agree with him, developed and deepened through the years despite long separations. Adorno was a gifted pianist and versatile musician; he helped Thomas Mann to write the sections on music theory that appear in his *Doctor Faustus*. In 1932, supported by Tillich, he helped Max Horkheimer found the Institute of Social Research. It was in the field of philosophical sociology that Adorno was most creative, as his influential writings show. He always attributed his own success as a teacher to Tillich's pedagogical example.

Two other unusually gifted students were attached to Tillich in his Frankfort years: Gertie Siemsen, who majored in psychology and fulfilled her career as head of a women's prison in Berlin,

Paul Tillich's mother.
(Age uncertain.)

Paul Tillich's father.
(Age uncertain.)

Bad Schönfliess. Paul Tillich's childhood home from age 5 to 12.

Tillich and his sisters Elisabeth and Johanna. Ages: Paul 16, Elisabeth 9, Johanna 14.

(*Above left*) Alfred Fritz, Hermann
Schafft, Paul Tillich, 1910.

(*Above right*) Tillich dressed in Wingolf uniform, with younger officers,
1907.

(*Right*) Paul Tillich, his sister Johanna,
her fiancé Alfred Fritz, Wansee-
Berlin, 1910.

(*Left*) Alfred Fritz, Paul Tillich, seated. Army Chaplains, World War I, 1914–1918.

(*Below left*) Paul Tillich, *Privatdozent*, University of Berlin, 1920.

(*Below right*) Paul Tillich, Associate Professor, University of Marburg, 1925.

where she applied psychological insights to improve the lot of the individual prisoner; and Wolfgang Hochheimer, who became a Jungian analyst.

Tillich's successes in the classroom were enriched, perhaps even made possible, by the vital, progressive, liberal atmosphere of the university. The presence of illustrious colleagues such as Max Wertheimer in psychology, the classical philologist Karl Reinhardt, the sociologist Karl Mannheim, and the historian Ernst Kantorowicz, served to stimulate an ongoing debate which brought Tillich in contact with politics and science as well as philosophy. There were no artificial divisions between the faculties of medicine, philosophy, and the social sciences: each institute related easily to the next.[46] Professors visited one another's seminars in an informal way or directed them together. Tillich led seminars with such men as the sociologist Max Horkheimer, who was a *Privatdozent* when Tillich arrived in Frankfort and whom he sponsored for an appointment to a philosophical-sociological chair, a great innovation at the time. When Tillich was dean, in 1932, he helped Horkheimer become a director of the Institute of Social Research, although it was already dangerous to come to the aid of Jews. For these generous actions on Tillich's part Horkheimer was abidingly grateful.

Kurt Riezler and Tillich held a seminar on the Greek philosophers, vigorously debating opposite views of the demonic in human nature, or the sacred void in history. Years later Tillich said that when he asked why Riezler, the classically minded curator, had named a Protestant theologian to the philosophical chair in the university he replied with the opinion we noted earlier, that Protestant theology "provided a good entering door to philosophy."

For the first time in his career Tillich was exposed to science in a formal way through the work of the biologist and neurologist Kurt Goldstein and his colleague the psychologist Adhémar Gelb. Gelb and Goldstein had been favorably impressed by Tillich's lectures in Davos in 1928 and had applauded his appointment to Frankfort. The two scientists worked closely together on problems concerning the functions of the brain and personality, attempting to answer the question, "What is man?" They discovered, or came to realize, that a patient can be healed only if he is treated as a whole person. Together with Max Wertheimer, the two were proponents of the school of Gestalt psychology.[47]

Gelb was a tragic personality, exceedingly sensitive, subject to moods which alternated between exhilarated delight and melancholy. His friend Goldstein commented that he was like a Russian, capable of being only very happy or very sad. Tillich was grateful to Gelb for his first professional introduction to the meaning of existential psychiatry, a subject which his friends Eckart von Sydow and Heinrich Goesch had approached only from a subjective or personal point of view. After 1933 Gelb and his family fled to Holland, where he contracted tuberculosis and died in 1936, his work half-finished.

To Goldstein, whom Tillich greatly admired and with whom he remained in faithful contact throughout their lives, Tillich was grateful for many insights in the fields of organic and inorganic biology which he later included in his *Systematic Theology*.[48] Goldstein pointed to these pages with pride of ownership, saying that Tillich had not "stolen" his ideas but rather that they had thought about these things in the same way.

Men like Adolf Löwe, Karl Mannheim, and Friedrich Pollock were on the economics faculty, all lively, creative thinkers with whom Tillich continued his discussions on socialism and political matters.

Tillich himself was in the unique position of being the only theologian on the faculty of the university, a Christian scholar teaching philosophy in a secular setting. Despite this, he won the ear of his colleagues as easily as the attention of his students. They all had confidence in him; they admired his openness, they loved his humanity, some even became indebted to his political integrity. Horkheimer once said jokingly that there was a certain tiny shade in Tillich's voice which told one that he was a theologian. Tillich was "Paul among the Jews," accepted and admired.[49]

Together with his colleagues he became involved in two discussion groups typical of what was unique about the Frankfort experience, which Tillich later said made his years there among the richest of his career. The first was an informal seminar headed by the ironic Kurt Riezler. Tillich referred to this group as "classical-pagan." Its real name was the *Weisheitsseminar*, or "seminar on wisdom."[50] It was composed of men such as Karl Reinhardt and Walter Otto, the famous and influential Greek philologists, the physicist Madelung, and the jurist Hermann Heller. Graduate students also often attended. The discussions revolved around truth in all disciplines. Tillich faithfully came to the meetings, which lasted until long after midnight and during which, as in the second group, large quantities of wine were consumed.

Tillich considered himself a more or less peripheral figure of Riezler's circle, though it had the subject of philosophy in common with the second group, to which he felt he really belonged and which he described as "religious, philosophical, prophetic." Horkheimer, Löwe, Mannheim, Mennicke, Pollock, and Riezler, who came as "thought-provoker" ex officio, were all members. At their meetings debate raged back and forth in an extraordinary manner. The discussants fell like wild animals upon one another, attacking each other's ideas, calling them "impossible, unsubstantiated, meaningless." They hardly ever agreed, and they argued ceaselessly.[51] Despite uninhibited exchange and mutual attacks, the friendships between the members were never even slightly wounded, much less disabled.

This was especially true in Tillich's case. He was not without feeling about what others thought, but there was something in him that enabled him to hear contrary opinions without the slightest qualm. When he felt that his opponent was not merely being stupid or nasty, he always respected his opinion even when it differed sharply from his own. He was a pacific arguer. Adorno, who also belonged to this group, called him "Pacidius." Tillich always reasoned, remaining logical, Socratic, seemingly incapable of ill will toward anyone with whom he disagreed. Indeed, he was so open that he permitted Nazi students, so long as they proved themselves to be thinking persons, to take part in the discussions. The irony of the situation soon made its appearance: by 1933 the Nazis in their barbaric way had destroyed the discussion groups, the free atmosphere that allowed them to express their fanatical views, and the university itself.

Tillich's ability to debate flowered in the sessions with his colleagues. His sovereignty over large areas of knowledge, his sharpness of mind, his genius for organization, and his lack of bigotry were all part of what his admirers called his "presence," a quality which drew followers even when they were not especially interested in his ideas.[52] While he remained conciliatory in tone all his life, he was not completely unmoved by the criticism of his ideas, his work, or even his way of life. He was indeed sometimes greatly upset by it—stirred to anxiety, affecting an air of helpless wonder rather than anger or even annoyance, and expressing himself in deliberate careful questioning. He was not always comfortable with intellectual equals capable of challenging the soundness of his thought; partly because he himself sometimes questioned its validity. All this grew more pronounced the older and more famous he became.

In the two or three years that followed Tillich's establishment at the University of Frankfort he became widely known in Germany. He was invited to deliver many public lectures; he attended innumerable conferences; his travels all over the country brought him into contact with a variety of people and ideas. In Berlin on 10 November 1930, for example, he talked about "Cult and Form" at an arts and crafts exhibition. On the occasion of the Goethe Festival of the National Theatre in Mannheim in 1932, he delivered an address entitled, "Goethe and Classicism." At the traditional observance of the founding of the German Reich by Bismarck, on 18 January 1932 at the University of Frankfort, he spoke of "Young Hegel and the Destiny of Germany." For his friends Fritz and Lilly Pincus and Gunther and Claire Loewenfeld he gave a dedicatory lecture on the occasion of the opening of their modern house in Potsdam, stressing the balance between space and time achieved by the architects. It was entitled "Das Wohnen, der Raum und die Zeit, " or "Space and Time in Dwelling."[53]

Tillich also traveled frequently to Marburg in an effort to remain in touch with the discussion of theological ideas which was totally missing from his secular world in Frankfort. Yet when his friend Adolf Grimme, who had become Minister of Education in 1930, invited him to occupy the chair of systematic theology at the University of Halle, he turned the offer down.[54] Grimme, a religious socialist, was later imprisoned for his opposition to the Nazi regime. He remained Tillich's faithful friend.

The glorious quality of what Tillich referred to as his "secular years" included the beauty of the geographical surroundings of the city in which he lived: the Taunus hills, the Rhine and Main rivers, the innumerable quaint villages nearby. In Darmstadt, only an hour away by car, the Tillichs heard the première of Berg's *Wozzeck*. At home in Niederrad, a suburb of Frankfort where the Tillichs had a modern apartment on the Vogelstrasse, he collected a wine cellar of Hochheimer Rhine wine, of which he was exceedingly fond. The place was newly decorated with Mies van der Rohe chairs and expensive chintz curtains. Tillich bought his first car, a secondhand open Mercedes with leather seats and a bad engine, on which he spent far too much for lack of mechanical knowledge. This was replaced later by a blue Opel. Tillich, who obtained his first driver's license in 1930, was already forty-four and always a nervous, uncertain driver. He identified so intensely with the engine that in going uphill he literally pushed at the wheel. His wife soon became the family chauffeur, particularly later in America, but he continued as the director of any expedition, reading the road maps with great exactness and authority.[55]

In Frankfort Tillich had a special affection for a certain *Altstadt Lokal*, a restaurant in the old town where he experienced "the heights and depths of existence."[56] A friend of his was director of the *Städele* museum, one of the great art galleries he continued to frequent. But most of all he rejoiced in the numerous fancy-dress balls that sprang up each winter. The Tillichs entertained a good deal, chiefly as hosts to meetings of discussion groups. Once they gave a costume party on the first floor of their apartment. The invitations read:

INVITATION TO COSTUME PARTY
Frankfurt Niederrad, Vogelstrasse 11
Dialectics of Reality or
"Through Thesis and Antithesis to Synthesis,"
Evening of 27 February, 9 P.M. through
28 February, long after dawn.[57]

Those invited were asked to come dressed as their other selves; Adorno came as Napoleon, Riezler as a fascist in a brown shirt. Tillich greatly relished costume parties and longed for them nostalgically throughout his life in America. But the intellectual and human intercourse at the several salons to which he belonged in Frankfort were the climax of his social existence: a "meaningful, contentful" gathering. He was very fond of good conversation with interesting people, stimulated by good food and wine. The Tillichs were immediately included in the salon of Paul and Gabrielle Oppenheim, to which, he proudly noted, only the "most important people" were invited. Kurt Riezler and his wife provided a second such circle; they entertained their colleagues and friends surrounded by a spectacular collection of French Impressionist paintings, which prompted Tillich to recall his evenings with them as bathed in the "power of Being."

Abruptly and cruelly all this came to an end: the joyous, open discussions, the freewheeling debates, the costume balls and salons. The menace of National Socialist power, at first mere parody and shadow, suddenly became a grotesque and brutal reality. Although concerned for the future of their country, most German intellectuals hesitated to be touched by the odium of party politics. Many preferred to live in splendid isolation, intent mainly upon their pursuit of intellectual matters and the arts. When they finally acted, it was—as in many another national crisis—too little and too late. There were exceptions to be sure: a few perceptive and courageous persons, willing to risk their lives, threw themselves into active struggle against the Nazis, sacrificing their privacy and exhausting themselves in overactive days and sleepless nights— only to pay dearly for their courage later on.[58]

Encounter With Tyranny

Tillich had seen the rise of the National Socialist movement in 1919 alongside many revolutionary, reactionary, and terrorist organizations. Former German officers, soldiers, students, and other elements dissatisfied with republican, democratic, and parliamentary procedures rallied to Adolf Hitler's call. By 1920 the party's program was drafted: its emphasis from the beginning was on nationalism, the Germanic, and the working class. It set forth vaguely defined needs and a chauvinist expansionism, combined with a revolutionary call to the dissatisfied masses. The extremism of Nazi views and the propensity for wild propaganda of the party's leaders misled many German citizens into supposing it unimaginable that such ideas and such men could ever come into power.

Tillich himself was among them. With his increasing success, surrounded by admiring friends and colleagues, he assumed that he would remain at Frankfort for an indefinite period of time. Berlin was the only other place that attracted him. He thus deluded himself largely because of his oblique relationship to the world of practical politics.[59] During the 1920s, while the National Socialist movement was imperceptibly growing throughout Germany, he remained preoccupied with the theoretical and philosophical elaboration of the principles of religious socialism. He met regularly with other religious socialists, gave lectures and made radio broadcasts in which he expressed his political views, but avoided all practical engagement. This was because he felt that the most important part of politics was never expressed within the confines of a specific party. He yearned for a fellowship or alliance not tied to any particular party but representing the vanguard of a righteous social order imbued with prophetic spirit. While he did not shrink from certain practical duties that came his way, neither did he search them out—perhaps, he later admitted, to the detriment of his own theory. In the late 1920s the rapidly deteriorating socioeconomic and political situation in Germany and throughout the Western world, and the strong possibility that the National Socialist party would overwhelm the parties opposing it, forced Tillich and most of his friends to join the Social Democratic Party, which he did in 1929. Their mission as they saw it was to broaden the base of the party and rescue it from its semibourgeois conventionalism. Tillich joined without enthusiasm, nor did he become a very active member.[60]

Tillich's reluctance to become a party member grew out of his natural predisposition for theory and his affection for the boundary situation, but there was an even deeper reason. He had only with great difficulty transcended his father's sentimental and romantic adherence to what he considered a false application of Lutheran theology to political affairs. Indeed, in some ways he suffered from the same romantic attachment to nineteenth-century ways, although he was convinced that membership in the Social Democratic Party could provide millions of workers with a sense of community which they were unable to find elsewhere, even in the church. His own belated action to join the party made his rejection of his father's political views more overt than he liked.

Another political action in which he let himself become involved was the launching of a new magazine entitled *Neue Blätter für den Sozialismus* [New Leaves or "Pages" for Socialism], edited by August Rathmann, who surrounded himself with a board of editors of which Tillich was a member. Thus involved to the extent of party membership, publication, and lectures and broadcasts on socialism and the contemporary scene, Tillich continued to watch closely the moving stream of events, which became ever more threatening and turbulent.

In 1931 he had a dream which was an uncanny premonition of the consequences of a National Socialist victory for Germany. In Kampen, that summer, he and his friends had spent the night drinking wine, talking, dreaming out loud, reciting poetry, all on the theme of imminent doom. As they emerged from the cottage where they had gathered, at four in the morning, to watch the sunrise over the dunes, they were startled to hear Tillich say, "You will all see sheep grazing on the Potsdamer Platz one day." He had had in fact a dream in which he saw grass growing and sheep grazing on that busiest square in the center of Berlin. Fifteen years later, after the Allied invasion and the bombing of Berlin, he was excited and shaken to see that his dream had come true. A photograph in a New York newspaper showed sheep cropping grass in the Potsdamer Platz.[61]

Tillich's colleagues continued to admire his genius for systematizing political concepts and symbols, and prized his political integrity; yet the more they realized the potentials of German politics, the more they sensed in him a certain naïveté regarding political life. His friend Harald Poelchau saw in his attitude an almost childlike optimism, chastened only when Tillich was dismissed from his post.[62] Kurt Riezler, ever dry-witted and ironic, with bitter memories of the realities of political administration, regarded Tillich as a "sophomore" in politics. Günther Dehn was astonished when he heard Tillich speak at a conference on liturgical reform (Neuwerk Kreis) late in 1932. He unraveled his ideas about socialism with his usual extraordinary skill, totally wrapped up in his own world, apparently oblivious to the imminent threat, and failed to make even a single reference to the dangerous political situation. It was as though the Nazi movement did not exist for him at all.[63] Yet Dehn was mistaken.

In April 1932 Tillich and his friend Hermann Schafft, a leader of the Neuwerk Kreis, had written a remarkably bold letter to the Berlin Wingolf fraternity, denouncing them for their unwillingness to include left-wing-oriented students, or Jews by birth who were of Christian faith and for admitting only persons with extreme right-wing views. Schafft and Tillich judged the Wingolf position an affront to all Christian principles. They asserted, moreover, their own deep unity with Jews and socialists, friends with whom they had shared their own Wingolfite experience. They threatened to withdraw from membership unless the Berlin fraternity publicly avowed its error.[64] Thus Schafft and Tillich eventually resigned from the fraternity, which largely ignored their protest.

Tillich detested everything for which the Nazis stood, and his growing anger, usually hidden beneath carefully worded theoretical statements, was aroused in public a number of times, causing him to explode and frightening his friends and his wife, who felt he was endangering himself. On another occasion during a summer in Kampen, Tillich and his friends entered a local bar for a nightcap. Other patrons, already less sober, asked him, "Professor, can you tell us whether there are any Christians in the world any more?" Tillich shouted in reply, "No, not a single one. The only Christians in the world today are Jews!"[65]

Despite explosions and premonitions Tillich failed, as many German citizens also failed, to involve himself in consistent and continuous participation in anti-Nazi political activity. In several fiery exchanges, his friend Adorno urged him to reject Nazi language and ideology more directly.[66] He finally did so in his book *The Socialist Decision*. He wrote, "Should political romanticism and warlike nationalism become victorious, the self-destruction of European peoples is assured. *The task of rescuing European society from a return to barbarism is given into the hands of socialism.*"[67]

This book was Tillich's major contribution to socialist politics in these darkening years. It was the outgrowth of lectures he had delivered in various forums and contained a detailed and many-sided analysis of the ideological assumptions and principles determining the political debate in Germany. In the last resort, it was a plea for choices that would prevent the collapse of European civilization. Tillich was convinced, to be sure, that the capitalist system was the major source of all social ills, and he did not believe it could be saved. But he felt that the socialist masses had no choice but to align themselves politically in some way with the left wing of the bourgeois parties (Democrats and Centrists), if they did not want to be run over by dictatorships of the right or left. Tillich firmly opposed communism as well as National Socialism. He labeled the outlook common to both "political romanticism," a term probably borrowed from Carl Schmitt.

This was an influential political scientist who had forsaken his Marxist beginnings to become a spokesman and defender of Nazi political and economic programs in so far as they related to certain traditional German values—the "powers of origin" (*Ursprungs-*

mächte), as Tillich also called them: values embodied in the feudalist social order, and also others advocated by Nazi propaganda, such as honor, duty, and service, as well as whatever could be seen as related to "blood and soil" (*Blut und Boden*). Despite Tillich's deep and fearful awareness of the possibility that a new "barbarism" might sweep over Europe if no way could be found to prevent either a Bolshevik or a Nazi victory, he showed a sympathetic understanding for conservative as well as revolutionary romanticism. But in the end he bravely reaffirmed the "socialist principle," as he had explained and defended it since the beginning of the religious-socialist movement. Realism born of faith, he believed, demanded a decision for socialism.

The book did not appear until the end of 1932. Meanwhile, in July of that year, there occurred at the university the unforeseen incident which first directed the attention of National Socialists beyond the local level to Tillich personally, and subsequently to his writings. In 1932 Tillich was dean of the philosophical faculty. "I was," he later said, "a man of power." In July fighting suddenly broke out among the students. Storm troopers and Nazi students rioted and beat up left-wing and Jewish students until blood flowed freely. In the classroom where he was lecturing, Tillich was suddenly thrown back into his World War I role of dragging the wounded and the unconscious to safety. Shaken and enraged by the sight of violence, seized by a fresh recognition of the power of the irrational and destructive forces around him, Tillich made a public speech in defense of the left-wing and Jewish students, defending freedom of thought and action and demanding that the Nazi students be expelled from the university.[68]

The sight of the National Socialist uniform so infuriated Tillich that his friends often held him back to prevent him from becoming embroiled in trouble with brownshirts. Hannah, who had gone with a friend to a Nazi meeting to satisfy her curiosity about Hitler, persuaded her unwilling husband to hear him speak. Tillich did so and came away sensing great danger, and full of disgust at Hitler's vulgar and barbarous use of the German language.[69] Much later he wrote of Hitler,

At the time of our emigration it was not so much his tyranny and brutality which shocked us, but the unimaginably low level of his cultural expressions. We suddenly realized that if Hitler could be produced by German culture, something must be wrong with this culture. This prepared our emigration to this country and our openness to the new reality it represents.[70]

In the nine months that followed the student rioting, events on the national scene rapidly accelerated, ultimately catapulting the Nazis into the seat of power they had sought for fourteen years. The German nation, frustrated by economic chaos, embittered by territorial losses, and weakened by political controversy, saw the Weimar Republic come to an end. It was an irony of history that the Communists voted along with the Nazis in the attempt to destroy German democracy. By 30 January 1933, they had succeeded. President Hindenburg had appointed Adolf Hitler chancellor over a coalition government. On 27 February 1933 the Reichstag building was burned to the ground, giving Hitler the chance to blame the fire on the Communists and thereby rousing the specter of a Bolshevik revolutionary danger which he knew the masses feared. The new elections in March gave him his first clear majority, and in the new Reichstag meeting of 21 March 1933 he assumed the dictatorial powers voted him by parliament. Thus in a quite legal manner, to the accompaniment of huge marching bands playing German hymns or songs and supported by his goose-stepping troops, Adolf Hitler now inaugurated the Third Reich.

As it turned out, The Socialist Decision was written and published too late. When Hitler came to dictatorial power it was promptly banned and the publisher forbidden to circulate it. During the ensuing years a few copies were secretly handed from one person to another. The book thus had no noticeable influence. It is a noble document of Tillich's political outlook in the period between the two great world wars.

Publication of the Neue Blätter für den Sozialismus was also forbidden. Most of the professorial members of the board of editors, moreover, were suspended or dismissed from their professorships.[71]

128

In February 1933, a month before Hitler assumed dictatorial powers, Max Horkheimer urged Tillich on the basis of passages in his book on socialism as well as in *The Religious Situation* to embrace the first opportunity to emigrate or to be prepared to lose his life.[72] By April Tillich began to grasp the implications in an immediate way. On 18 and 25 March the *Frankfurter Zeitung* published two articles in which the writer viciously attacked the Johann Wolfgang Goethe University.[73] It was, he contended, an anti-German university; its heavily Jewish faculty was responsible for teaching unwary German students a sort of "cultural bolshevism." He retold and amplified in his own fashion the incident of student rioting nine months before, together with Tillich's condemnation of the Nazis. Tillich was specifically referred to as the "embodiment of the enemy," and his defense of left-wing students, as well as his pro-Jewish and prosocialist utterances and writings, cited as proof of his "unreliability." Moreover, one sentence from *The Socialist Decision* that Horkheimer had pointed out to Tillich was quoted in one of the articles.

Horkheimer and his assistants at the Institute of Social Research were considered equally dangerous and destructive. The most vicious attack of all was made on Kurt Riezler, who was scored for having participated as a member of the Bethmann-Hollweg government in a diplomatic mission to Russia. It was insinuated, not subtly, that Riezler was a Communist. The newspaper urged in nearly hysterical tones that the university be purged of elements that endangered German youth and society, to return it to its rightful place in the city where German emperors had once been crowned!

Tillich read the articles, tore them from the newspaper, and preserved them. For a while he wondered whether he ought to withdraw from membership in the Social Democratic party as a defense against possible reprisals on the part of the Nazi government, but he did not do so. While it was clear that the Nazis intended to avenge themselves upon their enemies, no one could be certain what form that vengeance would take, and Tillich still entertained a modicum of hope.

On 1 April 1933 Tillich was in Potsdam, where he spent the day with his friends the Loewenfelds and the Pincuses. The first Jewish boycott was in effect. At this time Protestant church taxes had been ordered collected by the state. When the official arrived at the house he asked to see Gunther Loewenfeld. Tillich berated him, shouting, "What right have you to come here to exact taxes? Here of all places!" The official went away bewildered, since he had no way of knowing that Loewenfeld was a Jew who had been brought up as a Protestant, and moreover that the others living in the house were also Jewish. Tillich's friends tried to calm him.[74]

On the same morning a more violent scene was being enacted at the University of Frankfort, which the S.A. troopers had occupied. Their purpose, it was declared, was to arrest all Marxists and Jews, thus cleansing the faculty and student body. Riezler was taken into custody but set free on the same day. He was suspended from his teaching duties for the rest of the summer, a fate soon to befall many others and which in nearly all cases turned out to mean permanent dismissal.[75]

A fortnight after the storm troopers had invaded the university, on 13 April the newspapers printed long lists of names of professors, artists, civil servants, officials—in short, all those whom the state considered its enemies.[76] Enemies of the state fell into two categories: first, left-wing intellectuals, members of the Communist or Socialist Parties, the politically suspect; second, the "racially" suspect, or Jews. All over Germany shock waves were breaking, casting upon other shores eminent and distinguished men, among them Bertholt Brecht, Ernst Cassirer, Albert Einstein, George Grosz, Wassily Kandinsky, Wolfgang Köhler, Thomas Mann, Erwin Panofsky, Max Reinhardt, Karl Ludwig Schmidt, and Bruno Walter.

Within the next year 313 full professors, 300 associate professors, and 322 *Privatdozenten*—a total of 1,684 scholars—were removed from German university circles.[77] Tillich's name appeared among those suspended in the first group on 13 April, along with many of his immediate friends—Horkheimer, Löwe, and Riezler for example—but also several non-Jewish colleagues in other universities: Günther Dehn, Paul Klee, Karl Mennicke, and Alfred Weber.

With cruel suddenness he and scores of others found themselves jobless, with no way of knowing what would happen next. They were all at the mercy of a state which was still in the process of substituting one bureaucracy for another, and were therefore plunged into a long period of uncertainty. Some, like Robert Ulich, had resigned before the Nazis could suspend them. Others, like Löwe and Horkheimer, fearful of imprisonment because they were Jews, had already departed for Switzerland in March. Tillich himself decided to stay and await further developments. He cherished the vain hope that the Nazi regime would last only a short time and that he and his friends might be reinstated. This was surely at times wishful thinking, a state of mind which endangered his life at least once, and which, strangely, did not cease until long after he had arrived in America. For the moment, despite all forewarning, he was still surprised that such things were happening. Much later he said of the first shock, "I stood before an abyss."[78]

On 19 April, seized with mild panic, Tillich wrote to his former student and friend Margot Faust, who lived with her husband in the Saargebiet. He expressed himself freely to her; her mail was not censored, as his already was.

> Perhaps you have in the meantime read that I have been suspended. This means the immediate cessation of my Frankfort existence since we are already unable to pay the rent. Please send us an urgent invitation to come to you at once. We must be able to prove, however, that we wish only to come to the Saargebiet. Please write very carefully. Let us know that it is possible for you to take in Erdmuthe. I do not wish to have Erdmuthe with us in case we are not allowed to proceed. Bring along an empty suitcase so that we can give you a fur coat and winter clothes. We want to put the furniture into storage and go to the Baltic Sea for a few weeks if we have enough money.[79]

Margot Faust complied with Tillich's wishes, and his daughter Erdmuthe was left in her care for the next six months. Tillich himself then took a hurried trip through Germany, restless and anxious, only to return to Frankfort in early May in time to witness the burning of books on the Nazi blacklist. *The Socialist Decision* was one of them. That event, together with the burning of the Reichstag, was a signal to all of worse horrors to come and a clear warning to those who remained opposed to the Nazi regime.

On that tenth of May 1933 Tillich, his wife, and some friends watched the eerie scene. Nine years later he described it vividly in one of his radio broadcasts to the German people:

> Many of you still have a picture in your minds of the events of that day. I myself experienced them from a particularly good vantage point and I would like to describe how the scene impressed me. It was in Frankfort on the Main. We stood at a window of the Römer, the ancient building where German emperors were crowned. On the square, which dates back to the Middle Ages, masses of people pushed forward, held back by black and brown shirts. A woodpile was set up. Then we saw a torchlight procession pouring out of the narrow streets, an unending file of students and party men in uniforms. The light of the torches flickered through the darkness and lit up the gables of the houses. I was reminded of paintings of the time of the Spanish Inquisition. Finally, a wheelbarrow or cart drawn by two oxen jolted or stumbled over the cobblestones, laden with books which had been selected for the offering. Behind the wheelbarrow strode the student pastor. When he halted before the stake, he climbed up and stood on top of the wheelbarrow and delivered the damning speech. He threw the first book on the burning woodpile. Hundreds of other books followed. The flames darted upward and lit up the dream picture that was the present. Time had run backward for two hundred years.[80]

Time continued to run backward in the months to come. The purging of the universities was followed by persecutions unequaled in German history: large numbers of Communists, socialists, liberals, Catholics, and pacifists were arrested, beaten, tortured, and either murdered or sent off to concentration camps. State and municipal governments were ousted and replaced by National Socialist administrations.

Toward the middle of May 1933 Tillich was instructed by a

high official of the new ministry of education to await a final decision regarding his professional status.[81] In this connection he was told that he could not accept an invitation he had received to lecture in Zurich, but must remain in Germany until his case was cleared. The Tillichs now decided to spend the summer months by the sea. They went first to Sassnitz on Rügen, an island off the coast of Denmark, later repairing to Spiekeroog, near Hamburg. In Sassnitz Tillich waited and wondered what would happen next, not yet knowing that in another country decisions were already being made on his behalf.

For in May, while books were burning in Frankfort, a meeting of great importance to Tillich and many other jobless German intellectuals was taking place at Columbia University in New York City.[82] Gatherings like it were taking place all over the United States, where the academic world was opening its doors to creative and distinguished early victims of the Nazi regime. At the Columbia meeting, attended by faculty representatives as well as Henry Sloane Coffin, president of Union Theological Seminary in New York, the chairman distributed a mimeographed list at the end of which stood Paul Tillich's name. Coffin volunteered to provide a post for Tillich for one year, on condition that Columbia University should also employ him in its philosophy department, provided that he could lecture in English. Coffin proceeded to check the Tillich bibliography at the seminary in order to acquaint himself with Tillich's point of view, while Reinhold Niebuhr, professor of applied Christianity at the seminary, then at the beginning of his fame, obtained more personal information about him: the nature of Nazi hostility to Tillich, the size of his family, his academic record, and the probable date of his arrival should the faculty cable him to come. Niebuhr's younger brother, H. Richard Niebuhr, professor of Christian ethics at Yale Divinity School, had translated Tillich's book *The Religious Situation* and had written an introduction to his thought. Apart from this Tillich was little known in America. Nevertheless, the board of directors of Union Seminary voted to extend an invitation to him. The Union faculty also met, discussed the matter, and voted that each professor would give 5 percent of his salary toward Tillich's stipend for the first year—a generous act, since the United States was in the midst of its own depression. Individual directors, sympathetic with the faculty decision, also contributed to the sum required.

Reinhold Niebuhr sent Tillich a cable extending the invitation (as conveyed in a later letter signed by Frank D. Fackenthal, secretary of Columbia University), stipulating that Tillich would not be required to lecture in the fall semester, but that he would teach a course of thirty lectures in the spring session. This would enable him to study English during the early part of the year and acquaint himself with his new surroundings and perhaps also accept invitations to lecture outside New York. The stipend, to be paid in twelve installments, consisted of $1,200. Union Theological Seminary was to provide living quarters.[83] The offer, generous for the time, provided Tillich with an extremely limited income but with a large apartment.

At the same time, Niebuhr asked Horace S. Friess, professor of philosophy at Columbia, who was planning to spend the summer in Germany, to arrange a meeting with Tillich. While on a traveling fellowship in Germany in early 1925, Friess had attended Tillich's lectures and had come away with a favorable impression of him. Friess himself taught courses in German philosophy at Columbia University from late 1925 on.[84]

Meanwhile Tillich waited in a beach house overlooking the Baltic Sea in Sassnitz, answering innumerable letters and entertaining visiting family and friends. He was in a state of growing uncertainty and despair. Upon hearing from Niebuhr around 1 July that a job and apartment awaited him in America, he began to turn over the invitation in his mind. The idea of leaving Germany was at first abhorrent to him. He felt that America, about which in fact he knew very little, was provincial and, despite the effects of World War I, isolated from the European world.[85]

Yet as the weeks passed and the power of the Nazi regime became increasingly entrenched, he realized that he might be foolish to turn down the only opportunity offered him to work. In discussions with friends that summer he found himself torn between wanting to stay in Germany and fleeing from unknown dangers which might come upon him if he remained. Adorno, who visited him in Sassnitz, urged him again and again to leave; he was astonished by Tillich's total lack of fear in the face of what he himself considered certain death, but was comforted by Hannah Tillich's adamant desire to depart. Others—for example, Tillich's young colleague Wolfgang Hochheimer—felt that he was endangered not so much by external threats as by his state of mind, his tendency to fall into anxiety and depression. The Harald Poelchaus, not yet as aware of the dangers awaiting them all, begged him to stay. Stressing that he was greatly needed in Germany, they urged him to join the underground resistance movement.[86]

As Tillich, wavering between his conflicting feelings and the growing necessity to act, finally made the decision to go to the United States, he was still hoping against hope that the Nazis would soon be evicted or defeated and that his post at Frankfort would again be available to him. There was no way of knowing, of course, how long they might stay in power, but this general uncertainty forced him to think through his own decision, which he postponed again and again. By the time Friess met him in September, Tillich had sent a telegram to Columbia accepting the offer; although he continued, characteristically and much to the distress of his wife, to speak as though his mind were still open. He did so in part so as to further clarify his own thinking; in part to assuage the deep feelings of guilt aroused by those of his friends who felt he should stay and help them in their struggle against the Nazi regime.

On 29 August Tillich wrote to the director of the Ministry of Culture, asking permission to leave Germany for a year in order to be visiting professor at Columbia University. He remained on Spiekeroog waiting for a reply and continued to study English, which he had already begun while on Sassnitz (postponing work on a book on metaphysics which he had planned to write that summer) in order to satisfy this major prerequisite for his year abroad. On 9 September the Prussian Ministry of Culture replied, granting him permission to leave the country provided no final decision regarding his status at the University of Frankfort was reached before his departure.[87]

In mid-September the Tillichs left Spiekeroog for Berlin, where they prepared to say farewell to family and friends. On the eighteenth Tillich met Horace Friess, who was staying in Freiburg and had agreed to meet him in the railroad station at Heidelberg, a compromise arranged so that Tillich would not have so far to travel. The two men paced up and down as they talked. While Tillich did not say in so many words that he had already accepted the Columbia invitation, he asked Friess so many detailed and practical questions that Friess privately came to the conclusion that the die was cast. Through him Tillich learned for the first time that he would be teaching only in the spring semester of 1934. Friess, satisfied that the conversation had been fruitful, returned to America; Tillich went back to Berlin.[88]

There he made a final effort to clarify his status, for the Ministry of Culture had still not notified him whether he would be dismissed. Although his appointment had been with Rust, the Nazi minister of culture, Tillich was ushered instead into the office of the director of the ministry, Dr. Wilhelm Stuckart, a young man of 31 years of age. He informed Tillich that it would be wise for him to remain out of Germany for two years at least. He also suggested that Tillich attempt to tone down the political implications of his ideas and books while he was gone. The two men also discussed the Old Testament and its relation to the New Testament. Tillich insisted on the necessity of including the Old Testament in the Christian tradition and made it clear that his views about Judaism were in direct opposition to those of the Nazis. He left the ministry with the impression that a year's absence might benefit him materially and personally, and that there was a possibility he would be reinstated. Stuckart had assured him that his case was not very serious.[89]

Tillich proceeded to the offices of North German Lloyd to pick up reservations for America he had made earlier. Then he went to meet his wife, who was waiting for him with Eckart von Sydow at the Café Kranzler, Unter den Linden. Without a word he threw the tickets on the table. Hannah, who from the beginning had urged him to leave Germany and had been still painfully uncertain as to what he would do, was so filled with delighted relief when she saw them that she gave five German marks to the first taxi driver she could hail.[90]

A long period of intense farewells followed. Tillich made other brief journeys to say good-bye to his many friends. In October, while in Dresden for a few days, he was trailed by the secret police. Driving through the woods to a luncheon at the Bienerts', he was stopped near the house by Bienert's secretary, who warned him that the secret police had just been there and were hoping to arrest him. Tillich had told Bienert that Goering was a drug addict. He had, moreover, been extremely critical of the Nazi elections and the burning of the Reichstag and the books, only to discover afterward that Mrs. Bienert, by then an elderly lady, had asked her hairdresser whether these things were true! The hairdresser, a convinced Nazi, had notified the secret police.

Tillich sought refuge at once in the home of his friend Robert Ulich, whose wife Elsa Brandström, the "angel of Siberia," he greatly admired. He waited there until dark, when he safely left Dresden for Berlin from a suburban station. Much later he was told that Mrs. Bienert had suffered keenly because of her carelessness. With a lack of generosity uncharacteristic of him he responded, "It serves her right!"[91]

Tillich spent the last weeks in Berlin attending to practical matters. He went shopping with Claire Loewenfeld for three days in search of all kinds of clothing. The Tillichs had sold many of their possessions in order to raise cash, only part of which they were permitted to take out of the country. Tillich, who was helpless when it came to shopping, normally relied on his wife to do it for him. She had asked Claire to help, since she herself was occupied with preparations for their departure. Tillich began to feel guilty at Claire's spending so much time with him, until she found a coat for herself on sale. During these weeks Tillich also met his friend Adolf Grimme, the former socialist minister of culture, as well as August Rathmann, who noted that Tillich's earlier optimism about the political situation had given way to a more realistic mood, but that he still clung to his hope for the *kairos*.[92]

Toward the end of October, increasingly depressed by the endless farewells, the Tillichs left Berlin. It was a cold, rainy morning. At the station to see them off were their friends the Loewenfelds and Pincuses, Tillich's sister-in-law Marie-Luise Werner, his childhood friend Eckart von Sydow, and his sister Elisabeth and her husband Erhard Seeberger. Tillich was strained, tense, quiet, almost desperate. He was more concerned about the fate of his Jewish friends than for his own. He begged von Sydow to take care of them. His father, from whom he had taken leave privately, was not at the station; the details of their last meeting—they were not to see one another again—were strangely repressed by Tillich. Indeed, he could never recall them.[93]

Tillich's melancholy journey then came swiftly to an end. In Frankfort, where they lived in the home of the banker Alexander Höchberg and his wife Ellen, another farewell party was given by Kurt Riezler, who as a "sublime joke" handed Tillich a copy of *Elmer Gantry* for shipboard reading. In Hamburg Tillich, his wife, and their daughter (safely brought back from the Saargebiet) spent their last two nights in Germany at the home of a pastor, one of Tillich's students.[94] There the last farewell was transformed by Tillich into a benediction, and his emigration became a blessing, not a curse. From this time on, in letters, in speeches, and in conversations he identified himself with Abraham, often quoting the biblical text, which he applied to himself: "The Lord said to Abram, 'Leave your own country, your kinsmen, and your father's house, and go to a country that I will show you. I will make you into a great nation, I will bless you and make your name so great that it shall be used in blessings. . . .' " (Gen. 12:1, 2)

5

Beneficial Catastrophe
(1933-1939)

A Second Death

The ocean voyage was swift and stormy. Tillich later reported that
he had never seen such high waves, nor passed through such fierce
storms, nor beheld such exotic rainbows.[1] He thought often of the
first words of the Creation story: "In the beginning of creation,
when God made heaven and earth, the earth was without form and
void, with darkness over the face of the abyss, and a mighty wind
that swept over the surface of the waters." (Gen. 1:1–2b)

Despite the stormy weather, Tillich enjoyed life on board ship.
He ate the superb food which was served in large quantities, not
missing a single meal, supporting his strong constitution with a
daily "Vasano" tablet in order to prevent seasickness. While his wife
and child were unhappily confined to their tourist class cabin, Tillich
walked for hours on deck, communing with the sea, visiting the few
intellectuals in third class; trying to learn English but discussing Hegel,
Schelling, and Goethe instead, and even dancing while the ship stood
on end.

On the afternoon of 3 November the ship, temporarily prevented from docking by a sudden thick fog, entered New York

harbor. Tillich found it extraordinary and sinister to hear the fog-horns of what sounded like countless ships invisible to the eye. From Eduard Heimann, who had already arrived and was waiting for him ashore, he received a telegram of welcome.[2] In the evening the fog lifted, blown away by icy northwest winds, unveiling the countless brilliant lights of New York and at closer range the Statue of Liberty with her flaming torch raised on high. The ship dropped anchor for the night. Next morning it moved into the Hudson River, and passengers were finally permitted to disembark. At dawn Tillich was once again overwhelmed by the sight of the city—now an ocean of stone with sharp contours—which was to be his home for the next twenty-two years, and which he was destined to love whether by moonlight or bathed in brilliant sunshine as it was on the morning he first stepped on American soil.

From that moment on, he plunged into days of bustling activity, only to find his worst expectations of the new world happily disappointed, his most cherished illusions about the people in it dispelled, and his new life crowded with one surprising event after another. Once ashore, the Tillichs were warmly welcomed by Horace Friess and his wife Ruth (the daughter of Felix Adler), the Eduard Heimanns, and Professor Martin Sommerfeld from Frankfort. With Friess's help the Tillichs and their twenty-five pieces of luggage (including Tillich's many books) passed easily and quickly through customs and were taken directly to their new home. As the Friesses' car moved north on Riverside Drive, Tillich noticed at once how disciplined the traffic was and commented on it. Within half an hour the party arrived at Union Theological Seminary, where Ursula Niebuhr, Reinhold Niebuhr's wife, and Henry Sloane Coffin extended their personal welcome. Tillich was totally mystified by Mrs. Niebuhr's Oxford accent, and always remembered with great fondness that she was the first person to greet him in his new home.

The apartment itself, to Tillich's utter astonishment, was large and sparsely furnished with beds, tables, and chairs contributed by various members of the faculty. As time went by, although the Tillichs purchased new household necessities, their various homes

in America were all simple and modern, producing a certain barren or monastic effect, neither luxurious nor particularly pleasing
to the eye, and never pretentious. To Tillich, accustomed as he was
to the physical scale of European living, his new place seemed
more like that of the Bishop of New York than of "a little professor."[3] Their first day in America ended in the Niebuhr household,
to which also Horace Friess and his wife had been invited, crown-
ing a reception which Tillich found charming in every detail.[4]

So completely did Tillich absorb himself in his new world in the
months that followed that for a time his yearning for home, to
which he had given ample expression during the sea voyage, was
submerged. His contract gave him freedom from the classroom
until early 1934, and he used his free time ingeniously, combining
intense study of the English language with an equally thorough
investigation of his new surroundings, conducted with unflagging
energy and boundless curiosity. By the end of December he had
inspected the entire city, visited New Jersey and Brooklyn, and
made weekend trips to Jones Beach, Long Island, and the sea.

He began with the seminary itself, established in 1836 by a
group of ecumenically minded Presbyterians eager for the cooperation of all Christians in the work of the Kingdom of God.[5] Tillich
was justifiably impressed by its location in the midst of a great
university. Flanked by Teacher's College and Columbia University
on the east across Broadway, by the Juilliard School of Music
(now part of Lincoln Center) on the north, and Barnard College
for women on the south, the seminary remained independent of
these institutions, but cordial academic relationships had developed gradually over the years. Tillich's own appointment to both
Columbia and the seminary stood as testimony to the fact.

To the west beyond the imposing structure of Riverside Church
on the drive lay Riverside Park, where Tillich walked for hours on
end, at first often in anguish about the German friends left behind,
and in a state of anxiety concerning his own immediate future.[6]
The sight of the graceful George Washington Bridge reminded him
of the Mainz Bridge over the river Rhine; and the spicy, changing
air of New York, even when cold and windy, exhilarated him. He

found New York air incomparable and "worthy of the capital of the world."[7] He was increasingly content, the more familiar he became with the city, to live in its northern section near the Hudson River, which reminded him of an ocean by the tides he observed one day when he and his family took a ferry ride. Everything enchanted him, even the seminary's neo-Gothic architecture, which he later criticized but which in the early days brought him comfort. It seemed paradoxical to be in the biggest city in the world and living not in a modern skyscraper but in a European, medieval, romantic setting. It made him feel at home.

Tillich's appreciation for his immediate surroundings was matched by considerable bewilderment about the inner structure and life of his new place of residence. Within its walls lived a tightly-knit community in which privacy was greatly cherished, and where the unwritten law against idle gossip was well obeyed throughout the decades. Yet the atmosphere was far from impersonal. Social relations among faculty members and students were encouraged by the gracious example of the aristocratic Henry Sloane Coffin: preacher, pastor, and—as president—friend to countless students who affectionately called him "Uncle Henry." Some meals were held in common in the refectory, where the portraits of former presidents gazed down somewhat pontifically upon each new generation. In James Chapel the church year was observed with various forms of Protestant service. Each morning at eight-thirty, students and faculty worshiped together, preaching, singing, and reading the gospel, the final prayer serving as a benediction on all as they went off to their classrooms together at nine. Sunday services at eleven, especially in the days of great preachers, from Harry Emerson Fosdick to Coffin and Niebuhr (Tillich's name was later added to this list) attracted people from all walks of life, of all religious faiths, from every part of the city.

The cohesion, the common purpose, and the tradition of this community soon swept Tillich into its embrace.[8] He adjusted to it with amazing swiftness, taking part at once in chapel services and attending lectures, particularly those of Reinhold Niebuhr, to whom he felt immediately attracted and whose thought he regarded as similar to his own. There was a double purpose in his attendance: he wanted and needed to become familiar with American theological ideas, but he needed even more to learn the new language. He regarded it as essential to listen to as many of his colleagues as he could. He also read a great deal, primarily the *New York Times*, which he quickly concluded was the greatest newspaper in the world; he was astounded at the huge Sunday edition, so large and costing so little.

English he found easy to read, hard to understand, and exceedingly difficult to speak—speaking was for him in fact sheer torture, and the learning process to which he was forced to subject himself at first slow. His attempts to teach himself the language on Sassnitz in the previous summer had provided him with the bare rudiments, and to speed him on his way the seminary secured the services of an English teacher in the person of a student named Carl Hermann Voss.[9] A great-great-grandson of Johann Heinrich Voss (the classical philologist who first translated Homer into German) and son of a German-American minister, Voss was bilingual, energetic, sympathetic, and patient. He liked Tillich and his family at once, ultimately becoming their great friend. Each morning Voss arrived in time for breakfast. Tillich was barely alert during his lessons, for he often stayed up until long after midnight discussing "the situation" with his many emigré friends, who were arriving weekly and who beat a hasty path to his door. The visits took their toll, and Voss, noting Tillich's weariness, frequently said, "Gosh, you must be in a fog!"—to which Tillich invariably replied, "Fog? Fog? What is a fog?" It was not merely fatigue and anxiety that made quick progress difficult. For Tillich persisted in speaking German whenever he could. But Voss and a second student, Harry Dorman, continued to work with him as often and for as many hours as possible.

In January 1934 Tillich made his first speech in America, but his pronunciation was so atrocious that hardly anyone understood what he was saying. The fact is that he never mastered either American pronunciation or idiom; his accent remained heavy until his dying day, and he often invented phrases which, while not correct idiomatically, were nevertheless imaginative and vivid. He was almost allergic to jargon or colloquial expressions, and whenever they were used in his presence waved his hands helplessly, looked nonplussed, and said, "Oh children, let's drop this!"[10] Yet he was exceedingly shrewd in his grasp of the meaning of words and almost always intuitively chose the correct American word for a German one when he needed to find it, often improving upon translations written by American colleagues.

His struggles with the language became the source of countless anecdotes as time went by. On one occasion he used the word "vacuum," pronouncing it "waykwoomb" to the general bewilderment of his audience. He said "crucification" instead of "crucifixion," "salvated" instead of "saved," "jok" instead of "joke," and on at least one occasion "blob" instead of "blurb." In 1948 he gave a major speech in which he made frequent reference to the "sacred void." One listener was utterly confused for he believed Tillich had said "sacred word" all along. In the late 1930s a former student's wife, who had not seen him for some time, complimented him on his ability to pronounce "world" and "word" correctly (an achievement of which he was inordinately proud), adding that his English had much improved since they last met. Tillich responded, "Oh, you consolate me greatly."[11] In the final year of his life, during a television appearance, the interviewer asked him to explain his role in the American theological world. Tillich replied, "I am the gadfly that stinjes." For a moment the interviewer looked puzzled, then realizing that he meant "stings," nodded in smiling agreement.

It would be erroneous to believe that Tillich remained entirely unsophisticated in his use of American phrases. Once during a Philosophy Club meeting in New York he surprised his colleagues by saying, "Here Hegel leaves us in the lurch." He was pretty pleased with himself for using such an idiomatic expression, and looked around the room to find people amused. Hoping to explain how he had come upon this phrase, he went on to say, "You see, I keep my ear to the soil."[12]

The outbursts of hilarity that often followed such characteristic and delightful misuse of words were almost never meant unkindly. American students and professors were generally sympathetic to Tillich's plight and patiently struggled to comprehend what he was saying, particularly in the early years when it was really difficult.[13] Toward the end of his career a certain impatience crept into public reaction, especially on the part of other emigrés who in the same period of time had come to master the spoken as well as the written word, and felt that Tillich had been unnecessarily careless and lazy.

On at least two occasions Tillich demonstrated in a classic way his failure to use the American idiom, revealing something about himself at the same time. During a discussion among Tillich, Niebuhr, and other colleagues, he said to one of them, "You agree with me." Niebuhr said at once, "No, Paul,—*you* agree with *him*." It took some time to explain to Tillich that English idiom in the circumstances required him to say, "I agree with you."[14] During rehearsal of a faculty Christmas skit (in a later year, when the Tillichs had acquired their East Hampton home), a scene was put on in which Tillich had been fired by Henry Van Dusen, then president, and was required to wonder sadly what he should do, now that he was jobless. "Why, you'll go to East Hampton, of course," quipped Van Dusen according to the script, whereupon Tillich replied in heartfelt tones, "Oh, how my students shall miss me!" He had changed his own line not consciously from "Oh, how I shall miss my students!"[15] This produced such a burst of merriment and applause that Betty Van Dusen, the author (Van Dusen's wife), shrewdly decided to leave it so. Tillich himself laughed as hard as the rest, once he realized what he had said.

He made swifter progress in writing English than in speaking it. By the end of December 1933 he began to write out the lectures scheduled for delivery in February. Voss and Dorman again came to his aid, but were faced suddenly by a new problem: Tillich's specialized vocabulary.[16] Terms such as "being" and "non-being" were utterly foreign to American theological students of the time, and the three men often found themselves in despair as they wrestled with the translation. It was the first time—but by no means the last—that Tillich's students, colleagues, or friends helped him set down his complex ideas in proper English language. In time the language itself simplified Tillich's difficult sentence structure and forced him to create new words in order to introduce his ideas to a new audience. Whether English made his ideas any clearer or more distinct remains doubtful.

As we have already seen, Tillich's obsession with learning English did not prevent him from continuing to explore the city. From the moment he saw it he had found it grandiose and fantastic. He became especially fond of the Empire State Building and Rockefeller Center (although they were both symbols of capitalism), but in general found much of the architecture plain and even ugly. On election day, in the year when LaGuardia was elected mayor, Tillich went to Times Square and was fascinated by the confetti falling from the skies, as well as by the Great White Way. He and his family explored the Battery, climbed the Statue of Liberty, and walked around Wall Street. They visited Chinatown, the Turkish and Romanian sections, and one evening went to Harlem with a group of tourists led by the owner of a German newspaper. That evening they saw a burlesque which Tillich felt was as good as anything he had ever seen in Paris. Indeed, this astonished him, for he was absolutely certain that America was a land of puritans, one of several prejudices he was never wholly able to shake. He was irresistibly drawn to the Metropolitan Museum of Art: the huge collection overwhelmed him. And when he discovered the Museum of Modern Art he felt instantly at home.

Yet it was the consistent and spontaneous generosity of his American colleagues that pleased and surprised him most of all. The informal manner of complete strangers who took him and his family into their homes comforted him. At first he naïvely assumed that the liberal atmosphere of New York was what made social life there so easy and pleasant; he imagined that everything west of the Hudson River must be provincial and dull. In the following fifteen years he learned to change his mind; in the process of transformation from emigré into world citizen he was forced to admit that his earlier view revealed his own provincial limitations. The American way of treating refugees as individuals, he said, was his first lesson in democracy.[17]

Tillich's first Thanksgiving and his first Christmas were spent in an American home where he admired the simple and charming way in which the holiday season was celebrated. It came to him as a great relief that Americans, too, celebrated Christmas with a tree. He purchased one, trimming it with great diligence, as was his wont. This annual sentimental encounter had always involved long and careful choosing, remodeling if necessary (removing branches or filling in empty spaces), and "architectonic" decoration with apples, silver icycles, and silver or gold balls (he had brought them along from Germany) brightened by the glimmering light of wax candles.[18] Trimming the tree was a ritual he reserved for himself in a strangely absolute way, barring his family from the room until he was ready to reveal it in all its splendor. For some unaccountable reason Tillich was convinced that wax candles were unavailable in New York, and in any case it was in fact against the law to use them. He compromised by using electric lights, but wrote home to his sister every year thereafter until the war interrupted all correspondence, asking for candles and Lindt chocolates and indulging in sentimental reminiscence. "I think of the times when we trimmed the tree together two days before Christmas Eve and then I brought out the building blocks and built a Christmas church . . . ancient mystique and bliss long since past. . . ."[19]

Tillich's genuine attachment to the traditional ways of celebrating the Christmas festival included also gifts to family and friends. He was not adept at buying presents for others but preferred to let them choose for themselves, or relied on the advice of a third person. His otherwise fertile imagination became strangely blocked when he tried to think of what he should give anyone, but whatever it was, he gave with the same generosity he admired so much in Americans, and with his characteristic carelessness of cost. He never failed to be in touch with family and friends everywhere during the holiday season, either by the spoken or the written word. Eventually, he and his wife adopted the American custom of sending out Christmas cards (in Germany it is New Year's cards).

They preferred unconventional designs, usually creating their own and always adding handwritten greetings.

Despite its beneficial aspects, Tillich's first Christmas was the most melancholy he had spent since World War I. Even surrounding horrors and death, he had felt then, could not erase the beauty and meaning of the lighted candles on his carefully trimmed tree. But in 1933, in the midst of peace and abundance, warmed in exile by friendships old and new, the Christmas lights did not for an instant ease his depression. It was not the absence of candles which brought on this grief but rather the official word of his dismissal from his post at the University of Frankfort.

In a letter dated 20 December the Nazi minister of culture informed Tillich that he was considered untrustworthy on account of his writings on socialism as well as because of his membership in the Social Democratic party, and would therefore not be permitted to hold an official position in Germany. This decision which finally deprived him of his professorial post and standing in Germany, came as a cruel blow rather than a release. Living in limbo, he had waited for it for months; he had indeed really hoped that it would not go against him. He therefore protested the decision in a long letter to the ministry.

New York City
606 West 122nd Street
20 January 1934

To the Ministry for Science,
    Art and Education
Department of Universities, Berlin

The communication dated 20 December 1933 concerning my dismissal from the civil service on the basis of No. 4 of the Laws of Reconstruction of the professional civil services has reached me here.

The communication is a great surprise to me; for various reasons, I had come to assume that such a step would no longer be considered by the ministry. On the basis of written and oral requests by the director of the ministry, Gerullis, I remained in Germany until the end of October, despite several invitations to teach outside Germany and despite the offer of a foreign professorship—all of which I rejected. I then accepted the invitation from Columbia University, having been given permission from the ministry to do so. Indeed, after this the director of the ministry, Jäger, assured me that he was convinced of my loyalty and that he thought that one year's stay in a foreign country would be of advantage to me both materially and personally. Finally, I heard from Dr. Kullmann in Geneva that Secretary of State Stuckart had assured him that my case was not at all serious and that I could expect a positive decision soon. I left Germany with this expectation. I have talked at length about my stay here in America with the Consul General here and our long conversation resulted in essential agreement between us. Furthermore, with the consent of the Consul General I accepted an invitation of Columbia University to give five lectures in the German language on the intellectual and spiritual bases of the present situation in Germany. Now it has become impossible for me to give these lectures because my dismissal has greatly disturbed my American colleagues, especially those who are earnestly striving to understand what is happening in Germany.

I must protest my dismissal in so far as it is based on section 4, which includes a judgment of national unreliability. I do this especally in view of the fact that it is stated in the law itself that my temporary membership in the former Social Democratic Party is alone no reason for dismissal. Indeed, there is no reason for assessing my scientific and political activities as nationally unreliable. On the contrary: in 1914, I volunteered and then took part in almost all great battles of the west until 1918. I have received the Iron Cross First Class. Later, I became co-founder of German Religious Socialism, on the basis of my experience with soldiers and officers in the trenches and on first-aid posts. As the theoretician of Religious Socialism I have fought throughout the years against the dogmatic Marxism of the German labor movement, and thereby I have supplied a number of concepts to the National Socialist theoreticians. Moreover, my last book was interpreted by the representatives of dogmatic Marxism as an attack upon them inasmuch as it points emphatically to the powers in man that bind him to nature. The fact that as a theologian I adopt the biblical criticism of an unbroken sway of national powers could be regarded as evidence of my national unreliability only if National Socialism had not identified itself with the program of "positive Christianity." This, however, is the case. Hence I cannot, in this connection either, agree that national unreliability has in fact been demonstrated.

In view of the fact that at the minister's advice I have rejected the offer of a new position and income and in view of the fact that as a result of the unusually long time it has taken to inform me, I have lost also other openings and on account of my resolute decision against becoming an emigrant, I have thus suffered great injury, I urgently request that I be informed as quickly as possible regarding the final decision about my situation. Should a revision of the judgment not be possible on the basis of the facts about which I have informed you herewith, it is necessary for me to find out whether, supported by an adequate pension, I can continue my work on dogmatics and metaphysics which I have begun in the German language and on German soil or whether I am to be forced to give up these plans and enter into the service of a foreign nation and culture.

[signed] Paul Tillich

It was not until 15 June 1934 that the Nazi ministry curtly replied:

I am unable to sustain your protest of 20 January 1934 against your dismissal from the civil service on the basis of no. 4 of the Laws of Reconstruction of the professional civil service of 7 April 1934.

[signed] Dr. Stuckart[20]

Thus Tillich's protest was of no avail. The paradoxical and contradictory letter itself, with its stilted and uncharacteristic style, was written in a moment of extreme anxiety about the future, after nearly a year of uncertainty. Tillich had waited overlong for a clear decision to be made, and had indulged in wishful thinking on the basis of his personal conversations with representatives of the Nazi regime, themselves not yet fully cognizant of the ultimately fatal direction in which their leaders were to move them. In the hectic weeks in New York, during which he had been only superficially distracted, Tillich suffered increasingly the tensions born of seeing one possibility after another dissolve and disappear. Once the slender chance that he might return to Germany was taken from him, when he had no assured permanent position in America, he fell victim to fear. Would he be able to earn a living in this foreign country—would he ever complete his own work in a language he was still trying to master?

The sometimes confused and imprecise tone of the protest seems to mar the image of a man of whom it was often said that he was the first non-Jew to be dismissed by the Nazi regime—a myth he never denied—and who was proud of his dismissal until the end of his life. Yet the letter reveals him, not as one proud of being singled out as an unreliable citizen and forced into emigration, but rather as the shrewd and practical man he was, caught in the ambiguities of history, reaching out to clear his name and trying to ensure that, failing all else, his pension would be available to him. The hero and the shrewd negotiator are one and the same.

The same man who wrote much later that life is ambiguous[21] was himself ambiguous in a startling way in this letter, particularly in his statement that the Nazis had borrowed their terminology from him. Yet even this was altogether in keeping with his personality and his tendency to remain open to all possibilities, not taking an absolute stand when the future was inscrutable. The historic events of the next six months showed him the vanity of his attempt.

It was in that winter that Tillich resigned from the Wingolf fraternity, as did his friend Hermann Schafft and many other anti-Nazi members. Tillich did so protesting the exclusion of Jews from the membership. Later the same year the Nazi laws against Jews were promulgated, depriving them of their rights as German citizens. In the spring, in a letter from his father, Tillich read the veiled and affectionate advice as a personal warning: "When an emigrant asks you whether you would advise him to return to Germany, I would in your place tell him not to, especially if he who asks the question is really attached to his fatherland. He would not feel comfortable here any longer."[22]

In May, at the conclusion of his first semester of teaching, Tillich was fortunately reappointed as visiting lecturer for a second year. Horace Friess and his colleague, John Hermann Randall, Jr., had attended the Columbia seminar to help him over the rough spots in his faltering attempts to communicate complicated ideas in a new language. Both there and at Union Seminary Tillich's classes, although small, were filled with keenly interested students who were struck by his great learning and seriousness of purpose. Although they did not always understand what he was saying, they sensed that it was important. Coffin shared his reactions with the Rockefeller Foundation, writing that while Tillich's English

> was very faulty when he arrived, he has worked hard at it and his lectures have been on the whole a success. Certainly the more recent ones have been very much appreciated by the students and he is now in a much better condition to be of use here than when he landed.

> He is entitled to a retiring pension under the German law unless that is denied him, but he is still a young man (in the forties) and it is quite possible that if he is not allowed back into Germany or allowed to resume his work there, he might be of use in this country; but his hope is that he may return. He feels and some of his friends feel that the present stringent action against all those who have not coincided with the nazi government will gradually be relaxed.[23]

In June Tillich, as always eager to be near the sea, expressed this desire to Friess, who at once invited him and his family, as well as their friends the Ulichs and the Heimanns, to Martha's Vineyard. Despite the unspoiled beaches and the privacy of the island, despite the nearness of the sea, the sadness among the homesick refugees was unmistakable.[24]

Then in late summer several shaking events in Germany forever deprived Tillich of his hope that the Nazi regime might be overturned. He read of President Hindenburg's death, the illegal persecution of powerful Nazi leaders by order of Hitler himself, and Hitler's assumption of absolute power. A ruthless and violent dictatorship had been unleashed, permitting no resistance, coolly removing or exterminating all who stood in its way. From this time forward, Tillich became fully aware that Germany was in the hands of the same terrible power he had seen written in the fanatic faces of the storm troopers before his departure. On this power and all its representatives he now turned his back.[25]

One of these was his lifelong friend Emanuel Hirsch. With an aggressiveness unusual for Tillich, he broke with Hirsch, who had failed not only to protest the laws promulgated against the Jews but had even gone so far as to describe Hitler as "the voice of God to the German people," a pronouncement which Tillich regarded as incomprehensible and abhorrent. In an exchange of open letters between the two men published in the *Theologische Blätter*,[26] an end was written to their friendship. Tillich found it painful to be forced to wound his old friend and so tried to cushion his attack by first confessing the personal difficulty he felt in writing the letter. He then pointed up their differences, listing the ideas, concepts, and phrases he accused Hirsch of having "borrowed," and denounced him for failing to fight the Nazis now that they had finally shown their true colors. Although after a second and final exchange in May 1935 the two men were in occasional brief touch, the break between them, painful for both, was never mended.[27]

In the years that followed Tillich continued to make speeches, preach sermons, and write letters in support of the enemies of the Nazi regime, but he always remained loyal to Germany itself. He never once wrote or spoke a word against his homeland, thus remaining faithful to a vow made shortly before his departure, "I will never write a single line against Germany."[28] He judiciously distinguished between the Germans and the Nazis, a distinction not every refugee or thoughtful person was willing to make.

Tillich's loss of position, friendship, and homeland wrought neither bitterness nor resentment in him, but plunged him into mourning for the past. At the end of his first year in America he was overcome with a feeling of darkness about the future. He wrote to a friend that he was enduring a "second death";[29] it was a death in some respects similar to the one he had experienced in the battle of the Champagne in 1915. That first knowledge of what it was to perish had been more immediate and threatening; the second was subtler and more bitter. Much in his new life was in order: a good beginning in the classroom, interested students, a growing command of English, many fine friends, interesting challenges, a bearable salary. All this, including his own acceptance of these benefits, did not change the fact that at times he stood in the very midst of death, and knew he needed to live and suffer through the past in order to find new meaning for himself. For the moment he stood between "no longer" and "not yet." More than ever he identified himself with Abraham, whose fate he learned to love and about whom he wrote these moving lines: "He is bidden to leave his native soil, the community of his family and cult, his people and state, for the sake of a promise that he does not understand. The God who demands obedience of him is the God of an alien country, a God of history, who means to bless all the races of the earth."[30]

If Tillich did not yet understand God's promise to him, there were countless other emigrés arriving in ever increasing numbers who did not comprehend it either. The first wave of German refugees consisted mainly of left-wing intellectuals and politicians, professors, artists, poets, musicians, and actors.[31] In many ways they were fortunate, for like Tillich they were often able to find immediate employment, not always commensurate with their previous positions but with the possibility of advancement. Some were confused by their new surroundings and subject to self-pity, even melancholia. Others were eager to meet the new challenges, and those whose command of English was adequate found themselves able to do so. Still others, particularly those who came later, assumed that they had somehow a right to employment on the same level as that which they had been forced to abandon. When they saw that this was impossible, especially in the late 1930s when the best positions in the academic world had already been taken, their unrealistic expectations were cruelly disappointed. Some became bitter, some never adjusted to their condition, a few committed suicide. Others, despite all adversity, became phenomenally successful: one of them was Tillich.

The characteristic that perhaps distinguished him most from many other emigrés was his willingness to embrace his fate, once he realized its inevitability. While at rare moments and in private he confessed to a "second death," he did not in general stoop to self-pity or idly complain about his condition. Nor did he expect special favors: he took the American experience upon himself, accepted it as it came, and never looked back. This attitude saved him from feeling cheated and freed him for his work.

To be sure, for years he was the "exiled emigrant," consciously and articulately aware that at the age of forty-seven, well known and well off, he had in the twinkling of an eye become poor, little known, and forced to begin at the bottom of the academic ladder. But he wasted no time and set out almost at once to remedy the situation. In the years that followed he worked industriously to establish himself in his new world in the hope of achieving a new academic success. It is interesting to note that he became known to a wider audience in America, not through his originality or productivity as a philosophical theologian, but as an emigré in relation to other emigrés.

At the outset his contact with the old world, which he was naturally unwilling to relinquish, was kept alive by continuing friendships with people who had also come from abroad: Arnold Wolfers at Yale, Eduard Heimann and Adolf Löwe at the New School for Social Research, Theodor Adorno, Max Horkheimer, and Max Wertheimer at Columbia; and Kurt Goldstein, who set up a private practice in New York, to mention a few. By the end of 1934 an increasing number of his friends and colleagues from Frankfort had arrived in this country, where they reassembled with regularity, mostly in Tillich's home, until their new professional appointments took them outside the city.[32] They resumed their familiar debates with Tillich at the center; his leadership was so taken for granted that Adorno, arriving from England by ship at five in the afternoon, was in Tillich's apartment by seven-thirty the same evening. The reunions between Tillich and his friends were not marked by any rehearsal of what had happened to them since their last meeting, but rather by an ongoing dialogue. They were chiefly interested in discussing the meaning of historical events and united in their common opposition to the regime that had brought about the ruin of their past. Beyond that, they had a resolute will to create something new.

The presence of Tillich's friends in America provided him with help, criticism, encouragement, and continuity on which he greatly depended. They made life easier for him, but in some ways also harder: his adaptation to America was somewhat impeded, his adjustment to the new world gradual, not immediate. Later he confessed that this slower process helped him to translate the values of the old world into the spirit of the new, something he suspected he could not have done had he at once abandoned the old values in favor of the new.[33]

The American depression of the 1930s was at its height. As the circle of emigrés grew larger and the difficulties of finding employment more intense, just as American stockbrokers were reduced to selling apples on street corners, so likewise many cultured Europeans and their wives had to perform menial labor to avoid starvation. The women became household servants or governesses. In one case, to Tillich's horror, a beautiful woman who came to see him had become a prostitute because she had no other means of staying alive.[34] The men too, particularly when they could not directly resume work in their own professions (as in the case of lawyers and physicians), were often forced to content themselves with less lucrative and to them less dignified ways of earning a living. Their common suffering was caused most of all by loneliness, confusion, and the sense of being cut off from any genuine community. This was a loss that Tillich's reception at Union had spared him, although the inevitable restrictions put upon him and his wife by the community there created, as we shall see, still other problems with which they both had to wrestle.

A friend of Tillich's, Else Staudinger, keenly aware of the anguish of many fellow emigrés, hit upon a new idea of organizing help for them. Sensitive and warm-hearted, she spent much time doing little services for others, finding them doctors, giving them clothes, and trying to build up their morale. She and her husband Hans Staudinger, a former high German government official who had become a member of the graduate faculty for politics at the

New School for Social Research and later was appointed dean, felt that the time had come for the emigrés to help themselves and each other. The main purpose of the organization they had in mind was to provide jobs for those who needed them by means of a referral service and to put newcomers in touch with one another— in short, to draw all refugees into a community. Accordingly, on 25 November 1936 "Self-Help for Emigrés from Central Europe" was founded. Tillich later wrote that the name Self-Help had been chosen

> because we wanted to help a larger self than our own, the community of those who were the first victims of national socialism. We felt united in this group, not by clever devices of mutuality, not by senti-mental feelings of pity, but by the experience of an embracing "we" based on a common catastrophe, a common wrath against those who brought about the ruins of our past, and a common resolute will to create something new out of these ruins. This experience of a higher self has given rise to self-help, its name and its reality.[35]

Those who needed jobs presented themselves to the organization's leaders, who put them in touch with possible employers after as-certaining through personal interviews what sort of employment they were best suited for.

Tillich, a member of Self-Help from its inception, was chosen as its first chairman, a position he occupied for fifteen years. With great passion and devotion, he threw himself into this work at once, showing an administrative ability few knew he possessed. He identified himself with the fate of the Jews to such an extent that they were everlastingly grateful to him. On the other hand, he was brought in contact with many people from the old world whom he might not otherwise have met, and his eyes were opened to new depths of human anxiety and misery, and new heights of courage.

Tillich's generosity was soon made apparent to his colleagues at Union, who witnessed a steady procession of visitors to his office: people to whom he gave advice, for whom he sought contacts, people who never forgot his patience and encouragement. To many of the visitors, unrelated as they were to the academic world, he seemed like a creature from another planet as they looked around his office with its impressive collection of books, but they soon were won over by his warmth, humanity, and gentleness. They felt understood, not overawed. They found in him a pastor who was willing to listen. Those he counseled were made to realize that something deeper than mutual help was being given them: they were being helped, not because they were expected to return the favor, but simply because they belonged to a larger unity no part of which could be neglected.[36]

Of the endless number of refugees who came to him and whom he helped in one way or another, by finding them a job or making a contact for them, the case of Walter M. Mosse stands out as a good example of his ability to arrive at a fitting solution in a seemingly hopeless case. Mosse, the scion of an aristocratic, learned Jewish family which had for generations lived in Königsberg, had been a lawyer for the Berlin Philharmonic Symphony. He was very musical, and inordinately proud of having once been asked by Wilhelm Furtwängler to play in a concert with the second violins. He had come to America in the late 1930s, but was unable to practice law, his only means of support. When he turned to Tillich for help, while the two were talking the latter had a sudden inspiration. Perhaps Mosse could teach German to American theological students at Union, who were unhappily ill-prepared in foreign languages. Mosse responded with enthusiasm to this notion, whereupon Tillich picked up the phone and asked Blanche Britton, the able registrar, whether it would be possible for him to be thus employed. An arrangement was made at once, and for years Mosse taught what he called "theological German" to doctoral candidates, becoming a cherished member of the community until his death in 1973.

Not all problems were so readily solved, of course, and Tillich was often forced to admit failure and send his visitor on to another source of help. Indeed, as times changed, so did Self-Help. It developed over the years from modest beginnings in a small room on upper Broadway (with "one window, two flowers, and three fishes"[37]), where Tillich dictated a few letters once a week, to a larger organization with an office on Forty-second Street and Broadway, full-time help, and a permanent director: Toni Stolper, an indefatigable and imaginative volunteer. Over the years, too, the emphasis changed from help for refugees in America to help for displaced persons abroad after World War II. The need to search for jobs or help newcomers adjust ultimately gave way to other needs: for Care packages, or inexpensive vacation homes, and so on. Yet the main principle of Self-Help, as Tillich himself came to define it on the tenth anniversary of its founding, never changed: it sought to help where help was most needed, and succeeded supremely well where larger committees usually failed because they were unable to act quickly.[38]

Tillich's role as chairman was as flexible as the organization for which he worked: he was administrator, pastor, and speech-writer. As his name became more widely known among refugee groups he was often invited to speak at their public meetings, where he tried to encourage the downhearted, to remove any feelings of bitterness and revenge, and to interpret the meaning of historical events. When the Jewish persecutions abroad grew increasingly flagrant, Tillich emphasized over and over again that not the Jews alone but Christianity and humanism were also being put to death. As the years passed, he stressed more and more the need to look forward, as Americans did: to become involved in creative action in the present and not remain enslaved to the past. Although he progressed during these years from a European provincialism to becoming an American, he never ceased to identify with emigrés in such a way that he became a permanent symbol for them. The same people who spent time with him in his office later read his books and heard him lecture and preach, thus constituting his first large audience in America.

Shelter from the Storm

The new beginning, despite its manifold benefits, was something about which Tillich felt a certain ambivalence, largely because he was forced by circumstance to begin at the bottom of the academic ladder and once more work his way up toward the top.[39] He had come to this country with the conviction that he had nothing to learn from the new world, clad in the armor of certainty that German theology and philosophy (which to be sure stood in a commanding position at the time) represented a kind of perfection to be found nowhere else.[40] In his most pessimistic moments he had even doubted that he could complete his system in this country. He soon discovered that there was no permanent position immediately ready for him in the world for which he harbored this condescension (rarely if ever expressed in public), and the fact depressed him. On the one hand, he was deeply grateful to have a job at all; on the other, while he accepted his fate with grace, he bore a small, invisible grudge at being once again a *Privatdozent*. As it turned out it was four years before he was given tenure, another three before he was made a full professor, and by then, at fifty-four, he was only eleven years from normal retirement age.

Many factors coalesced to prevent an earlier marriage between Tillich's talents and the American academic world. As we have seen, the financial depression and his poor command of English were chiefly responsible, the first outweighing the second as time went on. The difficulty for many of his colleagues in comprehending his complex vocabulary and thought, and their inability to figure out what niche he might appropriately fill, were two other causes. He was clearly an extraordinarily gifted man, eager to be understood, ambitious and industrious, one who charmed his students almost at once.[41] The question his colleagues asked themselves was: What sort of man is he—philosopher or theologian? Skeptic or Christian? To the philosophers at Columbia, only a few of whom were familiar with and open to his thought, his point of view seemed too theological. They felt he belonged most properly "across the street" on the divinity faculty. There in turn Coffin as well as some of his colleagues wondered whether a man who stressed German and Greek philosophy as much as he did could play a constructive role in training candidates for the Christian ministry. At the time, such candidates comprised the large majority of students at the seminary, and it was their expert training that concerned Coffin most. Even after he had secured funds for a new appointment (he and his board were famous for balancing the budget to the penny), a question lingered in his mind, not as to Tillich's intellectual ability but as to the relevance of his thought to a seminary curriculum. To Coffin, Tillich's ontological language seemed too philosophical and too secular.[42]

As for Tillich, the more he became acquainted with the American scene, the more content he was to remain in New York and await advancement at Union. He had in fact no other alternative, and in the long run it proved a good opportunity. In the scarcity of depression few academic jobs were available even outside the city. Once when Niebuhr mentioned the possibility of his teaching elsewhere, Tillich threw up his hands in horror, sensing that he would be lost in the provinces. He had a need, he said, to be near New York's cultural life, his emigré friends, and the sea. Later he recalled this unbending attitude with some chagrin, declaring that he had been bold at the time.[43] It was partly instinct, partly naïveté about the rest of the country that made him react as he did; as it turned out, it was precisely in and through Union Seminary that he ultimately succeeded beyond his or anyone else's wildest dreams. It is quite doubtful that the circumstances in which his career now unfolded could have been duplicated anywhere else.

Once in America, Tillich's hopes for making his living as a philosopher in a university (to which he was more naturally drawn than to a divinity school) were gradually dispelled. At Columbia there was simply no room for his fascinating but peculiarly Teutonic ideas, so unfamiliar to colleagues and students alike. The many illustrious members of its Department of Philosophy were concerned, not with Schelling and the concept of Being, but with John Dewey and pragmatism. Irwin Edman, William P. Montague, and Ernst Nagel who were not predisposed to Tillich's thought, together with Horace Friess, John H. Randall, Jr., and Herbert Schneider who were, shared the decisive trait that they were Americans speaking to the American mind while Tillich was not. Nevertheless, for most of his American career he taught regularly at

Columbia and was proud of his long association with professors and students there. He gave courses on "Protestantism and Culture" and on "German Classical Philosophy," both tailored to attract students of varied backgrounds, age groups, and interests in the School of General Studies. He participated in two graduate seminars, one on myth and symbol, another on religion and mental health, both during and after World War II.

His participation in the graduate seminar on "The Cognitive and Religious Use of Myth and Symbol" is an episode that deserves mention. This occurred in the 1940s and 1950s, and although seemingly unimportant at the time, more than anything else it proved to be a breaking of ground. For eight years Tillich joined John Hermann Randall, Jr. in intensive cooperation; he liked to call it "teamwork."[44] It was, in fact, the first time that professors from Union and Columbia had collaborated in a seminar; this was a time when many in the Columbia philosophy department regarded theology with considerable skepticism if not scorn. Randall, well known for his encompassing knowledge of the history of Western thought and his sharpness of mind, was intrigued from the start by Tillich, whom he thought of as a "true-blue German Romantic";[45] he studied his thought carefully and was so impressed by it that he even paid Tillich the supreme compliment of attending his James Chapel sermons, making the short trek north from his Claremont Avenue apartment for only one other: Reinhold Niebuhr. Tillich, for his part, highly respected Randall; their association, chiefly professional, reached its zenith in the intellectual interplay of the seminar they gave together.

Randall was as eager to understand Tillich as Tillich was to present his ideas in the American vernacular to those who seemed immune to them. Accordingly, in the seminar the two men talked together about the role of myths and symbols in metaphysics and religion. Their goal was to persist in dialogue, inspired by the papers each presented at every meeting, until they had reached common ground.

Randall tried to talk Tillich's language, and the latter bent over backward to agree. But while Tillich spoke of the "human situation," Randall preferred "the fix man finds himself in."[46] The result was a fairly successful attempt to establish philosophical communication. Yet Randall was never wholly certain that he and Tillich were talking about the same thing, while Tillich always tried to believe they were! Randall responded particularly to Tillich's use of the psychological dimension; it seemed to him functional and therefore American. But while he wanted to leave students complacent in their faith, Tillich was reluctant to do so. After Tillich's refusal to restrict membership in the seminar, the students, fascinated by the discussions between the two men, arrived in even larger numbers, a consequence Randall generously attributed to Tillich's appeal, not his own.

Tillich's engagement with American philosophy was gradually enriched and enlarged through contacts with other universities and especially by his membership in the Philosophy Club, but he was accepted by only a small minority of philosophers in America, particularly when the general philosophical trend moved from pragmatism to linguistic analysis. Seen against this background, the seminar with Randall on the meaning of myth and symbol acquired a magic of its own.

Tillich's concern to remain in touch with the "old world" and with other institutions, as well as his curiosity about politics, domestic and foreign, were partly satisfied through his peripheral alliance with the New School for Social Research. A few weeks after his arrival in this country he met there with other emigré intellectuals to discuss both the German situation they had left and the new world to which they had come. For the next twenty years this "general seminar" attended by many visitors from other universities met every Wednesday; later for one term only.[47] The discussions were not always of a contemporary nature but dealt with scholarly themes as introduced by designated members of the seminar. Throughout the years Tillich was also invited to give courses in the graduate faculty of the New School, and delivered various public lectures there on subjects ranging from philosophy, art, and depth psychology to the effect of the space age or the nuclear bomb on Christian theology. While his association with the

New School was less intense than his link with Columbia, he always cultivated his contacts there, especially since they gave him
an opportunity to continue his friendship with men like Heimann,
Löwe, Riezler, and others who were all members of the faculty.
Yet he said from the very first month of his life in America that he
was glad fate had brought him to an established institution of
learning rather than to a school he regarded as new and without
roots.

Union, the "established institution," Tillich considered at the
beginning primarily as a shelter, where he was generously made to
participate in the life of the community.[48] He was at first a phenomenon sought after and observed with interest by students and
faculty alike. The community itself was small—sometimes around
250, never in those days exceeding 300. It became considerably
larger only after World War II. In 1933 Henry Coffin and other
members of the faculty were aware that historical accident had
brought into their midst a distinguished colleague for whom they
felt a serious responsibility, and for whose services they were paying a very small price. From 1933 to 1937 he was reappointed
from year to year as a visiting professor. His salary was subsidized
by two grants from the Rockefeller Foundation and the Emergency
Committee for Displaced Persons, which gave aid to hundreds of
learned refugees until they were fully employed. Coffin, whose
hope it gradually became to appoint Tillich to a chair as soon as
one became vacant, worked industriously with the Rockefeller
Foundation through Harry Emerson Fosdick, securing as much
money as he could and openly expressing his compassion for Tillich's restricted and insecure position. In fact, that income for
several years did not exceed $3,500 a year,[49] but with the apartment the seminary continued to supply, and in times of fairly
stable prices, Tillich and his family maintained a bearable standard
of living which he supplemented by means of lectures elsewhere.

However, his colleagues, except for those with private incomes,
were not much better off. Between 1931 and 1939, for example,
they were forced to take a cut of 10 percent in salary on at least
two occasions, as was indeed true of many professors in those

years. Most of them, like Tillich, did not succeed in earning ade-quate—or in some cases even large—salaries until after the end of World War II.

If it was not possible for Tillich to live as well as he had in Germany, it was also not easy for him to adjust to the new com-munity in which he had found immediate shelter. He did so in a quiet way, never imposing himself, never dominating, always co-operating, but finding everything considerably more difficult than he publicly admitted.[50] He had come to this country as a con-firmed individualist, estranged from the ecclesiastical and theolog-ical world of his youth by years of service in various university settings where he had come and gone when, where, and with whom he pleased.[51] From this open yet isolated existence, fate had brought him to a small community where it was almost impossible to do anything unobserved, and where the atmosphere was some-times that of the "strangling fellowship" celebrated in student oral tradition. This characteristic fact of seminary life was something to which Tillich's wife, eager to retain her freedom of action and little interested in the religious aspects of the community, was unable to adjust completely. She preferred to seek her friendships outside. Tillich, who was naturally gregarious and greatly enjoyed encoun-ters with his students, felt not so much stifled as anxious at being constantly observed. He never got over the feeling of being watched or—so to speak—listened for, even long after his retire-ment. A year before his death he warned friends about to be married, "Don't hold hands when you walk through the quad-rangle—you never know who is standing behind the curtains!"[52]

The very attentiveness that would be natural toward a spectacu-larly vivid and charismatic figure, and toward anyone whose speech was hard to understand and sometimes funny, might well become rather haunting. To avoid being understood by eavesdrop-pers, largely a figment of his imagination, he spoke German when-ever he could, especially on the phone, an instrument he consid-ered his mortal enemy and through which he found it quite difficult to communicate. His irrational feeling that American society was made up of rigid moralists—that one had to be exceedingly careful about what one did, said, and wrote—was never alleviated, despite the fact that he met countless individuals whose behavior contradicted his prejudice.

Members of the seminary community were quick to sense Tillich's preference for his own friends, most of whom were emigrés and all intellectual. He enjoyed the European soirée of the style to which he had become accustomed in Frankfort, and was generally ill at ease at formal gatherings, which he felt tended to be somewhat stuffy. He also disliked the separation of the sexes. He was immediately included in Ruth Nanda Anshen's salon in New York and eventually rejoined the Oppenheim salon when it was revived in Princeton. A student of Whitehead's, a writer and philosopher, Mrs. Anshen was a slender, striking woman, always elegantly dressed, with an exotic vocabulary and an uncanny facility for conversation with men and women from many fields of intellectual endeavor, whom she generously entertained in her Manhattan town house throughout many years. Eventually she launched several series of books by distinguished thinkers, many of whom became her friends. She and her scientist husband, Ralph Brodsky, were exceedingly close to the Tillichs (she once described their relationship "as one family"), whom they provided with clothes and other necessities at the beginning of their life in America. The Brodskys, moreover, brought Tillich himself into contact with many interesting people outside the seminary circle, and showered him with a devotion he returned.[53]

Once in the late 1930s the Tillichs tried to introduce a party in the German style to the seminary community, and to their great disappointment it was a failure. They invited lawyers, poets, psychoanalysts, musicians, aristocrats, emigrés, philosophers, and theologians, seating them in mixed groups next to one another at little tables arranged on the roof of the seminary.[54] Tillich introduced each guest with a brief description of him or her. He meant to be amusing, but was in fact esoteric and strangely awkward. The guests did not relate easily to one another and a stiff formality prevailed—precisely the atmosphere the Tillichs had wanted to avoid. After this failure they never again tried to duplicate or transfer the European experience.

While Tillich's social relations to his colleagues, with few exceptions, were friendly but muted and formal (he did what was expected without sacrificing his independence), his professional ties were a continuing source of joy and satisfaction to him. In all his years at the seminary he had few if any disagreeable experiences,[55] largely because his own pacific tendency did not permit even sharp differences of opinion between himself and more "orthodox" colleagues to develop into personal friction. When men like James Muilenburg and others criticized his ideas severely as being too Greek and possibly un-Christian, Tillich became concerned at possibly being misunderstood but never retaliated in a fierce or angry way. Niebuhr's repeated attempts to set up Tillich's thought only in order to pounce upon it and knock it over engaged them in a lifetime of jovial exchange, innocent of ill feeling even after they became conscious of the great distance between their points of view. For many years the voice of Tillich's younger colleague and personal friend, David E. Roberts, who understood his thought from the inside and interpreted it to others with consummate clarity and skill, sustained him, especially in the 1950s when existentialism was being attacked by men like Henry Van Dusen as destructive, misleading, and dangerous for student morale (the suicide of a sensitive student was what he had in mind) and the Christian faith.

Van Dusen, known as "Pit" to his friends, succeeded Henry Sloane Coffin as president of Union in 1945. A Main Line Philadelphian and friend of John D. Rockefeller III, he had sensed ever since his undergraduate days at Princeton his destiny in this position and had for years combined being Coffin's "crown prince" with leadership in the ecumenical movement, into which he had been thrust by his teacher William Adams Brown. A tall man with large, handsome features, Van Dusen and his wife Betty, the former Elizabeth Bartholomew of the Scottish map-making family, were gracious and generous people who entertained with great flair. Tillich had a special fondness for Betty Van Dusen, who painted fine portraits of professors and their children, was a devotee of Gilbert and Sullivan, a competent actress, and a lively director of the annual Christmas skit. Her critical and enterprising spirit convinced him that she was unlike some of the stuffy, bourgeois ladies of the faculty to whom he did not respond favorably. For Van Dusen, to whom he became indebted for many a favor, Tillich had great respect tinged with awe. Their relations were friendly though not close. But when Van Dusen criticized existentialism, Tillich took it personally.

For the most part, Tillich felt surrounded by an atmosphere of essential harmony. He only "failed" to cooperate with the seminary community in so far as he was unable (or unwilling) to grasp the intricacies of administration, whether in the registrar's office or in the committee room.[56] In faculty discussions he was reticent about expressing his opinion, whether on curriculum changes or faculty promotions, and did so only when urged. His colleagues, aware of his puzzlement in the face of such tasks did not press them upon him, referring them instead to others more willing and able. To them Tillich sent students whose questions he was unable to answer, to them he forwarded the books he felt unable to review; indeed, to them Tillich owed a great debt of time. Seventeen years after his arrival in America, Tillich praised even the more restrictive elements in seminary existence which he could not escape, as a necessary discipline and a corrective to the extreme individualism of his earlier academic career. By then he realized that Union had given him an invaluable introduction not only to the American way of life but also to American methods of study.[57]

The one place where Tillich felt instinctively at home was the classroom. One of his earliest American students once said that if Tillich were to languish in bed with a high fever, one had only to remind him of his students and he would miraculously revive.[58] His earliest students, occasionally joined by Coffin, Niebuhr, and other interested faculty members, came more to observe than to learn from the stocky, square German professor, his friendly eyes peering at them through horn-rimmed glasses. Tillich's custom of reading from a prepared manuscript had not changed since his days as a *Privatdozent* in Berlin. His voice was heavy, his patience monumental, his manner authoritative yet mild. He rarely struck the pose of the unapproachable German professor, although he was capable of doing so, particularly as his fame grew. His listeners however had to strain their attention in order to understand him; his thought as well as his speech were utterly foreign to them. Once a student complained that he could not understand Tillich's English lectures because his theology was so abstract, whereupon a classmate reassured him, "That's all right, he can't be understood in German either."[59] Two other early students, Albert T. Mollegen and Clifford Stanley, who later became skilled interpreters of his ideas, were at first so baffled by what Tillich was saying that after each class they ran across the street to a small café, where over a cup of coffee each deciphered for the other what—if anything—he had understood. Mollegen, recalling their efforts many years later, said, "Oh, it was the blind leading the blind!"[60]

These were not the last Union students forced to wrestle to uncover the meaning of Tillichian terms. Carefully selected from colleges all over the United States and Canada, Union students had uneven educational backgrounds. Many were hindered by inadequate training in languages and history: few had studied Greek, Latin, or Hebrew. Until 1945, when the curriculum expanded to include many foreign students as well as an increasingly large group of candidates for master's or doctoral degrees, most of them were preparing for the Christian ministry and in pursuit of practical training in biblical studies and homiletics. Those interested in theology at all were thinking in terms of the social gospel and social ethics. Tillich soon realized that the American theological enterprise was the reverse of what it had been in Germany: formerly queen of the sciences, theology had become the handmaiden of social ethics.[61]

No one symbolized more perfectly the spirit of the times than Reinhold Niebuhr. Speaking eloquently, while moving like a whirling dervish—foe of Henry Ford and exploitative capitalism, friend of labor, advocate of moderate socialism, sometimes candidate on the Socialist ticket—he was in the ascendancy. Tall, blonde, with bright blue eyes, when he spoke from lectern or pulpit he resembled an eagle ready to swoop down on his audience. Niebuhr was in fact in the process of transforming the American theological map from overoptimistic progressivism and liberal pacifism (whose adherents thoroughly disliked him) to a "radical," i.e., realistic, interpretation of the human situation, its deficiencies, and its conflicts. Keenly aware of man's pride, pretentiousness, and self-righteousness, he combined a hopeful outlook with realistic action, accepting the fact that earthly justice is always partial and each practical resolution of human conflict always the result of compromise. Thoroughly biblical and American (he was the son of a German-born Midwestern preacher), Niebuhr fired off lectures and sermons without note in hand, his face contorted, his body in perpetual motion. His emphasis on corporate ethics, Christian action, and social justice as well as his leadership of a group called Fellowship of Socialist Christians and editorship of its journal, *Radical Religion*, were all perfectly matched to the temper of the times.[62] Throughout his career, Niebuhr and his beautiful wife Ursula (a biblical theologian who presided over the religion department at Barnard College for many years) frequently opened their home to students and intellectual discussion groups, which often included such diverse and creative personalities as W. H. Auden, Lionel and Diana Trilling, and Hubert H. Humphrey.

Tillich represented a fascinating contrast to Niebuhr; the quiet, scholarly professor who pondered the ideas that lay behind human action, who constructed and elaborated theory and sought to formulate ultimate truth, seemed almost antithetical to the new world. Eager, as always, to demonstrate the relevance of his speculations, he proceeded to introduce bit by bit into the Union classroom esoteric German idealist and Greek philosophies, depth psychology, and existentialism. The students responded by returning to hear him in increasing and admiring numbers. Whether he lectured on the image of man or the history of the philosophy of religion; whether he was presenting "Church History from the

Reformation to Modern Times," a required course he gave in con-
junction with the church historian John T. McNeill, or leading his
seminars on Luther or Calvin, or developing his own systematic
theology, the story was always the same. He skillfully wove his way
in and out of theological or philosophical spheres, preparing each
lecture with great care and allowing time for discussion and questions after class. McNeill, incidentally, was an impeccable scholar
who emphasized historical *fact*. He once quipped that his part of
their joint course was "inevitable," while Tillich's, which emphasized the *meaning* of historical events, was "irresistible."

Students of the thirties, forties, and fifties reacted to Tillich in a
characteristically uniform way: they were captivated by his learning, mesmerized by his thorough analysis of ideas and movements,
and flattered by his willingness to answer their questions. They
were impressed by his interest in everything from dance to depth
psychology and felt supported in their own quest for life's meaning
by his frank admission that doubt was a reality even for him. What
attracted them more than anything else was Tillich's great talent
for making ancient or contemporary movements, whether in art,
politics, or science, relevant to their own situation. Finally, like
others before and after them, most were drawn—a few repelled—
by his extraordinary "power of being."

Students at Union and later at Harvard and Chicago, as well as
the larger audience Tillich eventually won for himself, were
stunned by the apparent originality of Tillich's thought.[63] Those
few who pursued their studies to deeper levels came to realize that
he himself had not created many of the terms he used, but had
borrowed them from other thinkers and by subtle transformation
made them his own. They also learned that the assumptions of
such men as Plato, Aristotle, Plotinus, and Augustine, in whose
world Tillich lived, were in fact the foundation stones of the the-
ories of value they accepted without question—of values, indeed,
which were often the consequence of ideas originating in Greek
times. The words and concepts Tillich sought to convey therefore
sometimes awakened an inner response even in the uninformed. At
a time, in short, when liberal theology and the social gospel domi-

nated the American theological scene, Tillich's erudition and synthesizing view of idealism and existentialism provided a certain depth of dimension to the prevailing theological mood.

Tillich was dismayed by the students' lack of training in philosophy and metaphysics, but he "loved them from the first day" for their openness to him and his ideas, their informal demeanor, as well as for their serious purpose.[64] Among the large number who heard him speak over the years not all returned his love, but most paused long enough to give attention to one who came to be regarded by a man no less than Reinhold Niebuhr as "a giant among us."[65] Some were instinctively inimical to Tillich's thought and person: those, for example, who interpreted the Bible too literally felt threatened by his notion that Christ was a symbol and that his power remained undiminished even if it should turn out that Jesus of Nazareth never existed. Or they were made anxious by his criticism of their belief in progress, so characteristic of the easy optimism of American Christianity, which he rejected by emphasizing the reality of evil powers and demonic structures in the world and in man.

Parallel to this reaction, Tillich's popularity among students, at first slight, became greater as the years passed. Yet only a small nucleus of his admirers ever came close to him, and none became his "disciples" in the sense of taking up any original part of his thought—for example, "the method of correlation"—and developing it further. It is a curious fact that, despite his great popularity, Tillich trained relatively few doctoral candidates himself, either at the beginning, when he was still unfamiliar with the American way of preparing such candidates, or at the end, when lack of time became an even more stringent reality for him. In the halls of Union, toward the end of his tenure, could be heard a not infrequent complaint that he was too busy to give students private interviews. Some, admitted to his poorly lit and crowded office, felt uncomfortable in his presence and were suddenly unable to express themselves, their minds gone blank in the face of the seemingly uninterested, preoccupied man who sat opposite, playing with a paper clip or shaving a wax candle with his finger nail. Those who made a definite impression upon him, whether because of their interesting faces or because they had demonstrated unusual skill in understanding, felt more welcome. There were also the rare few who came to him totally baffled by his work and to whom he patiently explained his meaning, thus winning them as friends and devotees. The chasm between those who came close to him and those who did not was revealed in the surprise and confusion of the former at discovering that the Tillich they knew had two quite different faces. Moreover, he remained distant from the mass of students. Unlike Niebuhr or other faculty members, he never joined them around the refectory tables at noon. Instead he repaired to his apartment and consumed the main meal faithfully prepared by his wife, and as the days grew more crowded and the nights longer, took a brief nap.

Tillich's introduction of philosophical theology into the Union curriculum paved the way for others to join him, resulting in a sort of department within the theological field. The first was his friend Richard Kroner, who had remained in Germany voluntarily despite Hitler, a fact which temporarily angered Tillich and nearly ended their friendship.[66] Kroner was reluctant to leave his new house in Kiel and did not feel endangered until a friend, finance minister in the Nazi government, warned him that also those of partial Jewish descent, of whom he was one, did not have long to live. It was already 1939 before Kroner finally emigrated. In the spring of 1940 he was offered a position in Montreal, Canada, but he could not assume it because, though a refugee, he was a German citizen and enemy alien and Canadian public opinion was unfavorable. He soon discovered that the best positions in the American academic world had already been taken by those who had preceded him; his expectation of an immediate professorship was disappointed, a fact it took him years to accept.

Kroner, who had supported Tillich's appointment to Dresden when the latter's heretical views endangered his career as a theologian, was now helped in turn by Tillich, who recommended him to Union. Kroner was always genuinely grateful to Tillich, but a certain distance grew between the two men in the years that followed.

Kroner's progress up the academic ladder was even slower than Tillich's; for years he was an adjunct professor. Because of his specialization in the narrow field of German idealism as well as his inability to adjust to the American scene (in many ways, he remained the prototype of the German professor), he never found a wide audience or even national recognition. Within the seminary, where his advocacy of the "primacy of faith" appealed to men like Henry Coffin,[67] and where he was regarded with great respect, his classes were filled primarily with graduate students. For several years he gave a seminar on Greek and Christian tragedy in association with David Roberts. In one session it came about that one took the side of Aeschylus and the other of Job in a dialogue lasting an hour and followed by a question period for a second hour. The students were fascinated by their intellectual pyrotechnics.

Roberts, the third member of the philosophical wing of the department, was a young, brilliant, articulate theologian with round, smiling features and versatile talents and interests. He was a superb teacher, an effective and popular preacher, and a skillful writer. His book *Psychotherapy and a Christian View of Man* was a pioneering effort which many scholars still accept as the finest introduction to the field in print. His course on the history of philosophy helped prepare interested students for the more rarefied air they were to breathe in Tillich's or Kroner's classes. Roberts and his wife, the sensitive and artistic Eleanor, or "Elli," became Tillich's personal friends. Tillich felt at home with the young scholar and his death in 1955 not only cut off Roberts' promising theological career but deprived Tillich of a staunch ally on the Union faculty and in the department itself.

In 1935, when Tillich was still little known in this country, he was eager to introduce himself in writing. His first attempt badly misfired. His search for identity in a new world prompted him to set down an autobiography (his first of three, as it turned out)—a literary form which came naturally to him. In a concise, poetic, and self-conscious essay entitled *On the Boundary*,[68] he described the origins and development of his thought. Here, in the hope of making himself better understood, he revealed his complex nature in all its ramifications. In this book as in few others he wrote, Tillich stands before the reader as he was, without pretense, his mask discarded. The more one knows about him, the more honest the self-revelation appears. From his critical old friend of Dresden days, Fedor Stepun, he received a note of high praise. "I read your little autobiography with particular interest; it is perhaps the best of your work so far as I know it. Perhaps I feel this because the unity of narration, thought, and self-knowledge comes closest to my own mode of writing. In some way or other we are all egocentric."[69]

In America the reaction was generally cool. The not fully adequate translation of the autobiography and the accompanying essays and the murky complexities of the concepts, particularly in the essay entitled "An Interpretation of History," created more confusion than clarity about Tillich's ideas and their relevance. The book sold poorly.

Tillich's father wrote on 9 September 1936, "I am busy reading your book *On the Boundary*, and I have already begun to dictate my reactions to it, but am making slow progress."[70] Johannes Tillich was suffering from depression and old age, teaching himself Italian to make the time pass, wondering aloud whether he had any new thoughts to think. At Christmas there was one last letter, then on 30 July 1937, at the age of eighty, he died. For three weeks thereafter Tillich dreamed that he was writing his father, as was his wont, about everything that was happening to him, sharing his thoughts and experience with one who had never ceased to observe his development with interest, admiration, and concern.[71] To his sister Elisabeth, in a rare expression of a universal human feeling or superstition, Tillich wrote, "I feel as though a roof had been removed from over my head."[72] It was his way of saying that his father no longer existed as his own protection from death. Johannes Tillich's critique of *On the Boundary*, if ever completed, is lost to us.

Henry Coffin was deeply impressed by the autobiography. It confirmed his opinion that Tillich was one of the ablest minds on the faculty, but he remained uncertain, again largely because of Tillich's Germanic and Greek emphases, whether his appointment to a permanent post on the faculty would be appropriate. Moreover, the board of directors, in whose hands the power of appointment and promotion lay, did not know what to make of Tillich's thought; accordingly they continued to postpone definitive action.

By 1936 a group of enthusiastic Union students became uneasy at the fact that, despite Tillich's increasing command of the language and his growing popularity, he had still not been given tenure.[73] Under the leadership of the articulate Holmes Hartshorne they drew up a petition, in March and again in November, praising his teaching and scholarship and urging the president to recommend Tillich to the board. Each petition bore approximately seventy-five signatures, and while they seem to have played some role in what followed, they were not in themselves unusual at a time when students were vocal about matters that moved them.

At the same time, Coffin suggested that Tillich explain his thoughts in relation to the theological curriculum then in force. Tillich replied, "I am a triboro bridge: systematics, philosophy, history."[74] It was then that Coffin hit upon the notion of creating a chair in philosophical theology (the first of its kind in this country) and appointing Tillich to this position. Tillich responded with enthusiasm, for his work in theology and philosophy, which had lain apart in Germany, was now recognized as a unity. Coffin's own ambivalences were never entirely resolved. When Tillich's first book of sermons, *The Shaking of the Foundations*, appeared (1948), Coffin expressed great appreciation of its Christian quality, only to fall into a state of outrage on reading the first volume of his *Systematic Theology* (1951), which confirmed his darkest suspicions that Tillich was not a Christian thinker but a Greek mystic who held the heretical views of Plotinian dualism, Hegel, and Schelling.[75]

Whether the student petitions, or Tillich's oral defense, or the availability of funds, or rumors that he had received an offer from another divinity school[76] finally turned the tide in his favor remains mysterious, but his promotion soon followed. On 9 March

1937, Tillich was informed that he had been appointed Associate Professor of Philosophical Theology for a period of three years at a salary of $4,500, and with the promise of a larger apartment.[77] His elevation to the status of full professor was postponed for another three years because of the protest of some conservative members of the faculty who remained unconvinced that his ideas were sufficiently biblical. Meanwhile, the students sent a third "petition" dated 4 May 1937 to Coffin and the board of directors. Coffin wrote about it to John Whyte of the Emergency Committee for Displaced Persons: "Students petition on many subjects but not often do they send out petitions of Thanksgiving."[78]

An Ear to the Ground

When Tillich arrived in this country, he was in most ways not very different from other intellectuals of the Weimar Republic. His views about Expressionism or politics, for example, were widely held. His originality was not so much in his point of view as in his ability to absorb forward-looking and radical trends of the contemporary mind, only to reformulate what he had assimilated in his distinctive systematic way. This reformulation made him sound more original than in fact he was; moreover, his ability to absorb enabled him to sense more quickly than most what was going on around him.

Through discussions with his students at Union he learned about the American mind and its uniqueness: namely, that it joined action to thought, tested theory by means of assessing its practical consequences, and regarded the Christian church as a social agent. These things naturally struck him at once, and it was not long before he began to alter his supposition that he had nothing new to learn in America. Since he saw his theologian's task as one of interpreting the ancient gospel to the mind of contemporary man, he felt compelled, once he realized that there was a unique American mind, to familiarize himself with it. He therefore began as soon as he could to sniff out the American scene, in three ways:

through travel, in discussion with students, and by intensive dialogue with colleagues in the Philosophy Club and the Theological
Discussion Group.[79]

Tillich's earliest travels were arranged in connection with invitations to lecture at colleges and universities, planned by the untiring
and forceful efforts of three contemporaries, all of whom were
sympathetic to him personally and interested in his thought while
not fully sharing it. These were Horace Friess, Reinhold Niebuhr,
and Wilhelm Pauck. Their influential, well-established positions in
the fields of philosophy, theology, history, and ethics put them in
touch with a network of connections which they opened up to him
from the beginning, largely out of simple spontaneous generosity.

Friess, in his position as chairman of the American Philosophical Society, was instrumental in setting engagements for Tillich in
philosophical circles. His polite and retiring manner smoothed
over many rough places. The two men never became close personal friends; in fact, after the visit to Martha's Vineyard in 1934
they saw one another infrequently on the social level, but their
relations were marked by mutual warmth and respect.[80]

Niebuhr—his colleague and "savior," as Tillich liked to call
him—was involved with countless ecclesiastical, social, and political groups all over the country and thus incessantly traveling,
preaching, and lecturing, and in an unusually good position to
recommend Tillich to others. Over the years he obtained lectureships for him, invited him to write book reviews, and arranged to
have his articles printed in religious journals; he also included him
in social action discussion groups such as the Frontier Fellowship,
making Tillich feel at once a part of what he liked to call the
American version of his "religious-socialist movement." Niebuhr
unfailingly encouraged Tillich in the early years when he was often
depressed by his professional situation, and generously joined others in heaping praise upon him when he became well known. Especially in the 1930s the two men shared a warm camaraderie,
walking on Riverside Drive, discussing their sharply different
points of view.[81] Niebuhr always remained suspicious of Tillich's
use of Greek philosophy and ontology, and he was somewhat

amused by his romantic attitude toward nature, indeed, regarded it as excessive, though Niebuhr was less indifferent to that aspect of the world around him than many have maintained. Tillich's fame came upon him at just the time when Niebuhr's career, which had exploded like a meteor across America, was slowed in 1952 by a crippling stroke; in the ensuing years the two men saw less of each other. At their last meeting before Tillich's death[82] they talked of eternity and what it meant, Niebuhr rejecting his friend's views as he had expressed them in the third volume of his *Systematic Theology*. Tillich never forgot the debt he owed Niebuhr for his support and encouragement.[83]

In the winter of 1934, Wilhelm Pauck, professor of historical theology at the Divinity School of the University of Chicago, paid a call on Tillich to welcome him to these shores. Pauck had been a student of Harnack's, and most particularly Holl's, at the University of Berlin when Tillich was a *Privatdozent* there, prompting Tillich in later years to refer to him erroneously as "my first student." Pauck had in fact attended only one of Tillich's courses, and the two had not met personally before 1934. By then Pauck, who came to America in 1925 as a foreign exchange student, had already set out on a career of his own. His "robust humanity," a phrase coined by his good friend Niebuhr,[84] and his ironic wit (Tillich called him "a rational Berliner") and practical sense were qualities with which Tillich empathized from the start. Their common heritage, including membership in the Wingolf fraternity, fostered an intimate friendship between two strikingly different men.

Unlike Tillich, Pauck had adjusted easily to the American way of life, rapidly achieving facility with spoken and written English.[85] Also unlike Tillich, Pauck read widely in American theology and philosophy, and sought out an understanding of American churches through sustained contacts with a variety of people. In short, he understood America to a considerable extent from the inside at a time when Tillich did not. Thus he became, as Niebuhr graciously put it, "Tillich's guide to America."[86] Undoubtedly it was his appreciation of their differences which led Tillich to make the generous statement that he never made an important decision without talking to Pauck first.[87] In later years Pauck's criticism of his metaphysics sometimes made Tillich uncomfortable, especially Pauck's understanding of the sources on which his ideas rested, but he was able to relax with Pauck, even to the extent of wondering aloud in his presence about the validity of his own achievements and the integrity of his way of life, at the same time comforted by their mutual understanding, loyalty, and laughter.

Tillich's first long journey in America, took place in the spring of 1935.[88] By 1940 he had seen the entire country. In the interim he had explored Chicago and the Midwest, the Southeast, New England, and finally the west coast, traveling as far northwest as Lake Louise in Canada. He traveled by bus, train, and car, whenever possible avoiding planes even when jet flights became popular. He climbed mountains and descended into canyons, he bathed in lakes and oceans, tramped through swamps, investigated villages, towns, and cities; he came to know the sights, sounds, and smells of a vast country, discovering at every turn something to contrast and compare with Europe. In his solitary peregrinations he came in contact with people in almost every walk of life; he asked questions, and he listened. In the thirties and forties, his travels were leisurely—he stayed in simple places, content with boardinghouse food, paying a dollar or two a night for a room; in later years, he was drawn to luxurious hotels in palatial surroundings, content to enjoy the comforts lavishly provided by the system he continued to criticize, namely, American capitalism.

Tillich's first sight of New England reminded him of the German landscape, with its gently rolling hills and density of small houses. In Chicago, even in sub-zero weather, he walked from the university campus to Lake Michigan, where he watched the forces of nature at work: he saw the abyss, sensed the depths, felt the dynamic forms in the pounding of the surf on the beach which made it seem like an ocean.[89] His other favorite haunt there was the Chicago Art Institute, to which he often returned with pleasure. The ugliness of Detroit was overshadowed by the fascination of the Ford factory; it seemed to him sheer magic to see a car put together so swiftly, but he later argued that factory workers were "thingified," his word for depersonalized, by their tedious labor. In March 1935 Tillich first experienced the South as a participant in a sociological field trip. In the company of Pauck and twenty-two professors and students of a social ethics seminar at the University of Chicago, he saw Lincoln's birthplace in Kentucky, the Mennonite settlements in Indiana, the cotton fields of Georgia and Alabama. He was fascinated by the faces of black people, noting that the mixture between blacks and whites produced the most interesting he had ever seen. In Tennessee the building of dams for the TVA project confirmed his belief that socialism would replace capitalism in America; while in Louisiana the group's hotel-room meeting with Huey Long, clad in green pyjamas, made him wonder whether an American dictatorship was imminent. In Alabama, Tillich insisted on stopping the car in which he was riding so as to sit by the water and watch the setting sun and the moonrise. Whereupon Pauck, always ready to tease, sang the popular ballad "Stars Fell on Alabama," a moment which for both remained unforgettable.[90]

After several days in New Orleans, which reminded Tillich of Montmartre and Marseilles, he left the seminar group and made his way by bus and train through Florida, the Carolinas, Washington, D.C., and on up to New York. The heat of St. Augustine reminded him of Sicily, and the palms and villas of Palm Beach overwhelmed him; the green Atlantic lured him barefoot through the town, only to reward him with the sting of a jellyfish. Washington impressed him as that rarest of things: a beautiful American city. By the time he reached New York he had seen twenty-five of the forty-eight states; America had become a reality for him. The history of the land and views of the landscape were now engraved on his mind and made everything more meaningful.

Yet it was not until 1938, when he reached the Far West, that he really fell in love with America. There people were more primitive, more vital, more friendly, more eager to speak to strangers than in the East. He was pleased that almost all the girls wore pants and even went dancing in them. In Estes Park, Colorado, where one early morning he walked all alone, he gained the false impression that no Americans walked. At noon he ate trout from a Rocky Mountain lake, at night watched the farmers with their sharply cut pioneer faces dancing in Estes Park. In Santa Fé he discovered the desert, was held spellbound by the most colorful sunset of his entire life. Shortly before his fifty-second birthday he descended on foot into the Grand Canyon, observing the great variety of vegetation and amused by those who rode horses or mules. By the time he had walked up again he felt dizzy, and soon discovered that he had undergone the greatest physical strain since the war, for which he paid dearly with an attack of lumbago that kept him in bed for several days in a friend's house in Berkeley.

After a conference in Carmel, which seemed to him as beautiful as the Riviera and ideal for retirement (an eventuality already very much on his mind), Tillich traveled from San Francisco to Lake Tahoe, Reno, and Mt. Shasta (which reminded him of Monte Rosa in the Italian Alps). Northern California and the West made him wish for Goethe's powers of description. He was so impressed by the variety and intensity of colors he had never seen before, reflected in mountains and lakes, as to be nearly beside himself.[91]

Two years later in 1940 accompanied by his family, he returned to California, spending several weeks near Carmel, where under the influence of the ocean he wrote his inaugural lecture as full professor, entitled "Philosophy and Theology." One evening, after a festive meal, he read the final version aloud to a group of friends who happened to be spending their vactions there, among them Ernst Kantorovicz, Kurt Riezler, and Wilhelm Pauck. Pauck was alone in not rejecting outright Tillich's thesis that the task of theology is "to ask for being as far as it gives us ultimate concern."

Throughout his life Tillich remained an indefatigable traveler, generally combining recreation with work. Many of his lectures were delivered and discussed at meetings held in resorts and retreats, old schools or castles, historic cloisters or churches. He never failed to explore the places he visited, and much of the mood and atmosphere of these locales entered into his thoughts, writings, and discussions—or, as he preferred to say, "debates."

It was natural for him to enjoy participating in conferences held in remote or unusual yet attractive places. The first such meeting he attended in America took place in June 1935 at Fletcher Farms in Proctorsville, Vermont.[92] It was attended by Harry Bone, Gardner Day, Reinhold Niebuhr, Clifford Stanley, Gregory Vlastos, Carl H. Voss, Henry Wieman, and others. Tillich was greatly agitated during the conference, first by what he understood to be a defense of dualism on the part of Wieman, maintaining—as Tillich erroneously thought—that good and evil were equally ultimate! This prompted him to call Wieman a "Parse" or Persian and sent him running for escape to the hills. But he also felt uneasy on this occasion because of the impending birth of his second child, and called his wife daily for reassurance. On 7 June a son was born, later the image of his father, who was named René Stefan. Reinhold Niebuhr baptized the infant a few weeks later in Lampman Chapel at the seminary.[93]

The high point of the Fletcher Farms debate was a discussion of the nature of God in which all the lecturers took part. Wieman, who then had an enthusiastic following, was convinced that Niebuhr and Tillich were "neosupranaturalists." He misunderstood Tillich's dialectical talk about the "immanence of the transcendent" and the irruption of eternity into time, and was baffled by Niebuhr's constant reference to biblical religion. Niebuhr in turn attacked Wieman sharply, rejecting his naturalism, while Wieman graciously listened and Tillich looked on. It was his first exposure to the style of American discussion groups, many of which he was to attend in the years that followed.

Tillich's relation with the Columbia University philosophy department ushered him, with unusual rapidity, into the Philosophy Club. The first meeting of this group, originally known as the Philosophy Club of New York City, took place on 7 February 1900 in the home of Felix Adler, its founder.[94] "My thought was," the latter declared, "in the selection to lay stress rather upon a common temper—earnestness and open-mindedness—than upon common opinions."[95] The great variety of the eminent minds that belonged to the club from the time of its founding shows how carefully Adler's intention was followed. Professors on the east coast, all the way from Brown University to Johns Hopkins, were elected to the society, which never exceeded twenty-five in number. When a member retired, moved away, or died, a new member was chosen to replace him. No one could volunteer to join; membership was by invitation, with the sole exception of Harvard University professors, who were automatically included.

In the earliest years of the society, men like Josiah Royce and William James, John Dewey and Bertrand Russell stand out on the roster; in later years Morris Cohen, Max Eastman, and Arthur Lovejoy; in Tillich's time, Horace Friess, James Gutmann, Carl Hempel, Sidney Hook, Paul O. Kristeller, Ernest Nagel, J. Robert Oppenheimer, John H. Randall, Jr., John E. Smith, Paul Weiss, and John Wild were among the luminaries who belonged. Only a handful of professors from Union Theological Seminary were elected to the society at any time, chosen on the premise that they had demonstrated philosophical learning and talent. William Adams Brown, Eugene Lyman, and A. C. McGiffert were among the earliest. Reinhold Niebuhr was elected late in his career, in April 1944, after the publication of *The Nature and Destiny of Man* finally convinced some club members that he was, after all, a philosopher as well as a theologian.

Over the years, these productive men in their varying fields of psychology, history, physics, or theology, met on the third Friday of every month between October and May to combine a rigorous exchange of ideas with excellent food, wine, and conversation. The setting, with its formality, open-mindedness, and ritual procedure was ideal for Paul Tillich. In his day (he was elected in the late 1930s or early 1940s, the precise date not being recorded in the minutes), the sessions took place at the Columbia University Faculty Club, gathering at precisely four in the afternoon. Between four-fifteen and quarter of five the members consumed tea and toast; there were always two kinds of toast, one with cinnamon, one plain, as there were always two kinds of jelly and also marmalade. During tea the business of the club was conducted by the host, who along with the writer of the paper for that meeting was a different person each month. Between quarter of five and quarter of seven the author, introduced by the host, read his paper aloud.

The host then, beginning at his left and ending at his right, called on each member to present comments. Each was restricted to two and a half to five minutes of comment. During this ritual, which no one was allowed to interrupt, the author of the paper listened and prepared his final response, which was not permitted to exceed fifteen minutes. The procedure was never altered in the slightest. By seven in the evening dinner, accompanied by sherry or wine and tobacco (Antonio and Cleopatra Princess cigars and two or three brands of cigarettes) was served. Conversation around the table was always lively: often between smaller groups, sometimes —but rarely—including all. By eight-thirty dinner was usually over and the members separated.

This exceedingly civilized society became Tillich's primary means of meeting American philosophers as well as his main source of American philosophical ideas, which despite the friendly encouragement of his colleagues he chose not to seek by reading the books in which they appeared, an avoidance for which he was repeatedly criticized. The club also became a forum for Tillich's own thought. Sometimes this enraged his listeners as in the case of Montague's negative reaction to a paper on "The Two Types of Philosophy of Religion"; sometimes it befuddled them, as in the case of G. E. Moore, who claimed he had not understood a single sentence of Tillich's paper on "Existentialist Philosophy";[96] yet sometimes, too, it delighted them, as in the case of his last lecture on art.

It took a little while, of course, for American philosophers to become acquainted with Tillich's philosophical posture. There were those who from the start had reservations about him, but their appreciation grew as they learned more of his position. Gutmann, himself a Schelling expert, Hofstadter, an aesthetician, and

Randall were his particular fans. Ernest Nagel, the logical positivist, chiefly interested in science, was highly respectful of Tillich but did not go along with what he had to say. Certain elements in his thought, especially those derived from German Romantic philosophy and from the Kantian theory of knowledge, seemed particularly alien to the Americans. As time passed, Tillich was increasingly encouraged to relate his special point of view to the American way of thinking in order to achieve a greater impact in this country.

Tillich's own response to the papers presented was as ritualistic and formal as the rules of the club required, and entirely in keeping with his own personality. In his criticisms of others' efforts he always tried first to express appreciation, no matter how deeply opposed he was to their position. He always thanked especially anyone, for example, who presented a paper on technical, logical, and methodological problems. His critical and constructive comments he phrased in his own terminology, speaking in an open and direct way that welled up from within, causing one member to observe that he was both childlike and venerable. He had great ability to penetrate to the essentials of a problem, even when it was foreign to him.[97]

Tillich's last paper, given on 17 October 1958, was entitled "Contemporary Visual Art and the Revelatory Character of Style"; it was delivered shortly after Reinhold Niebuhr's paper on "The Cold War and the Nuclear Dilemma." Tillich had brought along colored reproductions, so that the members could look at the pictures (which he placed on the wall around the room) while he was talking.

In 1962 he resigned from the club. He had rarely missed a meeting and was reluctant to abandon his membership, but because he had moved to Chicago for his final professional appointment, and frequent travels to the west coast and Europe also kept him away from New York, he felt compelled to do so, and was automatically made an emeritus member.

The Philosophy Club gave Tillich his introduction to American philosophical thought in all its variety and intensity, but his membership in the Theological Discussion Group set him down among the most active academic theologians of that generation.[98] Originally known as the "Discussion Group of the Younger Theological Thinkers," it came into being in 1931 under the auspices of John R. Mott, who as the leader of the International Missionary Council had observed the effectiveness of such groups in his work with the so-called Younger Churches in Asia. Among its members were Roland Bainton, Robert Calhoun, and H. Richard Niebuhr of Yale; John Bennett, then of the Presbyterian Seminary of Auburn, New York; Henry Van Dusen and Reinhold Niebuhr of Union; Douglas Steere of Haverford, George F. Thomas, then at Dartmouth; Angus Dun, then of Cambridge, Mass.; John Mackay, then a leader of Protestant missions in Latin America; Edwin E. Aubrey of Chicago, Francis P. Miller of Virginia, Georgia Harkness, then of Elmira College, and Virginia Corwin of Smith—all drawing together for the purpose of "full, frank, and leisurely discussion of ideas."[99] For some years the group, whose membership changed very little, met at Yale; later they convened at the College of Preachers, near the National Cathedral in Washington, D.C. Originally, Henry Van Dusen and then John Bennett were its secretaries, and when annual elections became too cumbersome Wilhelm Pauck became permanent chairman and secretary, an office he held until the group disbanded in 1965, and which earned him the name of "Papa Pauck."

In the course of time some members found it necessary to withdraw, when they moved to distant places or accepted posts with responsibilities that prevented them from preparing papers or attending the discussions regularly. Later some died and others became emeriti. Vacancies were filled by new elections, the general rule being that membership should never exceed thirty. When they first organized, most members were still relatively young and at the beginning of their careers. As the years went on, most of them advanced to positions of influence and leadership, representing a variety of philosophical, theological, and professional points of view. They produced a great number of books and articles and provided leadership to the various churches and denominations, to the several branches and councils of the Ecumenical Movement, to such educational enterprises as the Hazen Foundation, and—of course—to their own schools and faculties. Gradually the group came to be recognized as representing Protestant theological work in America, and on this account many of its members came in touch with the leading theologians of other countries. From time to time, when such leaders came to the United States as visitors, they were invited to attend the sessions of the discussion group in order to put them in direct touch with American theological thought, but also in order to induce them to expose their ideas to critical debate. Thus Archbishop William Temple was present at some meetings, and before him Dr. J. H. Oldham, secretary and one of the chief organizers of the celebrated International Missionary Conference at Edinburgh in 1910. The latter, in addition to other high ecumenical responsibilities, was also chairman of the Research Commission of the Universal Christian Council for Life and Work, in which capacity he organized the famous Oxford Conference on Life and Work in 1937. His influential colleague William Paton also came on one occasion; and Emil Brunner, at the height of his influence as foremost spokesman, next to Karl Barth, of dialectical theology (as neo-orthodoxy was then called), defended his teaching before the group. Throughout the years there were many such visitors.

The meetings of the theologians were as unceremonious as those of the philosophical society were ritualistic. On the first weekend of every November and March the members came together, at first rather tense and ill at ease with each other, soon becoming cordial, sharing all meals and debating in a lively, open, and stimulating way. At each meeting three papers, distributed in advance and dealing with aspects of a single theme (e.g., sin or salvation, and so forth) were analyzed and evaluated by a critic, appointed beforehand, and then discussed generally. The papers were debated on Friday evening and Saturday morning and afternoon. Sunday morning was reserved for a summary report and discussion. In later years the participants, more than well acquainted, spoke from notes in an informal way.

Tillich was elected to this society as early as 1934. American theologians were eager to have him share with them ideas which at first baffled and later fascinated them. Because of his linguistic ineptitude, Tillich formed the habit, maintained throughout his membership, of being silent until everyone else had exhausted himself. In the freewheeling debates the Niebuhrs and Pauck were generally in agreement, while Henry Van Dusen and John Bennett remained reservedly suspicious of the "German" mind. Tillich, the most comprehensive and subtle, yet also irenic mind of the group, always felt for a synthesis of what everyone else had said before him. His remarks were often long, but always reflected his own systematic philosophical and theological work.

In spite of Tillich's eagerness to learn what American theologians were thinking, and his faithful attendance in this group, his own mind, already fixed by the time he came to this country, was not greatly transformed or altered by what he learned. He was not really interested in reading American theological works, except for those written by friends or thinkers in his own field, and neither Pauck, Van Dusen, or others were able to persuade him to familiarize himself with the main trends of American thought or with individual modern thinkers such as Whitehead or Hocking or Dewey. Tillich simply demurred, partly because of the sheer toil of reading in the English language, and partly because he did not want his own ideas disturbed. What he did learn, through dialogue with his colleagues, he persistently translated into his own terminology, to the amazement, amusement, and sometimes frustration of others. He thus frequently reconciled their conflicting opinions.

The members of the group had of course originally been chosen precisely because they represented a variety of points of view. Their discussions canvassed the whole range of problems of the Christian faith, and they began at a time when naturalistic humanism was giving way to skepticism, relativism, and uncertainty. Then, as the catastrophic conflict in Europe erupted, they moved more and more toward a consensus as to the character of the crisis that held contemporary culture in its grip. They came to agree that the only solution was in fact the Christian faith, and formed several groups within the larger one to spell out all the implications of that agreement. These concepts were published in 1945 in *The Christian Answer;*[100] the leading chapter by Tillich entitled "The World Situation" contains his familiar ideas, but because it was thoroughly edited by Van Dusen it appears in barely recognizable Tillichian style.

When Tillich presented his first paper to the Theological Discussion Group, examining the world situation in his inimitable way, it so happened that J. H. Oldham was present. He and Tillich took to one another at once: Oldham was impressed by Tillich's analysis as well as by his concern for the future of Protestantism. Tillich quickly warmed to Oldham's enthusiasm for his point of view and expanded in his presence. Within a short time Oldham, in his capacity as organizer of the 1937 Oxford Ecumenical Conference and in search of consultants, invited Tillich to become a member of his preparatory commission, and Tillich, eager to be identified with the ecumenical movement, accepted at once. The preparatory work that had to be done in London and Geneva gave him his first opportunity to return to Europe since his emigration. For nearly five months, in the spring and summer of 1936, he undertook a sentimental journey through England, France, Holland, Italy, Belgium, and Switzerland, combining in his tireless way serious discussion with old German friends now scattered throughout the Continent, intense reunions with members of his family, and the visual and gustatory joys of old haunts. His wanderings sometimes brought him painfully close to Germany itself, but he remained safely outside.[101]

Hitler, with his growing military might, had just invaded and reclaimed the Rhineland from France, finding no resistance from the war-weary French and English, a pattern which, once established, repeated itself in the Sudetenland, Poland, and finally Holland and Belgium again, inevitably producing the deadly consequences of World War II. While in England working with Oldham and others on the commission, Tillich gave a lecture to British churchmen on mass disintegration and meaninglessness in which he analyzed the primary causes of National Socialism. He urged

England to abandon its pacifist posture and defend itself against the Nazi threat before it was too late,[102] and expressed his concern about the fact that in the prevailing climate of political regimes the Protestant churches remained ineffective.

In London he also discussed his idea of a religious association or league in which men of a common mind would seek to preserve what the churches, because they had become petrified in institutionalism, could no longer keep vital. The fellowship he had in mind (he used the term *Bund*) was much broader in conception than what preoccupied him earlier that summer, when he thought of it primarily in terms of a reaction to the Nazi tyranny. He felt that such an active alliance, which he discussed not only with Oldham[103] but with many others, could inject into Protestantism a spirit of social justice, a dynamic religious socialism which could not be realized by the churches in their mood of defense and retreat.

The idea ran like a motif through Tillich's personal encounters during his travels. He discussed it with Karl Mennicke, the most active member of the first religious-socialist group in Berlin, who had sought refuge in Amsterdam, where Tillich visited him. He continued the conversations with Wilhelm Stählin in Enschede, a Dutch border town where the two met.[104] Stählin, who had introduced Tillich to the Berneuchener movement, was now a professor at the University of Münster. He expressed his wish to retire; he felt helpless in the German church situation, unable to side with "German Christians," the Nazi sympathizers among churchmen, or with their opponents, the "confessing churches." He felt that the former threatened Christianity with destruction, while the latter were about to retreat into the "catacombs" of an outworn creedalism. His deepest wish was to become abbot of a Protestant monastery. It was obvious that he had long thought, like Tillich, of a religious association as a temporary means of preserving religious and spiritual power, to be brought forward and used at a safer time. The Berneuchener movement itself was such an "order" or "league," and its three hundred members had assumed personal responsibility for one another; Stählin, for example, had been assigned to be Frede Fritz's helpmate and confidant. His report on the growing doctrinal rigidity of the confessing church, which he secretly blamed on Barthian influence, shattered any illusions Tillich had as to its religious strength or power to unite all German Protestants against Hitler.

After a brief but friendly meeting with Barth himself in Basel,[105] Tillich sought refuge from the growing darkness around him by fleeing to Paris, drinking in the beauty of Cézanne's "mystical devotion to life" and visiting Negro nightclubs in the company of his friend Eckart von Sydow—in reunion also with Hugo Simon, the banker who had helped him in Berlin directly after the war. The idea of a new order reappeared when Kurt Riezler, also in Paris, admitted that he had on his part conceived of the idea of a religious association from the Greek cultural point of view, to bring together those who would carry on the humanistic tradition in order to save it.

Tillich's encounters with so many victims of the Nazi regime moved him, while in Geneva attending a seminar in a preliminary ecumenical conference, to give further expression to his anti-Nazi formulations in the face of German church figures.[106] Indeed, his presence in the same room with Hanns Lilje, leader of the Christian Student Federation in Germany, and Paul Althaus, the famous Lutheran theologian from Erlangen, seemed to Carl Stange, a stubbornly patriotic professor at Göttingen, a compromise for German Lutheranism.[107] Even Tillich's blissful reunion with members of his family who met him in Switzerland was overshadowed by the division of political opinion among them, prompting sharp clashes, disturbing his dreams. Moreover, his political views made Mrs. Froebe-Kaptein, president of the Eranos meetings which Tillich together with other specially invited philosophers, psychologists, and historians of religion attended in August near Ronco and Ascona in Switzerland, doubtful whether she should permit him to lecture.[108] Although the younger people in his audience responded affirmatively to what he had to say, he came away with the conviction that a sort of Jungian "unpolitical mysticism" was being practiced there.

In Ascona Tillich experienced the high point of his spiritual journey: his reunion with Hermann Schafft. The two fled from the ever present throng of people surrounding them to the top of Monte Bré. Early on the morning of Tillich's fiftieth birthday, a small orchestra assembled by Schafft played directly under his window the tune of an old Lutheran chorale in praise of the "golden sun" ("Die güldne Sonne, der Mensch hat nichts so eigen").[109] Tillich wept at the sound. The memory of his thirtieth birthday spent on the western battlefront, when at precisely the same hour of day the regimental band had played the folksong "Full Thirty Years Old Are You Now" ("Schier dreissig Jahre bist du alt") came floating back. It was as though a dam holding in all the emotions evoked by reunion with friends, conflict with family, and the sense of inevitable separation from home, now gave way, released by the sound of music. He found immediate comfort in the beauty of mountains, lake, and woodland, as well as through Schafft and other friends who surrounded him at breakfast with good cheer, song, and a plateful of fifty red candles. Many birthday letters, including a series of tributes from American and European friends, were delivered by the postman. His wife, aware that such birthday ritual was necessary to his happiness, had prompted their writing. The day, which began with music and tears, ended with a balcony discussion of the idea of progress, Tillich adopting for the sake of argument "the American point of view," followed by the responses of Hermann Schafft and another religious-socialist friend, Emil Blum. Nine days later, in Geneva, Tillich telephoned his father, and in a profoundly affectionate moment the two exchanged moving farewells. It was their last conversation.[110]

Shortly before Tillich's return to America in September he went to London and Manchester, where negotiations were under way for him to come to the University of Manchester.[111] His friend Adolf Löwe, a member of that faculty, was eager to have Tillich join it as a lecturer, a position which freed the occupant for much of his own work but did not guarantee a pension; the offer remained as unrealized as did Oldham's promise to appoint Tillich a director of the Oxford Conference.[112] At the time, in any case, it had seemed to Tillich, whose American contacts through the Federal Council of Churches had put him in touch with various phases of the churches' work for refugees, that a leading role in the ecumenical movement was somehow assured him. It turned out otherwise.

In 1937 Tillich returned to Europe in order to attend the Oxford Conference on Life and Work, acting as a member of the "Commission on Socialism and Communism and their Relation to the Ecumenical Movement." Reflecting upon this many years later, he said that he and his immediate friends had made a very important contribution to the ecumenical movement by persuading the commission to include in the final report to the conference the assertion that it was entirely possible that God was speaking more clearly through men concerned for social justice who were enemies of the church than through those who spoke in the name of the churches but exerted no social responsibility. It was characteristic of him that on the one hand he regarded himself as a representative and spokesman of the churches, and at the same time thought it within the realm of probability that some voices outside the churches spoke more clearly of God and his relation to human kind than those inside.[113]

It was perhaps because of this paradoxical stand that Tillich's active relation to the ecumenical movement came to an end. Despite the fact that he continued to have connections with the church, through discussions in committee meetings, through apologetic courses, and through regular preaching engagements, he was never a churchman but always the philosopher-theologian. Eventually he concluded that too many nonliberal theologians were represented in the ecumenical movement itself: men like Barth, for example, who for a long time received much recognition and exercised deep influence. Tillich's feeling came to the fore after the Amsterdam Assembly which organized the World Council of Churches. He was not invited to attend it, nor others that followed during his lifetime, and he took what he considered an intentional exclusion almost as a personal affront, expressing envy that others were included while he was not. He remained convinced from this time forward that Visser 't Hooft, then General Secretary of the World Council of Churches, disliked or disapproved of his theology and therefore stood in his way.[114] The contrary was the case. Union Seminary was strongly represented in ecumenical work, in 1948 and later, by three of its faculty members: Henry Van Dusen, Reinhold Niebuhr, and John Bennett, all active churchmen and publicly identified with the life of the churches to a degree that Tillich never was.

It was in fact his own position between the church and the world, a position from which he spoke to those outside the church more than to those who stood within it, that prevented him from becoming a force in ecumenical circles, and not any personal ill will toward his thought—although that, too, was sometimes expressed by conservative persons. Tillich's own paradoxical stand made his participation in the Oxford Conference at once his ecumenical début and his swan song.

Late that summer Tillich joined his wife in Switzerland. They spent several weeks near Mont Blanc, in the Italian and French Alps. Tillich's awareness (gained a year earlier) of the fear, uncertainty, and sense of meaninglessness prevailing in Europe was now sharpened. He felt more than ever that war was inevitable, and proved to be right. He was not to return to Europe for another eleven years.[115]

6

A Bridge to the World
(1939-1955)

War and Peace

In the summer of 1938 signs and portents announced the coming catastrophe. Northern lights appeared in the late summer sky; their like had not been seen, some recalled, since 1866 when Austria was conquered by Prussia. Carrion birds flew around the city of Vienna, and the weather was most unusual.[1] In the autumn Hitler and Mussolini signed the infamous Munich pact with France and Great Britain (prelude to the annexation of Czechoslovakia the following March). On 9 November, later to be remembered as the *Kristallnacht*, one synagogue after another all over Germany was burned to the ground, prompting countless Jews to flee, some succeeding, many failing.[2] In New York, Tillich broke his five-year moratorium on speaking in public about international politics. On 21 November he joined a Protestant gathering protesting Hitler's persecution of the Jews, and in an address entitled "The Meaning of Anti-Semitism" raised his voice on behalf of the true Germany, now defeated by the false or Nazi Germany. "After five years of silence I have spoken for the first time in a political meeting against those who have revealed themselves in these days as the real enemies of the German soul. And my speech has become a pledge for the True Germany."[3]

On 1 September 1939 Hitler marched into Poland, thus igniting World War II, an event which caused Tillich to remark, "Nowadays everything is done and nothing is declared."[4] Hitler's habit of attacking without first declaring his intentions still took Tillich, and millions of others, by surprise as did news of Nazi brutality, sending him into an emotional tailspin expressed in nightmares of "unimaginable torture" or states of depression which he overcame by walking on Riverside Drive or working until very late at night.[5]

By the time Hitler had occupied France, in the spring of 1940, Tillich was experiencing the early benefits of his emigration. On 4 March of that year he became an American citizen. In January 1939 Henry Coffin had written to the Emigration and Naturalization Service on Tillich's behalf in order to hasten the cumbersome, slow process, describing Tillich as a distinguished scholar, citing his great contribution to the 1937 Oxford Conference as well as Tillich's and his wife's devotion to America, which had now become the country of their choice.[6] In that year also Tillich was elevated to the rank of full professor, signaling the achievement of longed-for security and providing him with a larger salary, which gave him comfort but did not prevent him from complaining still of his "poverty."[7] Tillich's installation as Professor of Philosophical Theology took place in September, as tradition dictated, coinciding with the formal opening of the 105th year of the seminary, at four in the afternoon.

Yet a third benefit, namely, his first American honorary degree, came to Tillich in 1940. Aware of his consistent and stubborn refusal to wear a doctoral hood with his academic gown (in Germany professors wear velvet gowns and berets of varying colors but no hoods), Coffin in his official capacity as a trustee of Yale University arranged to provide Tillich with an American degree and hood of his own. Accordingly, Yale bestowed upon him the honorary degree of Doctor of Divinity on 19 June of that year, citing him as follows:

Paul Tillich, Professor at Union Theological Seminary, D.D.—In Germany, Dr. Tillich was known as a philosopher among theologians and a theologian among philosophers. He was a member of the university senate at Frankfort when 400 well-armed Brown Shirts came and beat up the radical students. He spoke out against the invaders, and, in his own words, "I had the honor to be the first non-Jewish professor dismissed from a German university and even at that time I was subconsciously aware that nothing could stop the Nazi advance!" He divides his time between research studies and untiring activity for the German refugees. His mastery of the relations between theology, philosophy, and various aspects of religion has been accomplished without sacrificing the distinctive emphases of the Christian faith and the unique place of Christian theology.[8]

On the same occasion Fiorello LaGuardia, then mayor of New York City, received a degree for making New York a "bigger and better place," and the American poet Carl Sandburg was similarly honored for his biography of Abraham Lincoln. Tillich was proud to be in such company, a pride shared by his personal friends, his Self-Help associates, and his Union colleagues, many of whom wrote to him on the occasion.

Europe's swift decline into the destruction of World War II coincided with Tillich's victory over his own "second death." He now understood his forced emigration as a providential new beginning. He was destined to declare frequently in the years that followed that "love is stronger than death," when his inner as well as outer identification with America, his undiminished love and compassion for the German people, and his conviction that Nazi power must be crushed forever, were fused in several ways.

After America joined the war, fighting Japan in the east and Germany on the western front, Tillich was invited by the Office of War Information (OWI) to write a series of addresses to the German people for the Voice of America. Between 1942 and 1945 he provided 109 talks, each roughly five pages or 1,500 words long,[9] an activity so wrapped in secrecy that not even his closest friends knew of it. In the talks, which were delivered on Sundays not by himself but by a speaker for the Voice of America, Tillich tried to make his "German friends" understand the injustice and hopelessness of Hitler's regime. He stressed the cruelty of the persecution of the Jews, the urgency for the Protestant church to resist Nazism, the need for Germans to face their own guilt. On 11 May 1942 he wrote of the rights of man, which the Nazis had taken away from the German people, and on 18 May of the same year was broadcast his graphically written and moving piece on the ninth anniversary of the burning of books.[10] Tillich explained on more than one occasion how democracy works and how Americans were willing to fight for it, and praised Roosevelt and the social policies of the New Deal. In nearly all his addresses he urged the German people to recognize their perilous predicament —to throw off the tyrant and be prepared to pay the cost of building a new order. Toward the end of the war, seeing the destruction of Germany, he begged its people to surrender and sue for peace before the entire country was destroyed. He frequently mentioned the tragic element in history, stressing especially the tendency of the German people to view their destiny as a nation in a despondent spirit (*Schwermut*). He hoped for a rebirth, a renewal, of the whole world; he hoped that, just as after World War I it had been possible to expect renewal because the time was ripe for it (*kairos*), a new *kairos* would come for the revival of justice in the world.

The talks were unavoidably marked by a great deal of repetition, but were nevertheless remarkable; they show how deeply and in how short a time Tillich had come to identify himself as an American with the American cause, discarding provincialism, yet at the same time extending a hand to his German brothers. It was not an easy task, and there is no way of knowing how many heard his words or changed their views or were strengthened by his courage. Yet the talks represent the main ideas that preoccupied Tillich during the war years, which he expressed more as an observer of the political scene than as one attempting to mold it as an active participant. Indeed, his political experience in America was disappointing and his contributions there proved ultimately ineffectual.

From the first Tillich obeyed the several rules he had set down for all emigrés in an address delivered in 1938.[11] It was necessary, he felt, for an emigré to see his own situation clearly and to rid himself of illusions either about his homeland or about America—in short, to become realistic in order to be able to act wisely and well as a citizen in a new world. He urged emigrés in particular to refrain from becoming involved in any American political party, and encouraged them to fight fascism through writing and speaking, without forming any large group which might cut them off from the American mainstream and make them appear to be a nation within a nation. His admonition to refrain from political activism grew partly out of his awareness that he did not himself comprehend American politics from within. Indeed, at the beginning of his American sojourn he depended on others, James Luther Adams for example, to supply him with information about what was going on so that he could speak and write in a relevant fashion.[12] He wanted to create an image of himself as a man with left-wing sympathies involved in the events of the times, not merely standing on the sidelines. But he remained cautious in going about it, in part because Coffin had advised him not to bother with political action on the American scene, which, since he did not understand all the practical consequences it would entail, might only get him into trouble.

For these reasons Tillich contented himself with adopting the role of an observer and critical analyst. He captured the attention of Kenneth Leslie, a Canadian of liberal, even radical social views who corralled him and several other Protestant theologians to write for *The Protestant,* a journal which he had founded in New York. In 1941 and 1942, glad to have an outlet for his convictions about the war and the postwar world, Tillich wrote numerous articles for Leslie, whom he regarded for a time as an intelligent and politically responsible man. He discussed war aims, stressed the allied Western nations' responsibility for Nazism because of the burden that the Versailles Treaty and war reparations had placed on Germany after 1919, and emphasized the need not only to conquer Nazism but to begin the construction of a new world order—indeed, a world federation. His article, "I am an American," an address originally delivered at a mass meeting in Central Park in New York, appeared in this journal.[13] His somewhat oversimplified rhetorical identification of the Orient with the past, Europe with the present, and America with the future demonstrated that he was beginning to think as an American and no longer as a German.

Despite contributions from Tillich and others, Leslie's journal did not build up a large following, and after a disagreement among the editors concerning policy toward Russia and communism it folded, sending Leslie back to Canada.

Tillich's ideas about the postwar world, propounded in the Voice of America broadcasts and in *The Protestant*, were also expressed in his one major political engagement in the United States. This was brief, stormy, and finally futile, putting an end to his political activities if not his interests. The episode concerned the activities of the Council for a Democratic Germany, founded in the beginning of 1944, which went out of existence in September 1945.[14] The war had moved from Hitler's early European victories, achieved swiftly by June 1941, toward the slow and costly reoccupation and liberation of Europe. Hitler's decision to invade Soviet Russia, a German ally, on 22 June 1941 (almost exactly 129 years to the day after Napoleon had done so in the last century) proved as fateful for him as it had been for Napoleon: from that time forward the war was lost. By 1944 Germany was surrounded on several fronts by the Russians in the east and the Allies in the west. As news crept out of Europe regarding the satanic horrors perpetrated on millions in concentration camps by the Nazis, and as Hitler's conquests in Europe and Africa were about to be undone, talk of unconditional surrender, the dismemberment of Germany, and the removal or destruction of all German industry became widespread. Men like the financier Henry Morgenthau, Roosevelt's Secretary of the Treasury, and the British foreign policy expert Vansittart advocated an extreme anti-German line of retribution.

Aware that total destruction of Germany was inevitable, Tillich and other German intellectuals in America became increasingly concerned about the prospects for a just and lasting peace in this climate of ill will and revenge for Nazi misdeeds against Germany as a whole. Accordingly, a council was formed of German emigrés of varied political outlook and persuasion, all victims of the Nazi takeover in 1933, all resolute opponents of Nazism from the beginning, in order to formulate a program for general European peace as well as for German reconstruction. There was a rumor that Thomas Mann had been invited to become president of the council but refused to join, maintaining that a friend in the U.S. Government had advised him against it.[15] After some dispute among the organizing members, Tillich was made provisional chairman and formulated the first proclamation of the council, a declaration which was rejected by Albert Grzesinski, a former socialist Prussian minister of the interior in Germany, who had himself unsuccessfully led an Association of Free Germans in 1941 and whose presence on the new council seemed questionable to some. The declaration, in any case, was printed in the first issue of the *Bulletin of the Council for a Democratic Germany*, published on 15 May 1944. A letter of invitation had been sent out to large groups of refugees on 27 April 1944, signed by Reinhold Niebuhr, William Jay Schiefflin, Jr., and Dorothy Thompson to invite them to endorse the newly formed council. An announcement to the press on 3 May 1944 stressed the three major points of the council's program: the study of practical measures for postwar political reconstruction of a democratic Germany; measures for purging German educational institutions, libraries, theaters, etc., of Nazi racist teachings, together with plans for the reorganization of German education within democratic channels; and finally a program of political unity to which all anti-Nazi forces in Germany could eventually adhere.[16]

The program was specifically against the economic and political dismemberment of Germany, but it envisaged a disarmed Germany that was expected to make good for Nazi crimes and aggression. It urged the reconstruction of Germany's productive power and opposed the deindustrialization and enslavement of its people.[17] In short, the program advocated the liberation of the German people so that they could find their own way toward establishment of a democratic order and appropriate institutions and policies.

Among the signers of the declaration were emigrés well known in their various professions: Bertolt Brecht and Heinrich Mann (writers), Frederick Forell (pastor), Werner Richter (educator), Veit Valentin (historian), Paul Hagen (research director of the American Friends of German Freedom), Erwin Piscator (stage director), and Elizabeth Bergner (actress). In addition, in order to lend their moral support, many American religious leaders and educators added their signatures, including John Bennett, Harry Emerson Fosdick, Alvin Johnson, William Allan Neilson, Reinhold Niebuhr, Wilhelm Pauck, Carl Hermann Voss, and others.

Behind this show of unity there raged in fact a fierce debate among the council's refugee members, who tended to be highly individualistic. As victims of Nazi oppression all had been unequivocally anti-Nazi from the outset; but practically all retained their former political outlook, most of them as Social Democrats or Catholic Centrists, although now American citizens. In joining the council they had agreed to exclude from it all political extremists, particularly left- or right-wing radicals—Communists or reactionary nationalists. But they were unable to achieve a common mind or a united front because the policy of exclusion failed. Sympathizers with communism did raise their voices and refused to cooperate, and the exclusion of some more conservative politicians—for example, the former chancellor Heinrich Brüning— proved divisive. When Tillich's declaration or manifesto was circulated, many intellectual refugees responded negatively to his idea of permitting Germany to create its own democratic government, and some were even in favor of extreme punishment. In the case of an especially strong protest from an unexpected source, namely Eduard Heimann, Reinhold Niebuhr responded in Tillich's place, saying that the Germans would have already paid the highest possible price for the misdeeds of their leaders: namely, the utter and complete destruction of their land, together with bankruptcy and unconditional surrender. Would they not have suffered enough?— Niebuhr asked.

There was protest also from persons in no way connected with the council. Rex Stout, president of the Society for the Prevention of World War III, issued a statement protesting the attempt of German political exiles to influence American public opinion with what they thought to be a creative solution of the German question.[18]

In the course of its short life the council itself did not achieve a consensus on any part of its program. Argumentative voices were persistently raised. Moreover, it was unable to get sufficient financial support, and the most influential leaders, namely Paul Hagen and Tillich, were criticized for not planning to return permanently to Germany, while encouraging others who had not succeeded in gaining a foothold in America to do precisely that. The council finally broke up under the impact of varying reactions to the Yalta agreement and because there was no majority opinion. Tillich's notion of a political balance in the group failed when the deep rift between Russia and the Western Allies became clearly visible. In the autumn of 1945 the Council dissolved, leaving several issues of the *Bulletin* as a footnote to history.

Among signers of the original declaration of the council was Trude Pratt, an American woman who later married the writer Joseph Lash (subsequently the biographer of Eleanor Roosevelt.) She had befriended the Tillichs soon after their arrival in this country, and it was through her that Tillich came to know Eleanor Roosevelt, who invited him to Hyde Park on several occasions.[19] Tillich expressed to her many of his ideas about the reconstruction of Germany, and she found them intriguing. She arranged a meeting between Tillich and her husband, which took place in 1944.[20] Tillich, accompanied by Adolf Löwe, Friedrich Pollock, and Hans Staudinger, all members of the graduate faculty of political sciences at the New School in New York, dined at the White House in the company of President and Mrs. Roosevelt, Vice-President Henry Wallace, and others.

Roosevelt, appearing at the party for cocktails, mixed martinis with a great flourish and was generally jovial and friendly, making small talk with his guests. Meanwhile Wallace, who seemed to Tillich to suffer from great melancholy, engaged him in conversation. "Your name is Tillich?" he asked. "Then you must be the author of the article on the demonic." Tillich said yes. Wallace replied, "I'm thrilled to meet you. It's an important idea. I'd like to understand it." Tillich explained it to him. Then dinner was served. Tillich sat at Eleanor Roosevelt's right, and while FDR chatted she succeeded in steering the conversation in Tillich's direction, whereupon he made a brief prepared statement on the reconstruction of Germany. Others supplemented what he said. Roosevelt replied that the Germans had fooled the Allies after World War I, but that this time America was in charge and Germany would have to do as it was told or suffer further bombardment. Tillich was shocked by Roosevelt's attitude. Coffee was served, and shortly before Roosevelt retired he wheeled himself over to the German professors and said, "We have great need of you. The Germans will require textbooks. I suggest that you write these textbooks for them." Tillich never fully caught the irony of this statement, but concluded later that the attempt to communicate his ideas to Roosevelt had been a failure because he was influenced by Stalin. After the president's departure there was general conversation with Wallace and Mrs. Roosevelt on the meaning and course of history, Wallace keeping the discussion alive by referring again and again to the concept of the demonic. It was a moment of fruitless glory for Tillich, but he recalled the meeting with a sense of pride as well as disappointment.

In 1945 Tillich was blacklisted by the U.S. Army because of his chairmanship of the Council for a Democratic Germany, this organization having been falsely identified by then as both pro-Communist and pro-German. Neither label was correct, and the army ultimately removed his name from its blacklist, but the episode as well as the postwar atmosphere in general depressed him and frightened him from the political scene.[21] After the war he felt the tragic more than the elevating elements of historical existence and lost the inspiration and interest for active politics. By then, also, he had come to feel that he was far from an effective understanding of American political problems.[22] By 1948, convinced that the postwar world, in which Germany had become divided in two dependent "colonies" standing between East and West, he suspected that a third world war was very likely. He announced that the productive time, the *kairos*, was over, that a "sacred void" existed, and that mankind must content itself with a period of expectant waiting. From then on Tillich's thinking emphasized an old interest of his, namely depth psychology, which unlike his dabbling in politics bore rich fruit; and he devoted himself almost entirely to the writing of his *Systematic Theology*.

After thirty years of disappointment, Tillich was driven to the conclusion that his program of religious socialism was too romantic for the times and that a more realistic way of living expectantly and hopefully in a vacuum had to be accepted. This feeling was reinforced by his first postwar visit to Europe in 1948.[23]

Return to Germany

During the summer months of the war years, Tillich had continued his exploration of America. Sometimes alone, sometimes joined by his wife and children, he revisited California, Massachusetts, Tennessee, and Maine. In 1943 the Tillichs spent their summer vacation in East Hampton, Long Island.[24] They enjoyed their stay, indeed, they liked it so well that they returned for several consecutive years. It was a fateful encounter. Only a hundred miles from New York, at the eastern end of the island with its old farms and hamlets, ponds and potato fields, highway and wind, East Hampton was immediately irresistible to him. The presence of oystermen, farmers, and rich summer residents, but especially the artistic atmosphere attracted him. Encouraged by the enthusiasm and initiative of his wife and by advice and financial assistance of a few friends, Tillich was able to purchase a house of his own at a relatively low price. It was primitive and stood on undeveloped land, within walking distance of the sea. By 1946 he envisaged this as his place of retirement. The house was slowly renovated, largely through the hard work of his wife, whom he regarded as the "soul and strength" of both this and their New York home.[25] Tillich's province was the outdoors: he planted the garden (he once remarked to friends admiring a little "victory garden" he had grown during the war, "And here is where I had my fight with the rabbits,"[26]) and a park of trees, his most prized possession. He once described himself as a pagan worshiper of trees;[27] indeed, he would go so far as to use money which might well have been spent on necessities to purchase a new tree. In 1947 the students in his course on religion and art collected enough for a copper beech tree, which he named the "Religion and Art" tree in their honor. It became one of the most beautiful in his grove.[28]

It was in East Hampton that Tillich rested and worked, writing in the morning in his own room, which together with the adjacent bathroom was off-limits to everyone but himself; walking on the beach in the afternoon, meeting friends under the large green umbrella he set up there. Most of his *Systematic Theology* was written in East Hampton. His wife provided him with space and undisturbed time, protecting him from too many visitors, arranging his days so that he could shuttle back and forth between ocean, post office, and garden; she prepared his favorite meals and deferred to his wish to be spared the duties of kitchen or home. While he enjoyed setting the table in the summer grape arbor, always delighting in his aristic achievement and encouraging his guests to admire it with him, he disappeared with the greatest rapidity once the meal was consumed. It was in East Hampton in the summers of his later life that Tillich was feted in an endless series of teas and cocktail parties. There, too, he first heard the news that the Allies had broken into Germany and that the European phase of the war was drawing to a close.[29]

After Germany's defeat the reopening of Europe to the world filled Tillich with foreboding; he recalled his earlier life in Germany with great clarity and could not imagine how the events between his departure and the present must have transformed the land and the people.[30] At first he found it difficult to communicate with many of his old friends and members of his family, when they wrote him from Germany in an outpouring of emotion. In endlessly long letters they told of their war experiences, the bombing, the poverty, their hunger and misery, their yearning for contact with the outside world. Frede Fritz wrote of his gratitude that his sons had returned safely home from the war; he was old and depressed.[31] Tillich's sister Elisabeth and her husband were alive in Berlin; their daughter Heide had reached safety only because a former student of Tillich's, then an army officer, escorted her and her group fleeing from the Russians across the Elbe River. He did this, the soldier told her quite flatly, only because he loved Tillich.[32] Hans-Jürgen Seeberger, Tillich's nephew, who later became a psychoanalyst, was held by the Russians and suffered years of imprisonment before he was released in the late winter of 1949. Marie-Luise Werner and other members of Hannah's family joined in the general reporting. Hermann Schafft, alive and well, wrote from Kassel where he was still working with incredible energy for the church. Fritz Medicus reported from Switzerland, thanking Tillich for his contribution to the Festschrift published in his (Medicus') honor. He also informed him of the tragic death of Friedrich Büchsel, his beloved fellow student, who had been shot by a Polish soldier attempting to abduct his daughter.[33] The letters began to arrive in 1945, and they never stopped coming.

Tillich replied to each and all, by personal letter or by a longer mimeographed circular letter. At first he was afraid of being rejected or misunderstood, but most of all he feared that his German friends might resent emigrés like himself who had chosen to identify themselves with America. He felt "a kind of dizziness" produced by the end of what had seemed a bad dream but turned out to be a horrible reality.[34] Referring to his earlier dream about sheep grazing in the ruins of Berlin, he wrote to a friend in London, "How literally my prophecy about the 'sheep' has been fulfilled!"[35]

The destruction, the hunger, the uncertainty, the darkness of the future confounded him, producing periods of despair as well as guilt that he had escaped what his friends and family had been forced to suffer.[36] He urged them to open themselves to the outside world so that they might be helped and thereby help others, including himself, in turn. Like countless other Americans, he did more than write letters; he sent food, clothing, coffee, chocolate, and cigarettes to the needy. He was deeply moved when a colleague of his at Yale asked him to provide the names of Germans particularly in need to whom he might send packages over a period of time. The first name Tillich supplied was that of Max Behrmann, a pastor living with his family in Hamburg, which had been almost totally devastated by allied bombing. To his colleague at Yale he wrote,

> Your letter to me was like the burning candles on our Christmas tree—light in the darkness. The darkness creeping from Europe over the ocean into the hearts of those who are in vital contact with many people in Europe is incredible. It has grasped me with a distress which often surpasses even the anxieties of my first year of emigration.[37]

Despite the letters, despite newspaper accounts and eyewitness reports of returning soldiers, it was not until Tillich returned to Germany that he fully realized the magnitude of the suffering people had undergone, and only then did the walls time and distance had erected between him and them finally fall away.

The journey itself took some time to arrange. Germany, a country split in two, was occupied by the military forces of the allied countries: England, France, and the U.S.A. in the west, Soviet Russia in the east. Only individuals on official business who had been approved by the American State Department were permitted to enter Germany, and while there they were obliged to report to the United States military government, which had its headquarters in Wiesbaden. Moreover, an invitation from a German institution was necessary. Many German-speaking professors were among the Americans who returned to Germany during these years in an attempt to help restore order and normal procedures and to initiate an exchange of ideas and also create a feeling of community in a broken land.

Tillich's opportunity, which he sought from the moment the war was over, came when the theological faculty of the University of Marburg and the University of Frankfort invited him to give lectures at their respective institutions for a number of weeks, and to deliver as many other lectures or informal talks in other places as time and energy would allow.[38]

By the spring of 1948 all was in order. Through the energetic mediation of Henry Van Dusen, the Rockefeller Foundation and World Church Service provided grants without which, Tillich later said, he could not have gone abroad.[39] The economy in America was in an inflationary spiral, Tillich's children were in private schools, he was paying off the mortgage on his East Hampton house, and despite his increasing income it was difficult to balance the budget.[40]

Cleared by the State Department, Tillich sailed for Europe on board the *Queen Mary* on 8 May; he returned to America on 10 September. Between these two dates he lectured for ninety-seven hours in nineteen different places, had personal talks and encounters with 357 people, and visited Paris, Basel, Bern, Geneva, Berlin, Hamburg, Munich, Cologne, Frankfort, Marburg, Nuremberg, Heidelberg, Kassel, Mainz, Göttingen, and London.[41] The sentimental odyssey set the style for Tillich's subsequent trips abroad: he revisited many of the same places, staying in the same hotels and seeing many of the same people in the years that followed. But he never again reached the heights and depths of feeling he experienced on his first return to Germany in fifteen years.

As the *Queen Mary* neared the French coast, Tillich felt increasingly alone, anxious, depressed. Not even Paris, the city of lights (which seemed to him dimmer than he remembered), brought him cheer. He viewed the paintings in the Louvre and elsewhere with his usual enthusiasm and thoroughness, but felt that Americans hung their paintings in a more effective way. Nor did the soft air of Paris, which he contrasted with America's aggressive winds, comfort him as it had in the past. The signs of the war had left their mark on the French people, who looked tired and shabby.

After Paris Tillich was never alone, and his great energy was put to good use. In Geneva, he visited Visser 't Hooft and dined with his old friend Adolf Keller, then seventy-six, robust despite a recent operation. In Bern he talked with Emil Blum and his wife, associates of religious socialism days. In Basel he had an unexpectedly jovial meeting with Karl Barth, who seemed to him much older, his face deeply lined. They conversed about theology and disagreed about the Resurrection; they talked of prophets and church administrators. A series of warm reunions took place with Karl Ludwig Schmidt, who was also teaching in Basel—from him Tillich learned details of the Germany he was about to see. All these meetings were a prelude to that moment, and as the train crossed the German border he became increasingly uneasy. In Frankfort the sight of destruction and defeat greeted him at every turn, rendering that once so familiar city strangely unreal. He joined a group of visiting professors from the University of Chicago at the Carlton Hotel, who had come to carry out an exchange program with the University of Frankfort. Wilhelm Pauck was their spokesman. Tillich and Pauck spent many hours together in the weeks that followed, lecturing daily, comparing notes on their experiences, visiting German friends. Their joy in the task they had assumed was overshadowed by the destruction they saw around them, and they were united in their common view that the Germans should be met with understanding and received into fellowship.[42]

From then on Tillich commuted between Marburg and Frankfort, and from there traveled to other towns on his itinerary. This was indeed the fate of all visiting professors: they were constantly underway from one place to another and everywhere found large and expectant audiences. Tillich divided his time, as did the others, between formal lectures and informal gatherings.[43] He soon learned that he was living in two worlds: he moved daily between the world of the conquerors and that of the conquered. The tensions produced by this alternation appeared in many little ways:

there was the constant problem of invitations—which to accept, which to reject; the problem of giving gifts and being tactful in doing it; and always the problem of understanding. He found communication easiest in his formal lectures, where distance between him and his audience established a certain objectivity that was not so readily achieved in more personal encounters. He carefully chose topics through which he could express what was most on his mind, lecturing on "Love, Power, and Justice," "Present Trends in American Theology," "Systematic Theology," "The New Being," and "Christianity, Humanism, and Socialism." At informal gatherings of personal friends, to which he was invited at every step, Tillich realized almost at once that his anxieties regarding his reception had been misplaced. Their unfailing generosity, their almost exaggerated hospitality (they brought forward their best in food and drink), conquered his fears. In such a setting he spoke often of his impressions and reflections on the world around him.

The ruins, the empty streets, the barrenness everywhere, and the ill-clad people constantly on the move in search of things to eat and wear, impressed him greatly. He found himself constantly trying to adjust himself to this world, eventually growing used to it and no longer noticing it. The sight of bushes and flowers growing in the midst of ruins, single walls or chimneys standing stark in the rubble, empty windows without window panes, yet clean streets (the Germans although they lacked machinery were compulsively rebuilding), produced in him a feeling of unreality. He saw men and women living in exceedingly crowded conditions and noted that the non-German displaced persons moved restlessly about looking for a welcome. He saw sad, sick, hungry faces everywhere. Many were blind or crippled. He noticed the rough hands of the women; a mixture of tidiness and messiness met his eyes everywhere. What struck him almost immediately was that whereas in France there had been many men, particularly of middle age, in Germany there were very few. Fate had meted out an exact and harsh justice: in exchange for millions of persons killed in Nazi concentration camps, it had taken millions of Germans. This fact

(Left) Paul Tillich, Institute of Technology, Dresden, 1928.

(Below) Elli Heimann, Paul Tillich, Erdmuthe Tillich, Eduard Heimann, Hannah Tillich. On Kampen, 1931.

(*Above*) One of many "sand-castles" which Tillich built.

(*Left*) Paul Tillich, emigrant. U.S.A., 1936.

Paul Tillich with his grandson, Ted Farris, 1963.

East Hampton. Tillich's house, with garden of trees.

Paul Tillich, Union Theological Seminary, New York. Last appearance there, 1965.

Paul Tillich and Theodor Heuss (President of West Germany) after Tillich received the Peace Prize in St. Paul's Church, Frankfort, 1962.

Paul Tillich, the main speaker at *Time*'s 40th anniversary dinner, with Henry Luce. 6 May 1963.

played a considerable role in the continuation of Tillich's friendship with German women, single, widowed, or divorced, for whom he felt a special responsibility and concern.

As time passed he came to know the twisted state of the German mind: the impassioned, bitter, unbalanced, and rarely objective reactions to their immediate past. The indifference of most Germans to their own fate was peculiar. They had reached the lowest level of human experience: their fear under Nazi oppression, their concern for their men during the war, the effect of bombing, starvation, the bitter-cold winter of 1946–47; their flight from the Russians, the rape of women—all this had created in the people an indifference even to death. They were able to master their outer but not their inner situation; that is why, Tillich concluded, they were now plunging into the ruins and rebuilding with such compulsive haste.

Tillich was welcomed everywhere: in his hotel-rooms letters, flowers, and berries in season awaited him. To his great relief the fact that he was an emigré created no resentment in old friends or new, so long as he did not judge or even condemn them. Yet he encountered considerable self-pity among the Germans he met. They were not really prepared to hear that other people had suffered too, believing that only they themselves had sacrificed; they had a curious inability to imagine what life was like for others. He soon gave up trying to talk of German guilt. It was the most sensitive point of all, in part because it had been discussed too often without full knowledge of what had happened, and in part because many Germans now felt themselves a cursed nation and preferred to maintain a distance from others. He also discovered that most of those to whom he spoke had not been Nazis, and that while few had had the courage to stand up against them, they refused to think of themselves as guilty. In fact, he suspected, their feeling of guilt was so great that they were forced to repress it. All this he learned in the course of his months abroad.

In Marburg Tillich was lunching one day with his colleagues Friedrich Heiler and Ernst Benz, when a woman came to his table. For a full moment he did not recognize her, and then suddenly knew her to be his sister Elisabeth. In the first joyous hours of their reunion, all she asked for when he offered to buy something for her in the PX was a comb. A day later Hermann Schafft arrived in a broken-down car with chauffeur. Schafft had been a Protestant minister in various parts of the province of Hesse, and had been made professor of religious education in a teachers' college shortly before the Nazis came to power. Since he had been a leading personality in the democratic groups of the German youth movement, they immediately dismissed him, and he became a minister in a small town near Kassel. The American military government discovered him in the first days of the occupation and made him a *Regierungsdirektor* or high government official in the field of education. After their reunion Schafft put himself at Tillich's service. Their private, almost exclusive friendship utterly unchanged, the two men spent many hours discussing the world situation and exploring the countryside between Marburg, Kassel, and Göttingen. The German landscape was almost the only thing that had not been transformed by the war, and Tillich found it wonderful to see.

His growing conviction that it was impossible to form creative relationships and community by judging the Germans, and that he and others coming from the outside had only one choice—namely, to deal with all, even those who had been pro-Hitler, in the spirit of outgoing love and patience—led him in mid-June to Emanuel Hirsch. It was in many ways the most moving meeting of the summer. Hirsch stood waiting for Tillich in his Göttingen garden. He was almost entirely blind, very old, his hair uncombed. The two men talked of their work, Hirsch's family, his blindness, the loss of a son in Yugoslavia. Hirsch still clung to his belief that Hitler had been sent to create a unified German nation. His forced retirement and reduced pension caused by his Nazi sympathies embittered him. Despite all, he had continued to be enormously productive, a feat Tillich admired. Their farewell was particularly moving for Hirsch, who wrote Tillich later in the year how often he thought of their meeting, and thanked him for the gifts he had sent: a bottle of wine, two bars of chocolate, and a piece of soap.[44]

A few weeks after this encounter Tillich flew to Berlin. From the air the city resembled a chessboard of ruins; large sections once so familiar to him were totally unrecognizable. Once on the ground, he experienced the past constantly merging with the present in what proved to be the most exciting weeks of the summer. In Harnack Haus, a guesthouse for visiting professors where outside the window of his room lilac and linden trees were in bloom, he lectured to an audience of four hundred persons, tightly packed in to hear him talk of "Christology and the World." Dozens of friends were in the audience, and in the weeks that followed Tillich met with them all, at his hotel or in their homes. His former students at Frankfort, Wolfgang Hochheimer, Harald Poelchau, and Gertie Siemsen; his former Halle classmate "Vater Rhein," his distant cousins, his wife's closest school friend, members of his family, and childhood playmates—all flocked to see and to hear him. Even his first wife, Grethi, appeared. She was very thin and aged; he still found her lovely. One morning, with his sister, he went to the Neunburgerstrasse where they had lived as children. The house was still standing and an elderberry bush still growing behind the garden wall. They walked through the open market place to find the Friedrich Wilhelm *Gymnasium*, where Tillich had gone to school, still there, as well as the *Konsistorium* where his father had worked. The appearance of Erich Harder, now seventy-five, one of his father's assistants many years earlier, more than anyone else moved Tillich even further back into the past; he used the occasion to confess how much he owed the older man for his spiritual and intellectual development.

Slowly the horrors of each and every story—all the same, each different—sank into Tillich's mind and heart. In Amersfoort (near Amsterdam) he heard from Mennicke's own lips the tale of his years in Nazi concentration camps; he wondered to himself how anyone could survive such experiences, about which he had not heard before so directly. In Hamburg Kurt Leese, Max and Hildegard Behrmann, and Maria Rhine told of the devastating bombing of the city, which took the lives of thousands of civilians in four nights. In Cologne Nelli Gelb evoked memories of the "splendid isolation" of Frankfort in the pre-Nazi years and told of the tragic death of her husband and the suicide of her son. Even a brief mountain-climbing vacation in Sils Maria, Switzerland, where Adolf Löwe read aloud the passages in Mann's *Dr. Faustus* which Tillich's letter had inspired, did not entirely free him from the steady assault of words rehearsing the war and its aftermath. Fedor Stepun arrived from Munich, dreading a possible Russian takeover of Europe and gripped by fear for himself on account of his friendship with Kerensky. He implored Tillich to arrange emigration to America for him; as it turned out, he lived out his life peacefully and productively in Munich.

There was not an hour of any day (he required only a few hours of sleep) when Tillich was alone, and his consistent acceptance in word and deed of those who felt unacceptable, who had expected him to judge, perhaps even reject them, aroused in them a devotion and affection often uncritically adoring, which grew in succeeding years to astounding acclaim. Everywhere it was the same, and the Berlin visit more than any other erased any feeling in him of being separated from the past; it was as though the fifteen years between meetings had never existed, as if time had stood still. In each and every meeting, almost, there occurred for him an instantaneous recovery of the past.

Tillich became a fixed point on the horizon of these German friends, a star by which they measured their own sometimes faltering position. In a world utterly disrupted, at least *he* remained unchanged, and for this they were grateful beyond measure. Nowhere has his effect upon them all been as perfectly expressed as in a letter written by Harald Poelchau's wife Dorothea.

I opened Paulus' letter with apprehension, and instead of rebuke and rejection I found the old friendship and compassionate criticism. How much Harald was formed by you when he was young I have discovered only since Paulus was here. Not only his theology but also his way of making decisions, of relating to people without any aggression, with an almost impersonal but warm love, all this comes from you.[45]

216

Nearly everything about Tillich had remained the same except for the way in which he expressed his thought. It seemed to many less abstract, more precise, more easily understood. His German had been influenced, many thought, by the English language and forms of expression. Whether or not this was the case, he found a ready response to his ideas as well as to his person in the Germany of 1948. The spiritual situation seemed to him surprisingly open and his own ideas peculiarly relevant, especially in Berlin.

That city had become the "center of the world," Tillich wrote on every postcard he sent to friends in America. An island between East and West, it was an ideal platform for Tillich, standing as he did on the boundary between opposing views. In his formal lectures, addressing himself to the present, he attracted young men in uniform without insignia, professional persons on the edges of the church, academic people, all shabbily dressed, all eager to hear him. The reaction to him everywhere, then as later, was highly favorable. His ideas were received with attentiveness and enthusiasm and were politely weighed in question-and-answer periods—which he sometimes referred to as "lively discussions," to the amusement of his colleagues. Even in the eastern sector of the city, where Tillich had addressed a group of socialists convened by August Rathmann and where Harald Poelchau sought to maintain contact through his work in the church, his ideas were still being discussed nearly a year after his appearance.

The only lectures he ever gave in Berlin that were not well received, so far as is known, were his four statements on "The Jewish Question: A German and a Christian Problem" (1953).[46] Here he analyzed the historical, social, and religious background of Germans and Jews, comparing their similarities and differences, trying to ascertain why the tragic conflict between the two peoples had arisen. He called for German confession, repentance, and national psychoanalysis! These notions were greeted with uneasy silence and open disagreement: it was a unique and unsurprising exception to the rule. Over the years, the demand for his personal appearance was exceeded only by a growing interest in his books.

Nor were the German universities oblivious to Tillich's presence. As early as 1946 the University of Halle had reinstated his title and academic honors, both of which had been rescinded by the Nazi oppressors.[47] Several universities invited him to return and teach for a term or longer. At the newly established Free University of Berlin and at Marburg, Frankfort, and Hamburg, plans were set in motion to lure him back to Germany. Largely because this summer visit of 1948 evoked in him a strong sense of responsibility for the postwar spiritual and intellectual development of the Germans, Tillich considered each invitation at length, carefully weighing the advantages and disadvantages that a decision to return might produce. Eventually he turned them all down, deciding to remain in America. German university administrators graciously accepted this decision for the most part, but it bitterly disappointed many of his friends. They had to content themselves with the fact that he had at least agreed to teach after 1951 in alternate summer semesters in Hamburg and Berlin.[48] These decisions were supported and applauded by his American colleagues. Most of them understood and shared his feeling of obligation to postwar Germany; nevertheless, they felt that his work would come to fruition only if he remained in America.

Harvest Time

In the early autumn of 1948, after brief visits in Paris and London, Tillich sailed home. As he crossed the Atlantic he began to assemble in his mind the many contradictory impressions of the spirit and mood of the German people and of the postwar world.[49] Despite joyous memories of his warm reception he was left with deeply pessimistic forebodings. The end of the war had not brought genuine peace; the German nation was split internally and externally; the people were sick, Tillich felt, and crying out to be healed. He doubted that the expectation of a new era of international cooperation could be fulfilled. This sense of a dark future was as genuine as the realization that gradually dawned on him that he was no longer a pilgrim or even an emigré, but had become a world citizen.[50]

By a remarkable concatenation of events, it happened that at the time when his sense of obligation to the old world was keenest he began to reap the benefits that fifteen years of concentrated thought, a sense of social and cultural responsibility, and sheer hard work had brought to fruition in the new world. His exposure to America, through his publications and lecture tours, had the cumulative effect that he was in continuous demand abroad: in the 1950s and early 1960s he lectured not only in Germany but also in Switzerland, Holland, Denmark, Scotland, and England.

As the schedule grew ever more crowded, Tillich began to think of Union Seminary as a bridge on which he encountered persons from every part of the world. He later applied the metaphor to his own work, describing it as a bridge between the American and European continents between which he shuttled.[51] Yet he became increasingly aware that while his audience abroad was as responsive as it had always been, America had suddenly opened up to him in a way and to a degree he had never dreamed possible. To a friend in Germany he wrote, "Harvest time is here; indeed I am now gathering in my harvest!"[52] Tillich explained this increase in his popularity in terms of a change in the intellectual climate. America, in its own postwar doldrums, no longer bustling with utopian optimism, now gave ear to Tillichian themes to which it had been tone-deaf in the early years of his immigration. There were other reasons: Tillich's language had changed, he was more easily understood, and he had learned how to relate himself to the American way of thinking. Moreover, his presence never ceased to exercise great magnetic power; it was an undeniably potent influence.

Thus only a few years before his retirement from the seminary, Tillich acquired a wide and enthusiastic public which clamored to hear him. At the same time the ideas that had grown to maturity in Germany and had remained essentially unaltered (although more clearly expressed in the English language) burst into print in an eruption of publications beginning in 1948 and ending in 1963.[53]

The first of these was *The Protestant Era*, a collection of essays drawn from twenty years of his philosophical and theological writings, translated from the German, published in 1948. Although only a few of the articles dealt directly with Protestantism, they all related to problems of religion and culture in which the Protestant spirit, or as he said, the Protestant *principle* expressed itself. Tillich posed the question whether the Protestant era was about to come to an end.[54] He pointed out that the harmony of society was a thing of the past and that man's manipulation of persons through industrial technology had resulted in widespread dehumanization —or, to use a German word he liked, *Verdinglichung*, characterized by ruthless competition, fear, despair, and meaninglessness. Mankind everywhere was in a flight to new authoritarianisms (either communism or fascism), a flight which indicated the need for a spiritual reformation. Such a reformation, he concluded, might sweep the Protestant churches out of existence, but the prophetic and critical power of the Protestant principle, itself everlasting, would remain, since it alone could find new ways of expression in the future. Tillich proposed religious socialism as a challenge to the churches, maintaining that a new philosophy of history was needed to cope with the existential situation.

This was his message, and it found a hearing, since America, despite its emergence from the war as the most powerful nation on earth, was deeply involved in the crisis of Western civilization. The book spoke to the times, and although it did not become a runaway best seller, it did make the larger impression Tillich had sought for so long.

As in the case of all his American books, *The Protestant Era* was the result of valiant group effort. Tillich himself acknowledged that it had come into being largely because of the industrious labors of James Luther Adams, translator and editor of the essays, a professor of theology then teaching at the Meadville Theological Seminary and the Federated Theological Faculty at the University of Chicago.[55] In preparing for his dissertation, later published under the title *Paul Tillich's Philosophy of Culture, Science, and*

Religion, Adams had gradually translated most of Tillich's German articles and essays.[56] He visited him in New York to ask about the meaning of specific words or phrases which seemed to have been used variously in one essay and another and which he wished to translate accurately. When Tillich was unable to answer all the questions Adams put to him, he concluded that Adams understood his thought more thoroughly than he himself did. Thus began a long cooperation and friendship which lasted until Tillich's death. Adams continued to translate pieces by Tillich and advised him in many ways. A Christian gentleman with a lively sense of humor, he became widely known on his own account as a champion of voluntary associations and liberal causes who selflessly combined theological learning with a social conscience.

In the late 1930s Adams had persuaded Tillich, then still concerned at being so little known in America, that a wider circulation of his ideas through the publication of a collection of his basic essays, drawn from both the German and American periods, would accomplish what the earlier *Interpretation of History* had failed to do. Tillich furnished a long introductory essay in which he described the development of his thought, and Adams wrote an accompanying piece—unfortunately pushed to the end of the book —in which with wide learning and poetic perceptiveness he analyzed Tillich's concept of history.

His prediction was now fulfilled. *The Protestant Era* was hailed as the most important work of religious apologetics to appear in America since Reinhold Niebuhr's *The Nature and Destiny of Man*.[57] The path to publication had been strewn with problems. For one thing, it was no easy matter to translate Tillich's abstract German into English, and even Adams's skillful handling of the materials needed correction by Tillich who, although his command of the English language was never complete, did have a shrewd sense for the meaning of words. He knew at once if the English translation was *in*correct, but did not always know how to correct it and therefore sometimes substituted one error for another. It was in this predicament that he turned to Pauck (to whom he dedicated the book). The two men spent many hours revising the

translations in the summer of 1941 while vacationing in Gatlinburg, Tennessee.

Once the manuscript was in publishable form, it was difficult to
find a publisher. Scribners, to whom Adams and Tillich turned
first, had published On the Boundary, but rejected the new manuscript after two years of deliberation, largely because two readers
of not inconsiderable stature in American Protestant ecclesiastical
and academic circles felt that there was no American audience for
Tillich's profound but ponderous ideas.[58] Finally Adams and
Pauck persuaded Fred Wieck, then editor at the University of
Chicago Press, to offer Tillich a contract. Wieck did so on condition that he would also sign a contract for the Systematic Theology. The bargain was struck (in itself not easy, since Tillich clung
to the notion that New York publishers were superior to those in
other parts of the country, besides which his circumstantial ways
made the very simplest business transaction sometimes difficult to
complete). The book was published and established Tillich on the
American map.[59]

Hegel has said that philosophy—"the owl of Minerva"—takes
flight only at dusk; as a case in point, The Protestant Era appeared
only after Tillich's preoccupation with the kairos, the right time for
creative action, had become a thing of the past. His personal failure to achieve influence in the sphere of politics as well as the
schizophrenic situation of the postwar world which paralyzed the
actions of men, made him feel that there was little any individual
could do to change the course of contemporary history.[60] It was a
feeling shared by many thoughtful men and women of contemporary society, who were sobered by humanity's inability to master
its fate, and despaired of the future. They began to turn the search-
light of investigation and inquiry upon themselves, asking why they
had come to such a pass. Concern for the reconstruction of society
moved into the background and was replaced by a quickly rising
interest in the existential and psychological analysis of man.
Efforts were made to establish the cause and discover the cure for
human failure and malaise. In poetry (Auden), the novel
(Camus), the theater (Williams, Miller), painting (Picasso), and

modern philosophy (Sartre)—indeed, almost everywhere existentialism came into its own, and the Kierkegaardian and Freudian concepts of *Angst* acquired new life.

In full accordance with the new mood, Tillich's interest in Freud, which he had nourished since 1919, first through von Sydow and later through Goesch, Gelb, and Goldstein, began to overshadow his interest in Marx. While he did not abandon his preoccupation with politics entirely, he exchanged it to a large extent for depth psychology. He no longer thought first of transforming society, but rather of healing individuals. Aware that a new way of interpreting history had been found when Marx questioned whether intellectual and moral ideas were independent of economic and social issues,[61] Tillich had never become a thoroughgoing Marxist; nor was he an uncritical Freudian. He insisted that Christian anthropology and theology must recognize the validity of Freud's basic methods and discoveries, but on the other hand pointed to the fundamental contradiction in Freud's position: his pessimism about the human condition and his optimism in believing that mental illnesses could be cured.

In America Tillich kept abreast of developments in the field of psychology through his membership in the Columbia seminar on religion and health, the practical and theoretical programs at Union, and finally his own friendship and association with both older and younger analysts and psychotherapists.[62] They were, he once said, a substitute for his earlier acquaintance with artists. Karen Horney was among the many with whom he had ongoing conversations. His admiration for her was movingly expressed in the memorial service after her death: "Those of us who have received the gift of her friendship will never forget what she made of herself. She was what the words of Jesus say, a light on a high stand which gave light to all in the house. It was this light radiating from her being which we have experienced whenever we encountered her."[63] Erich Fromm, old acquaintance of Frankfort days, with whom the Tillichs once vacationed in Mexico; Gotthard Booth, the distinguished physician to whom Tillich recommended many students and friends in need of counseling; Seward Hiltner,

Wayne Oates, and Rollo May were still others with whom he met either privately or in discussion groups. Of the last three, May, whose face Tillich found the most interesting of those in his first Union class, became a personal friend of the Tillich family. His work in particular reveals Tillich's direct influence.

As one of the few theologians to appear frequently before psychoanalytic societies and institutes, Tillich was warmly admired for his capacity to manifest empathy and comprehension for the art and science of healing. Even when they did not fully understand what he was saying, many psychoanalysts listened to him and were inspired by his ideas. It was however primarily to the psychotherapists and pastoral counselors that Tillich seemed "like a flashing streak of brilliance and lightning on the dark horizon of post-World-War-II theology and pastoral psychology."[64] He took the time and the trouble to attend their meetings. He opened the door to the use of psychological methods in theology; he discussed the implications of his concept of the "demonic"; he deepened the understanding of forgiveness by relating it to his ideas of being accepted and self-acceptance; most important of all, he made new distinctions between neurotic and ontological anxiety. For his work begun in the 1940s, and in "recognition of his outstanding contribution to the enlarged knowledge and deeper understanding of the relations between religion and health," the Academy of Mental Health and Religion on 17 May 1962 gave Tillich its second annual award.[65] By then he had decided that existentialist thinking provided the best grounds for fruitful discussion and co-operation between clergymen and psychiatrists.[66]

Tillich's thought about modern man did not stop with analysis. He defined man's existence or "what man is" in all its ambiguity but he also suggested a remedy; he defined man's essence, and concentrated his attention on "what man ought to be." Tillich had an answer for those living in a divided world, threatened by meaninglessness and imprisoned in the "age of anxiety," as immortalized in Auden's long poem of that title to which Tillich often referred as a perfect mirror of the times.[67] Tillich's answer was "the courage to be *in spite of*" death, fate, meaninglessness, or despair, each of which in various proportions has threatened mankind throughout the centuries.[68]

Like most of Tillich's ideas, "courage" had occupied his thought for a long time: since 1912, when he talked about it at the *Vernunft—Abende* in Berlin, and again since 1925, when for the first time he contrasted courage and melancholy or depression (*Mut und Schwermut*); but it came into its own much later in his masterpiece entitled *The Courage to Be*.[69] Tillich wrote the book (dedicated to his son René) during the summer of 1950 in preparation for the Terry Lectures which he delivered at Yale that fall. Two years later when the book was published it quickly became a best seller. Many said it was because of the catchy title, which attracted the modern reader, ever eager to discover instant solutions for his spiritual predicaments. But to naïve readers the first chapter presented an almost insuperable hurdle. There Tillich indulged in one of his favorite intellectual pastimes, defining the meaning of a word (in this case *courage*) by going to its roots and tracing its development throughout Western philosophy in several languages. The chapter presupposes considerable philosophical sophistication and is written in a concise, not to say cryptic or opaque, style. In later chapters however, which almost everyone found immediately understandable (or so they thought), he distinguished between the basic types of anxiety prevailing in the three main periods of Western civilization (antiquity, the Middle Ages, and modernity), and characterized modern man as subject to *angst* deriving from meaninglessness.

Tillich went on to say that although neurotic anxiety is often curable, existential anxiety is inescapable and must therefore be faced or accepted. For this man needs "the courage to be," namely, the courage to be part of a larger whole (society) as well as to stand alone (or to be himself); and finally, the courage to let himself be upheld by the creative power of being in which every creature participates.

In that period of gloom Tillich did not strike a note of undiluted optimism, but emphasized what he had already said earlier in different ways: the doubter, as well as the sinner, is justified. The last sentence of the book, "The courage to be is rooted in the God who appears when God has disappeared in the anxiety of doubt."[70] is a perfect description, not only of the fundamentals of Tillich's doctrine of God, but also of the personal struggle he shared with modern man but which, in contrast to many other theologians, he confessed in public. Men like Kurt Goldstein and John E. Smith considered such confession itself courageous. Many of Tillich's colleagues, perhaps strangers to doubt, were jolted by the book. They accused him in the classroom of being basically a Greek philosopher and not a biblically oriented Christian theologian.

The issue came to a head in a public debate at Union between two young professors, John Dillenberger and Edmond La B. Cherbonnier, the former speaking on Tillich's behalf, the latter representing his opponents. There was a large and curious student audience, and the debate stimulated discussion but changed few minds. Tillich's popularity at Union was at its height and remained so.[71] Nevertheless, he was somewhat alarmed by the clamor as well as by the fact that so many wrote him of their difficulties with the opening chapter. This prompted him to read his book again. Since he was almost always uninterested in reading his own published material, this was unusual. He said to a friend afterward, "I do not understand why people say *The Courage to Be* is a difficult book. I just finished reading it, and it reads like a novel."[72]

The "novel," actually a skillful splicing of theology and depth psychology, pushed Tillich's name into the limelight outside academic circles. He entered upon a healing activity of his own, through private conversations with students and friends and many others who were intrigued by his ideas. This earned him the title of "therapeutic theologian." Some psychologists accused him of being too philosophical, too unconcerned with concrete methods of therapy. Yet he was wide open to those who came to him seeking help. No stranger to inner conflicts and tensions, Tillich accepted humanity in all its foibles and weaknesses and—most important of all—did not make harsh judgments. The legend of his pastoral talents circulated and grew: a student is reported to have said,

"When I feel blue, I go to the movies, but when I'm really depressed I go to Tillich."[73] In the course of time he sent numerous persons to psychotherapists in cases he thought required treatment for which he himself felt and was inadequate.

In one instance his book *The Courage to Be* produced an almost miraculous recovery. A young artist, victim of drugs and alcohol, had attempted suicide. Her counselor, a friend of Tillich's, gave her a copy of the book, and she felt transformed by it overnight. She was introduced to him later and thanked him for his help. Since Tillich himself was convinced that suicide does not solve the problem that drives a person to it, and since he was against the act in principle, he was greatly pleased that his book had helped her so much, and asked to see her paintings—a request and show of interest which made her even more deeply grateful to him.[74]

The number of unhappy or distressed young people who passed through Tillich's office increased markedly; this made him recognize that people were indeed living in an age of anxiety and urged upon him a generally pessimistic view of life. He began to share Freud's suspicion that "man's happiness is not included in the plan of creation,"[75] and wherever achieved, is always ephemeral. He saw so much unhappiness, so much dislocation, that when a genuinely happy person came to see him he was apt to run jubilantly out of his office to announce the fact to secretary, assistant, or passerby. The occasions were rare. He was equally astonished when someone who had been psychologically troubled recovered and reached the goals that had formerly eluded him or her—love, marriage, or professional success. He celebrated these occasions, rejoicing in the triumph of "being" over "non-being" or good over ill. His pessimism did not paralyze him. On the contrary, the more numerous the symptoms of illness, the more he was inspired to proclaim his message of healing. For him, life's meaning and faith were real "in spite of" all opposites.

Tillich's healing message may be seen very clearly indeed in his sermons, which are the most widely read of his works and are regarded by many as his finest achievement. At the time of his arrival in this country, he had not preached since his days of service as a vicar and as an army chaplain during World War I. Moreover, although carefully trained in homiletics at the *Domstift*, so that he knew how to organize a sermon superbly well around a biblical text, he did not know how to communicate to American students in colleges, seminaries, or university chapels. His first sermons, given at Smith College and Mt. Holyoke, he said were a "complete disaster,"[76] not so much because of his struggle with the English language as because of his lack of understanding of what students were able to hear.

Church attendance had not been part of Tillich's life since 1919 —especially not in Frankfort, where he led a life of secular individualism. His "divine education," as he called it,[77] had been interrupted by World War I and was taken up again only at Union, where in the beginning he attended chapel services irregularly, finding most of the speakers too boring. After a time, Coffin suggested to him that he was missed in chapel and that most of the faculty found regular attendance there edifying. Tillich, who never ceased to respect authority, interpreted the suggestion as a command. From then on he never missed a chapel service unless he was ill or out of town, and learned to enjoy the habit of common worship.[78] He always sat on the left side of the chapel, near the front, turning his head from side to side in constant slow motion, giving the false impression that he was not paying attention. He enjoyed seeing students and colleagues and being seen by them. In pew and pulpit he learned what American students were able to take in, and taught himself painstakingly and laboriously how to preach to them, eventually becoming one of the most popular preachers to occupy the Union pulpit.

His preaching style was marked by vivid example, concrete analogy, and such keen psychological perception that individual listeners often felt that the sermon was addressed specifically to them. He wrote his sermons out in longhand, organized them systematically, and read them aloud in an even tone of voice. Yet their effect was mesmerizing, spellbinding—sometimes dramatic. The theologically sophisticated as well as the laymen had difficulty in following his labyrinthine thought: great concentration was necessary. His trick of defining words by starting from their root meaning and his ability to concentrate everything he knew on a given subject were inevitably part of the fascination he exercised. The listener who let his mind stray might find himself forever lost. Biblical passages, philosophy, current events, the state of man's mind, and concretely observed human experience constituted the subject matter with which Tillich wrestled. His message was not couched in abstract language but in meditatively poetic or psychological terms.

At Union and elsewhere the mixed audience of laymen and students reinforced Tillich's resolve to communicate in language understandable to everyone. Although he had begun to substitute philosophical language for traditional religious terms as early as 1909, when he found that to many people the old Christian words no longer meant anything, he learned in time that there were no real substitutes for words like "sin" or "grace."[79] Even the words of the great mystics, which he sometimes used, were not always appropriate he felt because they did not fully express the substance of the Christian gospel.[80] In the Tillichian vocabulary *sin* became separation, *grace* reunion, *God* the Ground and aim of Being and *faith* ultimate concern. People in the pew hearing that sin was not a single immoral act but a universal state of separation in which man found himself alienated from himself, from others, and from God, felt relieved and illuminated. Hearing that grace was not a virtue or a state of perfection but a state of reunion with that from which they had become separated, they felt comforted. Hearing that God was not "a being beside others" but "the Ground of Being" or "Being Itself," they may have felt somewhat confused— not always able to follow Tillich's use of abstractions—but were stimulated in their quest for understanding. At Union the philosophically inclined applauded Tillich's style, while the more conservative theologians were made uneasy by the untraditional language, preferring "God" to "Being itself," "Christ" to "New Being," and "Holy Spirit" to "Spiritual Presence."

Yet the very purpose of Tillich's use of unaccustomed philosophical or psychological words was to make the biblical text, on which his sermons were built and from which he never departed, truly understood, as he saw it.

The most important ingredient of Tillich's effectiveness as a preacher was the plain fact that he almost always preached to himself, and therefore to everyman. In some way or other each sermon-topic grew out of what he himself had experienced, directly or indirectly: he sometimes felt lonely in a crowd and sought solitude in nature, only to return to human company; he sought escape from the threatening presence of God through his work, only to find that it did not give him the full meaning of his life; he was afraid of being forgotten and tempted by yearning for immortality; he often felt he was the victim of his inescapable past and tried to live in the future; his depths were often unquiet when he needed to be at peace. The analogies are as numerous as the sermons; his experience, so self-consciously preserved, became an illumination for those who themselves were no strangers to doubt, insecurity, anguish, fulfillment, or joy, and their hearts were made glad to know that he too had stood in their place.[81] Only in his old age, when his concerns became a little faddish, did his sermons grow less powerful. In seeking to encourage young people in their nonconformist ways, he reaffirmed a prevailing trend but did not direct or transcend it.

Every spring for the last ten years of his life he preached the same carefully prepared new sermon at Harvard, Yale, and Chicago before finally coming to New York, where he preached at Union. He said he had learned from the New York world of theater that it was essential to try out or rehearse new sermons "in the provinces before opening night on Broadway."[82] Yet the sermons underwent few changes once they were written out. Only the second-to-last one, entitled "Life and Death," which he preached at Union Seminary in April 1964, was entirely rewritten the night before, keeping him up until three in the morning, not because he felt he had to revise it but because he had lost the manuscript on which he always depended.

In every congregation there were groups of friends to whom he had sent out postcards informing them of the time, place, and date of his sermon. Before each service, Tillich's eyes combed the congregation searching them out, and if a single one he had expected to be there was missing, he got in touch with him or her as soon as possible to discover why. He cared very much about the impression the sermons made, eagerly soliciting reactions, carefully reading the faces of those present or even the mail that came in increasing quantities in later years, and which he put in a manila file marked "Fan Mail." While at Union, largely because of the presence of so many personal friends in the city (most of whom were emigrés like himself), he initiated the tradition of post-sermon parties to entertain those who attended regularly as well as those who had made their way from out of town to be present. Slowly, over the years, the group, which included only a few Union colleagues, grew to more than fifty in number, and were to be found after the occasion in Tillich's apartment, sipping sherry or light wine and talking with him and one another. When Tillich moved to Harvard in 1955, Wilhelm Pauck, who had joined the Union faculty in 1953, entertained the after-sermon group until his wife Olga became too frail to handle the preparations. From then on until Tillich's death the event took place in the home of Samuel Terrien, professor of Old Testament, and his wife Sara, who had become admirers of Tillich and whose intellectual nimbleness and gracious hospitality he found stimulating and delightful.

The response to the sermons among Tillich's friends, students, and colleagues was almost always extremely favorable, and the demand for copies of what he had said on a given Sunday morning increased. Some wished to ponder what had been helpful to them, others to refresh their recollection of what had been said. It was largely to fulfill this demand that the first volume of sermons appeared in 1948, entitled *The Shaking of the Foundations*, and dedicated to Tillich's daughter Erdmuthe. Several of his most enthusiastic students, among them Elizabeth Cooper, William Fennell, and Mary Heilner, had revised and organized the sermons and chapel talks, spending many hours with their author, who was grateful for their "creative criticism,"[83] which he confessed had made publication possible. This time Scribners did not hesitate to publish what turned out to be the most popular of all the Tillich sermon collections. In 1955 a second volume appeared, entitled *The New Being* and dedicated to Mary Heilner, one of Tillich's most imaginative and perceptive students, who had served as sole editor. Finally in 1963 *The Eternal Now* was published (dedicated to the memory of Hermann Schafft), for which the difficult preparatory work was so sensitively done by Elizabeth Cooper Wood.

Tillich himself once said that his sermons manifested the "existential implications" of his theology.[84] The same may be said for the little talks or short sermons he delivered in connection with weddings at which he officiated, a custom he brought over from Germany. Those to be married frequently asked him to give such a talk, in which he always spoke directly to the bride and groom, whose inner life was often familiar to him. These talks have not appeared in print, but a characteristic passage from one such service may be quoted.

There is . . . a short sentence in the second chapter of the first book of Moses, the profundity and wisdom of which is not surpassed by any saying about marriage in all literature. "It is not good," says God, "that the man should be alone. I will make him a helpmeet for him." Meet for him—this means to suit him, to be a match for him or—as an old interpretation suggests—"answering him." Man, male as well as female, needs somebody who answers. But nothing in nature can do so. Nature returns to man what it has received from him. Man alone is able to answer man. A marriage is possible only if those united by it can answer each other. And the more they can do so the more perfect is the communion in which they live. Every word we say and every word we restrain implies an unbroken question to him whom we love and who seeks an answer.[85]

The Systematic Theology

It is an irony that Tillich expressed himself more convincingly in his sermons than anywhere else, including even his *Systematic Theology*.[86] Throughout the various stages of its development, which covered a period of more than fifty years, the system be came Tillich's driving passion, his "sword of Damocles," a "rock of infinite dimensions" lying on his shoulders,[87] an ocean of which he plumbed the depths. As a young man he told his bride that he would give up everything for her except his work;[88] in his middle years, he once left the manuscript of the *Systematic Theology* in a compartment on a train and was inconsolable until it was re-trieved;[89] in later life, on the occasion of Archbishop Temple's death, he was heard to remark, "Ah, and he understood my system —it is a great loss."[90] Tillich identified himself with his system to such a degree that many of his friends feared life would appear meaningless to him once he had externalized what for so long had lived inside his head.[91]

As it turned out, the general outline of the magnum opus he had first conceived in his twenties was brought to completion only two years before his death. There were long periods in which the work lay dormant, as well as moments at the end of his life when he feared he might not achieve his goal. The first sign of heart illness put him into depression and near-panic; the increasing number of lecture tours to which he committed himself and which he was unable to resist slowed him up even more; the swirl of parties, the myriad personal relationships from which at the end even he was unable to separate himself, all competed with that "ultimate con-cern," the systematic theology. Even more, a certain perfectionism on Tillich's part, a suspicion that anything as contemporaneous as this work might in the end turn out to be stillborn, combined to prevent its swift completion. One may say that Tillich finished "the system" in spite of himself!

During the period between his dissertations and the beginning of his military service, he had written out the outline of a systematic theology;[92] neither a *Summa Theologica* of the sort Thomas Aquinas had written nor a *Church Dogmatics* in the manner of Karl Barth. It was not unique or even unusual for a German theologian to be drawn to the systematic form. Since the days of Friedrich Schleiermacher, who set down the first modern Protes-tant system, hundreds of systems had sprung into being, particularly in Germany where the talent for intellectual architectonics flourished. Tillich's drive to be consistent, his desire to conceive of theology in its wholeness, and his wish to discover the coherence of symbols and concepts, were the motivations that led him toward the system as a form for which he had an inherent affection. His love of beauty, balance, and strength, his love of the aesthetic and the architectural, were all factors expressed in this work on which he delivered the first lectures while teaching at the University of Marburg in 1924. Later, in Dresden and Frankfort, distracted by the political situation and forced to apply himself to the needs of a philosophical curriculum, he temporarily abandoned it.

Paradoxically enough, his enforced emigration to a land which he had considered culturally and intellectually barren brought his precious plant to full bloom and fruition. What had lain dormant for so long (but by no means forgotten—every article, essay, or book review, every idea in Tillich's head was part of what the system became) was reawakened in America.[93] In alternate years, soon after his arrival, he gave a course on the three parts of the system, providing his students with a detailed outline of propositions or theses on which he commented freely in the classroom. The outline grew, the comments adjusted themselves always to the contemporary scene. In time he introduced into his theology the element of existentialist thinking. He was little influenced by American theological thought, which he considered at first too empirical and later too much concerned with linguistic analysis, not sufficiently systematic. In direct response to the spiritual situation he found in America, Tillich developed the "method of correlation," a methodological tool as old as apologetic theology, which became (to use his own analogy) the backbone of his system. He sought to satisfy two basic needs: the explication of the truth contained in the Christian message (this he regarded as centrally significant for all mankind) and the interpretation of this truth for every new generation. His awareness that all theology moved back and forth between these two poles made him an apologetic rather than a kerygmatic theologian. Moreover, although his system was not a restatement of biblical theology, he took the biblical message with utter and complete seriousness. His conviction that the meaning of Christian symbols had become increasingly opaque during his lifetime, coupled with his personal inability to accept the split between a faith unacceptable to culture and a culture unacceptable to faith, prompted him to interpret the articles of faith through cultural expressions. This was something, as we know, that he had done from the beginning of his career.

During Tillich's first fifteen years in this country, when he was not well known, his "real work" as he called it was the construction of his systematic theology. Yet he began the actual writing of an outline in the form of a set of propositions only after World War II. Even then he was uncertain that there was an American audience for the work he envisaged. Two things changed his mind: increased urging on the part of his students, colleagues, and friends, and the postwar atmosphere, which seemed to him at long last to "hunger" for systematic thinking, for unity and wholeness.[94]

In order to help get Tillich's work under way, his assistant John Dillenberger wrote down *verbatim* everything Tillich said in his lectures on the subject, using a self-taught shorthand. In this, Tillich's slow delivery proved a valuable asset. Then immediately after class Dillenberger dictated what he had written to an efficient typist.[95] This manuscript became Tillich's first draft, which being a literal reproduction of the spoken word was stilted and lifeless. Tillich labored for several years making minor and often major changes, sometimes rewriting whole passages completely, to achieve his goal. The first volume alone underwent several revisions. John Dillenberger and Cornelius Loew, a second assistant of Tillich's, edited the manuscript, the former concerning himself with documentation, the latter with style, both searching out errors, contradictions, and repetitions, and each spending many hours with Tillich in intense discussion. Albert T. Mollegen, by then a member of the faculty of Virginia Theological Seminary, also helped him with formal criticism and encouragement. On the basis of these suggestions, Tillich rewrote the first volume of his work, making the final revisions during the summer of 1949 and in the fall and winter of 1950. Tillich's secretary, Hilde Frankel, a woman of charm, character, and great ability, with an independent judgment of her own on which Tillich had for some time relied, typed each of the revisions. Her death from cancer shortly after the work was completed deprived him of one of his most loyal friends.

The same preliminary work was done by John Dillenberger alone for Volume II, when he and Tillich were colleagues at Harvard after 1955. Clark Williamson, Tillich's assistant at the University of Chicago, did similar work for Volume III. Williamson was provided with a fully typed manuscript and a detailed outline in the autumn of 1962. Tillich had spent most of the previous summer in East Hampton working on the book in his garden, by then lush and full. Williamson's instructions were to render the whole into idiomatic English without changing the Tillichian flavor. He later quipped that it was then for the first time that he understood the meaning of paradox. The two worked backward, beginning with part V, "History and the Kingdom of God," then moving to part IV, "Life and the Spirit," about which Tillich said that it contained a philosophy of life of which Schelling was the teacher and he merely the student. He was very reluctant to submit this last section to the publisher, but finally did so realizing he could not keep him waiting forever. This is a section with which he remained basically dissatisfied, and which struck many readers as tedious because of its repetitiveness.[96]

All this work of preparation, although rigorous and time-consuming, was done in a relaxed setting, accompanied by wine in Dillenberger's time and Jack Daniel's bourbon in Williamson's. For all who helped Tillich their efforts represented a labor of love (a few received remuneration), which he acknowledged in the introductions to his work and for which he was doubtless genuinely grateful; yet the amount and quality of help he received was unique in American academic circles, and one cannot be sure (as

Henry Coffin has pointed out) that Tillich was sufficiently aware of this fact.[97]

When Volume I was published in 1951 there was great celebration in the theological world. In New York, students crowded into the Union Theological Seminary bookstore around the beaming author, who obliged all with his autograph. H. R. Niebuhr described it as "a great voyage of discovery into a rich and deep, an inclusive and yet elaborated vision and understanding of human life in the presence of the mystery of God."[98] Although he commended Tillich for his consistency and "noble, closely reasoned and integrated presentation of the greatest theme in life,"[99] he and others found the work too difficult, too abstract, and too ontological. One characteristic reaction came, not from the pen of a theologian but from the poet T. S. Eliot, whom Tillich had met at the home of a common friend in London. Eliot had read the book twice, on sea voyages to and from South Africa, and was so impressed by its fertilizing effect on his mind that he thanked Tillich for writing it. He pointed out, moreover, that neither his New England Unitarian background nor his conversion to the Church of England had conditioned him to Tillich's work, but he considered it a great book nevertheless.[100]

The general acclaim with which Volume I was received did not prompt Tillich to turn out the second volume with undue haste. Six years passed before *Existence and the Christ* saw the light of day. He spent the summer of 1950 writing *The Courage To Be* and an autobiographical essay for *The Theology of Paul Tillich*, the first of a series on leading American theologians edited by Charles W. Kegley and Robert W. Bretall. The latter work, published in 1952, demonstrated that Tillich had by then become one of a handful of important figures in American philosophical thought; the editors ranked him with Dewey, Whitehead, Russell, and Santayana. Although the book contains many knowledgeable and interpretative articles, it was premature and inadequate—premature because Volumes II and III of Tillich's system were not yet in print, nor did anyone account for his German writings. Two pieces

were particularly illuminating: Albert T. Mollegen's essay on Tillich's Christology, which is generally accepted as the best apologia
for a position many regarded as gnostic, and Reinhold Niebuhr's
amusing analysis of Tillich's boundary-line stance:

> Tillich's greatness lies in his exploration of the boundary between
> metaphysics and theology. The difficult task of "walking the tight-
> rope" is not negotiated without the peril of losing one's balance and
> falling over on one side or the other. If Barth refuses to approach the
> vicinity of the fence because he doesn't trust his balance, Tillich
> performs upon it with the greatest virtuosity, but not without an
> occasional fall. The fall may be noticed by some humble pedestrians
> who lack every gift to perform the task themselves.[101]

There is also John Hermann Randall's crisp approval of Tillich as
a philosopher.

> Paul Tillich seems to me not only the ablest Protestant theologian
> of the present day, but also by far the most persuasive exponent of
> the philosophy of existentialism, and, what is more to the point, a
> real contributor to the present-day revival of metaphysical inquiry.
> His is a first-rate philosophical mind.[102]

In the summer of 1951 Tillich again went abroad, briefly visiting Germany where he lectured at the Institute of Politics at the
Free University of Berlin in May and June on "The Political
Meaning of Utopia."[103] After this "debut" in Berlin, he repeated
his perambulations of 1948 by including Hamburg, Düsseldorf,
Cologne, Bonn, Kassel, Marburg, and Frankfort on his itinerary
between the end of June and the middle of July, then abruptly
returning to East Hampton to prepare for one of the more demanding engagements of his entire career.

This was something that Henry Van Dusen, painfully aware of
the many distractions which were slowing up Tillich's progress on
the systematic theology, had skillfully arranged. In March 1951, in
reply to an inquiry from T. M. Taylor, Principal of the University
of Aberdeen, he had recommended that Tillich be invited to give
the coveted Gifford Lectures in 1953 and 1954, using Volumes II
and III of the system as texts. At the same time, Van Dusen and

the Union authorities granted him a sabbatical semester in which to devote all his time to this one task.[104] This unprecedented gift incidentally enabled Tillich to remain on the Union faculty a full year beyond retirement age.* He spent the summer and autumn of 1951 in writing the Gifford Lectures. A month before his sixty-fifth birthday he remarked in a letter to his friend Fedor Stepun, "Inasmuch as I shall be sixty-five years old this year, and there are some signs that I am not in the forties any longer, the anticipation of death (Heidegger) becomes an increasingly prevalent occupation of mine. And yet I say yes to every moment that is still given to me."[105]

Tillich's sense of declining vitality was not then apparent to anyone else; he interrupted his sabbatical semester and consequently his work on the system at least once. In the fall he gave the Richard Lectures in Virginia, later published under the title *Biblical Religion and the Search for Ultimate Reality*, a monograph of eighty-five pages which one of his colleagues, John C. Bennett, professor of Christian ethics and successor to Henry Van Dusen, later described as "Tillich's perfect book."[106] It is a defense of his own biblicism and a concise, fresh statement of his conviction that every theologian implies a philosophical position when he uses traditional and especially biblical language. It is an eloquent plea for the essential function of philosophy in religious thought, as Tillich himself had mastered it.

In May 1952 Tillich journeyed briefly to England to deliver the Firth Lectures on "Love, Power, and Justice" at the University of Nottingham. In this connection he also visited Cumberland Lodge in Great Windsor Park, where he lectured on "Man in Late Industrial Society" to an audience which included the Queen Mother Elizabeth and Princess Margaret. He was so charmed by them and so excited at being presented to them personally that he sent a cable home. *Love, Power, and Justice* was not published until 1954, after he had repeated the lectures at Union Theological

---

* Professors at Union normally retired at the age of sixty-five. But if they desired and the board of directors so decided, they could continue in their position for three more years when retirement became mandatory.

Seminary in Richmond, Virginia. Tillich characterized the difficulty he encountered in formulating this compact ontological analysis as having "surpassed almost everything I have experienced in my academic career."[107] Allowing for his tendency to exaggerate, he might have said the same of the confusion that attended publication of the little volume abroad. In a moment of unthinking generosity, he had promised the German translation rights to several publishers. His carelessness plunged him, two years later, into an almost inextricable difficulty, from which he was rescued by the kindly editors of the Oxford University Press in London and New York, who published the English and American versions. This impasse was one of several into which Tillich's absentminded dealings drove him; it led several concerned friends to urge him to appoint a literary executor in order to avoid future embarrassment.

Love, Power, and Justice was generally well received, and especially welcomed by no less a man of letters than the political analyst Walter Lippmann, who wrote to a friend,

> When I returned from California a few days ago I found the book which you were good enough to send me. It is most welcome, because I am just getting ready to go back to my book in which—at one important point—I have drawn heavily upon Tillich's "Systematic Theology."

> He is, I think, a very powerful thinker, and listening to him last winter in a long private debate with Maritain, which was organized by the Ford Foundation, I was struck in addition by his great gentleness.

> I need hardly tell you how happy I am to have the book from you.[108]

In 1953, a year after delivering the Firth Lectures, Tillich went abroad again, this time in the company of his son René, who had just graduated from Exeter near Portsmouth, N.H. They sailed to France on 20 June on the *Mauretania*.[109] In the whirlwind tour that followed, he combined sight-seeing with lecture appearances. He talked in Berlin, Munich, and Marburg, after which he enjoyed a brief respite in the Swiss Engadine Alps. Then he took part in conferences at Ascona and the Chateau de Bossey in Switzerland. Always lecturing, he traveled through Zurich, Basel, Cologne, Düren, and Düsseldorf to Denmark. After a brief visit to London, he finally arrived in Aberdeen on 1 November. Tired and depressed, he complained that he was sleeping in his thirty-fourth bed of the summer. He stayed at the Gloucester Hotel where his room was like a "monk's cell." There he rewrote his Gifford Lectures each day and evening until long past midnight, keeping his energies high on some wonderful sausage a friend in London had given him (the food in the hotel was only fair). Attracted by the romantic harbor, he walked along the beach, only to find that the cold wind aggravated a chest cold and cough which for several weeks had plagued him.[110] To add to his misery, as time passed he was unsure how the lectures were being received. Entitled "Existence and the Christ," they contained the material he intended for the second volume of his *Systematic Theology*. The lectures were delivered during November and early December, and although he was repeatedly assured that attendance was high, the audience seemed small. There were on average less than twenty in attendance. Nor did the polite and reserved Scots always tell him how they were reacting to his words. Despite the cold and the discomfort and his seemingly unresponsive listeners, Tillich persisted doggedly in his task. He enjoyed the welcome and hospitality of the university and even included in his full schedule several excursions to St. Andrews, Glasgow, and Edinburgh. By mid-December he was ready to go home.[111]

The following May, in order to deliver the second series of Gifford Lectures, after a full semester of teaching and lecturing in America, Tillich went abroad again. This time he took along his attractive daughter Erdmuthe who a few years earlier had married Theodore Farris, an educational administrator. Once there, he repeated the exhausting schedule which had tired and depressed him so much a year earlier, combining travel with lecture appearances and participating—among other things—in one of several centenary commemorations of Schelling's death. Although asked to present a paper at a large, formal conference in Bad Ragaz, where

Schelling died (20 August 1854) and where men of the caliber of Karl Jaspers, Gabriel Marcel, and Emil Staiger were appearing, Tillich was forced to decline. He had committed himself earlier to speak in Stuttgart, Germany, at a smaller conference in Schelling's honor scheduled to begin a day after the Swiss conference ended. The event took place on Sunday 26 September and represented for him a symbolic return to his intellectual beginnings. (The theme of tribute to Schelling in fact accompanied him throughout 1954–55: in January he gave a lecture entitled "Schelling zum 100 Todestage" [Schelling on the Hundredth Anniversay of His Death], to a group of German emigrés in Chicago, and in May a set of formal, abstract lectures, "The Existentialism of Schelling's Positive Philosophy and Its Significance for Today," at the University of Indiana.[112])

In October and November 1954 Tillich delivered his second series in the Gifford Lectures in Aberdeen, on "Life and the Spirit." The dates had been moved back so that he might be free to speak in Hamburg in December. This time, partly on account of the fine weather, partly because of an enthusiastic audience, he greatly enjoyed himself. His friendship with Professor MacKinnon and his wife enlivened his stay; moreover, MacKinnon's farewell speech "was so warm and understanding," Tillich said, "that I shall never forget it."[113] Tillich wrote to Principal Taylor in late November,

> The purpose of this letter is to thank you for everything you have done for me, first by asking me to be the Gifford Lecturer and then by making my stay at Aberdeen as nice and comfortable as you did.
>
> I want to repeat what I told you and Lady Taylor that this time I enjoyed Aberdeen much more than last time and shall have only the very best memories of people and place.
>
> But perhaps the greatest thing I have received from the nine weeks at Aberdeen was the occasion to concentrate without interruption on my main work.[114]

But there were inevitably more interruptions before the Gifford Lectures appeared in print. *Dynamics of Faith*, Tillich's popular summary of the basic theological views he had often repeated in earlier pieces, was only one of several commitments he was forced to complete during the very period in which he complained to friends that he simply had no time to work on "the system." This book was published in 1957 in the same year as Volume II of the *Systematic Theology,* which represented the first part of the Gifford Lectures. Tillich appropriately dedicated the latter work to the faculty of Union Theological Seminary in gratitude for his reception in 1933 and for the many years of teaching, writing, and learning there, as well as for the friendly cooperation between himself and his colleagues. Primarily, however, he wished to recall by means of the dedication that his Christology, the major theme of this volume, had been the center of discussions with students and faculty throughout the years.

Tillich's philosophical assumptions were challenged by Reinhold Niebuhr, for example, when he referred to Tillich as the "Origen of our period" because he sought to relate the gospel message to the disciplines of culture by means of ontological concepts.[115] Indeed, Tillich's Christology remained the most problematical and difficult point of his entire work, not only for himself but also for others; it often disturbed Union students who were more biblically oriented. Tillich seldom made it his practice to respond to his critics; in fact he proceeded in his work in almost utter disregard of those who cared enough about his system to commit themselves to a critique of its shortcomings.[116] While he always thanked them for taking the trouble to deal with his thought, the stones they threw made no visible mark on the structure of ideas he continued to erect.

He responded instead to the demand of many colleagues and students who increasingly pressed him for an outline of Volume III in the absence of the book itself. It was a time (the late 1950s) when courses on Tillich's thought were being introduced in the theological curriculum of many schools, and dissertations written on his system. More than ever, the need of many to see his work as a whole pressed in upon him. Moreover, the publishers were grow-

ing impatient with the seemingly endless procrastinations of their
author, who persisted in asking whether he should finish his work
on the system after all. The answer was always "Yes!"

In 1963 Volume III of the *Systematic Theology* containing
"Life and the Spirit" and a section on "History and the Kingdom
of God" was finally published. By then the early enthusiasm for
Tillich's unique contribution, so perfectly and sharply formulated
in the first volume and so heretically in the second, had given way
to increasing criticism, to which the author had grown sensitive. It
underlined his own gnawing doubt about the validity and finality of
what he had worked so long to achieve. Although to some the
volume represented the very acme of Tillichian perfection (one
scholar called it a perfect diamond[117]), for others it fell below
expectations.

Still others found it tedious in its overemphasis on the ambiguity
of life. This had reference to a section, about which Tillich himself
harbored grave reservations.[118] A young linguistic analyst, Paul
van Buren, wholly unreceptive to the Tillichian world of ideas,
declared in his review in the *Christian Century*, the most influential of popular religious journals, that the system was irrelevant
and useless in American scholarship.[119] Daniel Day Williams, the
sensitive and generous Whiteheadian theologian who had by then
succeeded Tillich at Union, and who was more inclined toward a
positive reception of Tillich's views, agreed to write an answering
review—partly because he felt that an injustice had been done to
his great predecessor's work and partly because Tillich lay ill in a
Chicago hospital and was unduly disturbed by van Buren's criticism. Tillich felt that Williams' review was an adequate answer to
van Buren, but he was nevertheless beginning to fear that his work
was being relegated to the "dustheap of the past" even before his
death.[120]

Tillich's own description of Volume III as "an incompleteness
of the completed" is a confession which strikes the note of his
acceptance of finitude, a note of resignation and relief rather than
of achievement.[121] He had agonized over it, grown bored with it;
had continually wished to change and nearly failed to finish it.

(His trips to Greece as well as Japan, among other adventures of the spirit in the 1950s, had on more than one occasion inspired him to say that his entire system had to be rewritten in the light of his new visions of the ancient and Eastern worlds.) Yet he lived to see his unique and magnificent intellectual creation accepted by even very critical minds. One scholar compared it to a pyramid, another to an ocean, and still another, J. H. Randall, Jr., the formidable historian of philosophy, declared it to be "beyond doubt the richest, most suggestive, and most challenging philosophical theology our day has produced."[122]

7

The Ambiguity of Fame (1955-1965)

The Crest of the Wave

When in 1953 Tillich had celebrated the twentieth anniversary of his arrival in America, he was fully conscious of the fact that the new world which had taken him in had finally opened up for him in a dramatic way. He was grateful and delighted by his new influence and eager to have it continue. Moreover, he felt a great responsibility to the people and the land that had made his late harvest possible. To this he paid tribute in a letter to Ludwig Metzger, the minister of education in Hesse, Germany who had for so long tried to entice Tillich to Marburg. In declining the invitation, Tillich showed a shrewd instinct for recognizing his own *kairos*.

> America has accepted me in these last years to a degree I never anticipated and in a way that few emigrés experience. It would be irresponsible to interrupt the process of this reception at this time. I see myself fulfilling the function of a bridge between the Anglo-Saxon and the German theological world. I must remain true to my fate of emigration.[1]

In the following months, he found himself increasingly preoccupied with his inevitable retirement from Union Seminary, a prospect he openly dreaded. Despite his repeated insistence that he was growing old and tired and that he felt unable to fulfill the demands of his schedule, he was reluctant to relinquish the influential role at which he had worked so hard and long. A quiet old age spent in East Hampton did not appeal to him, nor did the limitations of a reduced income. He was by no means a poor man; his books were selling well, and he could look forward to receiving a German as well as an American pension, but he was anxious, nevertheless, at the prospect of more limited financial circumstances. Then, less than a year after his letter to Metzger, income and influence were not only extended but enlarged to a degree he himself had never anticipated. The academic interests of Nathan Pusey, president of Harvard University, as well as the forceful persuasion of Henry Van Dusen combined to save him from the boredom and "poverty" of idle old age.

At the time, Pusey was planning to appoint another University Professor, as the title ran, to the Harvard faculty.[2] The University Professorships had been inaugurated by President Conant in 1936 in order to bring five or six distinguished productive scholars representing interdisciplinary areas to Harvard at the same time. Such scholars were free to teach as much or as little as they wished and were reappointed from year to year, depending on the state of their health, until they reached the mandatory retirement age of seventy-five. University Professors, moreover, were the personal choice of the president alone and responsible in an informal way only to him. Pusey was eager to appoint such a man and set about in search for one; in his capacity as acting dean of the Harvard Divinity School, an institution in need of strengthening and in process of reorganization, he was also in search of a "star," a shining light, in the field of theology. As it turned out he fulfilled both intentions with the same man.

Henry Van Dusen, then a member of a committee which had been set up to make recommendations regarding the Harvard Divinity School, drew Pusey's attention to Tillich's availability.

Pusey did not know Tillich personally (they had met only once, briefly, in the mid-1940s at Lawrence College), but had read many of his books and was greatly interested in the man and his thought. At first he invited him to teach at Harvard for a period of one semester each year. Meanwhile Van Dusen, hoping to retain Tillich's services at Union, proposed that he teach there in the capacity of visiting professor for the second semester or term. Tillich, who had little appetite for commuting between the two institutions, deliberated for some time whether he should accept one, the other, or both invitations. Then Pusey shrewdly made him an offer he was unable to refuse: to be University Professor at Harvard, full time and at a handsome salary.[3] Tillich's hesitation abruptly vanished. He accepted Pusey's invitation with alacrity and turned Van Dusen's down. The latter, who felt he had been the victim of a double-edged betrayal, was briefly angered that Tillich had been snatched from him in this way, but quickly reconciled himself to the new situation and arranged instead to have Tillich lecture at Union during several summer sessions in later years. Tillich's appointment to Harvard was announced in April 1954, a full year before the retirement he now no longer dreaded. Congratulatory messages from all sides poured in throughout the summer, following him across the Atlantic as he sailed to deliver his second series in Gifford Lectures, and to many of them he replied on his voyage home.

During his last semester at Union, feeling encouraged and in a mood of excited anticipation, Tillich remained absorbed in preparations for his move, responding to his normal routine with energy and éclat. The time was not without its rude shocks: the tragic and untimely death of two loyal friends, David Roberts and Mary Heilner, which served as a painful reminder of the reality and power of illness. The need to heal mankind was a theme he therefore intoned in his commencement sermon at Union, when he encouraged the graduating class to "heal the sick, cast out demons."[4] In his farewell address to the Union board of directors, Tillich confessed that Union was his "home" and that no matter where he went it would remain so.[5] It was a tribute to Union which he repeated seven years later even in his farewell address to Harvard University.

Of the constant round of farewell parties which stretched out into the summer, the last brought together in Tillich's home some of his closest friends in America: Kurt Goldstein, Adolf Löwe, Eduard Heimann, and Wilhelm Pauck and their wives. Each of these men had remained independent of Tillich; each bore the distinction of seeing and accepting him as he was; on each Tillich had depended for criticism and support; and to each in many ways he was indebted. Pauck made the after-dinner speech, sending him on his way to the last great chapter of his career.

That summer, by way of reply to Richard Kroner's congratulatory letter, Tillich predicted: "My old age will not be a quiet one, at least so far as I can tell, and in any case a quiet old age would not have been something for me. . . . But after my seventy-fifth birthday I will read only Greek."[6]

His premonitions were only partially fulfilled, for from the time of his arrival at Harvard until his death he never again found time for Greek—a euphemism for moments of meditation and tranquility. In that decade he addressed and enjoyed the largest audiences of his career; he traveled and lectured in the Orient, in the Middle East, Europe, and America, and became the recipient of honorary degrees and medals.[7] He enlarged his already wide circle of friends and acquaintances and cooperated with those wishing to erect monuments to his name.

At Harvard Tillich occupied an office "big enough for dancing" as he proudly described it, first in the Semitic Museum, a dark old vine-covered building, later on the top floor of the Widener Library, a grey stone edifice with matching Greek pillars in the center of the campus. He once confessed to his colleague Paul Lehmann, (the extraordinarily gifted and complex theologian who inclined his heart to Karl Barth), that although he loved his office he felt guilty that it was so much larger than anyone else's. When Lehmann replied that it showed how great a man Tillich was, the latter said at once, "In ten years, no one will be interested in my theology any more."[8] In a way the spacious office, flooded with light and with a view to the open campus, was a symbol of the new freedom in which Tillich visibly expanded. Unlike another University Professor, the great Greek classics scholar Werner Jaeger, who concentrated primarily on research, turning out his incomparable three-volume *Paideia*,[9] Tillich was from the start a public figure. A distinguished theologian set down in a larger context, he was no longer hemmed in by the requirements of a seminary community; he was utterly free from any obligation to the church and constantly in touch with a variety of disciplines without having to identify himself with any of them. Accordingly, his position on the boundary between religion and culture was strengthened.[10] In his many conversations with the members of other faculties (business, science, medicine, and law) he displayed an untiring curiosity, and as of old relished fencing with unsympathetic or critical faculty members.[11] A certain lack of sympathy for him and his ideas existed, particularly among some scientists and in the philosophy department. Soon after his arrival a protest was registered in the *Harvard Crimson*.

> From what was the high position that science held under President Conant, the field has definitely dropped in prestige in the last few years. The appointment of such men as philosopher Paul J. Tillich to University Professorships has made some science men uneasy. They have pointed to the fact that since physicist Percy Bridgman retired from his University Professorship last June, his chair has remained vacant. But, more specifically, their fear is crystallized in Tillich, because, some of them say, he represents a modern religious attitude that places much of the blame for the state of the world on science and urges greater attention to other values.[12]

Certain members of the philosophy department, with which Tillich was otherwise proud to ally himself, were cool toward him. Some of the philosophers and their students, more interested in logical positivism than in classical idealism, were cordial to Tillich personally but regarded his ideas with disdain. One philosopher went so far as to call Tillich's thought "unintelligible nonsense."[13] These critical views merely challenged Tillich to introduce his ideas to the various schools. Once or twice a year he delivered formal addresses there, in which he skillfully spliced the seemingly unrelated disciplines. At Harvard Medical School he once spoke on "The Concept of God"; at the Business School, on "The Theology of Business"; at the Department of Social Relations, on "Conformism, Protestantism and the Present Religious Resurgence"; at M.I.T., on "How Science in the Last Century Changed Man's View of Himself," and finally, at the Fogg Art Museum, on "Modern Religious Art and Modern Religious Art History."

Although Tillich prided himself on never going to church at Harvard, just as he had prided himself on going to chapel every day at Union, he lectured at the Harvard Divinity School, attended its faculty meetings, and was greatly interested in the "political" situation as it developed there under the leadership of Dean Douglas Horton.[14] Moreover the presence of a number of old friends on the faculty, among them James Luther Adams, John Dillenberger, and Paul Lehmann, ensured him a warm reception. Those who registered private disapproval of Tillich's thought did so in part to defend their identity against the threat of his enormous success. Tillich enjoyed the exchange that grew out of intellectual differences, but he enjoyed even more being a threat to his Harvard colleagues— a threat which increased as time went on and was achieved largely in the classroom, where he consistently drew the largest number of students.

Twice a month, in his small cluttered Chauncy Street apartment, in the midst of beer cans and cigarette smoke, Tillich held a graduate colloquium or seminar for the doctoral candidates of the Divinity School.[15] For precisely thirty minutes (timed by an alarm clock) a doctoral candidate described the outline of his dissertation, then answered the questions of other students immediately afterward. Tillich, always the last to speak, gathered together dangling threads, going to the heart of the matter, and gave his own reactions to what had been said. For many, including Harvey Cox (now a member of the theological faculty at Harvard), Tillich's seminar became one of the most informative experiences of their lives.

At Harvard, for the first time in his life, Tillich lectured mostly to undergraduate students, presenting himself as a sort of Zarathustra speaking to the human dilemma. His lectures on the "Philosophy of Religion" and "Religion and Culture" were both very well attended, but his course on "The Self-Interpretation of Western Man" was his greatest triumph. He gave some part of it every year, spreading it over four semesters: "Early Greek Culture," "Late Ancient Culture," "Renaissance Culture," and "Modern Culture." It was his favorite course, for he had worked on it throughout his academic career. Eventually the several hundred Harvard students who registered for it were forced to arrive an hour before class time in order to find seats.[16] Tillich himself, for a time overweight and bearlike, always came precisely on time, shut the windows, coughed, fiddled with his papers, answered questions, and then lectured from outline notes on which he extemporized. His magical way of making the meaning of ancient ideas relevant to modern times never ceased to amaze and fascinate his listeners. His intellectual vigor and energy remained unimpaired until his last year at Harvard, when two serious illnesses visibly aged and weakened him, both physically and mentally.[17] Except for these times, he never missed a class. His impact on the undergraduates remained stunning until the end. Crowds of students lined up to see him walk to class; they often applauded when he finished speaking, and habitually quoted the somewhat exaggerated statements he made at this stage of his life—e.g., "Marienbad is the movie of the century!" His "disciples" or followers on campus and in the Divinity School read his work diligently, but many quoted what they had read without thinking it through for themselves. When he gave the Ingersoll Lecture on "Symbols of Eternal Life," Memorial Chapel was packed and there was an air of expectancy as he rose to speak. At the end of his first year, members of the Phi Beta Kappa society on campus invited him to be their dinner guest and presented him with its key, making him an honorary member. At his last public lecture at Harvard, on 3 May 1962, there were about 450 students and visitors in the audience. He spoke on "Religion and Art since the Renaissance," illustrating his talk with paintings by means of color slides. When he had finished, he bowed to thunderous applause and accepted a bouquet of flowers which had been thrown onto the platform.

Tillich often confessed that Harvard had made him famous.[18] He disliked the word nearly as much as he disliked being called a genius, insisting that the only criterion for fame was being instantly recognizable to a New York taxi driver. By that definition he knew he was only temporarily in the limelight, not famous. The fact remains that his popularity on campus attracted the attention of the Harvard publicity machine, and the two continually fed each other. Tillich received, accordingly, hundreds of invitations, most of which came directly through the president's office. Although not self-effacing, Tillich was modest enough to admit that he owed Pusey a great debt, and he never ceased to thank him for having invited him to Harvard in the first place.[19] Tillich was away from the campus so often that he reacted defensively to an article published in *Time* in which reference was made to "wandering professors" from Harvard. He wrote to Pusey at once.

22 December 1960

Dear President Pusey:

Perhaps the article in the December 19th issue of *Time* magazine (p. 60) has been brought to your attention. Since according to my experience, a letter to the editors has no effect, I write you in order to set the record straight in case you should receive criticisms from Board members or others.

1. According to my secretary, the average of invitations I get in some weeks is 15–20, but, of course, not always. Under these circumstances, I have to turn down at least ninety percent of all invitations.

2. In all my academic life, I have only once received $1000.00 for a lecture. Actually, it is now in the last several years $200 to $250. But, of course, I never accept any money if I am invited by student groups or churches without a large budget.

3. The outside engagements in no case had the consequence as long as I have been in Harvard that I dropped even one lecture or seminar hour.

4. The fact that I was engaged this past October and November every weekend (about which I told you when we met on the street the other day) is true. But the word "regularly" is utterly misleading and for the next semester I have cancelled more than half of my outside engagements, and for the next academic year, my last in Harvard, I have not accepted anything except one or two foundation lectureships.

5. As Dean Bundy rightly says, the speaking trips enrich my teaching here by the fact that I have gained a deeper insight into the religious situation in the colleges and universities of this country. At the same time, I have been able to help many of the newly developing religious departments in the colleges and even the state universities. For this reason I felt justified, especially in my position as University Professor, to accept some of the most urgent invitations.

Respectfully yours,

Paul Tillich

On 11 January 1961, President Pusey replied to Tillich's letter as follows:

Dear Mr. Tillich:

Your name had never once crossed my mind in connection with the article in *Time* regarding wandering professors. In any case your University Professorship should entitle you to special exemptions! We are very fortunate to have you with us here at Harvard and I have complete confidence that whatever you do on the outside will be done for the right reasons and will contribute to a much better understanding of religious matters in the colleges and universities of this country and abroad.

Nathan Pusey[20]

For seven years, Tillich was drawn away from Cambridge by the lure of large audiences and ample fees. Nearly every weekend he traveled to nearby or distant points: Boston, New York, Chicago, Los Angeles, Santa Barbara, Berkeley. He arranged his schedule so that he could teach on Tuesdays, Wednesdays, and Thursdays, leave Cambridge (if possible by train) on Thursday afternoon or evening, and return on the following Monday. His assistants, successively Walter Leibrecht, Robert Kimball, and Paul Lee, kept overzealous students at bay, corrected papers, and attended to publication problems. The services of a full-time secretary, a luxury he had never enjoyed earlier, helped keep him abreast of his ferocious schedule.

To be sure, Tillich repeated many of the same lectures and sermons; he was sometimes forced to cancel long-held appointments, and many of his appearances were informal discussions or conversations requiring little previous preparation. Nevertheless, much younger men would have found the peripatetic existence a strain, and Tillich often did.

Representatives of the older generation were among those who turned out to hear him on the college campus at Harvard, among them his wife, their new friends George Brewster the architect and his wife Joan, Robert Ulich, and others. Inasmuch, however, as his audiences at Harvard and elsewhere were made up primarily of college undergraduates, he felt an obligation to address himself to their questions. He was convinced that they were asking "the right questions" about "the meaning of our life, the conflicts of our existence, the way to deal with anxiety in our life, the feeling of guilt, the feeling of emptiness."[21] He naïvely felt that the United States would be able to solve its social problems, but that the solution of individual problems remained a wasteland; thus he continued to speak on "Religion and Psychiatry" and "The Meaning of Health." When on 12 January 1960 he gave the Foerster Lecture on "The Immortality of the Soul" at the University of California in Berkeley, between three and four thousand attended. Three years later, on another visit to Berkeley, he reported that 7,500 listeners turned out.

On a less successful occasion in 1958, his conversation with J. H. Randall at Amherst College on "The Cognitive and Religious Use of Myth and Symbol" disappointed the students because the two men did not really debate but agreed too readily.[22] But such disappointment was rare; Tillich himself was convinced that he spoke to the situation in which the students found themselves. He held their attention as hardly any other theologian in America was able to do at the time. During these years, America was symbolized for him by the long series of couples waiting for him at railroad stations or in airport lobbies, who entertained him in their homes and encouraged and applauded him. They were mostly former students from Union and Columbia, or old German or American friends too numerous to name. It was their collective and individual devotion to him that he cherished most about this country at the end of his life.[23]

Certain other topics also preoccupied Tillich in his Harvard years. In 1960, on the occasion of an art festival at Yale, he spoke on "The Image of Man and Contemporary Art." In the same year he attended the centennial celebration of the Massachusetts Institute of Technology and lectured on "How Has Science in the Last Century Changed Man's View of Himself?" In 1962, he gave the four Bampton Lectures at Columbia University, entitled, "Christianity and the Encounter of World Religions." Perhaps the least original of Tillich's published work, the book represents an interest resurrected from earlier years. Another such interest was politics. Inspired by the new era of high intellectual standards introduced by the Kennedy administration in 1961, Tillich raised his voice once again on political matters. He was one of a group of intellectuals invited to attend the Kennedy inauguration and was seated on the platform reserved for special guests—in full view of Jacqueline Kennedy's profile, which he greatly admired. He later wrote to President Kennedy as follows:

The invitation to me as one of one hundred and fifty came as a complete surprise and I felt greatly honored by it. Fortunately, I was able to accept it and to participate in all the activities on the day of the inauguration. The source of deep satisfaction was the fact that the new president and his wife expressed their desire to cooperate with representatives of the arts and sciences. This very fact had an impact on me to become more active in political thought as a writer, philosopher, and theologian. The feeling I have had during the last 12 years that such participation had no consequence was considerably reduced by this invitation.[24]

Tillich's newly ignited interest in politics was short-lived and of little effect. On 16 October 1961 he participated in Eleanor Roosevelt's educational television program entitled "Prospects of Mankind." On that occasion, in the company of Secretary of State Dean Rusk and James Reston of the *New York Times*, he discussed the Berlin wall and the use of nuclear weapons to defend that divided city. Tillich's assertion that a war fought with atomic weapons could not be ethically justified because it would destroy what one wished to defend, was rejected as unrealistic by Rusk and Reston. In his column of 24 October 1961, the latter wrote that he preferred the judgment of Reinhold Niebuhr who said, "If the democratic nations fall, their failure must be partly attributed to the faulty strategy of idealists who have too many illusions when they face realists who have too little conscience."[25] A year later, Tillich had a similar exchange with Egon Bahr, the West German secretary of state whom he met in Berlin in the home of Claus Schütz, husband of Tillich's niece Heide Seeberger and later mayor of Berlin. There he encountered the same reasoning and resistance to his "pacifist" stance. Although he remained skeptical about the possibilities of peace in a nuclear age, and although his enthusiasm for political participation was soon dampened by the assassination of John F. Kennedy, Tillich did speak out for peace on one final occasion. On 18 February 1965, a few months before his death, he participated in a conference entitled "Pacem in Terris" convened by Robert M. Hutchins, president of the Center for the Study of Democratic Institutions. The purpose of the convocation was to explore pathways toward fulfilling Pope John XXIII's great encyclical of Easter Week, 1963, which had injected a dynamic new stimulus into the discussion of major political issues, including disarmament, nuclear weapons, racial equality, and human rights. Tillich's brief paper, later published in the spring issue of *Criterion*, was pessimistic and warned against utopian expectations.

World Traveler

During the last ten years of his life, Tillich traveled about the world to far off places he had never seen before: Greece in 1956, Japan in 1960, Egypt and Israel in 1963. A projected trip to India was canceled in 1962 because of illness, and Tillich never saw that country. His experiences in each region made profound impressions upon him, releasing myriad reactions which he recorded in travel reports composed for his friends. Greece he saw in his seventieth year, a birthday he celebrated with groups of friends in various places all year long. The sights of Greece overwhelmed him.[26] He was convinced, after seeing the Parthenon, that the pagan gods were real, not as existential beings but as creative forces. The perfectly proportioned, small human form of Greek sculptures pleased and surprised his eye. The unity of nature and religion, nature and culture, tragedy and the greatness of man, all penetrated his consciousness. Having seen the Erechtheion, a temple of classic style on the Acropolis at Athens, he wrote to a friend,

This is one of the most attractive places of the Acropolis. It is older and gentler than the Parthenon. Some revisions of my theology are now unavoidable. I should write "On the Reality of the Pagan gods." Nothing can be compared with the unity of landscape and architecture in Greece.[27]

During the winter of 1956-57 the Tillichs visited Mexico, but he reported very little on his experience there, only that he enjoyed the company of Erich Fromm and the warm waters of the Pacific, and had concentrated for four weeks on his "system."

His trip to Japan, on the other hand, served to widen his horizon as much as his transplantation to America had done twenty-seven years earlier.[28] He had never been to Asia before, and his curiosity about a totally foreign culture overcame his initial reluctance to travel so far at his age. Thus when the invitation to lecture there was extended he accepted, insisting on the companionship of his wife, on whom he increasingly depended and whose interest in Eastern religion and arts surpassed his own. Any hesitation he had about the enterprise vanished upon his arrival in Japan. His working program had been so carefully arranged by the International Exchange Committee, his taxing schedule so evenly spaced between days of sight-seeing and public appearances, that he found himself under less strain than he had anticipated. The permanent presence of an interpreter, the daily assistance of a secretary, and the frequent help of a guide (usually an art critic) smoothed his path and heightened his appreciation at every step. The infinite patience, politeness, and friendliness of the Japanese people at all levels captivated and charmed him beyond measure.

Thus in 1960, between May and July, Tillich spent eight weeks, first in Tokyo, then in Kyoto, presenting his basic theological ideas at ten universities and preaching in several churches. He lectured most often on religion and culture and philosophy of religion, in response to requests which had been made for these topics, and he soon found it necessary to make last-minute drastic changes in his material to ensure communication to a non-American culture. In delivery each lecture alternated between English and Japanese, a cumbersome process entailing teamwork with his interpreter: Tillich explained the lecture to him beforehand, and the actual address lasted from two to two and a half hours. Despite this exhausting ordeal for both speakers and listeners, the fairly large Japanese audiences were attentive and eager. On one occasion Tillich was especially moved to see students listening from outside an overcrowded room, putting up their umbrellas against the intermittent showers.

He had many opportunities to meet Christian leaders, some of whom he knew from Columbia University, some of whom had been former students of his; in his contacts with them he experienced for the first time in his life what it must have been like to be an early Christian in a pagan country. But what he found most stimulating was the discussions with Shinto and Buddhist scholars and priests who opened up the mind of the East for him. He visited their temples, observed and joined their ritual and ceremony, was

entertained by their dances and dramas, and heard their abbots
and masters explain their theology. An especially memorable discussion took place, Tillich later reported, when the Zen Master
Hisamatsu, whom he had known at Harvard,

> showed us the famous seven-hundred-year-old rock garden connected
> with his temple. The garden, not larger than a large oblong court-
> yard, is surrounded by a wall with astonishing colors, produced by
> nature in about five hundred years. The floor is gravel, raked in an
> oceanic pattern, but most important are fifteen rocks, ordered in
> groups of two or three or more in perfect proportions of distance,
> height and depth. Soon the chief-priest of the temple, Mr. Hisa-
> matsu and I fell into a discussion for more than an hour about the
> questions of whether the rock garden and the universe are identical
> (the position of the Buddhists) or non-identical but united by par-
> ticipation (my position). No amount of reading can replace such an
> experience.[29]

Tillich was especially attracted to Buddhist mysticism, which he
directly experienced as similar to Christian mysticism, whereupon
he concluded that although the principles of identity and participation were exclusive, "the actual life of both Christianity, especially in its Protestant form, and Buddhism, especially in its
monastic form, could receive elements from each other without
losing their basic character."[30] Zen Buddhist painting, which reminded him of Schelling's concept of "essentialization," and the
small-scale perfection of Buddhist architecture especially pleased
his eye. The Japanese landscape with its rolling hills and mountains and the absence of flat plains reminded him of central and
southern Germany. The ancient capital of Kyoto, where he spent
three weeks which he said were among the most intense of his life,
recalled Florence in its landscape and art treasures. Upon his return to America the many precious gifts presented to him and his
wife were visible reminders of what he called a volcanic experience. Shortly after coming home, he wrote,

> Before all the impressions have settled down in me, I cannot formu-
> late what it has meant; and even then probably others will notice

the influence of Japan more than I myself. But I know that something has happened: no Western provincialism of which I am aware will be tolerated by me from now on in my thought and work, and I am grateful to the Japanese friends who worked for a long time to make my trip and this insight possible. I can tell them that I have learned to love Japan and her people.[31]

Tillich's spiritual experiences in Japan confirmed his conviction that "one cannot divide the religions of mankind into one true and many false religions. Rather, one must subject all religions, including Christianity, to the ultimate criterion of a love which unconditionally affirms, judges, and receives the other person."[32]

He was soon to put this conclusion to a test. His visit to Israel three years later in 1963 corrected for him much that he had long imagined about the birthplace of the Judeo-Christian tradition. Before his departure in September, he decided to include Egypt in his itinerary. This turned out to be a mistake. At the time there was tension between Jordan and Egypt; consequently the Jordanian embassy revoked the visa already granted, thus preventing Tillich from seeing the old city of Jerusalem. Moreover, the promise on behalf of the Islamic Foundation of New York to arrange several lectures for him in Cairo did not materialize. Tillich and his wife were left to fend for themselves. Furthermore, the heat Tillich normally found bearable and even stimulating was so formidable that it weakened and exhausted him. Yet the visit was not without its rewards. The pyramids and their "superhuman greatness," which he could not help but admire, were not what made the strongest impression upon him, but rather the claim of infinite life he saw expressed in the mummies of the pharaohs, their wives and noblemen. Later he wrote, "One admired, but one also felt that this is no real victory over death. These faces, in their state of arrested decay, are extremely vivid and often very powerful (as good portraits can be) but they belong to the past, and their presence is that of the past, revived for the present but not belonging to it."[33]

They flew to Israel via Athens, where he compared the artifacts of Greek civilization with those of Egypt, experiencing "a kind of homecoming when the human measures reappeared in temples and statues and the quantitatively superhuman ceased to represent the divine."[34] Their trip through Israel was extremely well organized by the Israeli Foreign Office. Transportation was provided in government cars with guides, hotel arrangements had been made in advance. The sight of Lake Gennesaret (the Sea of Galilee), the mountains around Jerusalem with the city on them, the Dead Sea, and the Negev near Elath were for Tillich the most impressive parts of the Israeli landscape. The intense blue and beautiful shape of Lake Gennesaret so attracted him that he tried to prevent the driver from proceeding. Later he wrote, "I am conscious of the fact that the historical memory concerning Jesus who did most of his teaching in the villages and on the hills around this lake, contributed much to the deep impression on me."[35] Looking out one night from his balcony in the King David Hotel, when the full moon lit up the darkness, Tillich saw in his mind "Jesus and the disciples walking to Gethsemane."[36] The dusty Arab villages replaced what had always lived in his consciousness as replicas of small German villages and towns, and he felt that these new images would change for him the character of the biblical stories. At the same time, the behavior of a guide in Nazareth who insisted on showing him the very spot where the Annunciation had taken place made him feel that his lifelong attempt to deliteralize the Bible was confirmed in that moment as in no other. In a rare show of anger, the usually tolerant Tillich refused to follow the guide.[37]

Tillich was privileged to meet with a number of representatives of the Israeli government, including Abba Eban. But his encounter with Martin Buber, whom he had known since 1924, most deeply moved and excited him. Their philosophical and theological dialogue at widely separated times and places (in Germany, New York, Boston, and elsewhere), about the word "God" and its irreplaceability, about I–It and I–Thou, and finally about Israel's future, had mutually enriched them. They respected one another, and assumed and accepted their religious differences. As the evening they spent together in Buber's book-lined study drew to a close, Tillich asked him if he had any plans to visit America or

Europe again. When Buber answered quietly but with a certain emphasis, "No," Tillich sensed that it was their final meeting.[38]

Toward the end of October Tillich, temporarily exhausted by a diverticulitis attack, bade farewell to Israel. He spent the next two months at the University of Zurich, where he replaced the erudite and dapper historian and theologian Gerhard Ebeling, head of the Institute of Hermeneutics. For reasons not entirely clear Tillich's seminar lectures were not well received, to his dismay and Ebeling's surprise.[39] Between seminar sessions, perhaps feeling intuitively that this was to be his last visit abroad, he traveled to other Swiss and German cities and towns seeing family and friends. On 22 November, shortly before a planned trip to Berlin, the news of President Kennedy's assassination reached him; he felt so wounded and shaken by this shocking example of the violence he abhorred that he canceled his travel plans, only to renew them a few hours later. On the very same day Karl Barth had written him a cheery postcard confirming a date they had set.

> You are welcome on December 1. Where shall we begin when we meet again and see each other face to face? With the troubles of old age which now assail both of us? Or with the Ground of Being which concerns both of us unconditionally? Or with the difficulties you have with my books and I have with yours? Or with the Battle of Gettysburg which gives me much to think about and the address Lincoln gave there? Or with the horrible book of the Bishop of Woolwich? Or with the queer Institute of Hermeneutics which the Zurichers have built around Mr. Ebeling, and which now has the honor to put you up as its guest? Or with the question whether you will be able to match me in soon becoming a great-grandfather? However this may be, I rejoice in the expectation of walking in your company from heaven through the world to hell: "With all deliberate speed" as Father Goethe has providentially instructed us.[40]

The bantering, rapierlike thrust of Barth's good humor enlivened their meeting. Then the two parted, never to meet again. On his return to America Tillich excitedly reported to Wilhelm Pauck, "Barth and I are friends again!"—a reference to their quarrel about the Nazis in the 1930s. Whereupon Pauck, ever desirous of documentary proof, asked, "What is the evidence for this?" Tillich replied in utter earnestness, "He accompanied me to the tram halt."

Tillich was frequently honored by the academic community during his last decade. In 1954 he received the degree of Doctor of Letters from Harvard University. It was the third honorary degree bestowed upon him by an American school: ultimately that number grew to twelve. Two foreign universities followed suit; the University of Glasgow, which presented him with a Doctor of Divinity degree in 1951, and the University of Berlin, which honored him five years later on the occasion of his seventieth birthday with the degree of Doctor of Philosophy. Of them all, the last was the most meaningful and precious to him.

His entire life, as he said in his acceptance speech, had been bound up with Berlin, in dreams and in reality.[41] Since the day when the young boy from a small town had arrived there, the city of Berlin had been the symbol of all his yearning and fulfillment. It had instilled in him a love which had not been broken or disrupted by external or internal demonic powers. It was the place to which he had returned with most eagerness in 1948, and with all its divisions and tensions it remained his *Heimat*, his homeland. It was for this reason that he always wore the doctoral ring which the theological faculty of the University of Berlin had presented to his father. On it were inscribed the Greek words *Phos*, and *Zoé*— "Light" and "Life"—meaning "Let the light shine in order that life may abound." His father had willed him the ring, and he had worn it with great pride since 1937.

In 1956 Tillich was presented with two further honors, personally handed to him in Washington, D.C., by the ambassador of the Federal Republic of Germany to the United States: the Goethe medal of Frankfort and the Great Order of Merit of the West German Republic. Along more amusing lines, in his seventieth year he was given an affectionate tribute written by Ruth Nanda Anshen and signed by a group of friends in New York. Mrs. Anshen invited them all for the presentation of this honor, some time after Tillich's birthday (which he had spent in Switzerland),

and had asked them to sign the scroll. Eduard Heimann's signature came last, since he absolutely refused to sign the somewhat intricately worded appreciation until he had thoroughly understood the meaning of every word.[42]

German tributes continued to multiply, largely as the result of several factors: Tillich's summer round of lectures at German universities revived an interest in his ideas and stimulated discussion in a setting which men like Barth and Bultmann had pretty much dominated for several years. The German press was flooded with articles about him, especially on his sixty-fifth, seventieth, and seventy-fifth birthdays. Written by Maria Rhine, Dolf Sternberger, Adolf Müller, and others, all admiring friends, these rehearsed Tillich's life and work with German thoroughness and often in sentimental and exaggerated fashion. The Evangelisches Verlagswerk, publishers of Tillich's collected works, also fed the press with a great deal of publicity concerning him and his books. All this bore ample fruit. In 1958 the Hanseatic Goethe prize, awarded annually to a person whose lifework contributed to understanding among nations, was presented to Tillich.[43] The ceremony was held in Hamburg's City Hall: in the flower-filled room Professor Helmut Thielicke, theologian at the University of Hamburg and a warm admirer of Tillich's person and work, was the main speaker. He ended by saying, "So today we greet with honor and joy Paul Tillich, and I may well say our *own* Paul Tillich. His friends regard him as a wanderer between two worlds, and we rejoice that Germany is the world in whose soil he is rooted."[44]

Thielicke's reminder that the Germans once again claimed Tillich as their own was repeated in 1962. In an hour of personal triumph he received an honor that crowned all others: namely, the Peace Prize of the German Publishers Association. This coveted prize,[45] a symbol of German freedom and democracy, is presented annually to one who strives for peace and understanding between peoples. It was given to Albert Schweitzer in 1951; in later years to Martin Buber, Carl Burckhardt, Thornton Wilder, and Victor Gollancz, among others in that distinguished company. The ceremony honoring Tillich, as on previous occasions of the award, was the final act of the annual Frankfort book fair, itself as old as the discovery of print and the printing press. It took place in St. Paul's Church, Frankfort, on a warm September day.[46] Tillich was, of course, there in person. Ambassadors, churchmen, poets, librarians, relatives, and friends were assembled. Dr. Theodor Heuss, president of the West German Republic, and Werner Böckelmann, the mayor of Frankfort, were also present. Werner Dodeshöner, chairman of the German Book Publishers Association, led off with the first of four speeches (each so long that Tillich was forced to rush his own in order to meet the television deadline). Dodeshöner cited Tillich as one who "by means of the spoken and written word has tirelessly served the idea of peace, and who after the war reopened to the outside world the gates of German scholarship which, misled and blinded, we ourselves had closed."[47]

Otto Dibelius, the aged but still formidable Bishop of Berlin, gave the *laudatio*. The presence of this courageous churchman who had personally informed Hitler that he would have nothing to do with Nazi lawbreakers was a sign that Tillich had become more acceptable to German churchmen; indeed Dibelius's fulsome praise was such that those who had earlier feared his presence might arouse indignation in East Berlin, where he was unpopular on account of his anticommunism, were greatly pleased. Among other things, he said, "You have remained a German thinker, and yet you have become an American who has not failed to relate himself responsibly to American philosophical and theological tendencies as they have developed in that country." He ended on this note: "In your person a tie between two peoples has been forged for which I know no parallels. . . . The Peace Prize can be given to no one more worthy of it than the great pastor of broken men of today, the German and American theologian and philosopher, Paul Tillich."[48]

Dressed in a formal black suit and white tie, flushed with excitement, Tillich, "the man of the hour,"[49] rose to speak on a subject close to his heart: "Boundaries."[50] He reminded his listeners of the boundaries (or limits) that lie within and between all persons, ideas, and nations—boundaries which must first be acknowledged, then conquered. In a prophetic mood, he urged Germans, now a secure and affluent people in whose country few traces of the war remained, and where talk of division had been pushed underground, that they must not rest within the boundaries of their prosperity, forgetting their brothers on the other side. He urged them to cross the spiritual, intellectual, and whenever possible also the geographical boundaries between East and West, and to secure a lasting peace by tearing down the walls that separate one from the other. He invited the Germans in the Democratic German Republic who were listening to do the same. Moreover, he exhorted the German people to take upon themselves the full responsibility of their political fate, and to remain open to the healing powers of eternity always available from the other side of that boundary which all men must cross and accept. In conclusion, Tillich said, "And it is my wish for the German nation from whom I come and whom I thank for this honor, that it may keep itself open, recognizing its own true character and its calling, and fulfilling its destiny within the ever-changing boundaries of reality."[51]

To enthusiastic applause Tillich, beaming and supremely happy, walked out on the arm of President Heuss. Later he met with many friends who had traveled from near and far to hear him. Among them was Wilhelm Stählin, whom Tillich had last seen in 1936 near the German border. Stählin later wrote, "The way in which Tillich spoke of the boundary as a basic concept of his thought, and of our need to acknowledge and conquer boundaries, was regarded by many witnesses of that hour as a masterpiece; in any case, it brought me great spiritual satisfaction in form as well as in content."[52]

Tillich was surprised that German audiences so eagerly accepted his admonitions regarding the necessity for political participation. Widespread coverage in the press on the following day continued to applaud him; there was a large demand for copies of his speech, and the ensuing publicity sharply increased the sale of his German books.

By 1962, many of Tillich's books were again available in German owing to the Herculean efforts of the Evangelisches Verlagswerk, its editor Friedrich Vorwerk, and the publisher and business manager Paul and Willy Collmer, who succeeded Vorwerk after his death. The Evangelisches Verlagswerk had sprung into being in 1947. At the time Tillich's ideas, banned by the Nazi regime, were virtually unknown in Germany except to a small circle of friends and admirers. Paul Collmer, who had known him at the University of Frankfort before the war, was eager to build up a distinguished publishing list and therefore interested in making Tillich's major German writings (1919–33) available again. He also wanted to publish his major American writings in German translation, including the *Systematic Theology*.[53] August Rathmann, then acting as Tillich's literary agent in Germany, helped negotiate contracts for the publication of several American manuscripts which were being translated by some of Tillich's former students, then all very much in need of income.[54]

As Tillich's appearances in Germany created an ever increasing demand for his books, a more ambitious plan was set into motion, namely, to publish his collected works (*Gesammelte Werke*). Paul Collmer first discussed this plan with Tillich in 1958, at the same time suggesting Renate Albrecht, a translator of his writings who had demonstrated great organizing ability, as chief editor for the project.[55] As successor to Rathmann, Mrs. Albrecht, an energetic and efficient woman, fell heir to a time-consuming and highly complex task. She collected the German texts, sought permission to reprint them, rode herd on the translators, and edited the final manuscripts. Tillich retained ultimate authority over all texts, but as it turned out he was not prepared to spend much strength or time on the inevitable problems that arose, involving as they did hours of correspondence and conference. Indeed, he displayed comparatively limited interest, not only because of his constitutional indifference to his completed work, but also because of his hectic schedule. He suggested the theme and title of each volume and personally decided whether or not to include any given piece.

Since he wanted to acquaint a large readership with his ideas, he automatically rejected book reviews and discussions as well as his two dissertations (although he was eventually persuaded to publish one of them), preferring to include only what he regarded as "important."[56] Yet the original plan, as it developed further in meetings between him and Mrs. Albrecht on both sides of the Atlantic in 1961, 1963, and 1964, expanded from six volumes to fourteen! Thus all Tillich's previously published work, together with a few select hitherto unpublished manuscripts, is included in this collection. The final volume of the series contains an index for the other thirteen, a complete bibliography, and a listing of unpublished manuscripts and tapes held by the two Tillich archives.[57]

The first volume of Tillich's *Gesammelte Werke* [Collected Works] appeared in 1959. In America a *Festschrift* in his honor, entitled *Religion and Culture* and edited by Walter Leibrecht, was presented to him at an elaborate reception at Harvard on 12 February attended by many of the contributors, publishers' representatives, and friends.[58] The book includes articles by twenty-four of Tillich's distinguished contemporaries in several fields, pointing to the great diversity of his interests and influence. In the spring, a collection of Tillich's finest essays, spanning his entire career and touching on each of his important ideas, appropriately entitled *Theology of Culture* and edited by Robert Kimball, prompted Reinhold Niebuhr to hail him as

by general consent the most creative philosopher of religion of our generation . . . a very seminal thinker when he is dealing with the relation of religion to art, to psychoanalysis, to politics, and to education. He reveals, in considering every subject, the breadth and depth of his erudition and the wisdom of his judgments.[59]

A similar judgment came to be widely shared even outside learned circles. An impressive indication of this occurred on 16 March when Tillich, looking vaguely uncomfortable and overweight, appeared on the cover of *Time*,[60] his books in the background and a skull (the illustrator's invention) on his desk. The accuracy of the accompanying story in that issue of the magazine pleased him and inspired a display of his ponderous sense of humor.

I have read your article on the castle builder and fence sitting theologian, Paul Tillich, and I must say that you did an excellent job about this man of whom I have a slight knowledge. It is astonishing how much material you brought in partly by direct, partly by indirect communication. I think your presentation of his system was as clear as it could be, and the personal sections as rich and warm as they could be. I heard that Mr. Tillich has received many congratulations about the article.

Now I must admit that Paul Tillich is the writer of this letter. He thanks you.

Paul Tillich[61]

In the same year the death of his closest friend, Hermann Schafft, and of Karl Mennicke, cofounder of the *kairos* circle, saddened and frightened him, momentarily casting a shadow over his own success and bringing to mind his own finitude.[62] On the occasion of his seventy-fifth birthday two years later, the annual flood of birthday greetings accompanied by photographs and placed in an album by Tillich's wife included a perceptive word on the matter from Richard Kroner,

Since death is a farewell to everything we have enjoyed, done, admired, and loved, I hope that you will be able to live through the preparation for this end without fear and without mourning. There is not only the courage to be but also the courage not to be, and the second is most certainly the only religious one, even when we reject all pictures that religion offers us in order to inspire us with this courage. And so onward! as Goethe in his old age was accustomed to end his letters.

Your Richard[63]

It was not entirely without fear or sorrow that Tillich set about preparing for the end of his Harvard career. In his seventh year there his wife underwent a serious operation from which she recovered only slowly, and he was hospitalized by a severe attack of diverticulitis. The illness, which he feared was a harbinger of death, prompted him, not for the first time, to cast his eye upon the posthumous Tillich and his work, that "phantom" about whom words of high praise were printed in newspapers, journals, and magazines, filling him with joy one day and grave misgivings the next.[64] In discussions with James Tanis, then librarian of the Harvard Andover Library, concerning the lack of space for his large professional library in East Hampton, the two agreed to solve the problem by establishing at Harvard an archive in Tillich's name. Upon his retirement therefore Tillich donated the great majority of his books, as well as his professional and personal correspondence, to the archive. After his death, nearly all his notebooks, published and unpublished manuscripts, medals, honors, photographs, and any similar materials that bore witness to his long, eventful life were placed there.[65]

Tillich's last weeks at Harvard in 1962 found him caught up in a whirl of activity and celebration. The month of May was filled with "glorious, heartbreaking, and tumultuous"[66] events, his final lecture, student farewell parties, packing, and leave-taking. The farewell dinner given in his honor by the Harvard divinity faculty on 24 May turned out to be "one of the great evenings of his life."[67] An elegant dinner was served to a hundred friends and colleagues in the Busch-Riesinger Museum, while a string quartet played Mozart and Haydn. Informal talks were given by Samuel Miller, James Luther Adams, Rollo May, Wilhelm Pauck, Nathan Pusey, and others. While Tillich, overcome by joy and excitement, replied, a noisy thunderstorm disturbed and interrupted him, accounting only in part for his halting, unsystematic response. He was too deeply moved by the occasion to recover his composure entirely. It was, he said,

the most difficult speech I ever was asked to give, a speech in surroundings that—of almost all my experiences in my long life—are those nearest to a dream of heaven—among friends, among bearers of spirit and beauty, among the beauty created according to the eternal images called Ideas by Plato. And then from above the music, that music of Mozart I have sometimes called "the dance of the eternal essences in the Heavenly Spheres." And I am asked to answer the words that have moved me so deeply, stories of the past and evaluations of the present. How can I answer?[68]

With a heart full of gratitude, he thanked his listeners. Thus did the years of Tillich's "fulfillment," as he referred to them in his little talk, come to an end.

Illness and Death

In June Tillich moved to East Hampton for the summer months. Many of his friends had advised him to spend his retirement years in his newly winterized house, but an idle existence without teaching seemed unimaginable to him. It was with considerable readiness, therefore, that he accepted an invitation extended to him by Jerald Brauer, then dean of the Divinity School of the University of Chicago, to become the first Nuveen Professor of Theology. The professorship had been set up by the directors of the banking firm John Nuveen & Co. and named in the founder's honor. In October Tillich and his wife moved to Chicago, where for the next two years he was "the distinguished theologian in residence." A white-haired, leonine elderly gentleman, increasingly thin and slow in movement, he very much looked the part. He lived in a large, expensive Windermere Hotel apartment with a view of Lake Michigan, and each morning at nine, clad in one of his new Saks Fifth Avenue suits, with briefcase in hand, he walked or took a taxi to the Divinity School. Brauer, who had been an early assistant of Tillich's at Union and was an ardent admirer, provided him with a suite of offices and a full-time secretary to help him answer the twenty to thirty daily letters he received. Indeed, throughout these brief years in Chicago Brauer's friendly, ebullient presence, which he generously provided by the hour to Tillich, was a comfort to the old gentleman.

In the Divinity School itself Tillich taught one course in each of the fall and spring quarters, and in his final year he cooperated with Mircea Eliade in a seminar on the history of religions. He spent the winter quarters of 1963 and 1964 in Santa Barbara, California, where he conducted a seminar.[69]

In his last years, because his concepts had by then been so widely disseminated, Tillich confined himself to graduate seminars and public discussion groups in which he answered questions and encouraged students to enlarge upon their own ideas. In an effort to husband his strength, moreover, he accepted only the most challenging and lucrative of the many speaking engagements that continued to come his way.[70] When Henry Luce unexpectedly asked him to be the principal speaker at the fortieth anniversary party for *Time* magazine in 1963, Tillich found the invitation irresistible. He had been called to Luce's attention several years earlier by Henry Van Dusen and his middle son Hugh (then a young editor at Harper & Brothers), when Luce asked them to name the most influential Protestant thinker in America. Luce, the son of missionaries to China, was a member of the Union board of directors; his interest in Protestant theology came at first hand. He soon became an admirer of Tillich. Having placed his picture on the cover of *Time*, he now did him the honor to ask him to speak on "the human condition." Tillich was greatly impressed by the "astonishing lack of prejudice in the American tradition,"[71] as demonstrated by Luce's choice of a German-born intellectual with whose political philosophy he disagreed. The assignment was not an easy one: the glittering audience before whom he appeared on 6 May at the Waldorf Astoria Hotel in New York City, composed of 284 subjects of *Time* cover stories in every field of endeavor, included few intellectuals. His Eminence Francis Cardinal Spellman pronounced the invocation, and Van Dusen the benediction; Luce was toastmaster. Each guest was introduced, with his or her "cover" projected on a huge screen. There was rapt silence as Tillich, seated on the dais next to Adlai Stevenson and not far from Douglas MacArthur, rose to deliver his remarks, entitled, "The Ambiguity of Perfection."

Pointing to the ambiguous character of all high achievement, Tillich hammered home to his audience the idea that the human condition is ever ambiguous, an "inseparable mixture of good and evil, of creative and destructive forces, both individual and social . . . there is nothing unambiguously creative and nothing unambiguously destructive. They accompany each other inseparably."[72] The same was true, he continued, of the one-dimensional culture of which they were all a part. It was a free society, to be sure, but one without depth: its ceaseless expansion, whether into outer space or on the production line, had created an almost irresistible temptation on the part of everyone to produce in order to produce still more. Tillich exhorted the producers of cultural goods to stop moving in this one-dimensional direction—to come to a halt in order to "enter creation and unite with its power,"[73] in short, to add the vertical line of depth to the horizontal line of extension. In a direct reference to his own role as a Socratic gadfly, he pointed out that the creative critics of contemporary society no longer needed to fear martyrdom, but were instead forced to "fight against being absorbed by the culture as another cultural good."[74]

The audience of high achievers applauded loudly, but word later circulated that few of them had grasped Tillich's meaning. He understood his analysis only too well, particularly as it applied to himself. He was aware that his belated fame was itself ambiguous, an inseparable mixture of good and evil, of creative and destructive forces. The capitalist society which he characterized as lacking in depth was the same society that had enabled him to reap unusual and manifold benefits, the very epitome of which was his appearance at the *Time* dinner. As if unaware of all he had said on many occasions about the crisis of capitalism and bourgeois culture, the avowed religious socialist willingly mingled with the wealthy, influential men who represented this civilization, accepting their applause and favors.[75]

The many rewards to which Tillich fell heir in his last decade— perhaps precisely because they came so late in his life—wrought a subtle but discernible change in him. Hidden under his unpretentious dignity and gentle warmth, a metamorphosis had taken place: he had begun to believe what he saw written and heard spoken about himself. From that time on, he became less and less able to resist exaggerated praise, contemporary fads, the wiles of publicity, and the magnetism of wealth. At times he was strangely inflexible and omniscient in manner; he sometimes assumed the pose of the "famous man" glancing Narcissus-like at his own image. He knew this about himself, and some of his friends knew it too. At times, when it was late and he was tired, in the company of one of them he would ask, "Am I a phony? I fear so."

Such moments of doubt regarding the efficacy of his work and the deservedness of his success were companions to the confessions he made late at night to his wife concerning his dalliance with women.[76] These moods of self-doubt were genuine enough, merging ultimately in the fear that continued to haunt him: that his own salvation was uncertain, that he was a sinner who would be excommunicated from the Kingdom of God.[77] From this conviction at times no one could dissuade him. Yet by morning, after such confessions and tribulations of spirit, he had forgotten them and was once again ruled by the twin temptations of his life.

Although Tillich fell for his public image and was finally impressed by his own importance and influence, in private he remained childlike and unspoiled. His genius for friendship, his fidelity to innumerable men and women, his concern for each and every one, continued to the end. Although the time he was able to share with each inevitably lessened, the quality of his generous and intense communication did not. Sometimes, at the expense of energy and health, he stayed up until the small hours in order to continue one more conversation. In his friendships he himself found comfort and respite from the pressing demands of his career and from the superficial social occasions often connected with them, which he knew to be ephemeral. Indeed, on one level of his being he needed, more than any of his friends, *not* to be left alone. However fleeting such moments of rest with another person, they became times in which he ceased to flee from himself and was present for the other. It was largely for this reason that his many friends continued to love him, even as he grew increasingly willing to live with what he called "Paul Tillich, the object."[78]

A month after the *Time* anniversary dinner, Tillich and his wife flew in a private plane to New Harmony, Indiana, a little village on the Wabash river twenty-nine miles west of Evansville. Originally called Harmonie, it had been founded in 1814 by a group of German pietists led by George Rapp.[79] They had leveled the trees, drained the swamps, and planted rich farmlands. In 1824 the Rappites, as they were called, sold their land to a Scottish industrialist, Robert Owen, who aspired to provide a socialistic intellectual community for the promotion of the arts and sciences. He renamed the village "New Harmony" and for a time attracted men of talent to form a new community. But his scheme for establishing a utopia in the "western wilds" did not succeed, for he had failed to take into account inherent human selfishness; its members were soon fighting among themselves. Disappointed, he returned to England, where he spent the balance of his life lecturing and writing.

In 1950 Mrs. Kenneth Dale Owen, wife of Robert Owen's great-grandson, began to play an important role in the restoration of the tiny village. As director of the Robert Lee Blaffer Trust, established in memory of her father, a founder of the Humble Oil Company, she was eager to make New Harmony the center of a cultural renaissance. She began to restore the village buildings and to erect contemporary historical monuments as well. In that connection she commissioned Philip Johnson, the celebrated American architect, to build an interdenominational church. He designed a brick-walled flagstone terrace which came to be known as the "Roofless Church," although he himself thought of his creation as art for art's sake.[80] Within the high brick walls stands a shrine cast in the shape of a canopy, resembling a tent, attached to rounds of cement on the ground and puffed out as though blown by the wind from within. In place of an altar (originally intended for the inside of the canopy) stands one of Jacques Lipchitz's masterpieces, a bronze sculpture of the Madonna entitled "Descent of the Holy Spirit." Small bushes and trees are planted opposite the shrine near the huge main gates, also designed by Lipchitz. According to the sculptor's intention it is a processional gate to be opened only when musicians, actors, or singers for a festival or drama make their ceremonial entrance. Christian symbols woven into the gate design include a black cross, wreaths of thorns and roses, the Greek letters Alpha and Omega, and the Lamb of God. In place of a roof there is the sky.

It was to see this church and to participate in a service on Pentecost in 1963 that the Tillichs had been invited to fly to New Harmony. Mrs. Owen, a long-time admirer of Tillich, whom she had first heard speak at Union Seminary, had been formulating plans to honor him as a representative of the renaissance in which she was so keenly interested. She had commissioned the architect Frederick Kiesler to design a "Cave of the New Being" (an idea inspired by Tillich's sermon "The New Being"), and she had selected, opposite the Roofless Church, the ground for a future Paul Tillich Park, both of which she invited him to dedicate.[81] Upon his arrival (he later confessed that he had experienced great "fear and trembling" en route[82]) Tillich felt instantly at home. The landscape unaccountably reminded him of eastern Germany, and he was profoundly impressed by the Roofless Church, where on the morning of 2 June he addressed approximately 350 persons. Referring to the cave, of which only a model existed, he spoke of it as the symbol of a new reality: a mother's womb, or even a grave. He said about the church itself that "this alone justifies the century in which we are living—that our century is not only able to produce bad imitations of former centuries, but that it is able to create something born in our time, understood in our time, and great in symbolic power in all directions."[83]

In the afternoon Tillich and a small group proceeded to a small hill or knoll which had been built up as the ground for the future Paul Tillich Park. In accepting Mrs. Owen's plan for the park, Tillich had suggested that she

> plant a few beautiful trees, among them two Japanese cedars in memory of my visit to Japan, and two birches, because under birch trees I read Schelling's philosophy of nature. Perhaps also a walnut tree and a few lilac bushes and a Christmas tree. Unfortunately, there are no linden trees in this country, otherwise one could take one of them because of the memories that are bound up in them for

me. You must know that I am a quasi-pagan lover of trees. And if you want to name the park for me, then let a stone be put there, either a bust of myself, or with several sentences from my books, or both.[84]

In his dedication of the park that afternoon, Tillich said, "I, Paul Tillich, give my name to this place and dedicate the ground of this park and of the Cave of the New Being to a New Reality conquering what is estranged and reuniting what belongs to each other. In the power of the spiritual presence."[85] The "Cave of the New Being" was never completed, but the Paul Tillich Park became a reality: a grove of fir trees among which several large rocks are scattered, with sentences from Tillich's sermons carved in the stone. At the end of one path winding through the grove, by an open field, a bust of Tillich has been placed, the work of the sculptor James Rosati.

During the two remaining years of his life, Tillich was the object of sharp criticism as well as high tribute. He suffered a steady and irreversible physical decline at the time when there were signs that his own influence was beginning to wane. On 6 March 1964, a colloquium was held in his honor at the Cathedral of St. John the Divine in New York City. In the presence of nearly a hundred distinguished scholars from various fields, three former students— Rollo May, John E. Smith, and Clifford Stanley—presented lengthy papers, interrupted by afternoon tea and dinner.[86] Tillich, startlingly thin and tired, had just recovered from a severe diverticulitis attack but thoroughly enjoyed the occasion, listening attentively to every speaker and pausing later to regret only that they had been too uncritical of him.

On 15 March, after preaching a sermon on "Life and Death" in the James Chapel at Union Seminary, he once more heard words of praise and affection, this time from Wilhelm Pauck at the presentation of a life-mask of his face created by Ralph Brodsky and donated to the seminary. Pauck, in an attempt to avoid a funereal atmosphere, reminisced of the time when he had driven Tillich to Maine to prove to him that there were forests in America: he himself had paced the beach restlessly wanting to move on while Tillich sat on a rock staring at the ocean in meditation. At the time, Pauck continued, neither of them dreamed that one day a mask of Tillich would be made to commemorate him. John Bennett, the gentle champion of liberal causes, by then president of the seminary, proudly accepted the gift, declaring that despite the claims of Harvard and Chicago Tillich would always belong to Union.[87] A duplicate mask was presented to President Pusey at Harvard on 22 March and now hangs on the door of the Tillich Archive in the Andover Library. At the time, Tillich openly spoke of the emerging differentiation between Tillich the subject and Tillich the object, declaring that he was learning to live with the latter.

While the vast majority of Tillich's contemporaries continued to praise him, "as he walked towards death he . . . heard also a rumbling chorus of criticism."[88] Men like Bishop Stephen Neill, Kenneth Hamilton, Paul Edwards (who in his role as a linguistic analyst once wrote of "Professor Tillich's confusions"), and some younger theologians spoke harsh words of his system, questioning its value, wondering aloud whether his great construction was indeed communicating the gospel, and generally answering in the negative. Although he accepted such criticism graciously in public, in private it irritated him. In such a state of mind, a few months before his death, he wrote to his friend John E. Smith, whom he regarded as his most brilliant pupil,

Long ago your contribution "Philosophy of Religion" to Paul Ramsey's book "Religion" came to me. It was just in the moment when I prepared my departure from Chicago for Springfield and East Hampton. Only after I had settled down could I read your marvellous analysis of the modern scene and of my own position within it. About the latter (which Hannah also read with admiration) I can only say that my biographer (which now Pauck is supposed to be) will follow your lead. I am astonished how much factual knowledge and understanding you have of me! Thanks, thanks. You know how much ignorance and non-understanding I have to meet in the public criticism of my ideas. You are an oasis in a desert in this respect.[89]

A lung infection, a severe bronchitis, and indications of an increasingly serious heart condition put Tillich into Billings Hospital in Chicago on several occasions between January and June 1964. This prevented him from delivering a lecture he had been invited to give at the opening of the new galleries and sculpture garden of the Museum of Modern Art on 25 May. Wilhelm Pauck read the piece for him. Recalling the great moment in which he had discovered the museum in 1933, Tillich praised its "embodiment of honesty in creative expression, both in architecture and in the arts for which architecture gives the space and frame."[90] In this talk as well as in another he gave a year later to the National Conference of Church Architects, he rehearsed ideas he had first expressed at the beginning of his career in 1919. Stressing that "the arts open up a dimension of reality which is otherwise hidden, and they open up our own being for receiving this reality," he continued: "Only the arts can do this: science, philosophy, moral action and religious devotion cannot. The artists bring to our senses, and through them to our whole being, something of the depth of our world and of ourselves, something of the mystery of being."[91] He went on to declare that, as in many other fields, so in art and architecture the death of traditional concepts had given way to a period of "sacred emptiness" into which God has withdrawn.

> Saying that God has withdrawn implies that he may return. Then he will disappoint those atheists who believe that he has confirmed atheism by his withdrawal. What may have happened by the victory of secularization is that his wrong image has been destroyed by himself. Therefore, the expression of church buildings should be "waiting for the return of the hidden God who has withdrawn."[92]

In the autumn of 1964, after a quiet summer in East Hampton, Tillich returned for his third and last year to the University of Chicago. On 2 March 1965 he received an utterly unexpected invitation from Jack Everett, then president of the New School for Social Research in New York, to become the first occupant of the Alvin Johnson chair of philosophy there. He was offered a comfortable salary supplemented by a furnished apartment, in return for which he was expected to hold one seminar and give one public lecture course each semester for an indefinite number of years. At about the same time, he received another invitation from the University of California in Santa Barbara. His temporary inability to decide between the two was a topic of discussion between him and many of his friends for some time. Most of them, sensing how fragile he had become, advised him to retire altogether. Then on 8 April, having first promised Jerald Brauer to remain at Chicago until the end of the centennial year of the Divinity School, he accepted Jack Everett's invitation.[93]

The degree of doubt about his decision that lurked within Tillich is shown in the letters he wrote that spring and summer. To a friend in Germany he declared, "Except for the summer months, my life here in America is a net in which I struggle but from which I cannot escape."[94] To Eduard Heimann he joyfully announced his new post.

> Now I must tell you something surprising. I have received a call from the New School to occupy for a limited time the Alvin Johnson chair and I have said yes in principle. It is too much for me to continue to commute between East Hampton, Chicago, and Santa Barbara, and I think of New York as a suburb of East Hampton. As I dictate this I think of your first letter in which you encouraged me to come to New York. Hannah calls this event the "great circle of my existence." What do you say?[95]

Several days later, he wrote to Adolf Löwe,

> There is much I look forward to and there are some things I fear, for example the city, which is a new development for the hard-boiled city slicker I am. The many attacks moreover on my time and strength continue. One can say no to many things, but the little bit which simply cannot be avoided is still too much.

> I should gladly have begun in the fall but it was absolutely impossible to do so without an inner break. Hannah, who loves the symbol of the circle, marvels at the fact that in a certain way my life in America returns to its beginnings. It is all inwardly very exciting, gratifying, and problematical.[96]

There were references, too, in nearly every letter Tillich wrote in this period to the fact that he would begin his eightieth year in August. He spent his last summer in East Hampton, allowing only one break, namely, his participation in the Ministers' Conference at Union Seminary for four days in July. Some who attended later remarked that he seemed less vigorous than formerly. Indeed, to nearly everyone he appeared intensely preoccupied, his eyes seeking something far away, his mind still alert but often elsewhere. In July Martin Buber died. In September Kurt Goldstein died, at a time when Tillich himself was experiencing a wave of heart attacks. Nevertheless, he went into the city to attend the memorial service, quite shaken by the event. Later that month he and his wife drove to Chicago, where a heart specialist confirmed that there was a definite change in his entire physical condition, including his heart, and that extreme caution was indicated. Tillich promptly canceled all his commitments except for his seminar at the university. A trip which would have taken him to Europe, and his wife to India, was postponed. In a letter dated 7 October he reported on the situation to his many German friends,[97] but remarked that he still hoped for a reunion with them. He added a personal note to each; the one he addressed to Ernst Bloch is doubtless the most revealing. "Finiteness permitting only hope against hope has laid hold of me. Perhaps it is better so for me. I am given time to feel that there is still hope."[98]

On 11 October, at eight in the evening, Tillich made his last public appearance.[99] He spoke on "The Significance of the History of Religions for the Systematic Theologian," under the auspices of the Centennial Alumni Conference on the History of Religions sponsored by the Divinity School. The lecture was given at Breasted Hall in the Oriental Institute. Tillich was in good spirits and spoke with passion, perhaps remembering that his doctoral dissertation had dealt with the significance of the history of religion for Schelling's thought. Afterward Joseph M. Kitagawa, the historian of religions, a man of charm and learning, invited the Tillichs, the Eliades, and others to his home. There Tillich went into the kitchen where Evelyn Kitagawa was preparing hot food.

He sat on a kitchen stool and reminisced, recalling that as a child his mother used to tie him to a kitchen stool while she did her housework. "I still feel most at home in the kitchen," he said, engaging his hostess in conversation for over half an hour and quietly sipping Scotch whiskey. Later he joined the others, leaving for home around midnight. At three or four the next morning he had a heart attack and was rushed to Billings Hospital in critical condition. Ten days later, on 22 October 1965, he died.

On that day, realizing that the end he had so dreaded was near, he asked his wife not to leave him. "Today," he said, "is dying day." Terribly weakened, he touched the Greek New Testament she had brought to his bedside along with his most precious possession, a German Bible. He asked and received her forgiveness for his transgressions. They recited together a little German poem they used to say together on their walks around their East Hampton garden, and the knowledge that he would never do so again made him weep. Then he recovered his equilibrium and joked with the doctor, declaring that he would be an ascetic that day and not eat anything at all. At seven in the evening he expressed a desire to walk a little. The nurse helped him sit up, he dangled his legs over the edge of the bed, then lay down and quietly died,[100] experiencing what he himself had once so perfectly described:

> Our anxiety puts frightening masks over all men and things. If we strip them of these masks, their own countenance appears and the fear they produce disappears. This is true even of death. Since every day a little of our life is taken from us—since we are dying every day—the final hour when we cease to exist does not of itself bring death: it merely completes the death process. The horrors connected with it are a matter of the imagination. They vanish when the mask is taken from the image of death.[101]

Within an hour Tillich's death was announced on major television channels and radio stations. A lengthy obituary appeared on the front page of the *New York Times* the next morning, his portrait by Halsman staring at the reader. In Berlin, Cambridge (Mass.), Chicago, Marburg, and New York memorial services were held, attended by crowds of mourners.[102] His body was cremated and the ashes interred in the East Hampton cemetery at the spot he had shown his sister a year earlier. Although no plans had been made during his lifetime for any other burial place, his widow and immediate family came to feel that his spirit would be best commemorated in the park bearing his name.[103] His ashes were therefore, reinterred on Pentecost Sunday, 29 May 1966, in the Paul Tillich Park, New Harmony, Indiana, which became his final resting place.

Death takes a man away from the living and gives in return his completed image. We see him for the first time in his entirety only when he is no longer alive. The many facets of Tillich's kaleidoscopic image are mirrored in countless words spoken and written after his death.

In the *New York Times* a brief editorial accompanied his obituary, in which the writer stressed Tillich's uniqueness. "It was the exceptionally broad canvas on which Paul Johannes Tillich worked that distinguished him from so many modern theologians. This patient scholar took as his subject all of life. . . . As an admirer put it, 'Paul Tillich's contribution is the successful interpretation of Christian truth for an age of doubt.' "[104]

In Berlin Harald Poelchau paid eloquent tribute to Tillich, saying that he was a "genius of friendship."

> To be a genius of friendship is a dangerous thing. There is the danger of disappointment, the danger of excessive burden: often one had to protect him from many people who made demands on him, especially in his last years as his physical strength, above all of his heart, declined. Even then, he was compassionate until the last, counseling, loving, and I might well add, praying with a large circle of friends.[105]

In Cambridge, Massachusetts, James Luther Adams spoke of Tillich's integrity.

> It is difficult to say whether or not Tillich has elicited a following that may be called the Tillichian School. But there are few people who have become familiar with him inside the churches or outside

them who have not been quickened to a new awareness of the light to the Gentiles and of the darkness visible that corrupts and enervates the heart of man. Certainly, this impact coming from the mind and spirit of Tillich is in large part due to our recognition of the originality and the patient integrity of this man. He was himself a living example of the divinely given power and courage to be . . .[106]

But Tillich himself wrote perhaps his most fitting epitaph when he set down these lines,

. . . in the anxiety of having to die is the anxiety of being eternally forgotten.

Is there anything that can keep us from being forgotten? That we were known from eternity and will be remembered in eternity is the only certainty that can save us from the horror of being forgotten forever. We cannot be forgotten because we are known eternally beyond past and future.[107]

A Chronology of the Life of Paul Tillich

1886, 20 August	Born, Starzeddel, Germany
1898–1901	Attends Humanistic *Gymnasium*, Königsberg
1901–1904	Attends Friedrich Wilhelm *Gymnasium*, Berlin
1902, 23 March	Is confirmed
1903, 24 September	Mother's death, Berlin
1904–1909	Studies at universities of Berlin, Tübingen, Halle and again at Berlin
1906–1907	First chargé of Wingolf Fellowship
1909, Spring	Passes first church board examination
1909, 1 January —Autumn	Assistant to Pastor Klein, Lichtenrade
1910, 22 August	Receives degree of Doctor of Philosophy, University of Breslau
1911, 1 April —1912, 31 March	Vicar in Nauen
1911, 16 December	Passes examination for degree of Licentiate of Theology, University of Halle
1912: January	Receives degree of Licentiate
27 July	Passes second church board examination
18 August	Ordained minister of the Evangelical Church of the Prussian Union, Berlin
1912–1914	Assistant preacher in the Moabit or workers' district of Berlin and in Berlin-Lankwitz
1914, 28 September	Marries Margarethe Wever

1914, 1 October —1918, August	Army chaplain, World War I, Western front
1918, 10 June	Awarded Iron Cross First Class
1918, August–December	Army chaplain in Spandau, Berlin
1919–1924	*Privatdozent*, University of Berlin
1919, 16 April	First public lecture on his own thought. Kant Society, Berlin: "On the Idea of a Theology of Culture"
1919–1920	Participates in founding religious socialist circle, Berlin
1920, 5 January	Death of sister, Johanna
1921, 22 February	Divorce from Margaretha Wever
1924, 22 March	Marries Hannah Werner Gottschow
1924–1925	Associate Professor of Theology, University of Marburg
1926	Publication of *The Religious Situation*
1925–1929	Professor of Philosophy and Religious Studies at the Dresden Institute of Technology
1927–1929	Adjunct Professor of Systematic Theology, University of Leipzig
1929–1933	Professor of Philosophy, University of Frankfort Participates in founding and editing of *Neue Blätter für Sozialismus*
1929	Joins Social Democratic Party
1932	Publication of *The Socialist Decision*
1933: 13 April	Suspended by Nazi government
3 November	Arrives in New York, U.S.A.
20 December	Dismissed from Frankfort professorship
1933–1934	Visiting Lecturer in Philosophy, Columbia University, New York
1933–1937	Visiting Professor of Philosophy of Religion and Systematic Theology, Union Theological Seminary, New York
1934	Joins Theological Discussion Group
1936	Publication of *On the Boundary*
1936, 25 November	Participates in founding of "Self-Help for Emigrés"—elected first chairman
1937, 30 July	Father dies, Berlin

1937	Oxford Conference on Life and Work
1937–1940	Associate Professor of Philosophical Theology, Union Theological Seminary, New York
In late 1930s or early 1940s (unrecorded)	Joins Philosophy Club, Columbia University, New York
1940–1955	Professor of Philosophical Theology, Union Theological Seminary, New York
1940, 4 March	Becomes American citizen
1942–1944	Radio broadcasts to the German people, Voice of America
1944	Participates in founding, and elected chairman, of Council for a Democratic Germany
1946	Acquisition of East Hampton land and house
1948	First post-World-War-II visit to Germany Publication of *The Protestant Era*
1951	Publication of *Systematic Theology*, Volume I
1952	Publication of *The Courage to Be*
1953–1954	Gifford Lectures, University of Aberdeen, Scotland
1955	Retires from Union Theological Seminary, New York
1955–1962	University Professor, Harvard University
1956	Visit to Greece
1957	Publication of *Systematic Theology*, Volume II
1959	Publication of first volume of *Gesammelte Werke* [Collected Works]
1960	Visit to Japan
1962	Retires from Harvard University Receives Peace Prize, German Publishers' Association, Frankfort
1962–1965	Nuveen Professor of Theology, Divinity School, University of Chicago
1963	Publication of *Systematic Theology*, Volume III

	Dedicates Paul Tillich Park, New Harmony, Indiana
	Visit to Israel and Egypt
1965: 11 October	Last public lecture: "The Significance of the History of Religions for the Systematic Theologian"
22 October	Dies of a heart attack, Billings Hospital, Chicago
1966, 29 May	Final interment, New Harmony, Indiana

Abbreviations

A few abbreviations by initials have seemed convenient for the Notes, in view of frequent reference:

G. A.	Göttingen Archive
G. W.	*Gesammelte Werke* [Collected Works]
H. A.	Harvard Archive
O. B.	*On the Boundary*

Short or abbreviated titles (as, "Auto. Refl." for "Autobiographical Reflections") are used for most works cited more than once in a chapter. With repeated mentions in the same chapter of Paul Tillich's various writings his last name only is used. Other members of the family are clearly designated by first name or initial.

Notes & References

Translations into English are by the authors and references to the Bible are to the New English Bible (NEB), unless otherwise indicated. Materials noted as being in a "private collection" are held by the authors unless stated otherwise.

CHAPTER 1. DREAMING INNOCENCE

1. Birth certificate. Paul Tillich Archive, Andover-Harvard Theological Library, hereafter called Harvard Archive or H. A.

2. Johannes Oskar Tillich, b. Berlin, 3 June 1857, d. Berlin, 30 July 1937. Married Wilhelmina Mathilda Dürselen, b. 5 April 1860, d. Berlin, 24 September 1903, on 1 October 1885. Documents H. A.

3. Letter to his parents from Johannes Tillich, dated afternoon 21 August 1886. H. A. Another reference to the infant's illness occurs in Johannes Tillich's diary, October 1886. G. A.

4. Paul Tillich, "The Destruction of Death," in *The Shaking of the Foundations* (New York: Charles Scribner's Sons, 1948), p. 170.

5. Paul Tillich, "Forgetting and Being Forgotten," in *The Eternal Now* (New York: Charles Scribner's Sons, 1963), p. 34.

6. Paul Tillich, "Love Is Stronger than Death," in *The New Being* (New York: Charles Scribner's Sons, 1955), pp. 172–73.

7. Wolf-Dieter Marsch, ed., *Werk und Wirken Paul Tillichs: Ein Gedenkbuch* (Stuttgart: Evangelisches Verlagswerk, 1967), p. 37. Adorno points out that even Tillich's intimate friends found it impossible to imagine that he might one day die!

8. Paul Tillich, *The Courage to Be* (New Haven: Yale University Press, 1952), pp. 13–14.

9. Tillich, "Love Is Stronger than Death," p. 174.

10. Information about Tillich's forefathers from an unpublished *Stammbuch* or genealogy prepared by Johannes Tillich. H. A., Göttingen Archive (hereafter called G. A.).

11. Paul Tillich, *My Search for Absolutes* (New York: Simon & Schuster, 1967), p. 39.

12. Information about Tillich's parents, grandparents, and early childhood primarily from interviews with Paul Tillich; also with Elisabeth Seeberger and

Hans-Jürgen Seeberger. Birth and death certificates H. A. See also Paul Tillich, *On the Boundary* (New York: Charles Scribner's Sons, 1966), pp. 13–15. Paul Tillich, "Autobiographical Reflections," in C. W. Kegley and R. W. Bretall, eds., *The Theology of Paul Tillich* (New York: Macmillan Co., 1952), p. 8.

13. On 23 August 1898 Johannes Tillich wrote to his parents informing them that Paul was about to be sent away to boarding school, then added, "Denkt Euch, dass meine Orchester-Komposition von der hiesigen Kurkapelle morgen gespielt werden soll, ich hatte sie zu diesem Zweck für volles Orchester gesetzt. Grosse Spannung bei allen Bekannten und bei mir." [Just think, my orchestra composition will be performed tomorrow by the local spa orchestra. To this end I composed it for full orchestra. My friends and I are all intensely expectant.] H. A.

14. Johanna Marie Tillich, b. 11 February 1889, d. 5 January 1920. G. A.

15. Elisabeth Johanna Mathilda Tillich, b. 20 June 1893.

16. Interview with Elisabeth Tillich Seeberger.

17. Tillich, "Auto. Refl.," p. 6.

18. Tillich, *O. B.*, pp. 18, 30.

19. Ibid., pp. 19–20.

20. Eckart von Sydow, *Die Kunst der Naturvölker und der Vorzeit*, 3rd ed. (Berlin: Propyläen Verlag, 1922). Other titles: *Form und Symbol*; *Expressionismus*.

21. Tillich's autobiographical writings are: *On the Boundary*, "Autobiographical Reflections," cited above, and the "Author's Introduction," *The Protestant Era*, trans. and ed. James L. Adams (Chicago: University of Chicago Press, 1948). The first chapter of the posthumously published *My Search for Absolutes* (New York: Simon & Schuster, 1967), is a slightly modified version of "Autobiographical Reflections."

22. Tillich, *O. B.*, pp. 24–25.

23. Ibid., p. 27.

24. Oscar Wilde, "The Selfish Giant," *The Portable Oscar Wilde*, ed. Richard Aldington (New York: Viking Press, 1946). Interview with Gerda Erdmann.

25. Interview with Kurt Leese.

26. Paul Tillich, "The Yoke of Religion," *Shaking of the Foundations*, pp. 93–94.

27. Paul Tillich, "What Is Truth?" *New Being*, p. 65.

28. Tillich, *O. B.*, pp. 15, 36–37.

29. Paul Tillich, "Who Are My Mother and My Brothers?" *New Being*, p. 108.

30. Interviews with Paul Tillich, Elisabeth Seeberger, and Maria Klein Rhine. Tillich's nickname for Johanna, "Wumming", sounded like "woman". He thought of them as identical in meaning.

31. See *O. B.*, pp. 46–47. Interview with Elisabeth Seeberger.

32. Documents H. A., G. A.

33. Paul Tillich to Thomas Mann, 23 May 1943, in *Blätter der Thomas Mann Gesellschaft*, no. 5 (Zurich, 1965), pp. 48–52. See also Tillich, "Auto. Refl.," pp. 11–12: ". . . in my student years the fraternity gave me a com-

munion (the first after the family) in which friendship, spiritual exchange on a very high level, intentional and unintentional education, joy of living, seriousness about the problems of communal life generally, and Christian communal life especially, could daily be experienced. I question whether without this experience I would have understood the meaning of the church existentially and theoretically."

34. Paul Tillich to Johannes Tillich, Tübingen, May 1905: "Der Jammer ist nur, dass ich so wenig zur Arbeit komme. Der Vormittag ist von Kollegs besetzt, der Nachmittag von Spaziergängen. Denn ich kann es nicht übers Herz bringen, bei strahlendem, wolkenlosem Himmel und einer Natur, die mir bei jedem Schritt wie ein neues, unbekanntes Wunder entgegentritt, zu Hause zu bleiben. Stundenlang streife ich, meist allein, durch unbekannte Wälder, Wiesen und Berge, und geniesse, was ich ein halbes Jahr mit Schmerzen entbehrt habe. Die Obstblüte hat ihren Höhepunkt schon überschritten, die Stachelbeeren fangen an zu reifen, die Eichen sind ganz grün. Zum ersten Mal wird mir das Rätsel gelöst, warum der Mai von den Dichtern so gerühmt wird." H. A.

35. Alfred Fritz, "Erinnerungen an Paul Tillich," in Paul Tillich, *Gesammelte Werke*, ed. Renate Albrecht, 14 vols. (Stuttgart: Evangelisches Verlagswerk, 1959–75), XIII: 541.

36. Tillich, Introduction, *Protestant Era*, pp. xiii–xiv. See also O. B., pp. 47–48.

37. Interview with Heinrich Meinhof.

38. Information on Wingolf Society from interviews with Heinrich Meinhof, Ernst Rhein, Eberhard Röhricht. See also Hans Waitz, *Geschichte des Wingolfsbundes* (Darmstadt: Johannes Waitz Verlag, 1904). The German word *kneipen* means to drink.

39. Paul Tillich to Johannes Tillich, July 1907. Private collection.

40. Paul Tillich, "Hermann Schafft," in *Herman Schafft: Ein Lebenswerk* (Kassel: Johannes Stauda Verlag, 1960), pp. 11–16. Part of this moving tribute has been republished in G. W. under the title "Erinnerungen an den Freund Hermann Schafft," XIII: 27 ff.

41. Interview with Claudia Bader.

42. Tillich, "Hermann Schafft," p. 11.

43. Interviews with Maria Klein Rhine, Paul Tillich, Gisela Walker.

44. Interviews with Heinrich Meinhof.

45. Lichtenrade memories: interviews with Maria Klein Rhine and Paul Tillich; excerpts from letters by Richard Wegener to Maria Klein Rhine, 1951. H. A. See also Tillich, O. B., pp. 40 ff. Disputed dates, G. W., (*Ergänzungsband*) V: 110.

46. Dostoevsky's *The Brothers Karamazov* enjoyed great popularity at the time, and Wegener was referring in a symbolic or analogical way to the Grand Inquisitor as he is described in Ivan's story told to Alyosha. The reference was not literal; the Grand Inquisitor was a person of unquestioned authority, and Johannes Tillich clearly fitted this description.

47. Claus Siebenborn, *Unter den Linden*, 1647–1947 (Berlin: Oswald Arnold Verlag, 1949), p. 122. See also Hans-Joachim Schoeps, *Rückblicke* (Berlin: Haude & Spenersche Verlagsbuchhandlung, 1963), pp. 23, 58–60.

48. Paul Tillich to Frau Pastor Klein, quoted in G. W., XIII: 20. "Ich möchte Ihnen und Herrn Pastor noch einmal meinen herzlichen Dank aussprechen für die schöne Erinnerung, um die ich durch Sie reicher geworden bin, und den Vorrat an Kraft, aus dem ich hoffentlich noch lange schöpfen kann. Die Zeit in Lichtenrade erscheint mir als eine Art goldenes Zeitalter voll ungetrübten Naturgenusses und seliger Sorglosigkeit."

49. Günther Dehn, *Die Alte Zeit: Die Vorigen Jahre: Lebenserinnerungen* (Munich: Chr. Kaiser Verlag, 1962), pp. 100, 117–19, 120–21.

50. Letter from Paul Tillich to Johannes Tillich, May 1910, Thursday, Corpus Christi: "I arrived here [Breslau] Wednesday afternoon and went first to the hotel and then to the university, in order to see Kühnemann. He was very kind and showed great interest in my paper, and gave me advice. In the evening I was alone and went to bed early. Thursday forenoon I went to see the city and also the Corpus Christi procession. Then I went to the Dean, Dr. Baumgartner, who is Professor of Philosophy. He is a Roman Catholic priest. He thought I had not given myself enough time to prepare for the examination. Then I went to the Hebrew teacher, Praetorius, who said that he was acquainted with a man name Tillich in Frankfort and who sends greetings. He insists that if at all possible, I take an examination in Hebrew and biblical Aramaic. After this, I went to see the historian, who proved to be quite difficult. He expects me to know modern historical literature and primary sources at least of a certain period. . . . Everyone said that the oral examination is not easy. This means that I must show mastery of, first, history of philosophy (Kant, Plato, Schiller); also logic and psychology. The examination lasts an hour and fifteen minutes. Second, Hebrew; third, Aramaic. Examination lasts half an hour. Fourth, history, examination half an hour. I cannot possibly get ready for this within a month. I may get by with two. . . . This means that I should take the examination at the end of July. In this case, the problem of knowledge of Aramaic can easily be solved. Uncle Horn is good in Aramaic and he is ready to teach me the principles of this language during the next eight days. Then I should make out Aramaic passages without difficulty. I would then stay here another week and cram Aramaic day and night. The following three weeks I plan to study history and philosophy in Berlin." Private collection.

Tillich crammed for two months. In Berlin, his sister asked him questions while the two rowed on the Wannsee. Interview with Elisabeth Seeberger.

51. Tillich was appointed *Hilfsprediger* or substitute preacher by the Evangelical Consistory in Berlin from 18 August 1912 to 14 May 1913, and again from 20 August 1914 to 30 September 1914. H. A.

52. Interviews with Elisabeth Seeberger, Paul Tillich, Gisela Walker.

53. On 16 September 1912 a skit entitled "Der Prozess," [The Trial] written by Emanuel Hirsch and Paul Tillich, was presented in honor of Johanna's marriage to Frede Fritz. A merry bit of nonsense, it concerned the groom's allegation that his bride had been passively resisting the influence of his ideas. After a great deal of punning and discussion the president, Tillich, decided that the obligation the bride owed to her groom and the wife to her husband

could be simply defined: in all areas except that of spiritual beauty, the wife was to obey the husband and to be influenced by his decisions. G. A.

54. Tillich, O. B., p. 60. Emphasis supplied.

55. Ibid., p. 61. See also Maria Klein Rhine, "Tillich der Apologet," G. W., XIII: 544 ff., also 33–34, 59–60.

56. Johannes Tillich to Paul Tillich, 21 August 1913. H. A.

57. Rhine, "Tillich der Apologet," p. 545.

58. Maria Klein to Paul Tillich, 3 October 1913. H. A.

59. The engagement announcement read as follows: "Die Verlobung ihrer Tochter Margarethe mit Herrn Lizentiat Dr. Paul Tillich zeigen an Wilhelm Wever, Königlicher Domänen-Pächter, Mathilde Wever, geborene Hausmann, Januar 1914." [Wilhelm Wever and Mathilde Wever, née Hausmann, announce the engagement of their daughter Margarethe to Dr. Paul Tillich, Licentiate, January 1914.] Wever leased a royal domain. H. A.

60. Undated statement by Father Wever: "Die Vorgeschichte zur Verlobung ist bekannt, die schärfsten Gegensätze haben sich wieder einmal angezogen und führen hoffentlich zu einer glücklichen Ehe." H. A.

61. Margarethe Karla Mathilda Katharina Maria Wever, b. 8 April 1888. Married to Paul Tillich in Butterfelde, 28 September 1914. H. A.

CHAPTER 2. THE TURNING POINT: WORLD WAR I

1. Carl Zuckmayer, Als Wär's ein Stück von Mir. Horen der Freundschaft (Vienna: S. Fischer Verlag, 1966), p. 203. See also Barbara Tuchman, The Proud Tower (New York: Macmillan Co., 1966), p. 240.

2. Paul Tillich, "Principalities and Powers," in The New Being (New York: Charles Scribner's Sons, 1955), p. 52. "When the German soldiers went into the First World War most of them shared the popular belief in a nice God who would make everything work out for the best. Actually everything worked out for the worst, for the nation and for almost everyone in it."

3. Paul Tillich, "Autobiographical Reflections," in C. W. Kegley and R. W. Bretall, eds., The Theology of Paul Tillich (New York: Macmillan Co., 1952), p. 7. "What was still lacking in discipline was provided by the army, which trespassed in power and social standing upon the civil world and drew the whole nation from earliest childhood into its ideology. It did this so effectively in my case that my enthusiasm for uniforms, parades, maneuvers, history of battles, and ideas of strategy was not exhausted until my thirtieth year, and then only because of my experiences in the First World War." See also Paul Tillich, On the Boundary (New York: Charles Scribner's Sons, 1966), pp. 21–22.

4. Interview with Paul Tillich.

5. Details of Paul Tillich's experiences in World War I are from documents in the Harvard and Göttingen Archives as well as from interviews with Erich Pfeiffer and Tillich himself. See also Tillich's "Bericht an den Herrn Feldprobst," in Gesammelte Werke, ed. Renate Albrecht, 14 vols. (Stuttgart: Evangelisches Verlagswerk, 1959–1975), XIII: 71–79.

6. Zuckmayer, *Als Wär's*, p. 228.

7. On 18 February 1915 Tillich sent his Aunt Margaret Tillich a poem reflecting his yearning for home in the eastern plains of Germany.

> Denn nach Osten sehnt ich mich von Jugend auf,
> Wo die weiten Ebnen Wehmut hauchen,
> Wo in Abenddunst die Moore hauchen,
> Wo die Sonne glühend anfängt ihren Lauf.
> Lasst mich fliehen aus des Verwesens feuchtem Dunst
> Aus der alten Schönheit Trümmerstätte,
> Von der Wache an dem Sterbebette,
> Lasst nach Osten mich, gewährt mir doch die Gunst.
>
> H. A.

8. Paul Tillich to Maria Klein, 22 February 1915: "Das wahre Erleben hat seine Wurzeln im Schmerz und das Glück ist nur eine Blüte, die sich dann und wann eröffnet." H. A.

9. On 26 May Tillich drew a detailed map of the army station, and later sent it to his father together with a description of yet another move, furniture wagon and all, which took place on 31 May. H. A. For a capsule description of the daily existence of a soldier in World War I, see Zuckmayer, *Als Wär's*, p. 217.

10. Paul Tillich to Johannes Tillich, 21 August 1915. H. A.

11. Paul Tillich to Johannes Tillich, 21 August 1915. H. A. Interview with Erich Pfeiffer.

12. Unpublished sermons, H. A., G. A.

13. Paul Tillich, G. W., XIII: 78.

14. Paul Tillich to Johannes Tillich, 19 December 1915. H. A.

15. Paul Tillich to Johannes Tillich, 13 January 1916. H. A.

16. Paul Tillich to Johannes Tillich, 2 June 1916. "Um uns tobt die Hölle! Jede Vorstellung versagt." H. A.

17. Tillich, "Principalities and Powers," *New Being*, p. 50.

18. Paul Tillich to Maria Klein, 27 November 1916: "Ich habe immer die unmittelbarste und stärkste Empfindung in mir, nicht mehr eigentlich im Leben zu stehen. Darum nehme ich es auch night so wichtig! Einen Menschen finden, fröhlich werden, Gott erkennen, das sind alles Sachen des Lebens. Aber das Leben ist ja selbst kein Boden der tragfähig ist. Nicht nur dass man jeden Tag sterben kann, Du auch, sondern dass alle sterben, *wirklich* sterben,— und dann das Leiden der Menschen—ich bin reinster Eschatalog, nicht dass ich kindliche Weltuntergangsphantasien hätte, sondern dass ich den tatsächlichen Weltuntergang dieser Zeit miterlebe. Fast auschliesslich predige ich 'das Ende'. . . . Nebenbei erhole ich mich durch Aufkleben von Bildern und wissenschaftlichen Untersuchungen über das System der Wissenschaften." H. A.

19. Paul Tillich to Johannes Tillich, 10 December 1916. H. A. See also Zuckmayer, *Als Wär's*, pp. 249–250; Franz Marc, *Briefe aus dem Feld* (Berlin: Helmut Rauschenbusch Verlag, 1948), pp. 25–26.

20. D. Mackenzie Brown, ed., *Ultimate Concern: Tillich in Dialogue* (New York: Harper & Row, 1965), p. 153.

21. Zuckmayer, *Als Wär's*, p. 241. "Es war das Versagen einer Welt." [It was the failure of an age.]

22. So far as is known, the correpsondence between Tillich and his wife Grethi no longer exists. Only a few references to her are to be found in the H. A. In a letter to his sister Johanna during the war Tillich mentions that Grethi is more involved with Eckart von Sydow and Richard Wegener than with his own family. He laments this, saying he wishes she could help his father in his lonely widowhood, but realizes she cannot. The split between a soldier's fidelity to his wife or true love and his wartime amorous adventures was fairly universal. See again Zuckmayer, *Als Wär's*, p. 238. In one of Tillich's sermons he makes a reference to this problem as follows, "Hast Du Macht auch über die Lust in der Ehe um der Seele des Weibes willen, und ausser der Ehe um der Seele des Fremden Mädchens willen, hast du Macht über die Lust. . . . Wer ist stärker—deine Freiheit oder deine Lust?" [Do you control your lust in marriage for the sake of your wife and for the sake of the girl to whom you are not married? Do you control your lust? . . . Which is stronger —your freedom or your desire?] He goes on to quote 1 Cor. 6:12: " 'I am free to do anything,' you say. Yes, but not everything is for my good. No doubt I am free to do anything, but I for one will not let anything make free with me." H. A., G. A.

23. Paul Tillich to Johannes Tillich, 31 January 1917: "Am schwersten wird Dir wie mir die Seelsorge und die Predigt, während uns wissenschaftliche Arbeit und Aktensachen liegen. Du bist dem Wesen nach Konsistorialrat von jeher und ich Professor von jeher. Aber das Schicksal will, dass Du immer Prediger sein musstest, und ich einen grossen Teil meines Lebens, wenn nicht für immer, auch." And about his newfound passion for art: ". . . wie ich an meinen Bildern sehe, die mir jetzt das sind, was Dir die Musik war." [. . . as I can tell from my pictures which now mean to me what music meant to you.] H. A.

24. Paul Tillich to Johannes Tillich, 30 May 1917: "Das war eine Welt— eine ganze Welt von Seligkeit und Wirklichkeitsferner Unschuld." H. A.

25. Paul Tillich to Maria Klein, 14 October 1917. H. A.

26. Paul Tillich to Emanuel Hirsch, December 1917. *Emanuel Hirsch-Paul Tillich Briefwechsel, 1917–1918* (Berlin: Verlag Die Spur, 1973), p. 9.

27. Paul Tillich to Maria Klein, 5 December 1917. H. A.

28. Paul Tillich to Johannes Tillich, 18 December 1917: "Das gehört doch zum Schönsten, was wir von Dir bekommen haben, dass wir solche Erinner-ungen an Weihnachten haben können, und dass wir sie weitergeben können an andere." H. A.

29. Paul Tillich to Johannes Tillich, 2 April 1918. H. A.

30. Paul Tillich to Johannes Tillich, 13 April 1918: "Leib und Seele haben einen Knacks, der ganz nie zu reparieren ist, aber das ist ja nur ein kleines Opfer im Verhältnis zu den Millionen, die das Leben als Opfer geben." H. A.

31. Paul Tillich to Johannes Tillich, 31 May 1918. H. A.

32. Paul Tillich to Johannes Tillich, 11 June 1918. H. A.

33. These figures are reported by the U.S. War Department, February 1924. *Encyclopedia Americana*, vol. 29 (1974), col. 360.

34. Interview with Paul Tillich.

CHAPTER 3. BETWEEN TWO WORLDS

1. As he put it, "Für Jahre meines Lebens nicht nur Heimat sondern auch Mythos." See Paul Tillich, "Grenzen," *Gesammelte Werke*, ed. Renate Albrecht, 14 vols. (Stuttgart: Evangelisches Verlagswerk, 1959–1975), XIII: 423.

2. Interview with Paul Tillich. See also Carl Zuckmayer, *Als Wär's Ein Stück von Mir. Horen der Freundschaft* (Vienna: S. Fischer Verlag, 1966), pp. 312–13.

3. Peter Gay, *Weimar Culture* (New York: Harper & Row, 1968), p. 128. See also Hans Kohn, *Living in a World Revolution* (New York: Trident Press, 1964), p. 120. "Berlin seemed to me a place where the defeated authoritarian order had been replaced not by liberty but by license."

4. Wilhelm Lütgert to Paul Tillich, 28 November 1918. H. A. Tillich was army chaplain in Spandau (near Berlin) from August until December 1918. Interview with Paul Tillich.

5. Interview with Paul Tillich.

6. Clipping from a Berlin newspaper. H. A. "In der theologischen Fakultät habilitierte sich soeben Dr. Phil. Lic. P. Tillich mit einer Antrittsvorlesung über das 'Dasein Gottes und die Religionspsychologie.' "

7. Paul Tillich, circular letter, September 1919. G. A.

8. Interviews with Paul Tillich, Margot Hahl, Ilse Margot von Reuthern, Adolf Müller, Marie-Luise Werner. See also Adolf Müller, "Der Junge Privatdozent in Berlin," and Margot Hahl, "Studentin bei dem Privatdozenten: Paul Tillich im Nachkriegs-Berlin 1919–1922," G. W., XIII: 545 ff., 548 ff.; D. Otto Haendler, "Paul Tillich, der Mensch," in Wolf-Dieter Marsch, ed., *Werk und Wirken Paul Tillichs: Ein Gedenkbuch* (Stuttgart: Evangelisches Verlagswerk, 1967), pp. 61, 62, 64.

9. Paul Tillich often claimed that he had introduced the question-and-answer period into German academic life, but contemporary reports contradict this. He enjoyed and encouraged discussion, however.

10. Paul Tillich, "Autobiographical Reflections," in C. W. Kegley and R. W. Bretall, eds., *The Theology of Paul Tillich* (New York: Macmillan Co., 1952), p. 15.

11. ". . . one observes in Tillich the impulse always to form an architectonic structure, so one may observe it also in his whole system of thought. One is reminded of Goethe's famous characterization of the philosophy of Aristotle in which he compares it to a pyramid. Tillich's thought, as can most readily be observed in his *System of the Sciences*, also possesses a pyramidal quality." James L. Adams, *Paul Tillich's Philosophy of Culture, Science, and Religion* (New York: Harper & Row, 1965), p. 99.

12. Interviews with Reinhold Niebuhr, Albert Outler, Ruth Schmidt.

13. Paul Tillich, "Religion and Secular Culture," in *The Protestant Era*, trans. and ed. James L. Adams (Chicago: University of Chicago Press, 1948),

p. 57. The quotation as cited in the text of this book is translated from the original accurate German.

14. Tillich, "Auto. Refl.," pp. 14–15. Interview with Paul Tillich.

15. Interview with Margot Hahl who quoted this paragraph from a letter Tillich had written her.

16. Interview with Ilse Margot von Reuthern.

17. For Tillich's report, dated 27 May 1919, see G. W., XIII: 154–60. Bartels' letter, dated 12 July 1919, is in the H. A.

18. Der Sozialismus als Kirchenfrage: Leitsätze von Paul Tillich und Richard Wegener (1919), published in G. W., II: 13–20.

19. Interviews with James Luther Adams, Eduard Heimann, Adolf Löwe, August Rathmann, and Paul Tillich. See Also Günther Dehn, Die Alte Zeit, Die Vorigen Jahre: Lebenserinnerungen (Munich: Chr. Kaiser Verlag, 1962), pp. 212–13, 223; Paul Tillich, On the Boundary (New York: Charles Scribner's Sons, 1966), pp. 32–33; August Rathmann, "Tillich als Religiöser Sozialist," G. W., XIII: 565.

20. One of the most comprehensive articles on the kairos circle and the religious-socialist movement is by Eduard Heimann, "Tillich's Doctrine of Religious Socialism," in Kegley and Bretall, eds., Theol. of P. T., pp. 312 ff. See also Tillich, O. B., pp. 24, 75–78, and his "Auto. Refl.," pp. 12–13: "Another remark must be made here regarding my relation to Karl Marx. It has always been dialectical, combining a Yes and a No. The Yes was based on the prophetic, humanistic and realistic elements in Marx's passionate style and profound thought, the No on the calculating, materialistic, and resentful elements in Marx's analysis, polemics, and propaganda."

21. Interview with August Rathmann. See also his "Tillich als Religiöser Sozialist," G. W., XIII: 564–68.

22. Tillich, O. B., p. 26.

23. Ibid., pp. 27–28.

24. Adams, Tillich's Philosophy of Culture, p. 110. See also Paul Tillich, The Religious Situation (New York: Meridian Books, 1956), pp. 85–101.

25. Tillich, Relig. Sit., p. 89.

26. Interview with Margot Hahl.

27. Franz Marc, Briefe aus dem Feld (Berlin: Helmut Rauschenbusch Verlag, 1948), p. 75. See Wolf-Dieter Dube, Expressionism (New York: Praeger Publishers, 1973), for more on German Expressionism.

28. Tillich, O. B., pp. 27–28.

29. Adams, Tillich's Philosophy of Culture, pp. 66–67.

30. Paul Tillich, "Wahrhaftigkeit und Weihe in der Religiösen Kunst und Architektur," G. W., XIII: 445.

31. Paul Tillich, Theology of Culture, ed. Robert Kimball (New York: Oxford University Press, 1959), p. 68.

32. Paul Tillich in the classroom at Union Theological Seminary. See also his A History of Christian Thought, ed. Carl Braaten (New York: Harper & Row, 1968), p. 97.

33. Tillich, "Wahrhaftigkeit," G. W., XIII: 448. "Ich denke an Matisse, dessen Kapelle ich in Vence in Südfrankreich sah und die ich in ihrer Ein-

fachheit als grosses Kunstwerk bewunderte. Nachdem ich die Kapelle ver-
lassen hatte, sagte ich zu meiner Frau: 'Ich habe nichts daran auszusetzen, und
doch hat sie jemand gebaut, der keine Beziehung zur Kirche hat.' " See also
his "Honesty and Consecration," *Response*, 8, no. 4 (Easter, 1967). Here, as
in many other cases, the German is more accurate than the English, rendering the meaning more clearly.

34. Paul Tillich, *Systematic Theology*, 3 vols. (Chicago: University of Chicago Press, 1951–63), III: 197–98. Our quotation is slightly edited.

35. Interview with Lilly Pincus.

36. Tillich, "Auto. Refl.," pp. 13, 14. For a brief history of the authentic
Bohème (or "bohemian life") of Berlin, see Felix Henseleit, ed., *Berliner
Bohème* (Berlin: Ullstein, 1961). Between 1890 and 1930 this consisted of a
very few painters, poets, politicians, and actors: e.g., Ludwig Devrient, Theodor
Fontane, August Strindberg, and Else Lasker, who are remembered not for
their unconventional ways but for their achievements. When Tillich used the
word *Bohème* he was referring primarily to the disregard of conventions. See
also Tillich, O. B., 22–23; A. Rüstow, *Ortsbestimmung* (Zurich: E. Rentsch,
1957), p. 621; Paul Honigsheim, "Die Bohème," in *Kölner Vierteljahrs-
schrift für Soziologie*, III (1923–24); Robert Michels, "Zur Soziologie der
Bohème" in Conrad's *Jahrbücher für Nationaloekonomie*, 136 (1932), pp.
801–13.

37. *Diele*—"Das war der Name für kleine Bars mit Vergnügungsbetrieb,
die es an allen Strassenecken gab." Zuckmayer, *Als Wär's*, p. 313. Interviews
with Elisabeth Seeberger, Paul Tillich, Marie-Luise Werner.

38. Interviews with Waltraut Lefebre, Paul Tillich.

39. Interviews with Maria Klein Rhine, Elisabeth Seeberger, Paul Tillich,
Marie-Luise Werner.

40. Tillich divorced Grethi Wever on 22 February 1921. H. A. Except for
a brief meeting in post-World-War-II Berlin in 1948, they did not see each
other again. Interview with Paul Tillich.

41. Interview with Paul Tillich.

42. Margot Hahl, "Studentin," G. W., XIII: 549. Interviews with Margot
Hahl, Paul Tillich. See also Tillich, O. B., pp. 79–80.

43. Paul Tillich, "The Meaning of Joy," in *The New Being* (New York:
Charles Scribner's Sons, 1955), pp. 143–44.

44. Tillich, "Auto. Refl.," p. 14.

45. Paul Tillich in *Blätter für Religiösen Sozialismus* (May 1924), p. 18.
"Zweifellos besteht bei mir die Gefahr der deduktiven Gewaltsamkeit, der die
bluthafte Fülle immer neuer Anschauungen der Wirklichkeit fehlt. Diese
Gefahr kenne ich und suche ich durch immer neues Eingehen in das Leben-
dige und seine verschiedenen Seiten zu entgehen. So stehe ich in einem ununter-
brochenen und alljährlich mit grösster Energie erneuerten Konnex mit der
Natur, so kam ich zu einem intensiven Freundschaftsleben als Student, so
kam ich zur Bohème, zum Krieg, zur Politik, zur Malerei, und gegenwärtig
in diesem Winter mit grösster Leidenschaft zur Musik." It is noteworthy that
Tillich speaks here of his passion for music. He loved it but it never meant as
much to him as painting and architecture did.

46. Paul Tillich, "Heal the Sick; Cast out Demons," *The Eternal Now* (New York: Charles Scribner's Sons, 1963), p. 61.

47. Interview with Paul Tillich.

48. Emanuel Hirsch to Paul Tillich, 21 June 1921, 26 June 1921, and 28 June 1921. H. A.

49. Picture in H. A.

50. "Unsere Entschlafene war ein *suchender* Mensch, ein rechter Heimweh-mensch." January 1920. H. A.

51. Interviews with Maria Klein Rhine, Paul Tillich, Marie-Luise Werner. See Hannah Tillich, *From Time to Time* (New York: Stein & Day, 1973), p. 85.

52. Interviews with Hans Huth, Paul Tillich. The balls of this period were a very small facet of Berlin life, when everyone was still celebrating the end of the war. There was a certain status-symbol element in attending this particular ball. It was planned for students only, but guests were permitted. They had to pay high prices for tickets, which were hard to get since everyone who had anything to do with the arts wanted to go. Rich bankers, elderly persons, professors of mathematics or theology, and so on, were also to be seen there. See ibid., p. 80.

53. Interviews with Paul Tillich, Marie-Luise Werner, Ibid., p. 87.

54. Ibid.

55. Johanna Werner married Albert Gottschow (b. 26 June 1891) on 13 July 1920. Their son Albert Johannes, b. 5 June 1922, died very young. Documents, H. A.

56. Interview with Paul Tillich. See also ibid., p. 92.

57. Paul Tillich to Maria Klein, 1 January 1924: "Auch unsere Hochzeit wird nun hoffentlich bald möglich werden, nachdem vor einigen Tagen Hannahs Scheidung rechtskräftig geworden ist. Wahrscheinlich werden wir im Sommer nach Marburg gehen, wo ich den meist kränklichen Rudolf Otto vertreten werde." H. A. See also H. Tillich, *Time to Time*, pp. 95-97. Paul Tillich married Johanna Dorothea Werner Gottschow (b. 17 May 1896) on 22 March 1924 in Berlin. Documents, H. A.

58. Interviews with Marie-Luise Werner and Paul Tillich.

59. H. Tillich, *Time to Time*, p. 105. Interview with Paul Tillich.

60. D. Mackenzie Brown, ed., *Ultimate Concern: Tillich in Dialogue* (New York: Harper & Row, 1965), pp. 195-96.

61. Paul Tillich, *Love, Power, and Justice* (New York: Oxford University Press, 1954), p. 27. Letters written by P. Tillich to H. W. Gottschow in the 1920s substantiate this interpretation of Tillich's views on love and marriage. P. C.

62. Paul Tillich, "Spiritual Presence," *Eternal Now*, pp. 89–90. Interview with Paul Tillich.

63. Interview with Paul Tillich.

64. Interview with Paul Tillich. H. Tillich, *Time to Time*, pp. 123 ff.

65. Ibid., p. 202.

66. Interview with Paul Tillich.

67. Tillich, *Relig. Sit.*, p. 201.

68. Tillich, *Love, Power, and Justice*, p. 117.

69. Paul Tillich, "Who Are My Mother and My Brothers?" *New Being*, p. 108. See also his *Theol. of Cult.*, p. 69.

70. Interview with Paul Tillich.

71. Cf. H. Tillich, *Time to Time*, pp. 199–200, 242–43.

72. Paul Tillich, "God's Pursuit of Man," *Eternal Now*, p. 106.

73. Rollo May, *Paulus* (New York: Harper & Row, 1973), p. 65.

74. Paul Tillich, "You Are Accepted," in *The Shaking of the Foundations* (New York: Charles Scribner's Sons, 1948), pp. 161–62. John E. Smith, in a lecture at Union Theological Seminary in January 1971, spoke as follows of the sermon: "This same point is brought out even more forcibly in what I regard as Tillich's finest sermon, 'You Are Accepted,' which was preached originally in St. Paul's Chapel at Columbia University. There he speaks of God as the power which forgives and accepts us although we are in fact not acceptable or sufficiently good of ourselves to merit being accepted. Faith in the reality of God for him is the same as accepting the acceptance. And, indeed, according to Tillich, if we are accepted in the Divine life, who are we to reject ourselves?"

CHAPTER 4. SPLENDID ISOLATION

1. Tillich was associate professor of theology at the University of Marburg from 24 April 1924 to 30 April 1925. H. A. See also Paul Tillich, "Autobiographical Reflections," in C. W. Kegley and R. W. Bretall, eds., *The Theology of Paul Tillich* (New York: Macmillan Co., 1952), p. 14.

2. Interview with Harald Poelchau. See also Harald Poelchau, "Paul Tillich in Marburg," in Paul Tillich, *Gesammelte Werke*, ed. Renate Albrecht, 14 vols. (Stuttgart: Evangelisches Verlagswerk, 1959–75), XIII: 556.

3. Interview with Harald Poelchau.

4. Interview with Paul Tillich. See also Hannah Tillich, *From Time to Time* (New York: Stein & Day, 1973), p. 115.

5. D. Mackenzie Brown, ed., *Ultimate Concern: Tillich in Dialogue* (New York: Harper & Row, 1965), p. 32.

6. Interview with Paul Tillich. See also Paul Tillich, *My Search for Absolutes* (New York: Simon & Schuster, 1967), p. 29.

7. Tillich, "Auto. Refl.," p. 14.

8. Interview with Paul Tillich.

9. Interview with Richard Kroner. See also Tillich, "Auto. Refl.," p. 14.

10. Interview with Robert Ulich. Tillich was professor of philosophy and of religious studies at the Dresden Institute of Technology from 1 May 1925 to 31 March 1929. H. A.

11. Interviews with Paul Tillich, Marie-Luise Werner.

12. Dresden period. Interviews with Renate Albrecht, Nina Baring, Ellen Frankenberg, Hanya Holm, Richard Kroner, Fedor Stepun, Gertraut Stöber, Paul Tillich, Robert Ulich, Ilse Usener, Cora Wächter.

13. Cf. Renate Albrecht, "Tillichs Berufung nach Dresden," G. W., XIII: 558.

14.. Interview with Richard Kroner.

15. G. W., XIII: 582–83.

16. Interviews with Paul Tillich, Marie-Luise Werner. See also H. Tillich, *Time to Time*, pp. 123 ff. Erdmuthe Christiane Tillich was born on 17 February 1926 and baptized on 19 October 1926 in Dresden. H. A. For an anecdote Tillich often told about his daughter, see Brown, ed., *Ultimate Concern*, p. 194.

17. Interviews with Ellen Frankenberg, Richard Kroner, Paul Tillich, Cora Wächter.

18. Interviews with Paul Tillich, Cora Wächter.

19. Interview with Richard Kroner. See also Leonie Dotzler-Möllering, "'Tillichs Begegnung mit dem Ausdruckstanz," *G. W.*, XIII: 559 ff.

20. Interview with Richard Kroner.

21. See Dotzler-Möllering, "Tillichs Begegnung," *G. W.*, XIII: 561.

22. Paul Tillich, "Tanz und Religion," *G. W.*, XIII: 134 ff.

23. Interview with Hanya Holm, who became famous as the choreographer of many Broadway musicals, including *My Fair Lady* and *Camelot*.

24. Interview with Fedor Stepun.

25. G. W., VIII: 31–39.

26. Interview with Richard Kroner.

27. Paul Tillich, *On the Boundary* (New York: Charles Scribner's Sons, 1966), pp. 79, 80. Cf. also "One can only unite oneself with the demonic at the price of self-destruction: either the demon who lives in everyone and is prepared to destroy him is awakened, or the creative part of the demon, which makes it possible to talk about him at all, is unveiled, lifted out of the depths and thereby made empty. It is a peculiar experience: a speech about the demonic is followed by wildness or emptiness or both; the demon revenges himself because he has been characterized. Only the prophet who conquers him can name him without being harmed." From Tillich's Preface to *Das Dämonische* (Tübingen: J. C. B. Mohr, 1926).

28. Fritz Medicus to Paul Tillich, 3 June 1928. Private collection.

29. See also John Raphael Staude, *Max Scheler: An Intellectual Portrait* (New York: Free Press, 1967).

30. Interview with Ellen and Alexander Höchberg.

31. Interviews with Theodor Adorno, Horace Friess, Nelli Gelb, Kurt Goldstein, Wolfgang Hochheimer, Max Horkheimer, Adolf Löwe, Reinhold Niebuhr, Gertie Siemsen, Harald Poelchau, Paul Tillich, Robert Ulich.

32. Interviews with Adorno, Löwe, Horkheimer.

33. Paul Tillich's tribute to Kurt Riezler on his seventieth birthday, 11 February 1952. Unpublished MS, private collection.

34. Windelband, secretary of the Prussian Ministry of Science, Art, and Education (*Wissenschaft, Kunst, Volksbildung*) to Paul Tillich, 21 February 1929, 14 March 1929, 18 March 1929. Private collection. As earlier references to H. C. Becker (the Prussian Minister of Education) indicate, he favored Tillich for whom he had a great liking. These sentiments are reflected in a letter to Tillich dated 11 February 1930 in which Becker writes, "Die Bekanntschaft mit Ihnen gehört zu meinen schönsten Erlebnissen der letzten Jahre...."

Jedenfalls bringe ich Ihnen einen starken geistigen Respekt und eine warme, ganz rein menschliche Zuneigung entgegen." [My acquaintance with you is one of my most agreeable experiences in recent years. . . . At any rate, I have a great respect for your intellect and a warm affection for you personally.] H. A.

35. Bünger to Paul Tillich, 26 March 1929, Kurt Riezler to Paul Tillich, 23 December 1929. Robert Ulich to Paul Tillich, 8 February 1930. Private collection.

36. G. W., XIII: 84.

37. Interview with Paul Tillich. Tillich was professor of philosophy at the University of Frankfort from 1 March 1929 to 27 December 1933. Documents H. A. He was suspended on 13 April 1933 and dismissed on 27 December of that year.

38. G. W., XIII: 562–64. (19 March 1929).

39. Interview with Paul Tillich. See Tillich, "Auto. Refl.," p. 14; also University of Frankfort catalogues, 1929–1933.

40. Interviews with Theodor Adorno, Max Horkheimer, Paul Tillich. See Hans Driesch, Lebenserinnerungen (Basel: E. Reinhardt, 1951), p. 204. "War doch die Zeit von 1924, als die Inflation überwunden war, bis 1932 eine Blütezeit geistigen Lebens in Deutschland, wie sie selten eine Nation gesehen hat. Es gibt keine gemeinere und verlogenere Behauptung als die, jene Zeit sei ein Niedergang gewesen." [Once inflation was conquered, the period from 1924 to 1932 was a time when intellectual life flourished in Germany in a way rarely witnessed by a nation. There is no meaner or more mendacious an assertion than to say that that period was a time of decline.]

41. Interview with Theodor Adorno. See also "Erinnerungen an Paul Tillich," in Marsch, ed., Werk und Wirken, pp. 26–28.

42. Harald Poelchau. "Gedenkrede," unpublished MS, 20 November 1965. G. A.

43. Interview with Gertie Siemsen.

44. Interview with Theodor Adorno. See also "Erinnerungen an Paul Tillich." pp. 24–26.

45. Interview with Alexander Höchberg. "Humor ist Hoffnung im Wiedersehen."

46. Interview with Max Horkheimer.

47. Interviews with Nelli Gelb, Kurt Goldstein.

48. Paul Tillich, Systematic Theology, 3 vols. (Chicago: University of Chicago Press, 1951–63), III: 17–21. Interview with Kurt Goldstein.

49. "Paulus unter den Juden." Interviews with Theodor Adorno, Max Horkheimer.

50. Interview with Paul Tillich.

51. "Erinnerungen an Paul Tillich" in Marsch, ed., Werk und Wirken, pp. 29–30.

52. Ibid.

53. Paul Tillich, "Das Wohnen, Der Raum und Die Zeit," in Die Form (Berlin: W. & S. Loewenthal, 1933), 8:4–6.

54. Windelband to Paul Tillich, 5 March 1931. Private collection. See also

Eberhard Bethge, *Dietrich Bonhoeffer* (Tübingen: J. C. D. Mohr, 1967), p. 208.

55. Interview with Paul Tillich. Tillich's first driver's license is dated 30 June 1930, Frankfort am Main. H. A.

56. Interviews with Alexander Höchberg, Paul Tillich.

57. Einladung zum Kostümfest
Frankfurt Niederrad, Vogelstrasse 11
Die Realdialektik oder "durch Spruch und Widerspruch zur Einheit."
27 Februar Abends 9 Uhr bis 28 Februar lange nach Sonnenaufgang.
—Document H. A.

58. Carl Zuckmayer, *Als Wär's Ein Stück von Mir, Horen der Freudschaft* (Vienna: S. Fischer Verlag, 1966), pp. 451–53.

59. Interview with Paul Tillich. See also his "Grundlinien des Religiösen Sozialismus," in G. W., II: 91–120.

60. Paul Tillich, *On the Boundary* (New York: Charles Scribner's Sons, 1966), pp. 20–21.

61. Interview with Paul Tillich.

62. Interview with Harald Poelchau.

63. Günther Dehn, *Die Alte Zeit, Die Vorigen Jahre: Lebenserinnerungen* (Munich: Chr. Kaiser Verlag, 1962), p. 234.

64. Paul Tillich and Hermann Schafft to the Berlin Wingolf, April 1932. Private collection.

65. Interviews with Claire and Günther Loewenfeld and Lilly Pincus.

66. Theodor Adorno, "Erinnerungen an Paul Tillich," in Marsch, ed., *Werk und Wirken*, pp. 30–31.

67. "Siegt aber die politische Romantik und mit ihr der kriegerische Nationalismus, so ist der Selbstvernichtungskampf der europäischen Völker unvermeidlich. *Die Rettung der europäischen Gesellschaft von der Rückkehr in die Barbarei ist in die Hand des Sozialismus gegeben.*" Paul Tillich, "Die Sozialistische Entscheidung," G. W., II: 364. The latter sentence became a vivid source of offense to the Nazi journalists. See note 73.

68. Interview with Paul Tillich.

69. Cf. H. Tillich, *Time to Time*, p. 149.

70. Paul Tillich, *Theology of Culture*, ed. Robert Kimball (New York: Oxford University Press, 1959), pp. 163–64.

71. Interview with August Rathmann. See also his "Tillich als Religiöser Sozialist," G. W., XIII: 567.

72. Interview with Max Horkheimer. See also his "Meine Begegnung mit Paul Tillich," G. W., XIII: 568.

73. *Frankfurter Zeitung*, 18 and 25 March 1933.

74. Interview with Lilly Pincus.

75. Riezler, a Bavarian and a Roman Catholic, lived in Berlin until 1936 when, as a witness of the Olympic Games (which he described as a "Circus Maximus of 200,000 people"), he decided the time had come for him to emigrate. He moved to New York where he was reunited with many of his Frankfort friends and taught at the New School for Social Research until his retirement. See also Kurt Riezler, *Tagebücher, Aufsätze, Dokumente*, ed. Karl

Dietrich Erdmann, vol. 48 of the *Deutsche Geschichtsquellen des 19. und 20. Jahrhunderts* (Göttingen: Vandenhoeck, 1972).

76. Cf. *Manchester Guardian*, 19 April 1933.

77. Fritz K. Ringer, *The Decline of the German Mandarins: The German Academic Community, 1890–1933* (Cambridge: Harvard University Press, 1972), p. 440. "Nearly 1700 faculty members and young scholars lost their places (during the early years of the Nazi regime), among them 313 full professors." See also E. V. Hartshorne, *The German Universities and National Socialism* (Cambridge: Harvard University Press, 1937), pp. 87, 100; and Hans Meier, "National Sozialismus-Hochschule-Politik," in Helmut Kuhn and others, *Die Deutsche Universität im Dritten Reich* (Munich: R. Piper, 1966), p. 82: "Entlassungsaktion betraf 313 ordentliche, 300 ausserordentliche Professoren, 322 Privatdozenten. Insgesamt 1684. 56% aus rassischen und politischen Gründen suspendiert." See also in the same volume Wolfgang Kunkel, "Die Professoren im Dritten Reich," p. 115: "Linksparteiler sollten als 'politisch unzuverlässig' in den Ruhestand versetzt werden." [Members of left-wing parties were to be retired as "politically unreliable."]

78. Interview with Paul Tillich.

79. Paul Tillich to Margot Hahl, 19 April 1933. Private collection of M. Hahl. Tillich's assumption that his income would be cut off immediately turned out to be incorrect. He received a normal income until December of that year, and after his arrival in America retirement benefits were (for a brief time only) placed in a bank account in his sister's name in Berlin, to be held for him there.

80. Paul Tillich, "Läuterndes Feuer," G. W., XIII: 275–78.

81. Interviews with Paul Tillich, Horace Friess, Gertie Siemsen. Gerullis to Paul Tillich, 12 May 1933. Private collection.

82. Henry Sloane Coffin, *A Half Century of Union Theological Seminary, 1896–1945* (New York: Charles Scribner's Sons, 1954), pp. 134, 135. See also Charles Weiner, "A New Site for the Seminar: The Refugees and American Physics in the Thirties," in Donald Fleming and Bernard Bailyn, eds., *The Intellectual Migration: Europe and America, 1930–1960* (Cambridge: Harvard University Press, 1969). A letter signed by John Dewey (as temporary chairman of the Emergency Committee in Aid of Displaced German Scholars) and other members of the faculty "solicited opinion on the establishment of temporary fellowships at Columbia University for refugee scholars, asking whether the faculty were willing to contribute toward funds for this purpose. The response was immediate. 125 faculty members made contributions. . . . As a result provision was made to add four displaced scholars as visiting professors without financial responsibility on the part of the university. This group included the anthropologist Julius Lips, the archaeologist Margaret Bieber, the mathematician Stefan Warschawski, and the theologian Paul Tillich."

83. Frank Fackenthal to Paul Tillich, 16 August 1933. Central Files, Columbia University.

84. Interviews with Horace Friess, Reinhold Niebuhr.

85. Interview with Paul Tillich.

86. Interviews with Theodor Adorno, Wolfgang Hochheimer, Harald Poelchau.

87. Reference to Paul Tillich's letter to the Ministry of Culture, dated 29 August 1933, is made in the reply on official ministry stationery, dated 9 September 1933. Private collection.

88. Interviews with Horace Friess, Paul Tillich.

89. Interview with Paul Tillich. The substance of this paragraph was recalled by Tillich to the authors in 1964. He adamantly denied the allegation put forward by a colleague of his that he had seen Bernhard Rust or that Rust had offered him a post or tried to persuade him to remain in Germany.

90. In the 4 October 1933 issue of the *New York Times*, Nicholas Murray Butler announced the appointment of three German refugees as visiting professors for the year 1933–34. They were: Dr. Paul Tillich, Professor of Philosophy, Dr. Felix Bernstein, Professor of Mathematics, and Dr. Rudolf Schoenheimer, Professor of Biological Chemistry.

91. Interviews with Paul Tillich, Robert Ulich.

92. Rathmann, "Tillich als Religiöser Sozialist," G. W., XIII: 567.

93. Interview with Lilly Pincus, Paul Tillich, Marie-Luise Werner.

94. Paul Tillich, circular letter, 9 November 1933. G. A.

CHAPTER 5. BENEFICIAL CATASTROPHE

1. Paul Tillich, "Autobiographical Reflections," in C. W. Kegley and R. W. Bretall, eds., *The Theology of Paul Tillich* (New York: Macmillan Co., 1952), p. 16. Tillich's boat arrived on 3 November; he and his family disembarked the next day. See also Margaret Sterne's Foreword to James R. Lyons, ed., *The Intellectual Legacy of Paul Tillich* (Detroit: Wayne State University Press, 1969).

2. Interview with Horace Friess. This report of Paul Tillich's early impressions of America is primarily based on three circular letters he wrote to his German friends, dated 9 November 1933, 2 December 1933, and 4 February 1934; also interviews with Reinhold Niebuhr and Carl Hermann Voss as well as with Tillich himself.

3. Harold R. Landon, ed., *Reinhold Niebuhr: A Prophetic Voice in Our Time* (Greenwich, Conn.: Seabury Press, 1962), pp. 29, 30: "All of the Union professors had given me a little of their old furniture in the apartment which now the doctor has—by far the largest—I always had the feeling that I was in the apartment of the Bishop of New York and not of a little professor. In any case, I do not forget this. I want to mention that the first human being who greeted us in Union Seminary was Mrs. Niebuhr."

4. Paul Tillich, circular letter, 9 November 1933. G. A.

5. See Henry Sloane Coffin, *A Half Century of Union Theological Seminary, 1896–1945* (New York: Charles Scribner's Sons, 1954), for details.

6. Interviews with Paul Tillich, Carl Hermann Voss.

7. Interview with Clifford Stanley.

8. Interviews with Henry P. Van Dusen, Reinhold Niebuhr, Paul Tillich, Carl Hermann Voss. Union Theological Seminary of the thirties, forties, and

fifties, was a very different place from what it has become. Authoritarian and traditionally inclined, its administrators from the president down were in firm command. This gave order and coherence to a small community, although the close quarters (which some referred to as "strangling fellowship") also affected the atmosphere. It was under this confining atmosphere that the Tillichs and others sooner or later chafed. Today the community is larger and many of the earlier traditions have been overturned, producing more individuality but less community.

9. Interview with Carl Hermann Voss.

10. "O Kinder, lasst das!" See Coffin, *Half Century*, p. 138; also Walter Horton, "Tillich's Role in Contemporary Theology," in Kegley and Bretall, eds, *Theol. of P. T.*, p. 35. "It was hours later that I realized, after first listening to him, that 'waykwoom,' many times repeated, and the key to the whole lecture, was meant to represent the English word 'vacuum.'" Tillich's first public speech in English was delivered to a women's club in New Haven, Connecticut, an appearance arranged by Arnold Wolfers. He spoke on "The Religious Situation" and was barely understandable but nevertheless graciously received.

11. Interview with Clifford Stanley.

12. Interview with John E. Smith.

13. Rollo May in his book *Paulus* (New York: Harper & Row, 1973) describes the student laughter as mocking (cf. pp. 5, 6). Students and faculty contemporaneous with May deny this. In those early days as well as later it was almost impossible not to laugh at some of Tillich's gaffes, but for the most part this was not meant unkindly.

14. Interview with Clifford Stanley.

15. At Union Seminary, according to longstanding custom, Christmas entertainment was provided in alternate years by the faculty making fun of themselves or by students making fun of the faculty.

16. Interview with Carl Hermann Voss.

17. Interview with Paul Tillich. From the beginning to the end of his American sojourn Tillich was most appreciative of the spontaneous generosity of the Americans with whom he came in contact.

18. Interview with Paul Tillich. See also Hannah Tillich, *From Time to Time* (New York: Stein & Day, 1973), pp. 178–79.

19. Interview with Heide Seeberger Schütz. Paul Tillich to Elisabeth Seeberger, Christmas 1934. "Ich denke daran, wie wir zusammen zwei Tage vor dem heiligen Abend den Baum schmückten und ich dann die Baukästen herausbrachte und die Weihnachtskirche baute . . . alte Mystik und Seligkeit. Denkst Du auch noch an unser Schachspiel, immer ehe Väterchen uns hereinrief?" H. A. See also Paul Tillich, "Weihnachten," *Gesammelte Werke*, ed. Renate Albrecht, 14 vols. (Stuttgart: Evangelisches Verlagswerk, 1959–75), XIII: 105.

20. G. A. Different names and titles appear here because the Nazi authorities reorganized ministries and administrative offices. In this connection a change of personnel was unavoidable. Frequently official letters were signed with last name only. Private Collection.

21. See Paul Tillich, "Life and the Spirit," *Systematic Theology*, 3 vols. (Chicago: University of Chicago Press, 1951–63), III: pt. IV.

22. Johannes Tillich to Paul Tillich, 25 March 1934: "Wenn ein Emigrant Dich gefragt hat, ob Du ihm zur Rückkehr nach Deutschland raten könntest, so würde ich an Deiner Stelle dies verneinen und gerade auch dann, wenn der Frager an seinem Vaterland hängt. Er würde sich gemäss seiner bisherigen Einstellungen hier nicht wohl fühlen." H. A. Two days earlier he had written, "Ich verstehe, wie stark Du das deutsche Landschaftsbild vermisst." [I understand how much you yearn for the German landscape.] 23 March 1934. H. A.

23. Henry Sloane Coffin to David H. Stevens, 13 April 1934. Presidential files, Union Theological Seminary.

24. Interviews with Horace Friess and Paul Tillich.

25. D. Mackenzie Brown, ed., *Ultimate Concern: Tillich in Dialogue* (New York: Harper & Row, 1965), p. 59.

26. *Theologische Blätter* (ed. Karl Ludwig Schmidt), 13, no. 11 (November 1934).

27. At the birth of Tillich's son René, Hirsch wrote him as follows, 10 July 1935: "Die politischen und die persönlichen Gegensätze zwischen uns lassen sich nicht aus der Welt schaffen. Die bedeuten, dass das Verstehen in allen vitalen grossen Fragen unmöglich ist. Soweit es politische Pflicht und Ehre der eigenen Arbeit mir möglich macht, will ich die persönliche Gemeinschaft wahren. Herzlich Dich grüssend, Dein Emanuel." [The political and personal divisions between us cannot be undone. This means that an understanding on all vital, major questions is impossible. As far as political duty and the honor of my work allow, I want to preserve our personal friendship.] H. A.

28. Interview with Adolf Müller.

29. Paul Tillich to Lilly Pincus. H. A.

30. Paul Tillich, *On the Boundary* (New York: Charles Scribner's Sons, 1966), p. 13.

31. Joachim Radkau, *Die Deutsche Emigration in den U.S.A.; Ihr Einfluss auf die Amerikanische Europa Politik 1933–1945* (Düsseldorf: Bertelsmann Universitätsverlag, 1971), p. 23.

32. Paul Tillich to Elisabeth Seeberger, Christmas 1934. H. A. "Auch ist der alte deutsche Freundeskreis jetzt fast zur Hälfte hier. Wir haben zum Beispiel einen Diskussionsabend, der genau zu fünfzig Prozent aus den Teilnehmern unseres Frankfurter Diskussionsabends besteht." [Almost half of the friends of the old German circle are here. For example, we have a discussion group of which exactly 50 percent of the participants represent our Frankfurt discussion group.] Cf. also John H. Randall, Jr., "The Philosophical Legacy of Paul Tillich," in Lyons, ed., *Legacy*, p. 23.

33. Tillich, "Auto. Refl.," pp. 19, 20.

34. Interview with Carl Hermann Voss.

35. "Self-Help," unpublished MS, 25 November 1936. Private collection.

36. Tillich, "Auto. Refl.," pp. 19, 20. See also Otto Zoff, *Tagebücher aus der Emigration* [Diary of the Emigration] (Heidelberg: Lambert & Schneider, 1968), 12 January 1943: "Bei P. T. Ich lernte einen besonderen, reinen, wohlgesinnten Menschen kennen, in einem schönen, stillen Zimmer, das rings-

herum mit Büchern ausgefüllt ist. Seine Bücher aus Europa. Er war mir sofort gut gesinnt und will alles mögliche für mich versuchen." [In P. T. "I came to know an unusually honest, well-intentioned person in a beautiful, quiet room filled with books, his books from Europe. He showed immediate good will toward me and will try to help me in every way possible.]

37. Paul Tillich, address to Self-Help, unpublished MS, 11 February 1945. H. A. See also Toni Stolper, "Paul Tillich und die Selfhelp," G. W., III: 570 ff.

38. Paul Tillich, address to Self-Help, unpublished MS, 25 November 1946. H. A.

39. Interviews with Reinhold Niebuhr, John E. Smith, and Paul Tillich.

40. ". . . I wrote to a friend who had already left Germany: "There is everywhere in the world sky, air, and ocean.' This was my consolation in one of the most tragic moments of my life, I did not write: 'I can continue everywhere my theological and philosophical work,' because unconsciously I doubted whether one could do this anywhere except in Germany." Paul Tillich, "The Conquest of Intellectual Provincialism: Europe and America," *Theology of Culture*, ed. Robert Kimball (New York: Oxford University Press, 1959), p. 159.

41. Interview with Horace Friess.

42. Interviews with Reinhold Niebuhr, John E. Smith, Paul Tillich.

43. Interview with Paul Tillich.

44. Interview with Paul Tillich.

45. Randall, Jr., "Philos. Legacy of P. T.," p. 22. Interviews with John E. Smith, John Hermann Randall, Jr. See also Tillich, "Auto. Refl.," p. 16.

46. Randall, Jr., "Philos. Legacy of P. T.," p. 24.

47. Arnold Brecht, *The Education of Arnold Brecht* (Princeton, N.J.: Princeton University Press, 1970), p. 471.

48. Tillich, "Auto. Refl.," p. 17. Circular letter, December 1933. G. A.

49. See correspondence, presidential files, Union Theological Seminary, New York.

50. Interview with Henry P. Van Dusen.

51. Tillich, "Auto. Refl.," p. 17.

52. The authors, autumn 1964.

53. Interviews with Ruth Nanda Anshen, Paul Tillich.

54. Party list. H. A.

55. Interview with Paul Tillich. See also his "Auto. Refl.," p. 17.

56. Coffin, *Half Century*, p. 138.

57. Interviews with Paul Tillich, Henry P. Van Dusen.

58. Interview with John Dillenberger.

59. Interview with Reinhold Niebuhr.

60. Interviews with Albert T. Mollegen, Clifford Stanley.

61. Interview with Carl Hermann Voss.

62. Interview with Roger Shinn, who provided the following: "The Society originated as the Fellowship of Socialist Christians. It always seemed to me that its richness resulted from a fusion of two strains of thought. The first was Reinie's indigenous American Social Ethic, rooted in the liberal Social

Gospel, but then transformed by his appropriation of Marx and then Augustine and the reinterpreted orthodox tradition. The other strain was German Religious Socialism, represented by Paul Tillich and a number of other German exiles, most of whom taught at the New School for Social Research. The most important of these were Eduard Heimann, Hans Simons, Adolf Löwe. . . . There was great appreciation between the representatives of these two strains, but there was also enough tension between them to keep things interesting." Originally known as the Fellowship of Socialist Christians, the group changed its name on 21 May 1948 to "Frontier Fellowship: Christians for Social Reconstruction." In the autumn of 1951 the name was changed again to "Christian Action." The group closed its national office in 1956. The association published a journal entitled *Radical Religion*, the first issue of which appeared in the fall of 1935. Vol. 1, no. 1 includes an article, "Marx and the Prophetic Tradition," by Paul Tillich. In 1940 the publication changed its title to *Christianity and Society*. The last issue appeared in the summer of 1956.

63. Interview with James Luther Adams.

64. "Auto. Rel.," p. 26.

65. Reinhold Niebuhr, review of Paul Tillich's *My Travel Diary*, 1936 (New York: Harper & Row, 1970), in *New York Times Book Review*, 10 May 1970.

66. Interviews with Richard Kroner, John E. Smith, Paul Tillich.

67. Richard Kroner delivered the Gifford Lectures in 1939–40, on "The Primacy of Faith."

68. This autobiographical essay was published as the first chapter of a book under the title *The Interpretation of History* (New York: Charles Scribner's Sons, 1936). The contents were translated from the German. A revised version was published as a separate volume also by Scribner's in 1966.

69. Fedor Stepun to Paul Tillich, 1937: "Ich habe seiner Zeit mit ganz besonderem Interesse Deine kleine Selbstbiographie gelesen, die für mich vielleicht das Beste ist, was ich von Dir kenne. Vielleicht fühle ich so, weil diese Einheit von Erzählen, Denken und Bekennen meiner Art am Nähesten kommt. Irgendwo sind wir alle egozentrisch." H. A.

70. Johannes Tillich to Paul Tillich, 9 September 1936: "Ich beschäftige mich mit Deiner Arbeit 'An der Grenze; habe auch schon begonnen, meine Meinung dazu zu diktieren, aber das geht langsam." Johannes Tillich's last letter to his son is dated 23 December 1936. H. A.

71. Paul Tillich to Frede Fritz, 1937. H. A.

72. Interviews with Elisabeth Seeberger, Hans-Jürgen Seeberger. Paul Tillich affirmed that the meaning of the statement was positive: he thought of his father as one who protected him from his own death. It was not, as some have suggested, a relief to him that his father was dead.

Johannes Tillich's will is dated 4 April 1936. Paul Tillich and his sister Elisabeth Seeberger were the sole heirs. Tillich's inheritance was kept for him in a German bank in a closed account (*Sperrkonto*). H. A.

73. Correspondence in presidential files, Union Theological Seminary. Interviews with Henry P. Van Dusen, Carl Hermann Voss, Paul Tillich.

74. Interview with Paul Tillich.

75. Interview with Reinhold Niebuhr.
76. Interview with Henry P. Van Dusen.
77. It should be noted that before the happy decision was made to appoint Tillich to a teaching post in philosophical theology, the authorities considered him for the chair of "Christian Institutions." Tillich was apparently willing to cooperate. He believed that such an appointment would give him the chance to cultivate his interest in the history of thought and the theology of culture. Paul Tillich to Frede Fritz, 1 October 1935. G. A.
78. Presidential files, Union Theological Seminary.
79. Interview with John E. Smith. See also his "Paul Tillich," in Melville Harcourt, ed., Thirteen for Christ (New York: Sheed & Ward, 1963). Smith's chapter is a superbly clear and authoritative interpretation of Tillich and his American experience.
80. Interviews with Horace Friess, Paul Tillich.
81. Interviews with Reinhold Niebuhr, Paul Tillich. See also Landon, ed., Reinhold Niebuhr, pp. 30, 31.
82. At the wedding of Wilhelm Pauck and Marion Hausner, 21 November 1964.
83. Interviews with Reinhold Niebuhr, Paul Tillich, Carl Hermann Voss.
84. In private correspondence. Reinhold Niebuhr to Wilhelm Pauck.
85. Interview with Joseph Sittler.
86. Interview with Reinhold Niebuhr.
87. Interviews with Paul Tillich, Carl Hermann Voss.
88. Interview with Paul Tillich. Circular letter, 17 April 1935. H. A., G. A.
89. Interview with James Luther Adams.
90. Interview with Paul Tillich. He wrote most of On the Boundary on this trip.
91. Interview with Paul Tillich.
92. Interviews with Reinhold Niebuhr, Clifford Stanley, Carl Hermann Voss. See also Horton, "Tillich's Role," pp. 36 ff.
93. René Stefan Tillich was born on 7 June 1935. H. A.
94. Interviews with Horace Friess, Albert Hofstadter, John H. Randall, Jr., John E. Smith, Paul Tillich. All have supplied invaluable information on the Philosophy Club.
95. Minutes of the Philosophy Club.
96. "On one occasion he [P. T.] read a brilliant paper on 'Existential Philosophy.' Among the listeners were G. E. Moore, the distinguished representative of a very different philosophical tradition and language. When it came time for Moore to comment on Tillich's paper, he said, 'Now really, Mr. Tillich, I don't think I have been able to understand a single sentence of your paper. Won't you please try to state one sentence or even one word, that I can understand?' Moore's failure to understand was professional, and Tillich is clearly no Cambridge analyst." Randall, Jr., "Philos. Legacy of P. T.," p. 23.
97. Interview with Albert Hofstadter.
98. Interview with Henry P. Van Dusen. See also Tillich, "Auto. Refl.," p. 18: "Immediately after my arrival I was received into what is now the Theological Discussion Group and into the American Theological Society. I

want to express my thanks to the members of these groups for what the continuous discussion with them has meant and still means to me. It was in this fashion that I studied American theology—the way of the dialogue, which is, indeed, the dialectical way. After several years, I was asked to join the Philosophy Club, whose monthly meetings I almost never missed, and which gave me a dialectical introduction into the American philosophical life and its manifoldness and intensity."

99. Henry P. Van Dusen, ed., *The Christian Answer* (New York: Charles Scribner's Sons, 1945), p. vii.

100. Ibid., *passim*.

101. Tillich, *Travel Diary*.

102. Ibid., p. 45.

103. Ibid., p. 42.

104. Ibid., pp. 83–84.

105. Ibid., pp. 103, 104.

106. Ibid., pp. 143, 146.

107. Karl Stange to Landesbischof [Bishop] Mahrahrens, 29 May 1936: "Ich halte es für Kompromittierung des deutschen Luthertums, wenn Althaus und Lilje zusammen mit Tillich in Genf auftreten." [In my opinion German Lutheranism will be discredited if Althaus and Lilje appear in the company of Tillich in Geneva.] H. A.

108. Tillich, *Travel Diary*, p. 154.

109. Ibid., p. 162.

110. Ibid., p. 169, 29 August 1936.

111. Ibid., p. 177.

112. Ibid., pp. 178, 179.

113. Wilhelm Pauck, *Ecumenicity in Tillich's Theology*, the William Henry Hoover lectureship on Christian Unity (Chicago: Disciples Divinity House, 1974).

114. Interview with Paul Tillich. See also "Auto. Refl.," p. 18.

115. Paul Tillich, "A Historical Diagnosis: Impressions of a European Trip," *Radical Religion*, 2, no. 1 (1936–37), pp. 11–17.

CHAPTER 6. A BRIDGE TO THE WORLD

1. Carl Zuckmayer, *Als Wär's ein Stück von Mir, Horen der Freundschaft* (Vienna: S. Fischer Verlag, 1966), p. 65.

2. Hans-Joachim Schoeps, *Rückblicke* (Berlin: Haude & Spenersche Verlagsbuchhandlung, 1963), pp. 108, 109. "An diesem Morgen radelte ich stundenlang durch Gross-Berlin und besah mir das Werk der 'Reichskristallnacht.' Von einer brennenden Synagogue fuhr ich zur anderen, und überall sah ich nur schweigende Menschen stehen, die in die Flammen starrten. Manche hatten Tränen in den Augen, manche die Fäuste in der Tasche geballt. Das war das wirkliche Volk von Berlin. Ein alter Mann murmelte 'Gotteshäuser anzuzünden, das wird sich rächen, das wird ein schlimmes Ende nehmen.' In den nächsten Wochen ging dann die bitterböse 'Scherzfrage' durch Deutschland, 'Wissen Sie was NSKK bedeutet: Nach Synagogen kommen Kirchen.' " [On

this morning I bicycled through Greater Berlin and viewed the work of the "Reichskristallnacht." I pedalled from one burning synagogue to another, and everywhere I saw people standing silent who stared into the flames. Some had tears in their eyes, many had fists in their pockets. They were the real people of Berlin. An old man murmured, "Burning houses of worship will be avenged; it will come to a bad end." In the next weeks the bitter, angry joke ran through Germany, "Do you know what NSKK means? After the synagogues come the churches."]

3. Paul Tillich, unpublished MS, 10 November 1938. H. A. See also his "Die Bedeutung des Antisemitismus," *Gesammelte Werke*, ed. Renate Albrecht, 14 vols. (Stuttgart: Evangelisches Verlagswerk, 1959–75), XIII: 219. Tillich made this speech to a Protestant gathering of protest against Hitler's persecution of the Jews. Until then he had refrained from speaking publicly on political issues because he was an emigré who had not yet obtained American citizenship.

4. Interview with Clifford Stanley.

5. Interviews with Robert Handy, Paul Tillich.

6. Presidential files, Union Theological Seminary. Tillich's citizenship certificate is dated 4 March 1940. He was fifty-three years old, and described as fair with blue-grey eyes, blond hair, 5' 11" tall, weighing 160 lbs. H. A.

7. Paul Tillich to Frede Fritz, 1940 ("*Verarmung*"). G. A.

8. *New York Times*, 20 June 1940, p. 26. See also *New Haven Evening Register*, 19 June 1940.

9. Original MS, G. A.

10. See chap. 4, n. 80.

11. Paul Tillich, "Die politische und geistige Aufgabe der deutschen Emigration," G. W., XIII: 200–216.

12. Interviews with James Luther Adams, John E. Smith, Paul Tillich.

13. Paul Tillich, "I Am an American," *Protestant Digest*, 3 (1941), pp. 24–26.

14. For a complete account of the Council for a Democratic Germany, see the *Bulletin of the Council for a Democratic Germany*, published from September 1944 to May 1945. There were five issues in all.

15. On 12 April 1943 Thomas Mann wrote Tillich, asking him to describe theological education in Germany at the turn of the century. Mann was writing his novel *Dr. Faustus* and sought authentic details for the life of his hero, Leverkühn, for a time a theological student. Tillich replied in a long letter dated 23 May 1943, furnishing a detailed description of his own theological studies in Halle. Mann gave credit to Tillich as well as to Theodor Adorno, who had helped him with details on musicology. Tillich was later annoyed by the persiflage which Mann used to describe the theological world he loved so well. Mann's letter to Tillich is lost, but Tillich's to Mann is in the Mann Archive in Zurich; copies of the original are to be found in the Göttingen and Harvard archives as well as in the library of Union Theological Seminary. For more details concerning the relations between Tillich and Thomas Mann see Herbert Lehner, *Thomas Mann: Fiktion, Mythos, Religion* (Stuttgart: W. Kohlhammer Verlag, 1965), pp. 179–187.

16. *New York Times*, 3 May 1944.

17. "Declaration," *Bulletin of the Council for Democratic Germany*, 1, no. 1 (May 1944).

18. *New York Times*, 3 May 1944.

19. Interview with Paul Tillich.

20. Paul Tillich himself was uncertain of the precise date of this dinner at the White House.

21. See Paul Tillich, circular letter, September 1949, H. A., G. A.

22. Interviews with Reinhold Niebuhr, John E. Smith, Paul Tillich. Paul Tillich to Edgar Brightman, 9 January 1948: "I was, during the war, the Chairman of the American Committee for a Democratic Germany, consisting of all groups of refugees and sponsored by the American Association. After Potsdam the Committee was split for the same reasons for which the Great Alliance was broken. So I decided to resign from the whole action.

"There is no more Germany, but an American and a Russian colony, and this can be changed only by another war which to avoid was the purpose of my Committee."

"I have resigned from all politics in order to be able to write my Systematic Theology." Private collection.

23. Paul Tillich, circular letters, 1946. H. A. See also Eduard Heimann, "Tillich's Doctrine of Religious Socialism," in C. W. Kegley and R. W. Bretall, eds., *The Theology of Paul Tillich* (New York: Macmillan Co., 1952), p. 325: "After thirty years of disappointment, Tillich drew the conclusion that this time of ours is no *kairos*; that religious socialism, while right in the long run, is not applicable to the foreseeable future; that this is the period of living in a vacuum, which should be accepted and endured without attempts at premature solutions, and deepened into a 'sacred void' of waiting. This is a truly prophetic position. Tillich believes in the coming of the morning, but he does not say that it shall be we who shall emerge into it. The logic and honesty of this acceptance of defeat are unmistakable; whatever romantic enthusiasm may have crept into the original doctrine of the secondary *kairos*, its counterpart in the doctrine of the sacred void cannot be blamed for a lack of Christian sobriety." Others were more critical of Tillich's decision to abandon politics altogether; among them Reinhold Niebuhr, who felt that he had been too optimistic or utopian during the post-World-War-I period and was now too pessimistic. It is possible that Tillich's inability to heal his internal division was what ultimately made him so pessimistic about the external split of the world itself. See also Paul Tillich, "Autobiographical Reflections," in Kegley and Bretall, eds., *Theol. of P. T.*, p. 20.

24. Paul Tillich, circular letter, 12 October 1946. H. A. Interview with Paul Tillich.

25. Paul Tillich, circular letter, 12 October 1946.

26. Interview with John E. Smith.

27. D. Mackenzie Brown, ed., *Ultimate Concern: Tillich in Dialogue* (New York: Harper & Row, 1965), p. 16.

28. Sally Alexander to Paul Tillich, 13 August 1947. Private collection.

29. Interviews with Roger Shinn, Paul Tillich.

30. Paul Tillich, undated circular letter, probably 1946. H. A. Interviews with Elisabeth Seeberger, Paul Tillich.

31. Paul Tillich to H. S. von Ragué, 6 March 1946: "Von meinem Schwager Fritz habe ich inzwischen gehört, dass seine Anstalt in Teltow bei Berlin weitergeht. Er wird von allen Seiten als ein alter Mann mit weissem Bart geschildert, dünn und schwermütig. Aber er hat das Glück, dass all seine Kinder am Leben sind, wenn auch zwei davon in Gefangenschaft. Werdermanns Weissagungen über die kommende Katastrophe sind ja ganz in Erfüllung gegangen." [In the meantime, I have heard from my brother-in-law Fritz that his establishment is still in Teltow near Berlin. Everyone describes him as an old man with a white beard, thin and depressed. But he is lucky that all his children are alive, even if two are prisoners of war. Werdermann's prophecies about the coming catastrophe have all been fulfilled.] Private collection. Von Ragué was a Wingolfite living in Manchester, Michigan, at the time of this exchange.

32. Heide Seeberger became the wife of Klaus Schütz, later mayor of Berlin. Interview with Heide Schütz.

33. Fritz Medicus to Paul Tillich, 1945. Interviews with Marie-Luise Werner, Elisabeth Seeberger.

34. Paul Tillich to Lilly Pincus, 3 June 1945. He prefaced this exclamation by the following comments: "Many thanks for your letter. The feeling about the end of the European war is shared by all of us. It is a kind of dizziness produced partly by the end of a bad dream which was a horrible reality, partly by the extremely dark clouds concentrating on the horizon of the future. I am envious to hear about the beautiful things, nature and art, which you can reach without having to cross the Atlantic. We often ask ourselves whether it will ever be possible to see the remnants of the past in good old Europe." H. A.

35. Ibid.

36. Paul Tillich, circular letters, 1946. H. A.

37. Paul Tillich to Robert Calhoun, 10 January 1947. Private collection.

38. Paul Tillich, "Besuch in Deutschland, 1948," G. W., XIII: 364. Cf. also his unpublished MS, "The European Discussion of the Problem of Demythologization of the New Testament," p. 2: "I remember when I first came back to Germany in 1948, I was sitting with Professor Bultmann in the only room of his house remaining to him, and we shared the feeling that now we were the last two remnants of the old classical German theological tradition. It was of course sentimental, and not quite justified, but it was somehow real when we looked at the younger generation, because for them the break was almost total since they had no chance, in the years of the fight and the war, to continue the theological development from Schleiermacher and Troeltsch." H. A.

39. Paul Tillich to Henry P. Van Dusen, 27 April 1948. Presidential files, Union Theological Seminary. Tillich thanked Van Dusen for having secured $1,500 for him, without which he could not have made the journey. Between

December 1947 and April 1948 Van Dusen corresponded with the Rockefeller Foundation requesting a grant for Tillich, which it provided on 29 March 1948.

40. Paul Tillich, circular letter, December 1948. H. A.

41. Paul Tillich, "Visit to Germany," *Christianity and Crisis*, 8, no. 19 (1948), pp. 147–49. Interviews with Elisabeth Seeberger and the large majority of German persons listed as interviewed in the preface of this volume. Interviews with Paul Tillich.

42. See Marion Hausner Pauck, "Wilhelm Pauck: A Biographical Essay," in Jaroslav Pelikan, ed., *Interpreters of Luther* (Philadelphia: Fortress Press, 1968), p. 354. On Pauck's friendship with Tillich, see, pp. 353–60. Wilhelm Pauck to Olga Pauck, May 1948: "In Marburg, Richter turned up at a dinner which the Lord Mayor gave to the professors, and when I got back here on Sunday Tillich came into my room. Both are going to be in Marburg for four weeks and then go on to Bonn and parts north. Richter was the Ministerialdirektor again, but Tillich was very depressed." Private collection.

43. Tillich, "Visit to Germany."

44. Emanuel Hirsch to Paul Tillich, 16 October 1948: "Zunächst danke ich Dir herzlich für die Flasche Wein, die zwei Tafeln Schokolade, und das Stück Seife, das ich Mitte August in Deinem Namen erhalten habe . . . Ich denke auch sehr gern an Deinen Besuch bei mir zurück." H. A. An interesting note: Hirsch was the only one of nearly fifty German friends and relatives of Paul Tillich who refused to be interviewed for this volume, for he was incapable of compromise. He knew he would have to tell the whole truth or nothing, and was hesitant to divulge what he knew of Tillich's private life to anyone. Details of the 1948 meeting between the two men are from Paul Tillich and Gertraut Stöber, who acted as intermediary between them.

Tillich's charity toward those who had collaborated with the Nazis was demonstrated also in his judgment about Heidegger, which he expressed publicly many years later. "You cannot judge a philosopher in terms of his shortcomings in life. . . . The fact that Plato was foolish enough to become the advisor of the Hitler of his time, the tyrant of Syracuse, shows that you cannot identify a philosopher with his personal decisions." From "Heidegger and Jaspers," an unpublished lecture delivered at the Cooper Union Forum, New York, 23 March 1954, p. 6, as quoted in Paul Tillich, *Political Expectation*, ed. James L. Adams (New York: Harper & Row, 1971), p. xii, 7.

45. Dorothea Poelchau to Paul Tillich, 13 February 1949. Private collection.

46. Paul Tillich, "Die Judenfrage: Ein Deutsches und ein Christliches Problem," G. W., III: 128–70.

47. Gerhard Heinzelmann, dean of the theological faculty of Martin Luther University, Halle-Wittenberg, to Paul Tillich, 2 September 1946. Private collection.

48. Tillich rarely preached in Germany after 1948—not, as some have alleged, because he was not permitted to do so, but because in Germany he had no regular ministerial standing.

49. "Recently I spent three months in Germany and what I saw was a sick people, sick as a whole and sick as individuals. Their faces are shaped by burdens too heavy to be carried, by sorrow too deep to be forgotten. And what

their faces expressed, their words confirmed: Tales of horror, stories of pain and despair, anxieties dwelling in their blood, confusions and self-contradictions disturbing their minds. And if you look deeper into them you find guilt feeling, sometimes expressed, mostly repressed. For it hides itself under passionate denials of guilt, under self-excuse and accusations of others, under a mixture of hostility and humility, of self-pity and self-hate. The nation is split externally by the split between East and West which divides all mankind politically and spiritually. And the nation is split internally. Old hostilities are smoldering, new hostilities are growing, and there is no peace. A sick nation." Paul Tillich, "On Healing," in *The New Being* (New York: Charles Scribner's Sons, 1955), p. 34. See also his "Visit to Germany."

50. Paul Tillich, "The Conquest of Intellectual Provincialism: Europe and America," in *Theology of Culture*, ed. Robert Kimball (New York: Oxford University Press, 1959), pp. 159 ff.

51. Paul Tillich, circular letters, 1946–47. H. A. See also Tillich, "Auto. Refl.," pp. 17, 18.

52. See G. W., XIII: 329. "Die Zeit der Ernte drängt; hier ist jetzt Ernte!"

53. "But more obvious than the changes from the earlier to the more recent articles in this collection is the continuity of the main line of thought and the permanence of the basic principles. It sometimes strikes me (and this is probably a very common experience), when I read some of my earliest writings, how much of what I believed to be a recent achievement is already explicitly or at least implicitly contained in them." Paul Tillich, Author's Introduction, *The Protestant Era*, trans. and ed. James L. Adams (Chicago: University of Chicago Press, 1948), pp. x, xi. When in the middle or late 1940s Clifford Stanley and Tillich met after some years of separation, Tillich said, "Everything in my system is changed. You wouldn't understand anything." He referred to the introduction of his concept of "the new being." Then he immediately said, "Nothing has changed. You would understand it all." Interview with Clifford Stanley.

54. Tillich, Introduction, *Protestant Era*, p. xxix: "It was the 'estatic' experience of the belief in a *kairos* which, after the first World War, created or at least initiated most of the ideas presented in this book. There is no such ecstatic experience after the second World War, but a general feeling that more darkness than light is lying ahead of us. An element of cynical realism is prevailing today, as an element of utopian hope was prevailing at that earlier time. The Protestant principle judges both of them. It justifies the hope, though destroying its utopian form. In the spirit of such a realism of hope, Protestantism must enter the new era . . ."

55. Ibid., p. ix.

56. Interview with James Luther Adams and Samuel Miller. Adams' book was published by Harper & Row in 1965.

57. Paul Lehmann, *Journal of Religion*, 46, no. 1 (1966), p. 197.

58. Interviews with James Luther Adams, Henry P. Van Dusen. Presidential files, Union Theological Seminary.

59. John Dillenberger remembers seeing Wilhelm Pauck in 1946 at a meeting in Washington, D.C., holding a manuscript he had finished editing. Tillich was beside him, and Pauck said, "As soon as this book is finished, Tillich will begin the *Systematic Theology*." Interview with John Dillenberger.

60. "The schizophrenic state of mankind today is partly responsible for the schizophrenic state of many individuals. But it was mainly the state of individuals which took hold of my attention and thought in the last ten years." Paul Tillich, "On the Boundary Line," *Christian Century* 77, no. 49 (7 December 1960), p. 1437.

61. Paul Tillich, *The Shaking of the Foundations* (New York: Charles Scribner's Sons, 1948), p. 54.

62. "Auto. Refl.," pp. 18, 19.

63. Address delivered on 6 December 1952 at Karen Horney's memorial service. *Pastoral Psychology* 54, no. 34 (1953), pp. 11–13.

64. See Wayne E. Oates, "The Contribution of Paul Tillich to Pastoral Psychology," *Pastoral Psychology* 19, no. 181 (1968), p. 16. This memorial issue on Paul Tillich includes an interesting and illuminating series of articles by men such as Seward Hiltner, Daniel Day Williams, and others on Tillich and his relation to pastoral counseling.

Tillich also belonged to the New York Psychology Group, which met monthly for about five years beginning in 1940. Among the members were Ruth Benedict, Gotthard Booth, Erich Fromm, Seward Hiltner, Rollo May, David E. Roberts, and Frances G. Wickes. Many meetings were held in the Tillich apartment, some at the home of Harrison and Grace Elliott at Union. See Seward Hiltner, "Tillich the Person," *Theology Today* 30, no. 4 (1974). p. 383.

65. H. A.

66. "Almost every one of Tillich's theological concerns has direct bearing on psychiatry. I can illustrate this with only one or two examples. The first is the polarity of separation and union, the relation of individuality to participation. This derives from Tillich's philosophical anthropology, a theory that contains a number of elements which are parallel to psychoanalysis and child development." Earl A. Loomis, "The Psychiatric Legacy of Paul Tillich," in James R. Lyons, ed., *The Intellectual Legacy of Paul Tillich* (Detroit: Wayne State University Press, 1969), p. 85.

67. Paul Tillich, circular letter, 14 March 1950. H. A. Auden's *The Age of Anxiety* was published in 1947. See W. H. Auden, *Collected Longer Poems* (New York: Vantage Books, 1975), pp. 253–353.

68. Paul Tillich, *The Courage To Be* (New Haven: Yale University Press, 1952), pp. 32 ff.

69. See Paul Tillich, "Die Bedeutung Kurt Goldsteins für die Religionsphilosophie," in, G. W., XII: 309. Kurt Goldstein's influence on Tillich's book is here affirmed in Tillich's own words. Doubtless his conversations with many persons in the field of psychology helped him formulate his final conceptions of anxiety and courage as they appear in this volume.

70. Tillich, *Courage*, p. 190.

71. Interviews with John Bennett, John Dillenberger.

72. Interview with Mary Heilner.

73. "In Amerika sagte mir einmal ein Student . . . 'wenn ich ein Kümmerchen habe, geh' ich ins Kino; doch wenn ich an einem wirklichen Brocken würge, dann gehe ich zu Tillich.'" Helmut Thielicke, "Paul Tillich, Wanderer Zwischen Zwei Welten," in his *Der Spannungsbogen* (Stuttgart: Evangelisches Verlagswerk, 1961), p. 15.

74. Interview with Samuel Miller.

75. Loomis, "Psychiatric Legacy," p. 96. See also Dieter Wyss, *Marx und Freud* (Göttingen: Vandenhoeck, 1969), pp. 309–11.

76. Interview with Paul Tillich.

77. Interview with Paul Tillich. See also Tillich, "Auto. Refl.," p. 18; "Our Ultimate Concern," *New Being*, p. 153; and "Cultural Comparisons," in his *Theology of Culture*, ed. Robert Kimball (New York: Oxford University Press, 1959), p. 168.

78. "Auto. Refl.," p. 18.

79. "You Are Accepted," *Shaking of the Foundations*, p. 155.

80. Paul Tillich, O. B., pp. 65, 66.

81. See his "Loneliness and Solitude," "God's Pursuit of Man," "The Eternal Now," "Forgetting and Being Forgotten," in *The Eternal Now* (New York: Charles Scribner's Sons, 1963).

82. Interview with Paul Tillich.

83. Paul Tillich, Preface, *Shaking of the Foundations*.

84. Ibid.

85. Unpublished MS, private collection.

86. Th. Adorno in Wolf-Dieter Marsch, ed., *Werk und Wirken Paul Tillichs: Ein Gedenkbuch* (Stuttgart: Evangelisches Verlagswerk, 1967), p. 37.

87. Paul Tillich to James Luther Adams, 1 November 1949: "Thank you very much for the work you have done for me in talking with Mr. Wieck. I have received the letter from Mr. Wieck which, however, shows more giving-in than enthusiasm which I understand only too well. . . . Now the burden of the finishing of the first volume lies on my shoulders like a rock of infinite dimensions." Private collection.

88. Interview with Paul Tillich.

89. Interview with Marie-Luise Werner.

90. Interview with John E. Smith.

91. David E. Roberts, "Tillich's Doctrine of Man," in Kegley and Bretall, eds., *Theol. of P. T.*, p. 130. "Somehow Tillich, like God, manages to engulf distinctions without blurring them. He fully realizes (again, no doubt, like God) that such problems are met, in so far as they ever are, by living rather than by constructing systems. But it is a weird experience, which I have undergone many times, to have problems answered with great sensitivity and patience, by being brought into connection with some relevant segment of the system, only to discover later that I do not happen to be the man who carries this system around in his head."

92. Date uncertain, probably 1913.

In the Preface to Volume I of his *Systematic Theology* (p. vii) Tillich offers an explanation of what "systematic" thinking means to him. He says: "It has been impossible for me to think theologically in any other than a systematic way. The smallest problem . . . drove me to all other problems and to the anticipation of a whole in which they could find their solution." When he asserts, therefore, that "theology is the methodological explanation of the Christian Faith" (p. 15), he means to say that theology deals with an interdependent set of doctrines and symbols that form a unified or consistent whole in so far as they express the Christian message or the Christian faith. This is his definition of *systematic theology*.

When the unchangeable truth of the message (kerygma) is emphasized over against the changing demands of the human situation to which it is addressed, Tillich calls this *kerygmatic theology* (p. 4). But when attention is focused upon the human questions which are answered by the Christian message, he defines the theology as *answering* or *apologetic* theology (p. 6). This way of explaining the contents of the Christian faith through questions and answers that are "existential," i.e. questions and answers in which man is involved with his whole existence and which are therefore interdependent, Tillich calls the *method of correlation*.

A detailed and many-sided explanation of the nature, method, and structure of systematic theology constitutes Tillich's *Introduction* to his own system. (*Systematic Theology*, I, 3–71.)

93. Interview with Paul Tillich. See Introductions to the 3 vols. of his *Systematic Theology* (Chicago: University of Chicago Press, 1951–63).

94. Paul Tillich, circular letter, 14 March 1950. H. A.

95. Interview with John Dillenberger. See also Coffin, *Half Century*, p. 139.

96. Interview with Clark Williamson.

97. Coffin, *Half Century*, p. 139.

98. H. R. Niebuhr, *Journal of Religion*, 46, no. 1 (1966), p. 203.

99. Ibid., p. 205.

100. T. S. Eliot to Paul Tillich, 22 March 1954. H. A. This letter will most probably be published in a forthcoming collection of Eliot's letters.

101. Reinhold Niebuhr, "Biblical Thought and Ontological Speculation in Tillich's Theology," in Kegley and Bretall, eds., *Theol. of P. T.*, pp. 226–27.

102. John H. Randall, Jr., "The Ontology of Paul Tillich," in Kegley and Bretall, eds., *Theol. of P. T.*, p. 161.

103. Paul Tillich, circular letter, 2 May 1951. H. A.

104. Presidential files, Union Theological Seminary.

105. Paul Tillich to Fedor Stepun, 20 July 1951: "Nachdem ich in diesem Jahr 65 Jahre werde, und manche Anzeichen da sind, dass ich nicht mehr in den vierzigern bin, wird das Vorlaufen zum Tode (Heidegger) zu einer immer häufigeren Beschäftigung. Und trotzdem bejahe ich den Augenblick, der mir noch geschenkt ist." H. A.

106. Interview with John C. Bennett.

107. Paul Tillich, *Love, Power, and Justice* (New York: Oxford University Press, 1954), p. vii.

108. Walter Lippmann to Angus Dun, 30 March 1954. Private collection.

109. Paul Tillich, circular letter, 1952. H. A.

110. Paul Tillich's letters to Henry P. Van Dusen, Lilly Pincus, Adolf Löwe, Claudia Bader, et al., 10 November 1953. Private collection.
111. Interview with Paul Tillich.
112. Unpublished MS, H. A.
113. Paul Tillich to MacKinnon, 20 November 1954. Private collection.
114. Paul Tillich to Principal T. M. Taylor, 20 November 1954. Private collection.
115. R. Niebuhr, "Biblical Thought and Ontological Speculation," p. 217.
116. George Tavard, *Journal of Religion* 46, no. 1 (1966), p. 224.
117. Interview with Henry P. Van Dusen.
118. Interview with Albert C. Outler.
119. Paul Van Buren,. *Christian Century*, 81 (5 February 1964), pp. 177–79.
120. Interviews with Daniel Day Williams, Carl Hermann Voss.
121. Tillich, *Systematic Theology*, III: v.
122. John H. Randall, Jr., *Journal of Religion* 46, no. 1 (1966), p. 223.

CHAPTER 7. THE AMBIGUITY OF FAME

1. Paul Tillich to Ludwig Metzger, minister of education in Hesse, Germany, 29 September 1953: "Amerika hat mich in den letzten Jahren in einem Masse rezipiert, wie ich es nie erwartet hätte und wie es nur wenigen Emigranten zuteil geworden ist. Den Prozess dieser Rezeption in diesem Moment zu unterbrechen, wäre schwerlich zu verantworten. Ich sehe mich in der Funktion einer Brücke zu der angelsächsischen und der deutschen theologischen Welt. Ich muss dem Schicksal der Emigration treu bleiben." H. A.
2. Interviews with Nathan Pusey, Henry P. Van Dusen. Correspondence, presidential files, Union Theological Seminary and H. A.
3. Tillich began work at Harvard at a salary nearly double what he earned during his last year at Union, although it must be remembered that his rent-free apartment there made up for the difference. By the time he retired from Harvard in 1962, his salary had risen to over $25,000, which in addition to the income he earned through lectureships and publications meant he was more than comfortably off during a time of fairly stable prices. By special arrangement Harvard also increased his pension. H. A. Interview with Paul Tillich.
4. Paul Tillich, "Heal the Sick; Cast out Demons," in *The Eternal Now* (New York: Charles Scribner's Sons, 1963).
5. Paul Tillich, "Words by Paul Tillich," *Harvard Divinity Bulletin* 30, no. 2 (1966), p. 24.
6. Paul Tillich to Richard Kroner, 25 July 1955. "Mit einem ruhigen Alter ist es nun vorläufig nichts, wäre aber wohl auch sonst nichts gewesen. . . . Nach meinem 75. Lebensjahr werde ich nur noch Griechisch lesen." Private collection.
7. Tillich was mentioned in Ved Mehta's *The New Theologian* (New York: Harper & Row, 1963). Originally a *New Yorker* profile, this book includes in-

teresting characterizations of some of Tillich's contemporaries, among them Karl Barth, Dietrich Bonhoeffer, and Reinhold Niebuhr. It is noteworthy that Mehta's description of Tillich is not very flattering. Tillich also published an article entitled, "The Lost Dimension in Religion," in *The Saturday Evening Post* 230, no. 50 (1958), pp. 76–79. It drew the largest number of fan letters he had ever received, many of them from seemingly unstable persons. Finally, he was pictured in *Vogue*, February 1962, in the column, "People Are Talking About."

8. Interview with Paul Lehmann.

9. See Nathan Pusey, Memorial address, the *Harvard Divinity Bulletin* 30, no. 2 (1966), pp. 1, 2: "My next most vivid remembrance is of his [Tillich's] meeting with Werner Jaeger for the first time at a dinner I gave for the University Professors his first year here. Those two men were approximately the same age; both had studied in various German universities in the first decade of this century; each knew of the other; but they had not met. . . . Both men were Christians; both were emigrés from an older stable world of culture; a philosopher and a theologian, they enormously enjoyed each other that evening. To the rest of us they stood forth as very joyous *persons*, living exemplars of a great and honored tradition of learning."

Erik Erikson and Paul Tillich admired one another from afar, but unaccountably were too shy to introduce themselves. Accordingly Paul Lee, Tillich's assistant, invited them to his house one evening. On that occasion which both enjoyed tremendously, Tillich mentioned his concern about the faddish aspects of psychoanalysis, which Erikson felt was a criticism made in the true Freudian tradition. Ibid., p. 15.

10. Paul Tillich, "On the Boundary Line," *Christian Century* 77, no. 49, (7 December 1960), p. 1437.

11. Interview with Nathan Pusey.

12. *Harvard Crimson*, 7 March 1956, p. 6.

13. Interview with Paul Lee.

14. Interviews with John Dillenberger, Samuel Miller.

15. Interviews with Paul Lee, Paul Tillich. See also Harvey Cox, *The Seduction of the Spirit* (New York: Simon & Schuster, 1973), p. 264.

16. For Tillich's reception at Harvard: interviews with Winston Davis, Paul Lee, Kenneth Pease, Nathan Pusey, James Luther Adams, Paul Lehmann, John Dillenberger, Samuel Miller.

17. An intestinal ailment, diverticulitis, forced Tillich to eat pureed fruit and vegetables and large amounts of applesauce. A controllable lymphoma or swelling of the neck glands was treated by electrotherapy. He also suffered from occasional attacks of gout and was slightly hard of hearing in his last years.

18. Interview with Paul Tillich.

19. Interviews with Nathan Pusey, Paul Tillich.

20. Paul Tillich to Nathan Pusey, 22 December 1960, and Nathan Pusey to Paul Tillich, 11 January 1961. H. A.

21. Paul Tillich, as quoted by Austin C. Wehrwein, "Right Question Pleases Tillich," in the *New York Times*, 5 May 1963, 69:3.

22. Interview with John H. Randall, Jr.

23. Interview with Paul Tillich.

24. Paul Tillich to President John F. Kennedy. Undated. H. A.

25. James Reston in his Washington column, "Kennedy in the Middle on German Debate," the *New York Times*, 25 October 1961, 36:1, 3.

26. Paul Tillich, "Europäische Impressionen, 1956," *Gesammelte Werke*, ed. Renate Albrecht, 14 vols. (Stuttgart: Evangelisches Verlagswerk, 1959–75), XIII: 370–79.

27. Paul Tillich to Marion Hausner. Private collection. Tillich's ref. to "pre-classic" is wrong.

28. Interview with Paul Tillich. See also Tillich's long and extremely interesting report on his trip to Japan. Unpublished MS, 1960. H. A.

29. Ibid.

30. Ibid.

31. "Boundary Line," p. 1435.

32. Ibid.

33. Paul Tillich's report on Israel. Unpublished MS, 1963. H. A.

34. Ibid.

35. Ibid.

36. Ibid.

37. Interview with Paul Tillich. Ibid.

38. Paul Tillich, "Martin Buber: Eine Würdigung anlässlich seines Todes," in G. W., XII: 320–23.

39. Interview with Gerhard Ebeling.

40. Karl Barth to Paul Tillich, 22 November 1963, H. A. The reference in Barth's note is to Robinson's *Honest to God*, a little book which stirred up a great deal of discussion in Great Britain and elsewhere concerning Tillich's theology, discussion which some regarded as a help, others as a hindrance to the general understanding of his thought. Tillich himself wrote Robinson praising the book.

41. Paul Tillich. Unpublished MS, 1956. H. A.

42. Scroll in H. A.

43. The Hanseatic Goethe Prize was worth $2,300.

44. Helmuth Thielicke, *Der Spannungsbogen* (Stuttgart: Evangelisches Verlagswerk, 1961), pp. 23, 24. "So grüssen wir heute in Ehrerbietung und Freude Paul Tillich, und ich darf wohl sagen: unseren Paul Tillich. Uns als seinen Freunden erscheint er wie ein Wanderer zwischen zwei Welten, und es freut uns, dass wir in Deutschland die eine dieser beiden Welten sind, in deren Boden seine Wurzeln gesenkt sind."

45. Paul Tillich received DM 10,000.

46. 23 September 1962.

47. A little brochure contains the entire program of the Peace Prize ceremony. Cf. *Grenzen* (Stuttgart: Evangelisches Verlagswerk, 1963), p. 10. ". . . der in Wort und Schrift unermüdlich dem Gedanken des Friedens gedient hat und der nach dem Kriege der deutschen Wissenschaft die Tore nach aussen wieder öffnete, die wir selbst in Verführung und Verblendung zugeschlagen hatten."

48. Ibid., p. 16.

49. Cecil Northcott, "Paul Tillich's Germany," *Christian Century* 79, no. 41 (10 October 1962), p. 1219.

50. The German word *Grenzen* can also mean "frontier," "border," "limit."

51. Paul Tillich, "Grenzen," *G. W.*, XIII: 428. "Und es ist mein Wunsch für das deutsche Volk, von dem ich komme und dem ich diese Ehrung verdanke, dass es sich offenhält, seine Wesensgrenze und seine Berufung erkennt und im Wandel der Wirklichkeitsgrenzen erfüllt."

52. Wilhelm Stählin, *Via Vitae* (Kassel: Johannes Stauda Verlag, 1968), pp. 668–69. "Die Art, wie Tillich dann in seiner Dankrede von der notwendigen Wahrung und der ebenso notwendigen Überwindung der Grenzen sprach, ist von vielen Zeugen jener Stunde als ein Meisterwerk empfunden worden, und sie war jedenfalls für mich ebenso formal wie ishaltlich ein hoher geistiger Genuss."

53. The *Systematic Theology* was in fact published in a separate three-volume edition, not as part of the *Gesammelte Werke* [Collected Works].

54. Interview with August Rathmann.

55. See *G. W.*, vol. XIV for a complete history of the *G. W.* as well as for the most complete and up-to-date bibliography of archival contents: books, articles, essays, dissertations, tapes by and about Paul Tillich, published and unpublished. For the serious Tillich scholar this volume is a veritable treasure.

56. Interviews with Renate Albrecht, Paul Tillich.

57. In 1959 the Circle of the Friends of Paul Tillich (Kreis der Freunde Paul Tillichs) was established. Under the leadership of Carl Heinz Ratschow, professor of theology at the University of Marburg, who became the authority on whom Mrs. Albrecht depended after Tillich's death for editorial decisions, the circle has grown to include 236 members and is open to anyone desiring affiliation. Since its inception it has met annually on spring weekends in the Evangelical Academy at Hofgeismar, to preserve and continue Tillich's influence in Germany. Scholarly papers presented at these meetings were at first focused entirely on Tillich's ideas; more recently an effort has been made to broaden their content and perspective. The membership fee (now DM 20) helps to support the German Tillich Archive in Göttingen, presided over by Tillich's former student Gertraut Stöber, who is secretary of the society. The contents of this archive include originals or duplicates of nearly all Tillich's publications, correspondence and memorabilia, as well as current literature (doctoral dissertations) about him. Scholars from all over the world use the archive on a regular basis; at the moment 45 disserations (24 Roman Catholic, 21 Protestant) are underway. Work on unpublished notes and manuscripts of Paul Tillich is also in process. Many of his early lectures and notes are barely legible, written in pencil in small black notebooks, since they belong to a time when he had not yet determined to write clearly. He did so, incidentally, when he found he could not decipher his own notes. In this context, it is interesting that the natural handwriting of the young Tillich was cramped, although even. Later it became large and open but had the appearance of a scrawl.

58. Walter Leibrecht, ed., *Religion and Culture* (New York: Harper & Row, 1959).

59. See jacket copy, *Theology of Culture*, ed. Robert Kimball (New York: Oxford University Press, 1959).

60. He and his wife had cooperated eagerly, although not without some apprehension, with the editors and photographers who prepared this story.

61. *Time*, letters to the editor, 15 March 1959.

62. Paul Tillich, circular letter, February 1959. H. A.

63. Richard Kroner to Paul Tillich, 1961: "Da Sterben ein Abschiednehmen ist von allem, allem was wir auf Erden genossen und gewirkt, bewundert und geliebt haben, so wünsche ich Dir dass Du die Vorbereitung auf dieses Ende ohne Furcht und ohne Trauer durchleben kannst. Es gibt, glaube ich, nicht nur den Mut zu sein, sondern auch den nicht zu sein; und der zweite ist wohl der eigentlich religiöse, auch wenn wir alle Bilder ablehnen, welche die Religion uns anbietet, um uns diesen Mut einzuflössen. Und so fortan! wie Goethe im Alter oft seine Briefe abzuschliessen pflegte. Dein Richard." H. A.

64. Interview with Paul Tillich.

65. In this period, too, Tillich appointed a literary executor, Robert Kimball, and began discussions with his biographers.

66. Paul Tillich, circular letter, 30 June 1962. H. A.

67. Ibid.

68. Paul Tillich, "Words by Paul Tillich," *Harvard Divinity Bulletin* 30, no. 2 (1966), pp. 23, 24.

69. The seminar was taped and posthumously published by D. Mackenzie Brown, ed., as *Ultimate Concern: Tillich in Dialogue* (New York: Harper & Row, 1965).

70. Brauer had shrewdly introduced a clause into Tillich's contract protecting him from his tendency to accept too many outside invitations by setting a limit to their number. Interview with Paul Tillich.

71. Paul Tillich, "The Human Condition." Unpublished MS, H.A. Excerpts from this address, entitled "The Ambiguity of Perfection," were published in *Time*, 17 May 1963, p. 69.

72. Ibid.

73. Ibid., slightly edited to improve English.

74. Ibid.

75. In the 1940s James Luther Adams and Tillich attended a conference in palatial surroundings in Westchester, New York While relaxing on the terrace outside, enjoying a good drink, Adams said to Tillich, "How can a religious socialist so enjoy bourgeois privileges?" "Oh, but this is not *petit* bourgeois!" Tillich replied. Interview with Adams.

76. See Hannah Tillich, *From Time to Time* (New York: Stein & Day, 1973), p. 240.

77. Interview with Ruth Nanda Anshen. On several occasions Gabriel Marcel, Tillich, and Mrs. Anshen discussed Tillich's fear of death.

78. Interview with Paul Tillich.

79. Clarence P. Wolfe, *The Story of New Harmony*, 1814–1964. Privately printed brochure available in the New Harmony bookstore.

80. Rüdiger Reitz, *Paul Tillich und New Harmony* (Stuttgart: Evangelisches Verlagswerk, 1970), pp. 70, 71.

81. Jane Blaffer Owen to Paul Tillich, 1 February 1963, 8 February 1963, and 28 January 1963. H. A.

82. Paul Tillich, on the day of the dedication of the Paul Tillich Park in New Harmony, Indiana, 2 June 1963. Unpublished MS, H. A.

83. Ibid.

84. Paul Tillich to Jane Owen, Summer 1963. H. A. See Reitz, *P. T. und New Harmony.*

85. Reitz, *P. T. und New Harmony.*

86. A scroll signed by those in attendance is in the Harvard achive.

87. Henry P. Van Dusen, who had invited Tillich to become Fosdick Professor at Union for 1963–64 and was again turned down, this time in favor of Chicago, wrote to him on 15 August 1962 in the same vein. "Remember—once a member of the Union faculty, always a member of the Union faculty. We shall look forward to welcoming you back from time to time in the coming years." Presidential files, Union Theological Seminary.

88. Michael Novak, "The Religion of Paul Tillich," *Commentary* 43 (April 1967), p. 53.

89. Paul Tillich to John E. Smith, 9 July 1965. H. A.

90. Brochure handed out to guests at the opening of the new garden, p. 1. H. A.

91. Ibid.

92. Paul Tillich, "Honesty and Consecration," *Response* 8, no. 4 (Easter 1967), p. 210.

93. In his reply to Tillich's letter of acceptance, Jack Everett informed him on 13 April 1965, that he was scheduled to begin teaching at the New School for Social Research in March 1966. H. A.

94. Paul Tillich to Renate Albrecht, 12 April 1965: "Mein Leben hier in Amerika ausser in den Sommermonaten ist ein Netz, in dem ich zapple, aber aus dem ich nicht heraus kann." H. A.

95. Paul Tillich to Eduard Heimann, 13 April 1965: "Nun muss ich Dir noch etwas überraschendes mitteilen. Ich habe einen Ruf von der New School bekommen, den neu-gegründeten Alvin Johnson chair für eine Zeit einzunehmen, und ich habe im Prinzip zugesagt. Mir wird das Hin- und Herfahren zwischen Easthampton, Chicago, und Santa Barbara zu viel und ich betrachte New York als einen Vorort von East Hampton. Während ich dies diktiere, denke ich an Deinen ersten Brief, wo Du mich ermutigtest, nach New York zu kommen. Hannah nennt dieses Ereignis, 'den grossen Zirkel meines Hierseins.' Was sagst Du dazu?" H. A.

96. Paul Tillich to Adolf Löwe, 19 April 1965: "Es gibt vieles, auf das ich mich freue und einiges, wovor ich mich ängstige, z.B. die Stadt, was für mich, den ausgekochten Grosstädter, eine neue Entwicklung ist. Ferner die vielen Attacken auf meine Zeit und Kraft. Vieles kann man ablehnen aber das wenige, was fast unvermeidlich ist, ist immer noch zu viel.

"Ich hätte gern im Herbst angefangen, aber es war hier absolut unmöglich ohne inneren Bruch. Hannah, die das Symbol des Kreises liebt, wundert sich, dass in gewisser Weise mein Leben in Amerkia kreisförmig an den Anfang zurückkehrt. Es ist alles innerlich sehr erregend, beglückend und problematisch." H. A.

97. Paul Tillich, circular letter, 7 October 1965. H. A.

98. Wolf-Dieter Marsch, ed., *Werk und Wirken Paul Tillichs: Ein Gedenkbuch* (Stuttgart: Evangelisches Verlagswerk, 1967), p. 45.

99. Interview with Joseph M. Kitagawa. See also Paul Tillich, *The Future of Religions*, ed. Jerald C. Brauer (New York: Harper & Row, 1966), p. 7. Tillich's last public lecture, as well as three memorial addresses given in Chicago by Jerald C. Brauer, Mircea Eliade, and Wilhelm Pauck, are included.

100. H. Tillich, *Time to Time*, pp. 219–25.

101. Paul Tillich, *The Courage To Be* (New Haven: Yale University Press, 1952), pp. 13, 14.

102. Order of service and addresses delivered at each of the formal memorial services are in H. A. and G. A. A week or so before his heart attack, Tillich had encountered his colleague Joseph Sittler on the stairs in the divinity school and in the course of their conversation remarked that he would like to have Johann Sebastian Bach's "Alle Menschen Müssen Sterben" played at his funeral. His wish was fulfilled at the Chicago memorial service.

103. Announcement by the Robert Lee Blaffer Trust, New Harmony, Indiana. Unpublished MS, H. A. This announcement was sent to Tillich's many friends. In the spring of 1973 the Paul Tillich Chair of Theology and Culture was inaugurated at Union Theological Seminary, New York. The present incumbent is Tom Faw Driver.

104. *New York Times*, editorial page, 23 October 1965.

105. Memorial address by Harald Poelchau in Berlin. G. A.

106. Memorial address by James L. Adams in *Harvard Divinity Bulletin* 30, no. 2 (January 1966), p. 9.

107. Paul Tillich, "Forgetting and Being Forgotten," *The Eternal Now*, p. 34.

Index

Aberdeen, 241f.
Abraham, 138, 154
Absolute, 76, 96
Acropolis, 258
Adams, James L., xiii, 200, 220f.,
    251, 271, 284
Adler, Felix, 140, 183
Adorno, Theodor W., 115f., 119,
    122, 126, 135, 155
Aeschylus, 174
Agape, 91
Aisne-Marne, 50
Alabama, 181
Albrecht, Renate, 101, 268, 269
Althaus, Paul, 192
Ambiguity of life, 151, 244, 273f.
American philosophy, 185f.
American politics, 200
American theological thought, 188f.
Amiens, 50
Amsterdam Assembly, 194
Angst, 223
Anshen, Ruth Nanda, 166, 264
Antisemitism, 196
Anxiety, 224, 225, 283; of having to
    die, 285
Apologetics, 37
Apostles' Creed, 27
Aquinas, Thomas, 113, 233
Architecture, 120
Aristotle, 171
Art, 78
Art and architecture, 280
Art, Byzantine, 78
Art and science of healing, 223f.
Ascona, 192, 241
Athens, 261
Aubrey, Edwin E., 187

Auden, W. H., 170, 222, 224
Augustine, 171
Aure, 46

Bach, Johann Sebastian, 329, n.102
Baltic Sea, 8
Baring, Nina, 101
Barnard College, 101
Barth, Karl, 30, 62, 66, 70, 95, 96,
    99, 188, 192, 194, 211, 233,
    238, 249, 263, 265
Becker, Carl, 95, 110, 111
Behrmann, Max, 209, 215
Being Itself, 229
Bennett, John, 187, 195, 203, 239
Benz, Ernst, 213
Berg, Alban, 212
Bergner, Elizabeth, 203
Berlin, 9, 16, 28, 32, 33, 54, 55,
    57ff., 67, 96, 97, 123, 137, 208,
    215, 216, 217, 264
Berlin Philharmonic Symphony, 158
Berneuchener Movement, 191
Bethmann-Hollweg, Th. von, 110,
    129
Bible, 172
Biblicism, 239
Bienert, Ida, 106f., 137
Billings Hospital, 280, 283
Biology, 118
Blanchefosse, 48
Blätter für Religiösen Sozialismus, 74
Bloch, Ernst, 282
Blum, Emil, 193, 211
Blumhardt, Christoph, 69
Böckelmann, Werner, 266
Bohème, The, 81, 83, 301, n.36

Bonn, 38
Booth, Gotthard, 223
Botticelli, Sandro, 76, 97
Boundary, 59, 91, 250, 266f.
Boundary situation, 124
Bourgeois, 83; conventionality, 90
Bourbon, Jack Daniel's, 236
Brauer, Jerald, 272, 281
Breakthrough, Tillich's concept of, 77
Brecht, Bertolt, 58, 130, 203
Brewster, George and Joan, 255
Bridgman, Percy, 250
Brodsky, Ralph, 166, 278
Brown, William Adams, 167, 184
Brüning, Heinrich, 203
Brunner, Emil, 188
Brunstäd, Friedrich, 99
Buber, Martin, 262f., 265, 282
Büchsel, Friedrich, 84, 208
Buddhism, 260
Bultmann, Rudolf, 95, 98, 265, 317,
    n.38
Bund, 191
Burckhardt, Carl, 265
Burning of books, 132, 199
Burschenschaft, 20
Burse, 20
Butte de Tahure, 51
Butterfelde, 38

Café Josty, 32
Café Kranzler, 136
Café, Romanisches, 32
Cailette Forest, 49
Cairo, 261
Calhoun, Robert, 187
California, 182
Camus, Albert, 222
Capitalism, 56, 69, 274
Carmel, 182
Cassirer, Ernst, 130
Cave of the New Being, 278
Cézanne, Paul, 59, 76, 192
Champagne, 50
Chapel services, 228
Chartres, 78
Chateau de Bossey, 241
Cherbonnier, Edmond La B., 226
Chicago, 180, 186
Christianity, 260
Christmas, 7, 147
Christmas Eve, 46

Church, 177, 194
Church and socialism, 68f.
Coffin, Henry Sloane, 133, 140, 142,
    152, 160f., 164, 167, 168, 174–
    177, 197, 200, 228, 237
Cohen, Morris, 184
College of Preachers, 187
Collmer, Paul, 268
Collmer, Willy, 268
Columbia Seminar on Religion and
    Health, 223
Communism, 201
Conant, James B., 247, 250
Concentration camps, 201
Cooper, Elizabeth, 231
Cornelius, Hans, 109, 111, 113
Correggio, Antonio, 100
Correlation, method of, 172, 234,
    322, n.92
Corwin, Virginia, 187
Council for a Democratic Germany,
    201f.
Courage, 224f., 270
Cox, Harvey, 251
Crissier, 108
Cumberland Lodge, 239

Dance, 104, 121, 122, 171, 302, n.52;
    and Religion, 105; of the eternal
    essences, 272
Darwin, Charles, 8
Davos, 113
Dawes Plan, 111
Death, 1, 2, 18, 45, 51, 153, 261,
    270, 283, 284
Dehn, Günther, 70f., 125, 131
Delitzsch, Friedrich, 16
Democracy, 199
Demonic, the, 66, 81, 108f., 205
Demons, 79, 108
Depth psychology, 170f., 206
Detroit, 181
Dewey, John, 161, 184, 189, 237
Dibelius, Otto, 266
Dillenberger, John, 226, 235, 236,
    251
Disaster Bar (Katastrophen-Diele), 79
Dodeshöner, Werner, 266
Domkandidatenstift, 33
Don Juan, 82
Dorman, Harry, 143, 145
Doubt, 37, 226

Dresden, 100, 137, 234
Dresden Arts and Crafts School, 103
Dun, Angus, 187
Dürselen, Amalia (Tillich's maternal grandmother), 5
Dürselen, Gustav (Tillich's maternal grandfather), 5

East Hampton, 31, 66, 88, 206, 236, 238, 247, 271, 272, 280, 281, 282, 284
Eastman, Max, 184
Eban, Abba, 262
Ebbinghaus, Hermann, 53
Ebeling, Gerhard, 263
Ebert, Friedrich, 67f., 111
Ecstasy, 93
Ecumenical Movement, 188, 194
Edinburgh, 188
Edman, Irwin, 161
Edwards, Paul, 219
Egypt, 258, 261
Einstein, Albert, 130
Eliade, Mircea, 273
Eliot, T. S., 237
Elizabeth, Queen Mother, 239
England, 239
Enlightenment, 19
Eranos meetings, 192
Erechtheion, 258
Erikson, Erik, 234,n.9
Estes Park, 182
Europe, 201
Evangelisches Verlagswerk, 265, 268
Evansville, Indiana, 276
Everett, Jack, 280
Existentialism, 167, 168, 170, 185, 222, 234, 242
Expressionism, 8, 59, 76, 77f., 104, 105

Faith, 37, 229
Farris, Erdmuthe Tillich (Tillich's daughter), 241
Farris, Theodore (Tillich's son-in-law), 241
Fascism, 201
Fellowship of Socialist Christians, 170, 311,n.62
Fennell, William, 231
Fichte, Johann Gottlieb, 15, 19
Finite and infinite, 17, 88

Finiteness, 282
Firth Lectures, 239f.
Fischer Verlag, 58
Fletcher Farms, 183
Florence, 260
Ford factory, 181
Ford, Henry, 169
Forell, Frederick, 203
Fort Douaumont, 49
Fosdick, Harry Emerson, 142, 164, 203
France, 197
Francke, August Hermann, 19
Frankel, Hilde, 236
Frankenberg, Ellen, 105
Frankfort, 121, 123, 132, 135, 138, 211, 218, 234
Frankfort, St. Paul's Church, 266
Freedom, 83
Freud, Sigmund, 8, 59, 223, 227
Friedrich Wilhelm IV, 33
Friess, Horace S., 134, 135, 136, 140, 141, 152, 161, 178, 184
Fromm, Erich, 223, 258
Frontier Fellowship, 178
Furtwängler, Wilhelm, 58
Fritz, Alfred ("Frede"), (Tillich's brother-in-law), 18, 19, 24, 25, 39, 41, 60, 86, 102, 208
Fritz, Johanna Tillich (Tillich's sister), 41, 80, 84f.

Gatlinburg, Tennessee, 222
Gelb, Adhémar, 117
Gelb, Nelli, 215, 223
George, Stefan, 18, 58, 81, 103
Germany, 199ff., 205, 208f., 211f., 213, 218, 267
Gestalt psychology, 118
Gettysburg, Battle of, 263
Girgenti (Agrigento), 97
God, 96, 229, 262; flight from, 93; withdrawal of, 280
Goering, Hermann, 137
Goesch, Heinrich, 103f., 118, 223
Goethe, Johann Wolfgang von, 18, 19, 110, 120, 182, 263, 270
Goethe Museum, 110
Goldstein, Kurt, 117, 155, 223, 226, 249, 282
Gollancz, Victor, 265
Gorki, Maxim, 32

Göttingen, 214
Göttingen Archive, ix, 101, 326,n.57
Gottschow, Albert, 86
Grace, 93, 229
Grand Canyon, 182
Grand Inquisitor, 30, 294,n.46
Gray, Dorian, 109
Greece, 245, 258
Greek philosophy, 178
Greek thought, 171
Grieg, Edvard, 36
Grimme, Adolf, 121, 137
Grunewald, 85
Grünewald, Matthias, 78, 84
Grosz, George, 130
Grzesinski, Albert, 202
Guernica, 78, 91
Gutmann, James, 184f.
Gymnasium, Friedrich Wilhelm, 10

Haendler, Gustav, 59ff.
Hagen, Paul, 203, 204
Halle, 16, 19, 22, 47, 49
Hamburg, 138, 215, 218, 265
Hamilton, Kenneth, 279
Hamlet, 11, 32
Happiness, 43, 88
Harder, Erich, 12, 215
Harkness, Georgia, 187
Harlem, 146
Harnack, Adolf von, 60, 179
Harnack Haus, 215
Hartshorne, Holmes, 176
Harvard Andover Library, 271
Harvard Archive, ix, 271, 279
Harvard Crimson, 250
Harvard Divinity School, 247, 251
Hazen Foundation, 188
Hegel, G. W. F., 19, 107, 113, 120,
    144, 176, 222
Heidegger, Martin, 95, 98, 239,
    318,n.44
Heidelberg, 136
Heiler, Friedrich, 213
Heilner, Mary, 231, 232, 248
Heimann, Eduard, 70, 74, 140, 152,
    155, 164, 203, 249, 265, 281
Heller, Hermann, 119
Hempel, Carl, 184
Heraclitus, 97
Hermann, Christian, 81, 108
Heuss, Theodor, 266

Hiltner, Seward, 223
Hindenburg, Paul von, 128, 152
Hirsch, Emanuel, 30, 31, 53, 84,
    153, 214, 295,n.53
Hisamatsu, 260
Hitler, Adolf, 74, 123, 127f., 152,
    153, 190, 192, 196, 197, 199,
    201, 214
Höchberg, Alexander and Ellen, 138
Hochheimer, Wolfgang, 117, 135,
    215
Hocking, William E., 189
Hofstadter, Albert, 185
Hölderlin, Friedrich, 18
Holl, Karl, 30, 179
Holm, Hanya, 106
Holy, the idea of, 7, 78, 97
Homiletics, 228
Hook, Sidney, 184
Horkheimer, Max, 116, 117, 119,
    129, 131, 155
Horn, Trude, 25
Horney, Karen, 223
Horton, Douglas, 251
Humphrey, Hubert H., 170
Husserl, Edmund, 53
Hutchins, Robert M., 257

Idealism, German, 99, 174
Image of man, 97
Impressionism, 122
Independent Socialist Party, 68f.
Indiana, 181
Inflation, 111
Infinite and finite, 8, 88
Institute of Hermeneutics (Zurich),
    263
Institute of Politics (Berlin), 64, 71,
    74, 238
Institute of Social Research (Frank-
    fort), 116, 117, 129
Institute of Technology (Dresden), 98,
    112
Intuition, 84
Israel, 258, 261, 263
Italy, 97

Jaeger, Werner, 250
James, William, 184
Japan, 198, 245, 258
Japanese people, 259, 261
Jaspers, Karl, 242

Jerusalem, 9, 261, 262
Jesus, 262
Jews, persecution of, 151, 159, 196, 199
Job, 174
John XXIII, 257
Johnson, Alvin, 203
Johnson, Philip, 276
Jordan, 261
Judaism, 217
Judaism and Christianity, 71
Juilliard School of Music, 141
Justice, 170
Justification by faith, 19, 54
Justification of doubters, 19

Kähler, Martin, 19
Kairos, 51, 65, 73f., 138, 199, 206, 222, 316,n.23
Kairos circle (Berlin), 70
Kampen, 65, 100, 106, 124
Kandinsky, Wassily, 58, 106, 130
Kant, Immanuel, 15, 18, 19, 26, 113
Kantorowicz, Ernst, 117, 182
Kassel, 214
Keller, Adolf, 211
Kennedy, John F., 256, 263
Kennedy, Jacqueline, 256
Kiel, 112, 173
Kierkegaard, Sören, 116
Kimball, Robert, 255, 269
King David Hotel, 262
Klee, Paul, 58, 106, 131
Klein, Ernst, 29
Klein, Maria, 43, 51. *See also* Rhine, Maria Klein
Klemperer, Viktor, 101
Köhler, Wolfgang, 130
Königsberg, 10
Kristallnacht, 196
Kristeller, Paul O., 184
Kroner, Richard, 98f., 101, 104, 107, 112, 173f., 249, 270, 312,n.67
Kutter, Hermann, 69
Kyoto, 259, 260

LaGuardia, Fiorello, 146, 197
Lake Gennesaret, 262
Lake Louise, 180
Lake Michigan, 180
Lash, Joseph, 204
Lasson, Adolf, 16

Lee, Paul, 255
Leese, Kurt, 30, 31, 215
Lehmann, Paul, 249, 251
Leibrecht, Walter, 255, 269
Leslie, Kenneth, 200f.
Lessing, Gotthold E., 101
Lichtenrade, 29, 31, 32
Liebermann, Max, 111
Light and life, 264
Lille, 48
Lilje, Hanns, 192
Lincoln, Abraham, 198, 263
Linguistic analysis, 234
Lipchitz, Jacques, 276
Lippmann, Walter, 240
Loew, Cornelius, 235
Locke, John, 113
Loewenfeld, Gunther and Claire, 120, 130, 137, 138
Long, Huey, 181
Louisiana, 181
Love, 88, 92, 198
Lovejoy, Arthur, 184
Löwe, Adolf, 71f., 74, 118, 119, 131, 155, 164, 193, 204, 216, 249, 281
Luce, Henry, 273
Lütgert, Wilhelm, 20, 59, 102
Lutheran theology, 12
Lyman, Eugene, 184

MacArthur, Douglas, 273
Mackay, John, 187
Mackinnon, D. M., 242
Man, 224
Mann, Heinrich, 203
Mann, Thomas, 116, 130, 202, 216, 315,n.15
Mannheim, Karl, 117, 118, 119
Marburg, 86, 94, 97, 120, 213, 218, 245
Marc, Franz, 52, 77
Marcel, Gabriel, 242
Mardi Gras Ball, 85
Margaret, Princess, 239
Marienbad, 252
Marriage, 84, 87, 88
Martha's Vineyard, 152, 178
Marx, Karl, 59, 223, 300,n.20
Marxism, 149
Mattise, Henri, 79

May, Rollo, xii, 224, 271, 278
McGiffert, A. C., 184
McNeill, John T., 171
Medicus, Fritz, 19, 20, 34, 108, 113, 208
Mehta, Ved, 323,n.7
Meinhof, Heinrich, 19, 21, 26
Mendelssohn, Felix, 100
Mennicke, Karl, 70f., 119, 131, 191, 215, 270
Metzger, Ludwig, 246, 247
Mexico, 258
Mies van der Rohe, Ludwig, 121
Miller, Francis P., 187
Miller, Samuel, 271
Moabit, 36
Moissi, Alexander, 32
Mollegen, Albert T., 169, 235, 238
Monogamy, 80
Mont Blanc, 195
Montague, W. P., 161, 185
Monte Bré, 193
Montmartre, 181
Monte Rosa, 182
Montreal, 173
Moore, G. E., 185
Moralism, 114
Morgenthau, Henry, 201
Moscow, 110
Mosse, Walter M., 158
Mott, John R., 187
Muilenburg, James, 167
Müller, Adolf, 222, 265
Munch, Edvard, 76
Munich, 112
Music, 81
Mussolini, Benito, 196
Museums: Chicago Art Institute, 181; Goethe Museum, Frankfort, 110; Kaiser Friedrich Museum, Berlin, 76; Louvre, Paris, 210; Museum of Modern Art, New York, 146, 280; Metropolitan Museum of Art, New York, 146; Semper Gallery, Dresden, 100; Städele Museum, Frankfort, 121
Mysticism, 37, 84
Myths and symbols, 162

Nagel, Ernst, 161, 184, 186
Napoleon, 201
Nationalism, 40, 56, 69

National Socialism, 74, 122f., 127, 199, 200, 202
Naturalism, 183
Nazi brutality, 197
Nazi Germany, 196
Nazi regime, 132, 192
Nazi violence, 127
Nazareth, 262
Neuwerk Kreis, 125
New Deal, 199
New England, 180
New Harmony, Indiana, 176, 284
New Orleans, 181
New School for Social Research, 72, 155, 157, 163f., 280
New York, 141f., 146, 198, 230, 281
New York Times, 143, 284
Negev, 262
Neill, Stephen, 279
Neilson, W. A., 203
Neosupranaturalists, 183
Niebuhr, H. Richard, 133, 187, 237
Niebuhr, Reinhold, 70, 133f., 142, 145, 161, 162, 167, 168, 169f., 172, 173, 178f., 186, 187, 195, 202, 203, 221, 238, 243, 257, 269
Niebuhr, Ursula, 140, 170
Notre Dame, Cathedral of, 79
Novalis (Friedrich v. Hardenberg), 18
Nuclear weapons, 257
Nietzsche, F. W., 52, 96

Oates, Wayne, 224
Office of War Information (O.W.I.), 198
Oldham, J. H., 188, 190, 191, 193
Ontology, 240
Oppenheim, Gabrielle, 115, 122, 166
Oppenheimer, J. Robert, 184
"Order", religious, 191
Otto, Rudolf, 96, 97, 99
Otto, Walter, 119
Owen, Jane (Mrs. Kenneth Dale O.), 276
Owen, Robert, 276
Oxford Conference of Life and Work, 188, 190, 194

Pacifism, 170
Pagan gods, reality of, 250

Painting, 75, 78
Palm Beach, 181
Panofsky, Erwin, 130
Paris, 49, 108, 146, 192, 210
Parmenides, 97
Parthenon, 258
Party politics, 122f.
Paton, William, 188
Pauck, Marion (neé Hausner), x, xiii
Pauck, Wilhelm, xiii, 178, 179f.,
    187, 189, 203, 211, 221, 231,
    249, 263, 271, 278, 280
Peace, 257
Pfeiffer, Erich, 44, 50
Pharaohs, 261
Philosophy, American, 163
Philosophy Club, 144, 178, 183
Philosophy of life, 236
Picasso, Pablo, 78, 222
Pincus, Fritz and Lilly, 120, 138
Piscator, Erwin, 81, 203
Plato, 115, 171, 271, 318,n.44
Poltinus, 171, 176
Plötzensee Prison, 96
Poelchau, Harald, 96, 115, 125, 135,
    215, 217, 284
Pollock, Friedrich, 118f., 204
Potsdam, 130
Potsdamer Platz, 124
Power of being, 122
Pragmatism, 161
Pratt, Trude, 204
Privatdozent, post of, 59
Protestant, The, 200
Protestantism, 106, 220
Provincialism, 199, 261;
    European, 159
Psychoanalysis, 103
Psychotherapy, 226f.
Puritans, 146
Pusey, Nathan, 247, 271
Pyramids, 261

Raabe, Wilhelm, 18
Ragaz, Leonhard, 69
Randall, J. H., Jr., 152, 161, 162,
    163, 184, 238, 245, 255
Raphael, 100
Rapp, George, 276
Rathmann, August, 74, 124, 137,
    217, 268
Ravenna, 97

Realism, based on faith (gläubiger
    Realismus), 77, 127
Realism, New (Neue Sachlichkeit),
    77
Refugees, 154
Reinhardt, Karl, 117, 119
Reinhardt, Max, 32, 81, 130
Religion and culture, 220, 269
Religion and health, 224
Religion, dimension of depth, 64;
    substance of culture, 78, 105
Rembrandt, van Rijn, 100
Reston, James, 257
Reunion with Being itself, 92
Revolution, 55
Rhein, Ernst, 26, 215
Rhine, Maria Klein, 215, 265. See
    also Klein, Maria
Richter, Werner, 111, 203
Riezler, Kurt, 110f., 117, 119, 122,
    125, 129, 130, 138, 164, 182,
    192f.
Rilke, Rainer Maria, 18, 58, 81
Roberts, David E., 167, 174, 248
Roberts, Eleanor ("Elli"), 174
Robinson, A. T., 325,n.40
Rockefeller Center, 146
Rockefeller, John D. III, 167
Rockefeller Foundation, 164, 210
Romanticism, political, 127
Rome, 97
Roofless Church, 276
Roosevelt, Eleanor, 204f., 257
Roosevelt, F. D., 199, 204f.
Rosati, James, 278
Rubens, Peter Paul, 100
Rusk, Dean, 257
Russell, Bertrand, 184, 237
Russia, 201, 204
Rust, Bernhard, 136, 308,n.89
Rüstow, Alexander, 71

San Francisco, 182
Sandburg, Carl, 198
Santa Fé, 182
Santayana, George, 237
Sarajevo, 40
Sartre, Jean-Paul, 223
Sassnitz, 133f., 135
Schafft, Hermann, 16, 24, 25, 60,
    84, 125, 151, 193, 208, 214,
    232, 270

Scheler, Max, 53, 108ff.
Schelling, Friedrich Wilhelm Joseph, 16, 18, 19, 31, 34, 99, 107, 108, 113, 161, 176, 236, 241f., 260
Schiefflin, William J., 202
Schiller, Friedrich, 42
Schlegel, Friedrich, 29
Schleiermacher, Friedrich Daniel E., 29, 317, n.38, 233
Schmidt, Karl Ludwig, 130, 211
Schmidt-Rottluff, Karl, 84
Schmitt, Carl, 126
Schneider, Herbert, 161
Scholz, Heinrich, 62
Schönfliess, 6, 31
Schütz, Claus, 257
Schweitzer, Albert, 265
Schwegler, Albert, 15
Sculptures, Greek, 258
Secularization, 280
Seeberger, Elisabeth Tillich (Tillich's sister), 85, 175, 208, 214
Seeberger, Erhard (Tillich's brother-in-law), 7, 85, 86, 138
Seeberger, Hans-Jürgen (Tillich's nephew), 208
Seeberger, Heide (Tillich's niece), 208, 257
Self-Help for Emigrés from Central Europe, 157ff.
Shinto, 259
Sicily, 97, 181
Siemsen, Gertie, 116, 215
Sils Maria, 216
Simon, Hugo, 59, 192
Sin, 229
Sittler, Joseph, 329, n.102
Smith, John E., 184, 226, 278, 279
Socialism, 126, 170, 181
Socialism, religious, 34, 65, 69, 72ff., 149, 178, 191, 206
Social Democratic Party, 124, 149
Soden, Hans von, 97
Sommerfeld, Martin, 140
Sozialpädagogik, 113
Spandau, 55, 59
Spellman, Francis Cardinal, 273
Spiegelberg, Friedrich, 98
Spiekeroog, 133, 135, 136
Stalin, Joseph, 205
Stählin, Wilhelm, 191, 267
Staiger, Emil, 242

Stange, Carl, 192
Stanley, Clifford, 169, 183, 278
Starzeddel, 1, 5
Staudinger, Else, 156
Staudinger, Hans, 156, 204
Steere, Douglas V., 187
Steinweg Dance School, 104
Stepun, Fedor, 101, 107, 112, 175, 216, 239
Sternberger, Dolf, 265
Stevenson, Adlai, 273
Stöber, Gertraut, 101
Stolper, Toni, 159
Storm troopers, 130
Stout, Rex, 204
Stuckart, Wilhelm, 136
Student rioting, 128
Student societies, 20
Stuttgart, 242
Suffering, 43
Surrender, unconditional, 204
Sydow, Eckart von, 8, 79, 101, 118, 136, 138, 192
Symbols, 7, 76, 172, 235
Syracuse, 97

Tahure, 45
Tambach, 70
Tanis, James, 271
Taylor, T. M., 238, 242
Teltow, 25
Temple, William, 188, 233
Temptations of St. Anthony, 84
Tennessee, 181
Theocracy, 65
Theological Discussion Group, 178, 187f.
Theological training, requirements of, 29
Theology, 177, 322, n.92; apologetic, 37, 59, 101, 234, 322, n.92; biblical, 235; kerygmatic, 322, n.92; Lutheran, 124; philosophical, 173; systematic, 92, 95f., 114, 118, 222, 234, 322, n.92
Thielicke, Helmut, 265
Thomas, George F., 187
Thompson, Dorothy, 202
Tillich family name, 2f
Tillich forebears, 2
Tillich, Elisabeth (Tillich's sister), 6, 7

Tillich, Erdmuthe (Tillich's daughter), 102, 131, 231

Tillich, Hannah (Tillich's wife), xii, 85f., 87, 102, 127, 135, 137, 193, 207

Tillich, Johanna (Tillich's sister), 6, 7, 14, 36, 39

Tillich, Johannes Oskar (Tillich's father), 1, 3ff., 9, 12, 14, 22, 28, 30, 39, 151, 175

Tillich, Wilhelmina Mathilde (Tillich's mother), 1, 5, 283

Tillich, Paul: Birth in Starzeddel, 1; schooling 7, 10; university study, 16f.; training for the ministry, 16, 33f.; dissertations on Schelling, 16, 34; enters German army as volunteer, 39; appointed army chaplain, 44ff.; receives Iron Cross First Class, 55; determines to become professor, 15, 16; becomes *Privatdozent* in Berlin, 50, 59; professional career in Marburg, 94ff., Dresden, 98ff., Frankfort, 110ff.; activities as religious socialist, 67ff.; joins Socialist Party, 124; suspended and dismissed from chair at the University of Frankfort, 148; emigrates to U.S.A., 135, 138; protests dismissal, 149; appointed Professor of Philosophical Theology at Union Theological Seminary, New York, 197; becomes first chairman of Self-Help for German Emigrés, 157; identifies himself with the fate of the Jews, 157; becomes American citizen, 197; elected President of Council for a Democratic Germany, 201; meets with President F. D. Roosevelt at White House, 204f.; visits Germany but declines invitation to return as professor, 246; retires from Union Seminary, 247f. and is appointed University Professor at Harvard, 248; retires from Harvard and is appointed professor at the University of Chicago, 271f.; offered Alvin Johnson chair at New School for Social Research, New York, 280; suffers illnesses, 271, 278, 282, 324,n.17; death in Chicago, 283

Inaugural lectures: Breslau, "The Conception of the History of Religions in Schelling's Positive Philosophy," 34; Berlin, "The Existence of God and the Psychology of Religion," 60; Halle, "The Concept of the Supernatural in German Theology during the period of the Enlightenment," 37; Leipzig, "The Idea of Revelation," 107; Frankfort, "Philosophy and Destiny," 113; New York, "Theology and Philosophy," 182

First public lecture: before Kant Society in Berlin, 1919, "The Idea of a Theology of Culture," 64f.

Last public lecture: at the University of Chicago, 1965, "The Significance of the History of Religions for the Systematic Theologian," 282

Major lectureships: Bampton Lectures, Columbia University, 256; Foerster Lecture, University of California, Berkeley, 255; Gifford Lectures, University of Aberdeen, Scotland, 238f.; Ingersoll Lecture, Harvard University, 252; Terry Lectures, Yale University, 225

Addresses to the German People, 198f.

Sermons: *The Eternal Now*, 232; *The New Being*, 232; *The Shaking of the Foundations*, 176, 231

Books: *Biblical Religion and the Search for Ultimate Reality*, 239; *On the Boundary*, 174f., 222; *Christianity and the Encounter of World Religions*, 256; *The Courage to Be*, 225ff., 237; *Dynamics of Faith*, 242f.; *Gesammelte Werke*, 269; *The Interpretation of History*, 221; *Love, Power, and Justice*, 279; *The Protestant Era*, 220f.; *The Religious Situation*, 66, 90, 98, 129,

133f.; *The Socialist Decision,*
126ff.; *The System of the Sciences,* 51, 62; *Systematic Theology,* 63, 176, 179, 206, 207,
232f., 268, 341; *Theology of
Culture,* 269
Tillich's Socratic manner, 62, 119,
144, 274
Tillich's specialized vocabulary, 145
Tillich as author, 65ff., 220ff., 319,
n.53; builder, 7, 23; churchman,
53, 194; counsellor, 96, 158, 226;
debater, 67, 119f.; eschatologist,
51; examiner, 115; lecturer, 249,
252, 255, 259; patriot, 9, 198f.;
preacher, 32, 227f., 228f., 231;
teacher, 60ff., 107, 114
Tillich's residences: East Hampton,
145, 206f.; Berlin, 60, 79; Cambridge, Mass, 251; Chicago, 272;
Dresden, 103; Frankfort, 121;
New York, 140
Tillich's travels: Egypt, 261f.; England, 190f., 194f., 240; Europe,
190, 194f., 263; France, 108,
190f., 240; Germany, 209ff., 249,
258ff.; Greece, 261f.; Israel,
261f.; Italy, 97f., 190f.; Japan,
259ff.; Netherlands, 194f.; Scotland, 238f., 242; Switzerland,
113, 191ff., 195, 263ff.
Tillich's relations with father: 13,
15, 22, 30, 51, 53, 124, 175; last
meeting, 138; last telephone conversation, 193
Tillich's relations with mother: 13,
14
Tillich's relation with colleagues:
24, 167; critics, 243; friends, 24,
27, 82, 88, 153, 155, 256, 275;
students, 61, 95, 114, 119,
168ff., 172f.; women, 58, 82,
89f.
Tillich's character: 83, 91f., 274f.
Tillich's personal appearance: 60,
63, 109, 168f., 252
Tillich's attitudes toward: art, 47,
75, 186; Christmas, 47, 54, 147;
death, 2, 46, 54; doubt, 12, 275;
English language, 143ff.; German
people, 213; Jewish people, 71;
nature, 17f., 31, 179, 207, 277;

marriage, 38, 79f., 86ff., 89f., 90;
money, 112; politics, 67, 125f.,
religion, 7f., 50, 52f., 54; sex, 23,
81, 83, 92
Tillich's distinctive features: birthday celebrations, 43f., 193, 264,
270; dreams, 30, 97, 124, 175,
208; fondness for wine, 121,
236; handwriting, 326,n.57
Recreation: building sandcastles,
15, 66, 100, 106; dancing, 15,
105, 106; mountain climbing, 11;
sailing, 11, 14, 39; walking, 11,
12, 14, 26, 31, 96, 178, 182, 197
Tillich as recipient of: honorary degrees, 102, 197, 264; prizes:
Hanseatic Goethe Prize, Ham-
burg, 265; Goethe Medal, Frank-
fort, 264; Order of Merit of Ger-
man Federal Republic, 264;
Peace Prize of German Publish-
ers' Association, Frankfort, 265
Tillich, René (Tillich's son), 183, 240
Tillich, Oscar (Tillich's paternal
grandfather), 3
Time, 265, 273
Times Square, 146
Titian, 100
Tokyo, 25
Trench warfare, 44f.
Trilling, Lionel and Diana, 170
Troeltsch, Ernst, 60, 62, 317,n.38
Trust, Robert E. Blaffer, 276
Tübingen, 16, 17, 18
Turnip winter, 52
Twain, Mark, 32

Uhde, Fritz von, 76
Ulich, Robert, 99, 131, 137, 152, 255
Ullstein Verlag, 58
Unconditional concern, 107
Unconditioned, the, 96
Union Theological Seminary, New
York, 72, 133, 140, 164, 195,
219, 231, 248
Universities: Aberdeen, 238; Berlin,
16, 95, 179, 218, 238; Breslau,
34; California, Santa Barbara,
281; Chicago, 211, 236, 272,
280; Columbia, New York, 133,
141; Frankfort, 71, 96, 109, 110,
113, 117, 129, 130, 210; Giessen,

110; Halle, 19, 36, 102, 121, 218; Hamburg, 72, 265; Harvard, 97, 184, 247, 256; Leipzig, 107; Manchester, 193; Marburg, 94, 210, 234; Nottingham, 239; Zurich, 263
Utopia, 276, 338
Utopianism, 73

Valentin, Veit, 203
van Buren, Paul, 244
Van Dusen, Elizabeth, 145, 167f.
Van Dusen, Henry P., 145, 167f., 187, 189, 190, 210, 238, 239, 247f., 273
Van Gogh, Vincent, 76
Vansittart, Robert G., 201
Verdun, 49, 54
Vernunft-Abende, 31, 37, 225
Versailles Treaty, 200
Vienna, 196
Visser't Hooft, W. A., 195, 211
Vlastos, Gregory, 183
Voice of America, 198
Void, sacred, 206, 316,n.23
Vorwerk, Friedrich, 268
Voss, Carl Hermann, 143, 145, 183, 203
Voss, Johann Heinrich, 143
Vow, absolute, 88

Wächter, Cora, 105
Waldorf Astoria Hotel, 273
Walker, Gisela Fritz, 25
Wallace, Henry, 204f.
Walter, Bruno, 58, 130
War aims, 200
Wartburg, the, 21, 23, 27
Washington, D.C., 181, 187
Weber, Alfred, 131
Weber, Max, 62

Wedekind, Frank, 58
Wegener, Carl Richard, 29, 31, 37, 38, 80f.
Weimar Republic, 67f., 128
Weiss, Paul, 184
Werner, Marie-Luise, 86, 108, 138, 208
Wertheimer, Max, 117, 118, 155
Wever, Grethi (Tillich's first wife), 80f., 215
Whitehead, Alfred North, 166, 189, 237
Whyte, John, 177
Widener Library, 249
Wieck, Fred, 222
Wieman, Henry N., 183
Wiesbaden, 209
Wigman, Mary, 104
Wild, John, 184
Wilde, Oscar, 11
Wilder, Thornton, 265
Wilhelm II, 9
Williams, Daniel Day, 244
Williams, Tennessee, 222
Williamson, Clark, 236
Wingolf, 12, 17, 20ff., 27, 30, 38, 82, 84, 125, 179, 293,n.33
Wolfers, Arnold, 71, 155
Wolff, Christian, 19
Wood, Elizabeth Cooper, 232f.
World Church Service, 210
World Council of Churches, 194
World War I, 40ff., 205
World War II, 190, 197, 198

Yalta Agreement, 204

Zen, 260
Zuckmayer, Carl, 52
Zurich, 19